OWL

About the Author

David Oborne is Professor of Psychology at the University of Wales, Swansea, UK. He has published well over a dozen books in the areas of ergonomics and human computer interaction, as well as a wide range of specialist research publications. His research interests include the effects of the environment on human behaviour, the design of computer systems to accommodate the human operator, the effects of new working practices (particularly teleworking and other kinds of flexible working) on organisations and on behaviour at work, and on how the environment needs to be designed to fit the person.

ERGONOMICS AT WORK

THIRD EDITION

Human Factors
in
Design and Development

David J. Oborne
University of Wales Swansea, UK

JOHN WILEY & SONS

Chichester • New York • Brisbane • Toronto • Singapore

Other Wiley Editorial Offices

John Wiley & Sons, Inc., 605 Third Avenue,
New York, NY 10158-0012, USA

Jacaranda Wiley Ltd, 33 Park Road, Milton,
Queensland 4064, Australia

John Wiley & Sons (Canada) Ltd, 22 Worcester Road,
Rexdale, Ontario M9W 1L1, Canada

John Wiley & Sons (SEA) Pte Ltd, 37 Jalan Pemimpin #05-04,
Block B, Union Industrial Building, Singapore 129809

Library of Congress Cataloging-in-Publication Data

Oborne, David J.
     Ergonomics at work / David J. Oborne.—3rd ed.
         p.   cm.
     Includes bibliographical references and index.
     ISBN 0-471-95235-4 (pbk.)
     1. Human Engineering.   I. Title
  TA166.025   1995
  620.8'2—dc20   94–28236
                                         CIP

British Library Cataloguing in Publication Data

A catalogue record for this book is available from the British Library

ISBN 0-471-95235-4 (paper)

Typeset in 10/12pt Palatino by Mackreth Media Services, Hemel Hempstead, Herts
Printed and bound in Great Britain by Biddles Ltd, Guildford and King's Lynn

CONTENTS

PREFACE TO THE THIRD EDITION

Ergonomics is alive and well and living throughout the world. This is the clear message that arises after examining the diversity of material that has appeared over the past five years or so, since the second edition of *Ergonomics at Work* hit the bookstands. It is rare, these days, to see reference to new machines and systems without also reading about how 'user friendly' it is, how it has been designed with the 'user in mind', or even how it fits 'ergonomic principles'. Developers within both the developed and the developing worlds understand how important ergonomics can be for increasing people's performance, safety and comfort, and media and marketing personnel have a good grasp at the valued-added features that ergonomics can supply to their products and systems.

Despite its undoubted success, however, ergonomics must not rest on its laurels. While it is true that more people these days have heard of the discipline, it is equally the case that more people misunderstand the nature of the discipline. Too often ergonomics is seen as a simple synonym for 'adjustable', too frequently one reads about 'ergonomically designed' goods and systems that are really just the original designs with the addition of a few more hinges or slide bars.

As the first and second editions of this book demonstrated, and now the third edition too, ergonomics is far more than this. The first chapter emphasises that ergonomics is a concept, an idea, a way of looking at the world. It requires careful thought about the behaviours of all parts of the working system—people and machines—in order that they can exist and work together effectively. All three editions discussed areas where such aspects need to be considered—and how they should be examined.

But ergonomics is even more than this; it is more than a static idea. It is a living, developing concept and over the past few years, ever since the second edition of this book, the ideas that form its basis have developed in an evolutionary fashion—hence the need for a third edition.

As this book describes, our concepts about how we should interact with our world have changed. Since the 1950s and 1960s, for example, we have been through the 'knobs and dials' era, we have moved past the symbiotic communication period, and we have taken on board the cybernetics and systems approaches. Now we begin to enter a period of person-centricity in which we realise the importance of individual components within the system, and of the communication links between them, but we must emphasise the central nature of the most important component within the working system—people. Within the person-centred view, therefore, we recognise that people bring to the system a collection of individual features that can affect the subsequent interaction. Person-centred ergonomics, which this edition discusses, 'weights' the effects of the individual components according to the potential of the person in the system. It is from this end of the telescope that the concept of ergonomics is currently being viewed.

That is not to say, of course, that the details and principals discussed in the first two editions are obsolete—very far from it. They are as important today as they were five and ten years ago although, with the passage of time, more material is now available to support the arguments. The person-centred view of ergonomics simply reminds us that whatever happens within the system it is the individual human being who is the prime actor. As the reader progresses through this book, from the first to the last page, this fundamental feature should be remembered at all times.

David J. Oborne
Swansea, 1994

PREFACE TO THE SECOND EDITION

The first edition of *Ergonomics at Work* took an unashamedly evangelical stance. Through explanation and description of the available literature, its aim was to provide the reader with a reasonable grounding in the bases of ergonomics, and to illustrate the fundamental role that ergonomics (and its American sister discipline human factors) takes in the modern, industrialised society in which we live. Without doubt, space would not have been conquered, computers would not have been used effectively, working practices would not be as safe as they are without the rise and continued discipline of ergonomics. The first edition of this volume illustrated this fact.

But in only a short passage of time, an emerging and important discipline such as ergonomics produces considerable additional information as its disciples push back the frontiers of its knowledge. Over only the past four years, increases our knowledge concerning a number of different human activities with work have meant that an update and expansion of *Ergonomics at Work* has become necessary.

In this edition, a number of specific areas included within the first edition have been expanded: more details are provided relating to our body capacities in lifting and transporting loads, in our use of displayed material—particularly with the recent 'explosion' of electronic information systems—and of controlling the system. Further material has been included relating to the environment: lighting, noise and vibration, for example. Indeed, although throughout the book the chapters' structures remain essentially the same, considerable additional material will be obvious in a number of chapters. However, the basic crusading approach remains. This second edition still aims to convert people to the ergonomics view of the world. That is that people are at the centre of events; that systems will not be operated efficiently, comfortably or safely without understanding the basic behaviour of the operator within the system—what he or she can do and wants to do. Any working system, in the office, shop-floor, or organisation, that includes people interacting either with other people or with their physical environment needs ergonomics. This book explains why, how and where.

David J. Oborne
Swansea, 1986

PREFACE TO THE FIRST EDITION

Ergonomics experienced its birth during the Second World War and it is perhaps fitting that during this period the cry was continuously heard 'Give us the tools, and we will finish the job'. The 'job' then was particularly straightforward: victory over a fearsome aggressor. The present day 'job' is perhaps more diverse: victory over the oppressive forces which continue to make work less productive, less pleasant, less comfortable and less safe.

Today, Churchill's plea is as real as it was during the dark days of the Second World War. Modern work would be almost impossible without adequate tools: a screwdriver to turn a screw, or a hammer to force home a nail. Microscopes allow otherwise invisible objects to become visible; and computers supplement people's cognitive capacities to enable them to perform operations unthinkable a decade or so ago.

Unfortunately, however, machines suffer at least one major drawback, they have to be operated: the screwdriver must be turned, the hammer wielded, the microscope adjusted, and the computer programmed. The tools are useless without the energy and decision-making abilities of the human operator. Until the era arrives of machines which are able to carry out intelligent thought, make and take decisions and perform complex actions, the working system needs the help of 'man'. This symbiotic relationship between the human operator and the environment must remain.

This book is concerned with the way in which the working relationship can be adapted to perform at its most efficient. It will consider how the behaviour of both the operator in the system and the system itself can either enhance or reduce the system's effectiveness. In short it will examine the various ways in which the two major components in the system—'man' and 'environment'—interact and communicate with each other.

In some senses the book is intended to be evangelical in its approach. It does not set out to provide the reader with a comprehensive data bank with which he can design an environment. Rather it intends to present the fundamental aspects of man–machine interactions, and to explain ergonomics (and its American sister discipline human factors) and its role within the context of modern day work. It will emphasise aspects of the working situation which need to be considered, and explain the reasons why various solutions are proposed. It then hopes to motivate and to point the reader in the right direction to discover more about the various facets of the man–environment interaction within his own working system.

'Information' and 'communication' are the two keywords to this interactive process; one is transferred by the other. As the reader progresses through this book he should become aware of their importance. Without them no interaction can take place. More importantly if they are of poor quality, then very poor interaction will occur. Either of these lead to inefficient, uncomfortable or unsafe situations which are good for neither the operator nor the employer. After the first chapter which considers ergonomics in its widest context (its basis and history, its position amongst the disciplines, and its financial value), the following two chapters examine the way in which the human body allows the communicative processes to occur. Chapter 2 considers the communication channels from the environment into the operator, through the senses, while Chapter 3 examines the flow in the opposite direction, through the operator's limbs to the environment.

In the following three chapters, the behavioural aspects of these communication channels will be discussed. First communication between operators (primarily sensory); second communication between the environment and the operators (again primarily sensory) and finally communication between the operators and the environment (mainly using the limbs, but also sensory aspects).

Having considered these communication requirements in final detail, Chapters 7, 8 and 9 discuss the ways of arranging the environment to the operator's benefit—again to enhance the communication channels. In Chapter 7 the operator's immediate work area—perhaps the machine, the console or even the writing pad—is investigated. Chapter 8 then discusses the most appropriate ways of building up the workplace—which consists of many machines and men—again to enhance the communication. Finally, and possibly as an extension of Chapter 8, Chapter 9 considers the function and value of appropriate seating and posture at work.

At this point, then, the communication channels are open and are efficient. However, they do not operate *in vacuo*. Their efficiency can be affected, sometimes radically, by the environment in which the operator is expected to perform. Four environmental aspects are considered in Chapters 10 and 11: the vibration, the noise, the temperature, and the illumination. Although it is stressed that these are by no means the only environments at work, they are, perhaps, the most relevant for most operators.

The purpose of Chapters 12 and 13 is to demonstrate the importance of applying the ergonomic principles discussed and described earlier. Chapter 12 deals specifically with safety, and illustrates the cost to the individual, to the organisation, and to the nation, of unsafe behaviour and environments. It demonstrates how the disruption of efficient communication channels and the establishment of alternative and less optimal channels can reduce safety and lead to accidents.

Death, injury and substandard work, however, are not the only result of a lack of ergonomic considerations, as Chapter 13 illustrates. In many situations it can lead to reduced efficiency caused by poor feedback to the operator. In this way the maintenance of system effectiveness and the inspection process can suffer. Having roused the reader to consider his system more fully, Chapter 14 illustrates many of the pitfalls ready to trap the unwary investigator who has to deal with the behaviour of human beings as subject-matter in an experimental design. Armed with such information, however, it is hoped that the reader will be in a fit position to progress further in implementing ergonomic solutions to the man–environment interaction problems.

To paraphrase Churchill, after having read this book it is hoped that the reader will cry 'Give us the ergonomic tools, tools that have been designed so that we can interact efficiently with them, and we will finish the job more effectively'.

David J. Oborne

1

ERGONOMICS: ITS SCOPE AND FUTURE

At last, ergonomics seems to have come of age: it is difficult these days to avoid seeing or hearing some reference to it in the media. User friendliness, human-based technology, human factors—these terms are all synonyms for the basic notion that if we want the best out of people their technology and environment should be fashioned to fit their wishes, expectations and abilities. The message is gradually emerging in all areas of life that ergonomics has considerable value and that it can ease our interaction withour living and working environment and make our work more effective, safe and comfortable. But what *is* ergonomics? What are its central themes? What real use does it have, and why should it be considered at all? This book will address many of these questions.

To many people ergonomics is a concept, an idea. It is a way of looking at the world, of thinking about people and how they interact with all aspects of their environment, their 'equipment' and their working situation. Ergonomics takes as its central focus the proposition that since people inhabited this world well before machines (indeed, people *invented* machines), and since we want our interaction with our environment to be effective, it is only appropriate that we remain in full operating control of the system within which we are working. To ensure this outcome, and to ensure optimum interaction, the 'machines' and the working environment in which they operate must be designed to fit people's thoughts, wishes and abilities.

This is how ergonomists view working situations. By understanding how people behave at work, how they interact with their environment and their machines at both physical and emotional levels, working environments can be created that do not require more of the operator than the operator can give. When this happens, the ergonomic argument concludes, when people and machines are in harmony, productive output will increase.

ERGONOMICS VS. PROCRUSTES

The Devil's Advocate

Although this view of ergonomics is rapidly becoming understood and accepted, ergonomists have to accept that there is an opposing philosophy that is often espoused with equal strength. This argues that people are more adaptable than their machines and environments, that they can learn to interact with their situations more easily—and often more cheaply—and so it is easier to make people 'fit' in with their surroundings than the reverse. This is often called the 'Procrustean approach', a description that is borrowed from Greek mythology.

Once upon a time there was a Greek robber called Procrustes who had devised a cunning way of extorting money from weary travellers unfortunate enough to pass his door. He simply offered them lavish hospitality on the strict understanding that they would either sleep in one of his spare beds or they would pay for the food and drink they had consumed. If the offer of a bed was accepted, as most frequently it was, then Procrustes made an additional stipulation: that the traveller should fit the bed exactly. After being wined and dined the unsuspecting victim would be shown to the bedroom in which there were two beds; one was very long and the other very short—but neither was the correct size to accommodate the unfortunate person. Now Procrustes' trick became apparent even to the least intelligent. Unless the exorbitant fees were paid he would threaten to make his victims fit one or other of the beds—either by putting them on the short bed and cutting off their legs, or by stretching their bodies enough to fit the long bed. Needless to say, most tired travellers took the easy way out and paid up.

There is, of course, a moral to this tale. Ever since people first began to interact with the environment in any complex way, this kind of Procrustean approach to design has been widespread. Industrial man (and woman) in particular has constantly been 'tailored' to 'fit' the demands of the physical world, and most victims accept a fair degree of discomfort and disability without too much fuss. In metaphorical terms, arms have been elongated to reach inaccessible controls and perceptual abilities stretched to hear or see virtually inaudible or invisible signals. At the other end of the Procrustean scale, legs have frequently been cut to fit cramped workplaces and cognitive capacities shrunk to cope with monotonous tasks. It only needs a little thought to build a comprehensive dossier of Procrustean wrong-doings that have resulted in people becoming subservient to the needs of their environment, rather than the environment being adapted to people's needs.

Continued industrial and commercial expansion, and the increased complexity of both work and machines, have compounded such issues. Because of a poor 'fit' between the human operator and the environment, lives have been lost, productivity reduced, and errors incurred in many millions of cases. Until relatively recently the demands of the environment have been paramount, with the needs and abilities of the person in the environment being accorded secondary importance.

Contemporary Procrustes—the training approach

Over the years there has therefore been a prevailing view that people can be adapted in a Procrustean way to suit the needs of the working conditions— albeit using rather more humane methods than stretching or amputation. In our contemporary society, training people is often viewed as the ideal way of ensuring that they will be able to interact properly with their environment, despite the fact that they are frequently trained to work in less than ideal situations. Unfortunately, although training can have obvious benefits to a wide variety of settings, considerable evidence exists to demonstrate that training alone is not a useful precursor to high productivity. There are three reasons for this: first, the cost of training the operator to fit the environment; second, the effectiveness of this approach; and third, the possible disruption of performance that can occur when a person is placed under stress.

In financial terms, training people to perform either difficult tasks or tasks that are not designed with the operator in mind can be very expensive. Without an ergonomic approach, both errors and training time are likely to increase, and examples of this will be seen throughout this book. It is accepted, of course, that training schedules cannot be dispensed with altogether. However, as will be demonstrated, in the majority of cases training and production times can be reduced considerably if the environment is designed to reflect the operator's abilities and requirements.

Training by Procrustean methods is also suspect from the viewpoint of the effectiveness of its outcome. Although people can be trained to high levels of competence, training alone will not be sufficient to overcome the problems that can be created by insufficient thought being given to how the person and the process should interact. With increasingly complex plant and machinery the working behaviour after training may still not be effective enough if the operator's complete environment is not considered in sufficient depth. Further help is often needed in the form of appropriately designed and positioned controls, perceptible displays and other important features before the consequences of any training can either be maximised or maintained. For example, Ellis and Hill (1978) showed that although training could be used to help overcome the difficulties in reading seven-segment liquid crystal displays, the improved performance that was secured by the training programme reduced significantly over just one month without the opportunity for practice. When having to use less than optimum equipment, therefore, the skills learned through training can be difficult to sustain.

The final limitation of the Procrustean approach is one of the most important and, perhaps, the most insidious. No matter how well an operator has been trained, if the behaviours learned are inappropriate to the task they can easily become disrupted under stress so that the wrong responses may be made. For example, Murrell (1971) cites the case of a hydraulic press which was damaged during an emergency. To raise the press a lever needed to be pushed down, an action which is contrary to normal expectations (as will be seen in Chapter 7, it is usually expected that a control should be raised to make an associated part move upwards). Although the operator had been trained to carry out this action very efficiently under ordinary conditions, when the emergency occurred and the press needed to be raised in a hurry he forgot his training and reverted to the more 'natural' behaviour: he lifted the lever to raise the press. Unfortunately, this 'operator error' caused the platen to fall and the press was wrecked.

In most cases (and using normally accepted training regimes) no amount of training will overcome the tendency of an operator to 'do what comes naturally' under stress. Reasons for this occurring will be given later, but they relate primarily to the amount of 'attention' that the operator can give to any particular part of the task.

It is clear from these examples that training alone will not use the human operator's full potential. Only when training schedules are linked to a full understanding of the task being carried out, so that the work is designed to be in harmony with the operator's physical, cognitive and emotional capacities, will performance be optimal under a range of conditions. The role of ergonomics is to highlight this concordance between the environment and the operator, and to develop working systems that reflect this interaction. This is done by first understanding and measuring the human operator's capabilities and then arranging the environment to fit them. As Rodger and Cavanagh (1962) describe it, the role of ergonomics is to 'fit the job to the man' (FJM) rather than to 'fit the man to the job' (FMJ).

THE DEVELOPMENT OF ERGONOMICS

Birthdays have major significance in life—they represent the day on which a new entity entered the world—and this is as much the case for ideas and concepts as for people. The date when ergonomics was born can be pinpointed fairly accurately to 12 July 1949, when a meeting was held at the British Admiralty at which an interdisciplinary group was formed (called the 'Human Research Group') for those interested in problems of people at work (see Murrell, 1980; Edholm and Murrell, 1973). Later, at a meeting on 16 February 1950, the term ergonomics (from the Greek: *ergon* = work; *nomos* = natural laws) was adopted and the discipline could finally be said to be born. (It should be pointed out, however, that the name ergonomics is not new. Seminara (1979) shows that it was first used in Poland by Professor Wojciech Jastrzebowski in an article published in 1857.)

Of course, as with a human being, the fact that a birth has occurred implies that considerable thought and effort were expended prior to the big event. Like a living creature, an idea must be conceived, nurtured and developed properly before it is born. Happily ergonomics (and its American sister discipline, human factors) received considerable prenatal care over many decades.

Although the birth date of ergonomics can be fairly well defined, the gestation period of this new discipline was long and tortuous, and no precise date can be given for its conception (nor can its parentage be accurately recorded). However, the initial rise of interest in the relationship between people and their working environments could be said to have commenced at about the time of the First World War. Workers in munitions factories were essential in maintaining the war effort, but the drive for higher arms output created a number of unforeseen complications in the UK. The attempt to resolve these problems led, in 1915, to the establishment of the Health of Munitions Workers' Committee which included among its investigators people who were trained in physiology and psychology. At the end of the war this Committee was reconstituted as the Industrial Fatigue Research Board (IFRB), chiefly to carry out research into fatigue problems in industry. In 1929 the IFRB was renamed the Industrial Health Research Board and its scope broadened to investigate general conditions of industrial employment, 'particularly with regard to the preservation of health among the workers and to industrial efficiency'. It employed people who were trained as psychologists, physiologists, physicians and engineers and who worked, both separately and together, on problems covering a wide area. Areas studied included posture, carrying loads, the physique of working men and women, rest pauses, inspection, lighting, heating, ventilation and 'music while you work'—as well as selection and training.

Two features of the work carried out between the wars are important. First, it was at times interdisciplinary. Second, it was largely exploratory and, in a way, studied the 'natural history of industry'. So working behaviour, and its role in productive outcomes, was being explored even at this relatively early stage in the life and times of the ergonomics philosophy.

The outbreak of the Second World War in Europe saw a rapid development in the military field. As if the stresses of battle were not enough, however, the military equipment developed in response to the need to fight in different environments, with different kinds of people and using different approaches, soon became extremely complex and problematic. The operating speeds demanded, for example, were often so high that the additional stresses caused personnel either to fail to get the best out of their equipment or to suffer operational breakdown. The new and often complex ideas and activities that wartime generates led to misunderstandings and ineffective use of the very equipment and structures that were designed to facilitate the war effort. It became essential, therefore, for more to be known about people's performance capabilities and limitations under different conditions and within different working systems. Naturally this produced extensive research programmes in many diverse fields and it was as a reaction to the desire to draw together this new-found knowledge that the Admiralty meeting took place in 1949. With this meeting the modern discipline of ergonomics was finally born.

As this book will illustrate, from its birth ergonomics has grown into a mature adult, without whose help many of the industrial and manufacturing developments since the Second World War could not have been achieved so efficiently: safely harnessing natural energy supplies in often adverse environments; effectively exploiting communications technology; radically improving domestic design; and, of course, travelling beyond the confines of our world to conquer space itself. All of these activities and more would have been impossible without a consideration of the relationship between the operator and the working environment. Quite simply, all work needs to involve people at some stage or another, and people would be unable to perform effectively without considerable thought being given to the design of systems that will fit their cognitive and physical capacities.

THE SCOPE OF ERGONOMICS

Ergonomics thus developed via the interests of a number of different professions and it still remains a multidisciplinary field of study. To provide information about working behaviour and what people can and cannot do, it crosses the boundaries between scientific and professional disciplines and draws on the data, findings, principles and concepts of each. Present-day ergonomics can be considered to be an amalgamation of physiology, anatomy and medicine as one branch; physiological and experimental psychology as another; and physics and engineering as a third.

The biological sciences provide information about the body's structure: the operator's physical capabilities and limitations; bodily dimensions; how much can be lifted; the physical pressures that can be endured, and so on. Physiological psychology deals with ways in which the brain and nervous system function and determine behaviour; while experimental psychologists study the basic ways in which individuals use the body to behave, perceive, learn, remember, control movements, and so on. Finally physics and engineering provide similar information about the system and environment with which the operator has to contend. In many respects the chapters in this book will follow these influences.

From these areas an ergonomist takes and integrates information to maximise the operator's safety, efficiency and performance reliability, to make the task easier to learn and to increase feelings of comfort and satisfaction.

These criteria, however, are by no means independent. For example, efficiency depends on accuracy, but accuracy is not its only component—others include such factors as reliability, speed, effort and fatigue. Arguing in the same vein, ergonomics seeks to increase safety. In turn this should result in a reduction in time lost through accidents and (perhaps) a corresponding increase in (worker) efficiency. By the same token, however, safety will itself depend on efficiency. Indeed, this book will provide many examples that show how the margin of safety left in an operation is largely a function of the operator's speed or reliability.

A further aim of ergonomics is to consider features that lead to operator 'unpredictability', in other words to increase reliability. Thus the human operator should not only be fast and efficient at work, but reliably so. Again, although reliability is related to accuracy the two processes may be independent. An operator may perform a task accurately most of the time but, because of some intermittent action of the work situation, this accuracy may be unreliable.

The importance of ease of learning has already been discussed. A system which has been designed so that the individual tasks are easier to learn will reduce training time and costs, and may produce fewer errors under stress.

The final aspect, comfort, is a subjective feature that is becoming increasingly important in present-day situations and refers to a sense of well-being and ease induced by the system. The concept of comfort and the controversies surrounding its definition will be discussed in later chapters, but it is sufficient to point out here that an uncomfortable operator will be prone to errors and is likely to perform less efficiently.

In summary, therefore, the ergonomist's task is first to determine the capabilities of the operator and then to attempt to build a workable system around those capabilities. Only when this approach has been fully adopted can the spirit of Procrustes finally be said to be exorcised.

MAN–MACHINE SYSTEMS

Ergonomics seeks to maximise safety, efficiency and comfort by shaping the working environment to the operator's capabilities. By linking the 'machine' to the person in this way (and in this direction) a relationship is established between the two components so that the system presents information to the operator via the operator's sensory apparatus to which a response may be made in some way—perhaps to alter the machine's state via various controls. For example, to drive a car safely and efficiently along a road a relationship needs to be built up between the driver and the vehicle such that any deviation of the car from a prescribed path (which is determined by both the driver and the road's shape and conditions) will be displayed back to the driver via the visual (and perhaps auditory and tactile) senses. These deviations can then be corrected by limb movements via the steering wheel and perhaps the brake or accelerator pedal. In their turn the corrections will be perceived as information that is displayed to the operator, and the sequence is continued until the journey's end. In this way information can be seen to pass from the machine to the person and back to the machine in a closed, information-control loop (see Figure 1.1). This loop is fundamental to the concept of ergonomics.

Many examples of single man–machine loops can be seen in a range of different work situations. However, in modern-day working environments such single loops are generally combined to produce more complex behavioural systems which, being composed of groups of different components (both people and machines, and parts of people and parts of machines), have to be designed to work together. It is the ergonomist's task to preserve and to enhance the operation of these kinds of complex loops. For example, the speed of information transmission to the car driver may be

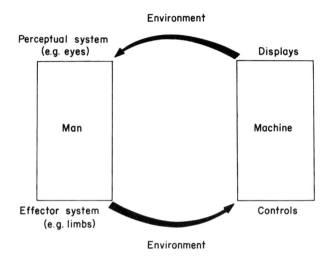

Figure 1.1 The 'man–machine' loop. The machine displays information to the operator who uses controls to affect the machine. The environment can interfere with the efficiency of this loop

increased (perhaps by clearer windscreens or by more understandable road signs) or the operation of a control may be made more efficient (perhaps by power-assisted steering or by altering the control, its position or dimensions). Similarly, knowledge about the antecedents and effects of, say, boredom might help to improve the driver's reactions to displayed signals; while understanding something of the behaviour of pedestrians will help in the design of vehicle systems, roads and footpaths that contribute to road safety and reduce the frequency and severity of pedestrian–vehicle contacts.

As well as illustrating the nature of the man–machine interaction, the car driver analogy suggests some of the problems that face ergonomists when attempting to design environments to fit the human operator. For many reasons the simple single man–machine loop does not exist in the 'real world'. Things are far more complex. In working situations many loops are often combined to produce more complex systems which, being composed of loops with different components (both operators and 'machines'), must be designed to work together. From an ergonomics viewpoint such combinations can create a variety of problems: two loops may act efficiently when considered in isolation but, when combined into a simple system, they might work antagonistically owing to unexpected interactions. For example, one loop may involve an operator pushing a lever in response to a deflection on a display, and a second might require a button to be pushed in response to a warning sound. Taken separately the two loops may work extremely efficiently: the display is well designed, the lever compatible with the operator's force capabilities, the warning sound audible and attention getting, and the push-button easy to use. When operating together, however, the two loops might interact to cause the operator's normally efficient behaviour to break down. For example, if put in the 'wrong' place, the operator's natural response may be to operate (incorrectly) the lever in response to the warning sound and attempt to change (unsuccessfully) the machine state by pushing the button. It is not too difficult to conceive how problems of this nature can be increased as the number of extra loops which are added to the system increase.

A second concern relates to how the environment interacts with these information-control loops. As Figure 1.1 illustrates, the system's physical and social environments can affect the efficient operation of these loops. For example, an operator's ability to see a message on a computer screen can be adversely affected simply by the sun appearing from behind a cloud and producing glare on the screen; noise can interfere with an otherwise audible auditory message; the presence of other people walking or talking nearby can disrupt concentration, and so on. Many hundreds of examples could be given to illustrate the fact that the quality of information transmitted from the operator to the system and back again is mediated by the environment.

For such reasons, the emphasis of modern, though traditional, ergonomics has been to investigate the operator and the environment as equal partners within the total working system, rather than to examine in minute detail the components which constitute any one man–machine loop. Traditional ergonomics, therefore, seeks to consider aspects of the job beyond a 'knobs and dials' approach, 'beyond the panel' (Murrell, 1969), to the man–machine system; that is, to the total interaction between the operator and the environment.

PERSON-CENTRED ERGONOMICS

Although in its traditional guise ergonomics argues that, for efficient operation of the system, individuals and their working systems should operate in close harmony, contemporary thinking suggests that even this seemingly innovative philosophy has its shortcomings. Recent arguments have advanced the thesis that the operator and the system are not equal partners at work; indeed, to consider them as being so in some way denigrates the most important component in the system—people—and reduces them to the level of inanimate components. Thus the modern, person-centred view of ergonomics argues that it is the person who controls the system, who operates it, steers its course and monitors its activities. In doing so it is the operator who has goals and wishes and who can change the system through abilities and whims. As Oborne *et al.* (1993) argue, it naturally follows that for the system to be effective it should be designed from the primary viewpoint of the operator—and not so much from a symbiotic (operator/machine) perspective. In short, the traditional man–machine concept is too simplistic for the operation of modern working systems that require people to be at the centre.

Discussing the human–computer interaction domain, for example, Eason (1991) argues that the basic man–machine viewpoint 'as a form of conversation between different kinds of participants' misses the rich complexity of the interaction. He points out that in the real world we interact with machines not merely to exchange messages but to engage in complex tasks. The man–machine interaction has a meaning which is over and above that which can be expressed by simple, straightforward analyses of the component parts. This meaning is injected into the system by both the operator and the nature of the task and its outcomes.

Wisner (1989) considers this viewpoint within the full domain of ergonomics. He argues that what is specific to ergonomics, as well as to psychology, is that it should consider more than just the specific 'properties of man'. Rather it should attempt to 'understand how man uses his own properties in terms of a story, his own story and that of humanity, the part of humanity to which he belongs'. Individual wishes and desires, motives and experiences are brought to a working situation and must be understood when considering the 'fit'. Even such factors as social background and culture play an important role.

The person-centred view of ergonomics, therefore, considers the interaction as one that is controlled and guided by the operator(s) in the system. In the course of their interactions with it, people bring to the system a collection of inherent strengths and weaknesses (including experiences, expectations, motivations, and so on) which themselves will interact with the system to change it. Often such features will be to the good of the system, from the viewpoint of such criteria as efficiency and safety. But sometimes they will include variability, fallibility and maybe even perversity—each of which is more likely to lead to errors and inefficiency.

Thus the traditional, almost mechanistic ergonomics philosophy can be said to have misperceived a critical perspective of the system in which it is involved—the operator and the attributes which he or she brings to the system in the wider sense. So, rather than just concentrating on ways of improving the information flow between individual components, person-centred ergonomics takes as its central point the need to accommodate the human attributes that the person brings to the system.

In many respects, of course, the traditional and person-centred perspectives can be viewed as being variations in emphasis as to which are the most important components within a system. The traditional view emphasises the individual as being almost subordinate to the system; the person-centred view concentrates on the individual as a unique controller of the system. By taking such a position, however, the person-centred approach loses none of its thrust towards the ideal of creating working environments that will fit the abilities and requirements of human operators.

Put another way, with others Branton (1983) has emphasised that human operators in a system inevitably turn it from being a closed-loop system to an open-loop one. Thus, instead of information flowing from one component to the other with (in theory) maximum efficiency for correcting deviations within the system, deviation corrections are effected by the operators on the basis of their 'mental models' of the system and its operation.

Oborne *et al.* (1993) point to four important features of the situation that can influence the process in this way. The person-centred approach views the human operator as: purposive, information seeking, uncertainty reducing and responsible. Such aspects of behaviour will aid people in their interactions with the system, particularly in determining the effects of their actions on the system and the nature and interpretation of the feedback arising from it. Indeed, these four features can be further divided:

Purposivity. The central tenet of this principle is that, despite frequent anecdotal evidence to the contrary, people at work are not merely passive beings who respond to incoming stimuli from the machine and the environment. They are 'doers' who are continually active, computing (sometimes even at a mathematical level) the implications of the incoming information and the nature of their responses to it. Thus individuals have a purpose in their interaction with the environment, and it is important to understand the nature of these purposes in order to design the system to accommodate them.

Anticipation and prediction. These features follow from the concept of purpose; they concern how the system is to be operated and controlled. When designing an interface between the operator and the system, for example, it is important to ensure that the operator can 'see' the results of his or her actions before they are carried out.

Interest and boredom. When viewing the operator as an active being it is important to consider the source of this activity. In this respect, interest plays an important role. Increased interest leads to a lowered likelihood of boredom and of subsequent errors. Indeed, Branton (e.g. 1983) and others have argued that reduced interest/increased boredom will lead to increased stress levels because the operator's 'mind' begins to wander. This in turn leads to 'mini panics' when the operator realises that a time slip may have occurred and becomes concerned about possible errors in that time.

Control and autonomy. Such concepts have an important tradition in the organisational psychology literature when dealing with individuals and work groups. They are equally important when considering the individual's interaction with his or her system. Thus, increased control over a situation results in reduced uncertainty of the outcome. Discussing the design of computer screens, for example, Branton and Shipley (1986) highlight the importance of control as a factor in stress causation and management. They postulated the development of a new 'breed' of individuals (Houston Men) whose lives revolve around interactions with these systems:

> Perhaps his VDU screen presents an illusory picture of the true condition of any plant or process deemed to be under control? Glued to his screen, how far can he actually control the reality out there? ... Our interest is not so much in what is actually shown to be on the screen but what is behind it, in what the display is supposed to represent to the operator. The processes to be controlled are at least one step removed from the controller's direct experience. The stress arises when these displays can no longer be trusted. The very remoteness from the end product generates feelings of helplessness, a condition often reported in the literature as stress.   (p. 1)

Responsibility and trust. A central aspect of the person-centred approach is that individuals act with responsibility when interacting with the system. Since this responsibility is towards the successful outcome of the goals, the information fed back must be of the kind and nature necessary to facilitate the desired outcome. The information received must be trusted by the operator, however. For example, Zuboff (1988) demonstrated that operators' lack of trust in new technology often formed a barrier that interfered with the effective use of the new systems. On the other hand, she also showed that operators sometimes placed too much trust in the system and failed to intervene when appropriate. Lee and Moray (1992) develop this concept further to consider an appropriate model for the design of automated systems based on the degree of operator trust that can be instilled in the working system. So again, the person-centred view of the relationship is being emphasised.

From the above discussion, it can be seen that the person-centred approach does not simply argue for a 'humanised' workplace. Rather the philosophy is to understand the factors which contribute to the operator's wishes and abilities in order to design the system appropriately. Each area illustrated above has important implications for the design of telematic systems for use in teleworking environments, as Table 1.1 illustrates.

WORK AND PERFORMANCE

The person-centred approach reminds us that people are the central components within the working system, and that they have aims, ambitions and motivations for both the work and for the system. These can be used to enhance total effectiveness, as long as they are accommodated within the system design.

It is clear, therefore, that the interaction between an operator and the system and environment is a very complex one. It now becomes important

Table 1.1 Essential human features of the person-centred approach to ergonomics

Purposivity	The technology design needs to reflect the use to which it is to be put. Designing an electronic mail interface for message archiving, for example, will lead to different considerations and conditions to one for real-time interactions.
Anticipation and prediction	The way in which information is displayed to the operator, and even the nature of the information displayed, should be such as to enhance the operator's needs to use the material to predict the outcome of the events displayed.
Interest and boredom	There are many ways which can be used to stimulate interest in the material being presented. Boredom can occur from both over- and under-stimulation.
Control and autonomy	Control over the situation is as much perceived as real. Most telematic systems remove the operator by at least one step from the situation being controlled; teleworking is likely to increase such remoteness.
Responsibility and trust	Since individuals *are* responsible for their actions, and since stress is likely to occur if the responsible individual is unable perform the task effectively, the technology needs to be designed after having understood the nature of the individual's feelings of responsibility and trust towards the task.

to question how this complexity can interfere with work performance—and the converse: how reducing the task complexity and creating a working environment that 'fits' the wishes and capacities of the operator can increase performance.

The relationship between the task's demands and the operator's performance can be described fairly simply by an inverted-U relationship as shown in Figure 1.2. As the figure illustrates, only when the demands fall somewhere within a middle range of complexity, intensity or whatever will performance be highest. The continuum that underlies the task demands aspect of the relationship is actually operator arousal—a concept that refers, essentially, to the amount of brain activity; indeed, it is often measured using electroencephalography (EEG). Thus, when a person is asleep or drowsy brain activity or arousal is low, and when under stress arousal is high (this is often accompanied by such physiological reactions as increased heart rate and sweating).

The importance of this relationship lies in the fact that an individual's arousal level is related to the amount of external and internal stimulation received. In this respect the nature of the task and the environment is clearly a varying source of stimulation, as also is the operator's own emotional state. So, during periods of low stimulation—perhaps from a boring job, or when signals are infrequent—the low levels of arousal are

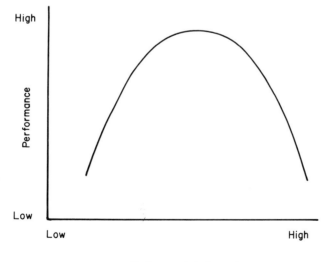

Figure 1.2 The hypothetical inverted-U relationship of environmental demands versus performance

likely to be reflected in low levels of performance. Similarly, cases in which the stimulation is too high can cause reduced performance levels. Too much noise, for example, or performing tasks that are difficult or stressful, or have been designed without considering the operator's needs, can help to increase arousal levels and reduce performance ability.

Unfortunately the inverted-U arousal/performance curve is only a general relationship. Both the shape of the curve and the level of arousal depend for optimum performance on characteristics of the operator and the type of stimulation. Personality and intelligence are just two individual characteristics that can alter the relationship. For this reason it is not possible to provide 'tables' of optimum arousal/stimulation levels. All that can be done is to recognise the existence of the relationship and to ensure that the working system neither over- nor under-stimulates the individuals concerned. For example, environments with very low levels of stimulation, like those with boring, repetitive tasks, can be enhanced by the provision of music (although, as will be seen in Chapter 10, the kinds of music played can be important).

Before concluding the discussion of the arousal/performance relationship, it should be emphasised that an operator obtains stimulation from a number of features at work: physical, physiological, social, personal, etc. Each can operate to raise or to lower the overall arousal level. Thus the value of an otherwise 'ideal' physical environment may be reduced if the operator's arousal is increased or lowered by the imposition of additional stimuli which induce or reduce arousal, such as bad social relationships with colleagues or worries at home. Such stressors, of course, may also be variable in their effect—acting detrimentally on one occasion and not on another.

As well as describing this task/performance relationship in terms of arousal, attempts have also been made to model the effects in terms of 'mental capacity'. In essence this descriptive model suggests that an operator brings to a task a limited capacity to perform. As long as the capacity is not exceeded the task will be executed efficiently. Performance will fall, however, if the task demands more than the operator can give, often because other, secondary, features of the situation intrude. Wetherall (1981) reviews the extent to which different types of secondary task can detrimentally affect various kinds of activity.

The essential value of this model is that it suggests that when performing a task some kind of trade-off often takes place between the demands of the task and those of the environment on the one hand, and the operator's own abilities on the other. The spare mental capacity model, therefore, suggests that any increased requirements made by less-than-optimum working situations can be compensated by additional operator effort. For example, an operator may normally be able to accommodate poor environmental conditions without any outward adverse effects simply because more of the limited spare mental capacity is used—the operator 'works' hard or 'concentrates' more. If the task and environment demand too much, however (perhaps other machines start up causing increased noise levels, and so increased stimulation), the spare mental capacity that was otherwise used by the primary task will be exhausted, with resultant reductions in performance. The additional work required, therefore, became the 'straw that broke the camel's back'. In terms of the philosophy of ergonomics, it is likely that a difficult task or one that does not 'fit' the operator will leave less spare mental capacity, and will be affected more quickly and to a greater extent than one that is easier or more appropriately designed.

The implications of these two models, therefore, are clear. Operators can generally adapt to work in less-than-optimum conditions—but only at a cost. As long as the environment does not demand more spare mental capacity than is available, performance will be maintained, although at a level which is related in some way to the arousing qualities of the task. Too much demand will reduce efficiency because of increased arousal and reduced spare mental capacity.

ALLOCATING FUNCTIONS BETWEEN MAN AND MACHINE

It is often argued that one of the first and most important questions in man–machine system design concerns allocating functions between the operator and the machine. Which functions of the system should be assigned to people and which to machines? Or, what kind of tasks can and should human operators be performing in a man–machine system?

In response to concerns such as these, a number of authors originally developed lists of operations which are carried out most efficiently by people and by machines (for example, Chapanis, 1960; Murrell, 1971). Taken together they suggest that human beings are better decision-makers, particularly when flexibility is required and unexpected events may occur; are able to improvise; have a fund of past experience; and can perceive and interpret complex forms involving depth, space and pattern. Machines, on the other hand, are highly efficient computing, integration and differentiation devices; can deal with predictable events very reliably; and are useful in hazardous environments. Even with modern computing equipment, many of these distinctions still hold true. Price (1985), for example, describes a number of these lists and evaluates their potential.

Although such lists can have some value in directing an ergonomist's thinking towards man–machine problems, and providing reminders of some of the characteristics that people and machines will bring to the system, they tend to lose sight of the basic nature of a system that contains humans and machines, how they interact, and the importance of the person-centred nature of systems design. For example, before deciding on the relative advantages and disadvantages of 'man' and machine one also needs to know something about the operator's preferences, expectations and responsibilities.

Chapanis (1965a) suggests three further problems. First, general man–machine comparisons can be wrong or misleading. In many cases the system itself determines the adequacy of its individual components. For example, the general statement that 'man' is superior to a machine for decision-making tasks is just that—a general statement. It cannot be true for all people or for all machines.

Secondly, it is not always important to decide which component can do a particular job better. Often the question should be 'is the component good enough for the job?' Fitts (1962) rephrases this question to ask 'which component will do an adequate job for less money, weight or power, or with a smaller probability of failure and less need for maintenance?'

Finally, general comparisons between people and machine give no considerations to trade-offs. There are many considerations that need to be taken into account when choosing between the two components, for example, weight, cost, size or availability. Variables such as these have to be traded off, one against the other, before the ideal system can be designed.

The question which may need to be asked, therefore, could be 'is it better to design a system which, because of size limitation, includes a human operator and less equipment, or would it be better to reject the human operator—thus losing some flexibility but being able to include more equipment?' Simple lists which compare the values of 'men' and machines separately do not help to solve this kind of trade-off problem.

The dilemma is best summed up by a statement made during a recent NASA mission to recover a satellite that had been 'lost' in space. Against all odds, the satellite was successfully retrieved by the mission commander (dangerously) reaching out and grabbing an antenna, after all the other, more mechanical, options had failed:

One of the benefits of having men up there is that if things go wrong they can repair them and rethink them, and if that doesn't work they can try again some other way.

(Barbara Schwartz, Mission Control Houston, 14th May 1992)

Again, the need for a person-centred approach to ergonomics becomes clear.

COSTS AND REWARDS

Deciding on the relative merits and effectiveness of 'men' and machines within a system is a difficult task which is made more complex when the question of their respective costs is included. At this point, therefore, it is appropriate to consider how ergonomics fares when it is subjected to some kind of cost–benefit analysis. Any manager who contemplates either implementing an ergonomics investigation or introducing a system designed to ergonomic principles is likely to have to justify the cost in relation to the rewards. (See *Ergonomics*, 1990, Parts 3, 4 and 5, for a comprehensive set of discussions relating to the issue of 'marketing ergonomics'.)

Chapanis (1976) points out that a full cost–benefit equation is extremely difficult to devise since many factors, some of them 'invisible', are involved when assessing the value of a system. Those which he considers important include, on the benefit side, the value of all goods and services produced by the system and the values which accrue from any incidental or 'spin-off' products. In addition, the impact of international health and safety legislation should not be forgotten; the production of unsafe systems—or even of systems that have the potential of directing behaviour in unsafe ways—can prove costly for the organisation in terms of fines and compensation. On the negative side of the equation Chapanis includes equipment costs, replacement or maintenance costs, operating costs, the cost of job aids, auxiliary equipment and manuals, of personnel selection, of training, of salaries and wages, of accidents, errors and breakages or wastage, and the social costs of implementing the system (for example, the long-term costs of pollution).

Many of these factors can be expressed in tangible, monetary terms. Others, however (for example, the cost of pollution, selection, accidents, and the like), are less quantifiable (see Chapter 12). Nevertheless they make important contributions to reducing the efficiency and productivity of a system and must be taken into account. Corlett and Parsons (1978) describe other criteria which ought to be part of the assessment. These include reduced stress and turnover costs, and increased work interest and satisfaction.

A further problem relating to the cost–benefit equation is that few well-controlled studies are available. From an economic viewpoint this is understandable—a redesigned piece of equipment, for example, which is thought to be better than its existing counterpart will naturally be used throughout the plant as soon as possible. However, it also means that comparative measurements of the system effectiveness with and without the new equipment and under otherwise similar conditions (pay, time of year, operator, etc.) are extremely difficult to obtain.

Despite these problems some studies are available which illustrate the cost-effectiveness of ergonomics. Sell (1977) describes detailed work which was carried out in the early 1960s at the British Iron and Steel Association to design overhead crane cabs. A problem which had occurred involved damage to railway wagons caused by drivers of some cranes swinging the magnetic hooks against the side of the railway truck. It was estimated that this damage was costing the company around £60 per week in wagon repairs. Simple observations showed the operator could not reach all his controls and, at the same time, look out of the crane to see the position of the magnet. By redesigning the position of both the magnet and the controls so that the operators could see the hook and reach the controls, the design fault was eliminated. Beevis and Slade (1970) have suggested that the modifications cost £270, which meant that the costs were repaid within about six weeks.

On the same theme, Teel (1971) describes the costs and rewards accruing from two separate ergonomics studies. The first evaluated the effectiveness of specially prepared visual aids in improving the performance of machine parts inspectors who examined precision parts for defects which might make then unsuitable for use. The cost of the study, of preparing the aids, was calculated to be $7200. The savings in the first year alone, however, were over $10 000. Since the production was to continue for three years, Teel argues that the total savings accounted for more than four times the cost of the study.

In the second study Teel considered the workplace of electronic assemblers: again according to ergonomic principles. When using a redesigned console the time taken by each operator to complete a task was reduced by 64 per cent, with 75 per cent fewer errors. The cost of the study was $4200, while the savings per year were calculated to be in excess of $28 000.

These are examples of the benefits that could be obtained from considering the work from the operator's viewpoint. However, as Chapanis' (1965a) list discussed earlier indicates, productivity benefits to a company may not always be measurable simply in terms of the number of units produced. For example, in some cases productivity may rise simply because all the workers remain at their jobs, rather than having to take time off through sickness or accidents. Even if a worker is only temporarily hurt by an accident, and takes perhaps half an hour off work to visit the sick bay or doctor, productive time is reduced by at least that time and probably more.

As an example of this problem, Drury *et al.* (1983) describe the design of a palletising aid to help in the manual stacking of boxes on a shipping pallet. The new aid reduced the amount of spinal compression due to lifting from about 250 kg to about 150 kg. Taking account of the number of spinal injuries that occur each year from lifting inappropriate weights and weight distributions, the authors calculated that the specifically designed aid would reduce spinal injuries by a factor of four. Relating this to actual costs per operator, they calculated that the expected cost of back injuries could be reduced from $503 per man year to $129 per man year—a saving of $374 per man year. They also computed the saving that their new design would make in terms of reduced cardiovascular strain: between $3000 and $4000 in eliminating relief (resting) time.

Finally, it should be remembered that in many circumstances appropriate ergonomics considerations are not merely desirable—they are sometimes critical and embodied in legal statutes. For example, Wilson (1983) discusses the concept of a manufacturer's liability for the production of safe consumer products and describes some of the costs incurred by manufacturers found to be contravening design safety standards. Consumer pressure groups in many countries create critical climates against which products are evaluated for both legal and commercial viability. Ease, safety and efficiency of use, and the extent to which the user has been considered in the product design, are frequently employed assessment criteria.

SUMMARY

This chapter has discussed how ergonomics, and its American sister discipline human factors, arose as a response to the need to consider how the human operator manages to cope with the environment. The important concept is that discrepancies between what the environment requires and what the operator can give should be resolved by adapting the environment to the operator, rather than the normal approach of making the operator suit the environment. When doing so, it is the person at the centre of the system who should be considered; his or her abilities, motivations, expectations and feelings are central to the effective operation of the system. When such basic changes are made, it is argued, then the efficiency, safety, comfort and productivity of the total man–machine system will be enhanced. The remainder of this book considers the various aspects of the system and the nature of improvements.

2

THE STRUCTURE OF THE BODY I: THE SENSORY NERVOUS SYSTEM

Put in very simple terms, the human operator can be said to be little more than a rather complex system of bones, joints, muscles, tissues, nerves and fluids. Such simplicity, however, belies the rich complexity of human life and form. The population of the world displays an almost infinite variability in body structures and in the individual ways in which the bodies are used—at both physiological and psychological levels. Since it is impossible to understand fully how a proper relationship between the human operator and his or her mechanical environment can be developed without some understanding of how the body is built and how it works, the purpose of this and the following chapter is to take this simplistic view of 'man'. After all, it is the arrangements and limitations of these bones, joints, tissues and nerves that define the body and will thus define the most basic concept of ergonomics: literally that of designing the environment so that it fits the person.

Putting to one side for a paragraph or two the person-centred input to understanding the system, it should be remembered that the relationship between people and their environment largely hinges on a complex closed-loop system. At its most basic level, this involves firstly the display of information from the machine to the operator: a light flashes, a colour appears, a sound is made, or a lever changes position. On the basis of this information the operator may have to carry out some action—pull a lever, push a switch, adjust a rudder, and so on. These actions transmit commands to the machine which alter the display and, with the presentation of information back to the operator, the loop is completed. (Returning to the person-centred input: it is the operator who then determines how the information should be interpreted and acted upon.)

The efficient operation of this closed-loop system requires the effective use of a number of body structures. First, there are the receptor agencies of the human body, the sense organs. Through these the information is initially passed to the operator and they represent a major potential site for errors and improvements. Secondly, the nerves carry information from the sense organs to the interpretation and decision-making areas of the brain, and from the brain to the muscles. Although they conduct this information very quickly, nerves have their limitations. Third are the body structures which carry out various actions—the effector processes. Once a decision to act has been made, the information is transmitted to the muscles which control the action of the bones, joints and tendons. In addition to the decision-making capacities, these effector processes represent possibly the greatest limitation to the operator's mechanical efficiency.

This chapter considers the structure and functions of the nerves and the sense organs. Chapter 3 deals with how the bones, joints and muscles are arranged and the limitations which they place on the body's movements.

SENSORY MECHANISMS

The basic unit that transmits all sensory information is the single nerve cell or neurone, which comes in many shapes and sizes depending on its position in the body. Each neurone consists of three main parts. First the cell body, which contains the nucleus; second, a mass of hair-like protrusions extending from the cell body, known as dendrites; and third, a long, single, thin extension of the cell body, the axon. This may be from less than a millimetre up to more than a metre long, and ends as dendrites. In many neurones, the axon is covered by a fatty insulating sheath known as the myelin sheath.

The chain of command, therefore, is for the cell body dendrites to convey information to the cell body itself. This is transmitted along the axon as a burst of potential differences to other dendrites at the far end, which are closely entangled with the cell body dendrites of the next neurones. The information is transmitted across the dendrite gaps (synapses) and so on throughout the body. The rate at which impulses travel along a nerve fibre depends on the thickness of the myelin sheath surrounding the axon and also, to some extent, on the diameter of the axon itself. When the sheath is thick the rate of travel may be as high as 20 m/sec, but if the sheath is very thin or non-existent the rate of travel could be as low as 0.6 m/sec.

The transmission speed through the body also depends on the number of synaptic gaps between the neurones, since the synapses create a slight delay in the transmission process. Although the synaptic gap is only of the order of 100 angstroms (0.000001 mm) the delay between the arrival of an impulse at the axon terminal and the initiation of an impulse the other side of the synapse can be in the order of $1/2$–1 msec. In that period, another impulse could be travelling a metre along the fibre.

THE SENSES

Various kinds of information are fed into the sensory system through receptors, which can be classified into two groups. The exteroceptors receive information about the state of the world outside the body and so include the eyes, ears and touch receptors in the skin. Using the same terminology, the interoceptors inform the individual about the body's internal state, for example its state of hunger or the fullness of the bladder. A specific subgroup of interoceptors which is of direct interest to ergonomists is the proprioceptors which are concerned with motor functions. These give information about the position of the body or parts of it in space and basically form two groups: kinaesthetic receptors in the muscles and tendons that supply information about the muscle and joint activity, and the vestibular system in the ears which informs the individual about the body's orientation in space.

Before describing the senses in more detail, it is useful to consider the difference between 'sensation' and 'perception'. Whichever sensory system is considered, sight, hearing, taste, touch or smell, the particular organ receives energy from the outside world, converts it into small potential differences and passes these along the system to the brain. This is the process of sensation (or reception). It is determined entirely by the stimulus quality and the particular organ and part of the nervous system, and it is an objective process. On entering the brain, however, the nerve impulses are interpreted to produce a recognisable pattern of sight, smell, sound, etc., and this process is considerably influenced by the individual's past experience, expectations, feelings and wishes. This (person-centred) process of perception is entirely subjective in nature.

Thus the distinction between sensation and perception is very important: simply presenting stimuli so that they will be *received* accurately does not mean that they will *perceived* accurately. Furthermore, although two people may receive and sense the same object, they may not have identical perceptions. The implications of this for the person-centred approach to ergonomics should be clear. This distinction will be emphasised again in Chapter 4 when discussing in more detail the channels of communication that can be set up by people.

THE VISUAL SYSTEM

Of all the senses, vision has been the most thoroughly studied, which is useful because it is probably the system that is most overloaded at work. In essence the system consists of two eyes, each connected to the visual cortex of the brain by an optic nerve (see Figure 2.1). The two nerves meet at the optic chiasma at the base of the brain, where part of each nerve crosses over and terminates in the visual cortex on the opposite side of the brain to the eye from which it originated. In fact, fibres from the left-hand side of each eye terminate in the left visual cortex and those from the right-hand side of each eye terminate in the right visual cortex.

The effects of this crossing of fibres may prove to be important when information is presented in very short periods of time or when extremely fast responses are required. For example, it is now fairly well understood that the two halves of the brain do not 'perform' equally well for all types of material: speech appears to be analysed better in the left half (hemisphere) while the right hemisphere is dominant with respect to spatial ability. In terms of material normally presented to the visual system, the left hemisphere is better than the right at analysing words, whereas there is

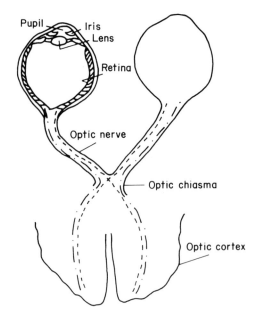

Figure 2.1 The eye and visual system, showing the pathways of portions of the optic nerve

some evidence to suggest that numbers are recognised faster in the right hemisphere.

Depending on the nature of the visual material, therefore, it might be acted on more speedily or efficiently if presented to one half of the visual field rather than the other. However, this right- or left-hand advantage is likely to be noticed only when very fast responses are required. Welford (1984) argues that a hemispheric advantage may also be useful in situations such as the left/right placement of road traffic signs, when fast reactions are often also required.

With regard to the eye itself, perhaps the easiest way to understand its structure is to compare it with a camera. A specific amount of light enters the eye through the pupil (aperture), the diameter of which is controlled by the coloured portion of the iris (stop). It is then bent and focused by the lens to fall on to the retina which acts as a photosensitive layer.

Although the analogy with the camera is suitable at a descriptive level, differences exist between the structure of the eye and that of a camera which mean that the eye has more flexibility:

- The eye's lens is in a fixed position relative to that of the photosensitive area—it does not have to be moved to and fro to focus on objects at different distances as is the case with a camera. Focusing is accomplished by the muscles that surround the eye and change its curvature.

- The photosensitive layer is curved, which compensates for the curvature of the lens. Both of these differences allow quicker and more efficient focusing.

- The pupil size is regulated by the iris. By influencing the amount of light able to enter the eye, along with the variable sensitivity of the retinal cells, the eye can operate over a far greater range of illumination intensities than can a camera which has to use a fixed type of film sensitivity at any one time.

- The retina does not have the same level of sensitivity to light over its surface; it is highest at the centre and decreases quickly towards the periphery. A photographic film of this type would produce a picture with very good detail at the centre only, with reducing quality as the image fell further from the centre. To compensate for this, the eye constantly scans the visual field using a set of six muscles attached to each side, above and below the eyeball. In this way, different images can be pointed at the most sensitive part of the retina in rapid succession.

Table 2.1 The properties of rods and cones (adapted from Morgan, 1965, and reproduced by permission of McGraw-Hill)

Rods	Cones
Function at low levels of illumination (such as at night)	Function at higher illumination levels (such as during daylight)
Differentiate between shades of black and white	Differentiate between colours
Most sensitive in the greenish part of the spectrum	Most sensitive in the yellowish part of the spectrum
More numerous in the periphery of the eye	More numerous in the central part of the eye
Sensitive to very weak stimuli	Mainly involved in space perception and visual acuity

- Finally, by using both eyes together it is possible to obtain binocular vision. This helps us to perceive spatial relationships between objects and the environment—so the eyes record in three dimensions whereas the camera can only 'see' in two.

Perhaps the most important part of the eye itself is the retina. This is the layer at the back which acts like a complex photodiode to convert luminous energy to electrical energy. It is made up of three layers of neurones, the most important of which is on the outside surface and contains two different neurones called rods and cones (so called because of their shape). These are the main receptor cells and, as shown in Table 2.1, they perform different functions.

A number of important points emerge from Table 2.1. First, because the rods, which function at low illumination levels, are primarily towards the periphery of the retina, we can see dim objects much more effectively if we look at them off-centre. This means that staring a little to the right or left of the object will help to focus it towards the periphery of the retina where the rod density is high. The corollary, of course, relates to the distribution of cones in the retina. These are the cells used for 'normal' vision and are more numerous towards the central part of the retina (known as the fovea). Since cones are the main receptors for differentiating between colours and are used in normal vision, it is important for maximum perception that visual information is presented centrally to the eye rather than to its periphery. Of course, the eyes can move around in their sockets to focus on an object but, before they can do so, the object has first to be seen. Images falling towards the periphery of the retina are less likely to be seen.

A second implication suggested by Table 2.1 is that our sensitivity to light changes with variations in the ambient illumination level. At some point, for example at dusk, responsibility for the conversion of light energy to electrical impulses switches from the cones to the rods. Thirdly, the rods and cones are sensitive to different wavelengths of light. These two latter points are important when considering how we adapt to light and dark.

Light and Dark Adaptation

Because of the two types of receptors in the retina (the rods and the cones), the human eye is able to function efficiently over an extremely wide range of illumination levels. Cone vision provides acute vision at daytime (photopic) levels of illumination, whereas rod vision allows for the high degree of sensitivity that is essential for seeing when light levels are low (scotopic). With increasing or decreasing luminance levels, however, there will always be a point at which one set of photoreceptors suspends operation as the other begins to take over. If the illumination change is relatively slow this adaptation to dark or light conditions is fairly smooth, but with fast changes in illumination the well-known experience of temporary blindness results. For example, moving from pitch darkness to bright sunlight sharply increases the illumination level falling on the retina so that the previously functioning rods cannot cope and the cones have not had a chance to operate fully. In this case the eyes normally have to be closed, or dark glasses worn, to allow them gradually to become adapted to the change in the light level, after which time the eyes can again function efficiently within a new dynamic range of intensities.

Because the cones react relatively fast, their light adaptation is often complete within a minute or two. Rods, however, are much slower, and dark adaptation may take half an hour or even longer, depending on the previous illumination levels. For this reason, dark or coloured goggles are often worn by people having to work in dark environments (for example, radar operators or maintenance people) for some time before entering the dark room. Red is the colour normally used because it is one which does not greatly affect the visual pigment in the rods. Thus the cones may operate fairly normally during daylight while the rods are able to become adapted for the dark (see for example Cushman, 1980).

Visual Movement Perception

There are many situations in which a human operator might need to perceive motion accurately. For example, a pointer moving across a dial, a vehicle along a track, or a falling object.

In general, movement can be perceived in two ways. In the first an object is kept in view by moving the eye, so the observer receives information about the object's speed and direction using information fed back from (proprioceptive) receptors in the muscles that surround and position the eye (this type of sensory information will be discussed in more detail later). The second way occurs when the eye is stationary and the object's image moves across the retina; the moving object is then perceived from the stimulation of different retinal cells. Under these circumstances the minimum velocity which can normally be detected is about 1–2 minutes of arc/sec. Faster movement causes the normal reaction of the eye to track the object as it moves across the visual field, and so movement information is obtained from the eye muscles.

The lowest level of movement that can be detected (the movement threshold) will be reduced considerably, by an order of approximately 10, if another (stationary) figure is present in the visual field. This provides a reference point against which the moving image can be compared and it is likely that other visual processes are also involved, perhaps concerning the ways in which we perceive spatial relationships.

Visual Spatial Perception

Perceiving the spatial relationships between a series of objects in the visual field is also normally accomplished by one or both of two processes. Visual cues are provided by different objects in the visual field, and proprioceptive feedback comes from accommodation and convergence of the eyes.

Two kinds of visual cues are normally used to perceive spatial relationships: binocular and monocular. In the former the images received by the two eyes are compared by the brain and the disparity between them is used to indicate the relative positions of objects in space. For example, if a near and far object are both directly in front of the observer and the eyes are fixated on the near object, when the right eye is closed the left eye 'sees' the far object as having moved to the left. Similarly, looking through the right eye only, the far object is observed to the right of its actual position. Interpretation of these two different images by the two visual cortexes provides the observer with information about the relative positions of the two objects.

An observer also uses a number of monocular cues to perceive spatial relationships, and each is related to past visual experiences. These cues include the relative sizes of objects (if two objects are the same size, the object further away appears to be smaller); covering and shadow (if one object is in front of another it may partially obscure it, or the degree of shadow may provide information relating to the distance between the two objects); and texture. Gibson (1950), for example, has argued that if there is any regular marking or visible texture in the object, such as on a patterned floor, this texture undergoes a transformation in perspective so that in the retinal image there is a gradient of texture density; the gradient suggests space.

In addition to binocular and monocular cues obtained from the images of different objects in the visual field, the fact that the eyes had to converge to fixate on the various objects also tells the observer about their relative position in space. Fixating on a far object, for example, causes double images of the near object and this disparity can be reduced by converging the eyes. This convergence may be used as a cue, implying that the second (nearer) object is nearer than the initial fixation point. Furthermore, the lens shapes are altered to accommodate the two, slightly different, images. The degree to which these two processes occur provides valuable information about the relative positions of objects in the visual field, and this information is obtained from the position (proprioceptive) receptors in the eye and lens muscle.

Visual Acuity

Having considered some of the principles underlying our ability to register spatial aspects of the visual scene, it is appropriate to turn to the topic of visual acuity. This is the process by which we can see fine details. Again many aspects of work require this ability—to register the fact that a very slowly moving pointer has moved; to detect differences in the position of two controls; to recognise the presence of an object in the visual field; to localise and to distinguish between two close objects in space, and so on. The three kinds of acuity most commonly recognised are line acuity (the ability to see very fine lines of known thickness), space acuity (the ability to see two spots or lines as being separate, in other words to see a space between the lines), and vernier acuity (the ability to detect discontinuity in a line when part of it is slightly displaced).

In essence three factors are important in determining the degree of acuity that we have under any given condition. First is the size of the pupil—acuity is fairly linearly related to pupillary diameter down to a value of about 1 mm. (High ambient illumination levels and some drugs, such as alcohol, may cause the pupil to be constricted and this could be an important factor for the safe and efficient operation of machines which require high levels of acuity.) A second factor is the light intensity reflected from the object (its luminance). An object which is, perhaps, too fine to be seen at all under low illumination levels may become clearly visible when illumination is increased. (As was mentioned above, however, too high a level of illumination is likely to cause the pupil to become narrowed so reducing acuity. Indeed, in many respects it is the contrast between the object and its background that is important—as will be discussed in Chapter 11.) Over normal illumination ranges, acuity varies linearly with a logarithmic increase in illumination between a visual angle (that is, the angle subtended by the object at the eye) of about 0.2–1.5 minutes of arc. Finally, and within limits, acuity is related to the time allowed to view the object; a reduced exposure time reduces acuity. The exposure times experienced in normal work, however, are usually above those needed for this to be a problem (above 200 msec at normal daylight levels of illumination).

Age and Visual Performance

The question of acuity becomes particularly important when considering how our visual senses fare as we become older. Unfortunately, from a fairly young age all visual functions are subject to deterioration. We can normally compensate for such losses, however, since increasing experience and familiarity with a given object mean that we require less information to recognise it. Nevertheless, as was explained in Chapter 1, such compensation might well bring with it further costs to overall efficiency.

A number of experimenters have investigated the course of visual depreciation and have shown that some of this reduction can be offset by increased luminance of the object. Lerman (1984), for example, noted that the cornea yellows with age and Weale (1963) demonstrated that this effect also happens to the lens. Both observations mean that the amount of light reaching the retina of a 60-year-old person is about one-third that reaching the retina of a 20-year-old person. Thus Bodmann (1962), for example, found that 50-year-old subjects needed illumination in the range 100–400 lux to perform as well as younger (20–30-year-old) subjects working in 2–5 lux illumination.

Data such as these, therefore, imply that careful attention should be paid to the design of visual tasks in order to take account of the variations in visual abilities among different age groups. In many visual tasks involving reading printed text, for example, it might be possible to raise the general level of illumination of the material to be read. However, even this practice could have some difficulties since sensitivity to glare also increases with age because of changes that occur in the eye, resulting in more light being scattered in the optic media (Hopkinson and Collins, 1970).

A further problem of decreased visual function with age relates to our ability to focus on objects at different distances—accommodation. This is normally performed by the ciliary muscles in the eye contracting and changing the lens shape. With age the functioning of these muscles may deteriorate, with the result that the nearest point to which the eye can be sharply focused (the 'near point') moves further from the eye (that is, we become long-sighted). In addition our speed of accommodation decreases with age, a problem that is particularly important, for example, when typing text at a computer keyboard. Thus, the eyes often have to move quickly between the material on the manuscript to the VDU screen. If the text and screen are at different distances from the observer, the eyes will have to accommodate rapidly if blurred images are not to result. These problems are not entirely insoluble, however, since the ageing effects can be ameliorated using appropriate spectacles.

Visual Flicker

In many cases the human operator may be called on to respond not to a visual stimulus with a relatively steady illumination level, but to one that flickers. Flashing warning or indicator lights are, perhaps, the most obvious examples of such displays. Flicker can also be a negative feature of some environments; as will be discussed in Chapter 11 excessive flicker from structures like fluorescent lights can be detrimental both to health and to working conditions.

Flicker is a temporal phenomenon; its perception depends heavily on the ability of the visual system to react to the fast changes in light intensity. In many cases, therefore, it may be considered to be a kind of acuity task, since the observer needs to 'perceive' the period of darkness between two flashes.

This task can be carried out fairly well for light flashes occurring relatively infrequently, when a flickering sensation will arise as a result of the separate flashes being perceived. As the flash frequency is increased, however, the flashes appear to merge to produce light which is indistinguishable from a steady state illumination. The frequency at which this occurs is called the critical fusion frequency (c.f.f) and depends on a number of factors. It is often used as a measure of visual performance and has been shown to range from about two to three flashes per second at very low illumination levels (that is, during scotopic vision using the rods) to around 60 flashes per second with extremely high levels (that is, during photopic vision). At the change-over point between scotopic and photopic vision, at illumination levels normally experienced at dusk for example, c.f.f. is around 15 flashes per second.

A considerable amount of experimental literature has built up regarding the parameters of c.f.f. (see, for example, Hopkinson and Collins, 1970; Riggs, 1972). The main results can be summarised as follows:

- C.f.f. increases linearly with the logarithm of illumination intensity over a wide range of light intensities (this is the so-called Ferry–Porter Law, see Kelly, 1961).

- When the levels of brightness of the stimulus and the surrounding area are the same, c.f.f. is at its highest. It reduces as the brightness difference increases.

- At very small visual angles, the c.f.f. increases linearly with the logarithm of the stimulus area.

- C.f.f. is relatively independent of wavelength (stimulus colour).

- C.f.f. reduces during dark adaptation.

- There is wide individual variability in c.f.f., but individuals are fairly consistent within themselves.

- C.f.f. is relatively independent of practice.

Colour Vision

A quick glance around a modern workplace will illustrate immediately the importance of colour. It is used to help the operator distinguish between different parts of the working area, controls, displays and parts of a display, files, action requirements, and so on. It can create mood (it is generally accepted that the reds and yellows are 'warm' colours whereas blues are 'cool') and, using contrasts, colour can help improve visibility.

Different colours are perceived as a result of the eyes receiving different wavelengths of light, either reflected from a coloured surface or emanating from a coloured light source. The normal eye can sense light in the visible spectrum with a range of wavelengths between about 440 and 700 nanometres (1 nm = 10^{-9}m). To these different wavelengths we attach various colour names, with the shorter wavelengths (around 450 nm) being described as 'blue' and the longer wavelengths (around 650 nm) as 'red'. The physical attribute of what is normally called colour is the hue.

The important dimensions of colour, however, do not simply end with hue. The saturation and luminance of the wavelengths contained in the light also have important implications for the quality of the colour experienced. The dimension of luminance is possibly the easiest to understand and refers to the amount of light that enters the eye. At one extreme the stimulus will be barely visible, at the other end it will appear almost painfully bright. Saturation, however, is less easy to conceptualise. It refers, essentially, to the amount of white light (that is, light containing all the visible wavelengths) contained in the light perceived. It is an index, therefore, of the hue's 'purity'.

Although the impression has so far been given that colour sensation depends entirely on physical parameters, this is not strictly correct. Firstly, the retina is not equally sensitive to different hues. This means that different colours of the same intensity will appear to be more or less bright according to their wavelength. When the eye is light adapted, the brightest spectral colour is at about 550 nm which gives a yellowish-green impression; the brightness progressively diminishes as the wavelength approaches either the 400 nm (violet) or the 700 nm (red) end of the spectrum.

Secondly, our cones in the retina and our interpretive mechanisms in the brain sometimes cause colour sensations to appear other than they actually are. Two phenomena are particularly important here: colour adaptation and colour constancy.

Colour adaptation refers to the process by which some colour sensations are altered by continuous exposure to others. For example, looking at a bright red stimulus for a few minutes and then at a yellow stimulus will cause the yellow to appear green. Gradually the eye will recover from the adaptive effects of the red field; the yellow content of the test field will gradually increase relative to the green and, after a few minutes, the field will again appear as normal. Similar effects occur through continuous exposure to green stimuli: a yellow field appears red. Along with this adaptation there will also be a reduction in brightness and changes in saturation. In both cases, it appears that the cones responsible for either red or green perception become adapted to one stimulus so that the other becomes dominant. (Most theories of colour vision suggest that there are specific types of cones in the retina that are sensitive to specific wavelengths.) Such effects, of course, have important implications for an operator who may have to spend a long time looking at a coloured display such as a computer screen.

Colour constancy is the term given to the psychological mechanism that leads us to see colour as we think it ought to be rather than as it actually is. For example, near a sunlit window a white ceiling of a room with a blue carpet will actually reflect quite a lot of blue light from the carpet. However, it will appear to have the same white colour all over because of the colour constancy effect.

The process by which all the colours and hues normally experienced are decoded are too complex to be explained here and, indeed, there are still large gaps in our knowledge of this area. Of more interest to the practising ergonomist is the proportion of the population who are deficient in their colour discrimination. These people, who represent about 6 per cent of the male and 0.5 per cent of the female population, may experience difficulty in work, particularly when colour is used to code various aspects of their machines.

Colour deficient people (note that the term 'colour blindness' is a misnomer since very few people are actually totally blind to colour) may be classified in a number of ways. The most common is on the basis of an ability to discriminate between the colours red, green and blue. People with normal colour vision can discriminate all three colours, hence they are called trichromats. The most common type of colour-blind individual is the dichromat: this person might confuse red with green, or yellow with blue (red–green 'blind' individuals are considerably more common than yellow–blue individuals). The relatively rare person who is totally 'colour blind' (about 0.003 per cent of the population) sees only white, black and shades of grey. Such a person is described as a monochromat.

The presence of 'colour blindness' may be fairly simply determined— perhaps the easiest way is to use cards which make up the Ishihara colour test. Each card, which needs to be presented under standardised conditions, contains a number of different coloured dots, some of which form a pattern—either a number or a wavy line. Because of an inability to discriminate particular colours the 'colour-blind' individual has difficulty in perceiving these patterns and the deficiency can be discriminated by an inability either to name the number or (for less literate subjects) to trace the wavy line. Although the test appears simple to administer, it must be emphasised that it produces valid and reliable results only in the hands of a skilled tester under controlled lighting conditions.

THE AUDITORY SYSTEM

If the eye can be likened to a camera, the performance of the ear can compared to that of a microphone. In this case the ear's main job is to convert the sound received in the form of air pressure waves into electrical patterns, which are then recognised by some kind of decoding apparatus. However, unlike the eye which is functionally superior to the camera, in many respects the human ear is inferior to the highly sophisticated modem microphones that are now available.

The ear itself is composed of three recognisable sections: the outer ear, the middle ear and the inner ear, illustrated in Figure 2.2. What most of us commonly call the ear is to the anatomist the pinna of the outer ear. Animals like dogs and cats can move this structure in different directions to help 'collect' sound waves. In human beings, however, the pinna is a less effective trapper of sound. The outer ear also consists of a tube which runs inwards from the pinna and terminates at the eardrum (the tympanic membrane). It is through these parts of the external ear that sounds are conducted to the middle ear and then to the inner ear.

The middle ear performs two functions: to transmit sound waves and to protect the inner ear. Sound wave transmission is carried out by three small

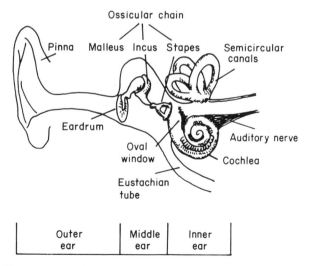

Figure 2.2   The structure of the ear

bones, the malleus, the incus and the stapes, which are collectively called the ossicular chain. They are so arranged that they span the middle ear, and connect the eardrum to a thin 'oval window' on the other side. For this part of the ear to function properly it is important that the air pressure remains the same as in the environment and this is achieved by a tube (the eustachian tube) which connects the inner ear to the back of the throat. However, sudden changes in the air pressure can close the eustachian tube, thus creating pressure differences between the middle ear and the outside atmosphere. The effect of this may be to cause the excruciating pain sometimes experienced by air travellers, and may even lead to permanent hearing damage.

The outer and middle ear appear to have the function not only of transmitting sound to the inner ear, but also of protecting it from having to operate with sound pressure levels outside its capacity. Kryter (1970) points to three ways in which this can occur. First, the action of the eustachian tube may prevent pressure waves which have fast (less than 50 msec) rise times being transmitted to the inner ear. (The rise time is the time taken for the sound pressure level to reach its maximum intensity—explosions can produce sounds with extremely fast rise times.) Secondly, the mass and stiffness of the ossicular chain are such as to prevent the transmission of pressure waves with exceptionally fast rise times (of less than 50 msec). Thirdly, if high-intensity pressure waves are experienced, small muscles in the middle ear can contract to stiffen the ossicular chain and attenuate the sound.

The inner ear performs two separate functions: hearing and maintaining posture (this latter function is discussed in the next section). The primary receptor organ for hearing is the cochlea, which derives its name from its coiled structure that is similar in shape to a snail shell. It tapers slightly along its length, with the broader end incorporating the 'oval window' of the inner ear, and is filled with fluid. Running the length of the cochlea is the basilar membrane which acts in a similar way to the ribbon in an old carbon ribbon microphone, sensing the vibrations created by the oscillating air pressure caused by the sound.

Opinions differ as to the precise mechanism of hearing. However, a simple model would suggest that the sound pressure waves are transmitted as vibrations across the inner ear from the eardrum to the oval window via the ossicular chain. These in turn set up hydrostatic travelling waves along the cochlea and basilar membrane, which cause the membrane to vibrate and its covering of hairs to be compressed. The sensation of pitch is produced because different parts of the membrane are sensitive to different frequencies: high-frequency sounds are perceived at the base of the basilar membrane while the apex is sensitive to low-frequency sounds. Loudness is discriminated by the extent to which the hairs are compressed.

Sound Localisation

Although the ear may act mainly in a mechanical way, our interpretation of what we hear is certainly not mechanistic. For example, just as our two eyes enable us to perceive depth, so having an ear on each side of the head enables us to tell from which direction a sound is coming. This information can be extremely beneficial. For example, in a dangerous situation being able to locate a warning sound, as well as registering its presence, could provide the 'split second' needed to take appropriate avoiding action.

As with visual depth perception we use cues to localise sound sources. Instead of being related to the size of the object, however, these cues are in terms of the different times taken by the sound to reach each ear.

It is possible to understand how sound localisation occurs by imagining a sound source positioned to the right of a fixed head. Because the source is slightly further from the left ear than the right it will take correspondingly longer for the sound pressure waves to reach the left ear. As the sound moves to the centre of the head the time difference is reduced. These time differences are sufficient to provide cues about the left–right location of the sound source. Furthermore, as well as the time cues there is likely to be an intensity difference at the two ears because of the shadowing effect caused by the head, which also provides cues about the position of the source relative to the two ears. Combinations of time and intensity cues, therefore, help us to localise sounds accurately.

Accurate localisation, however, only occurs when the second source is situated to the right or left of the listener. If the head is fixed, then front–back and up–down discrimination is poor. For this reason it is very important that the head is free to move to allow us to place the sound source along a left–right line relative to the ears. With head movement, of course, we can also integrate information derived from the neck and shoulder muscles (proprioceptive information) with that obtained from the time and intensity cues in order to localise the source more efficiently.

Tone and Loudness Discrimination

Frequency and intensity (and their corresponding subjective attributes, tone and loudness) are the two defining characteristics of an auditory stimulus.

However, our ability to discriminate between (and thus act upon) different sounds is limited.

In this respect it is possible to distinguish between two types of discriminatory process. First, *relative judgement*, in which there is an opportunity to compare two or more stimuli; for example, comparing two sounds in terms of their loudness or two colours in terms of their hue. In the second, *absolute judgement*, there is no obvious opportunity to compare the stimuli. In this case the task becomes more one of identification or labelling. As might be expected, people can make more accurate discriminations on a relative judgement basis.

In most work settings, discrimination is likely to be based primarily on absolute judgements. An operator may have to decide to press the 'red' button, react to a particular noise, or turn a specific control. Little opportunity for immediate comparison between stimuli exists in each situation. Unfortunately, however, our ability to make absolute discriminations between individual stimuli of most types is not very good. In this connection Miller (1956) refers to the 'magical number seven plus or minus two', implying that the range of such discriminations is somewhere around 7 ± 2 (or 5 to 9). Thus we can discriminate four to five sounds of different loudnesses and about the same number of different tones.

If different dimensions are combined, however, the number of absolute judgements that can be made is increased. For example, Pollack and Ficks (1954) asked subjects to discriminate between over 15 000 tones, each having different frequencies, intensities, durations, rates of interruption, on-time fractions and locations in space. Under these conditions their listeners could discriminate about 150 separate tones without error, although their accuracy diminished as more tones were added. Miller (1956) sums up these and similar results by pointing out that: 'as we add more variables (dimensions) ... we increase the total capacity but we decrease the accuracy for any particular variable. In other words we can make relatively crude judgements of several things simultaneously.'

In terms of auditory discrimination, therefore, the message is clear: our ability to discriminate between tones increases as we increase the number of dimensions carried in the meaningful sound.

THE PROPRIOCEPTIVE SENSES

The proprioceptive senses are those concerned with perceiving the body's own movement and with informing the individual of his or her position, and the position of the limbs, in space. In essence this sensory system is composed of two separate systems: the vestibular system in the ear, which is mainly concerned with maintaining the body's posture and equilibrium, and the kinaesthetic (literally, 'feeling of motion') system which consists of sensors in the muscles, tendons and joints that indicate the relative positions and movements of the limbs and of different parts of the body.

The proprioceptive system is frequently overlooked when considering an operator's behaviour in a working environment. This is possibly because no single visible organ is responsible as, for example, the eye is the organ for vision or the ear for hearing. In many respects the system provides 'unconscious' information. However, a lack of consciousness does not imply a lack of importance; the proprioceptive system is crucial for notifying the operator about what the body is doing, without each and every part of it having to be monitored. For example, we can walk and climb stairs efficiently because of kinaesthetic feedback from the muscles, tendons and joints used during locomotion; we do not have to look at our feet to know where to put them. Similarly, information from the kinaesthetic receptors in the hand, arm and shoulder muscles enables an operator to use a hand control efficiently above the head or out of sight.

The Vestibular System

Situated within the inner ear, just above the oval window of the cochlea, are sense organs which are collectively known as the vestibular apparatus. When describing this system it is usual to distinguish between two types of vestibular organs: the semicircular canals, and the vestibular sacs which contain the utricles. Each has a different structure and, to some extent, function. However, they have a common feature in that they do not provide direct sensation as do the eyes, ears or tongue. As any 'poor' sailor will know, for example, the sensations of dizziness and nausea which can arise when the vestibular apparatus is violently stimulated by vigorous rotation is not centred in the inner ear!

The semicircular canals in each ear comprise three, almost circular, tube-like structures that are attached to one another in the vertical and two horizontal planes. Each canal is filled with a fluid which, by virtue of its inertia, flows through the canal whenever the head moves in the plane of that canal. This provides information about the direction and rotational velocity of head movements, and the signals produced by the fluid movements also generate reflex eye movements, termed nystagmus, which help to keep the visual world stable. Syringing the external ear with water, for example, causes the eye to sweep slowly in one direction and then quickly back. (Interestingly, the water temperature determines the eye movement direction: hot water produces nystagmus with the quick phase to the side of the head being stimulated; cold water does the reverse.) Since each canal is part of a three-part system, when the sensations from all canals are integrated they will inform the person about the direction the head is moving as well as its speed. They can be conceived, therefore, as acting as both 'spirit levels' and angular speedometers which are capable of discriminating rotational movement in any direction as the head is moved.

The second organ, the utricle, is found in the utricular sac at the point where the three canals meet. The importance of the utricle is clear: it contains nerve endings necessary to preserve normal posture. As with the semicircular canals the utricle is filled with a fluid, but it also contains a flattish blob of jelly called the otolith which is covered with dense crystals. When the otolith moves in the fluid it probably stimulates hair cells around the cavity, which gives information about the head's orientation with respect to gravity. Thus the utricles inform the individual both about the tilt of the head and its linear displacement.

The vestibular receptors, therefore, enable us to maintain an upright posture and to control our body's position in space. The utricle informs the body about the static position of the head—whether we are upright, upside down or leaning over. The semicircular canals provide similar information about the head's rotation, its speed and direction and thus its equilibrium.

The Kinaesthetic System

Because people at work often need to know what different parts of their bodies are doing during any operation, the kinaesthetic senses form an extremely important system. This system comprises receptors situated in the muscles and tendons which convey information to the brain both about the extent to which these structures are being stretched and the rate of stretching.

Three kinds of kinaesthetic receptors are present in the body tissues. The first, which are spindle shaped, are located in the muscles and provide information about how much a muscle is being stretched and the rate of stretching. The second type of receptor is located at different positions in the tendons. These provide information about the extent to which a joint is moved so that, again, movement speed and direction will be indicated. The third kind of kinaesthetic receptor (the Pacinian corpuscle) is located in the deeper tissues. These furnish information regarding deep pressure and are sensitive to any deformation in the tissue in which they are embedded. In addition they can frequently be stimulated by a squeezing action whenever the body or the limb changes position, and they are thought also to be stimulated by vibration.

Each receptor provides the operator with some idea of where the body or limbs are positioned in space, without the operator having to see them. For example, by integrating information from the biceps and triceps in the arm one can tell by how much the arm is extended. Further information from the tendons and from the shoulder muscles will provide sensations that imply by how much the arm is having to be supported—in other words its position with respect to the horizontal.

The kinaesthetic system is also critically important in training and performing skilled motor behaviours. For example, Fleishman (1966) has listed eleven important ability traits, found by himself and his co-workers, which underlie a large range of physical skills. The names provided are arbitrary but, as Dickinson (1974) points out, many of the abilities either include kinaesthesis to a greater or lesser extent or are totally measures of different kinds of kinaesthetic sensitivity. The eleven factors are:

- *Control precision*: this factor is common to tasks which require fine, highly controlled muscular adjustments, primarily where larger muscle groups are involved.

- *Multi-limb coordination*: this is the ability to coordinate the movements of a number of limbs simultaneously.

- *Response orientation*: this ability has generally been found in tasks which involve rapidly discriminating direction and orientating movement.

- *Reaction time*: this represents the speed with which the individual is able to respond to a stimulus when it appears.

- *Speed of arm movement*: this is similar to reaction time but represents the speed with which an individual can make gross, discrete arm movements where accuracy is not required.

- *Rate control*: this ability involves making continuous anticipatory motor adjustments relative to changes in the speed and direction of a continuously moving target or object.

- *Manual dexterity*: this ability involves skilful, well-directed arm–hand movements and is involved in manipulating fairly large objects under speed conditions.

- *Finger dexterity*: this is the ability to make skill-controlled manipulations of tiny objects using the fingers.

- *Arm–hand steadiness*: this is the ability to make precise arm–hand positioning movements; the critical feature, as the name implies, is the steadiness with which such movements can be made.

- *Wrist and finger speed*: this ability could be called 'tapping' and relates to the ability to move the wrist and finger quickly in time with some external stimulus.

- *Aiming*: speed and accuracy of placement are critical features of this ability.

From this list, it can be seen that the kinaesthetic system plays a major role in training all kinds of skilled motor behaviour, since much of the development of complex motor skills depends on providing efficient feedback mechanisms. For example, in a skill like typing the feedback obtained from the kinaesthetic receptors in the fingers, arms, shoulder muscles and joints allows the operator to be able to sense where the fingers ought to be placed without any conscious placement needed. In addition, efficient use of the kinaesthetic system (in other words when the skill has been fully learned) enables the operator to be able to sense when a limb is in an incorrect position and rapidly move to the correct position. Car drivers, for example, have learned that the right foot controls the accelerator and brake and the left foot the clutch. It takes a conscious decision to operate the brake with the left foot and, when this is done, the driver often feels 'uncomfortable' in the lower leg and ankle.

As Dickinson's list suggests, the kinaesthetic system is also used in making skilled behaviour because of the information which it provides in relation to the timing of motor responses. In a large proportion of physical skills it is not enough merely to be able to predict appropriate responses; timing is also important for smooth performance. For instance, when hitting a moving ball the subject needs to anticipate the arrival of the ball and to time a response so that the ball is struck at a specific position. In addition to providing information about where the hand and arm are placed so that correct placement can be made, therefore, the kinaesthetic receptors inform the skilled ball-player about the speed and direction of the arm movement so that the correct point can be reached at the correct time.

At this juncture it should be emphasised that kinaesthesis alone is not enough to allow fully skilled behaviour to occur. Vision is also important— possibly because the visual system helps originally to calibrate the kinaesthetic system. A number of authors, for example Gibbs (1970) and Norman and Fisher (1982), have argued that as the skill is learned vision gradually gives way to kinaesthesis as the important system for monitoring limb movements. As will be seen later, this observation is important in relation to the development and maintenance of keyboard and other skills, and to the design of appropriate equipment. Furthermore, recent evidence suggests that although kinaesthesis has a role in response timing it is not a sufficient system alone. Vision is also crucially important for accurate motor aiming (Smith and Marriott, 1982) and in the maintenance of posture (Butterworth and Henty, 1991).

Finally, it should be emphasised that muscles operate many parts of the body in addition to the skeletal system, and the role of kinaesthesis in these muscles should not be overlooked. For example, the positions of the eye are maintained by muscles which attach the eye to the socket, and the kinaesthetic receptors in these muscles provide information about the degree and direction of the eye's movement. Furthermore, if the eye is fixated at a particular point kinaesthetic feedback from these muscles and those of the neck inform an individual of the body's orientation around the eye, and thus the orientation of the head. The role of the muscles' kinaesthetic system, therefore, should never be overlooked.

SUMMARY

This chapter has considered the roles of various aspects of the sensory nervous system in providing the channel for information to flow from the outside world to the human operator. Since they represent the first link in the man–machine system, the importance and modes of function of the visual, auditory and proprioceptive systems need to be understood before the efficiency of these channels can be increased. The next chapter will perform the same service for the body's motor processes—the communication channel in the other direction.

3

THE STRUCTURE OF THE BODY II: BODY SIZE AND MOVEMENT

The aspects of the body discussed in Chapter 2 essentially describe how the operator receives and decodes information from the environment; that is, the information transmission system that represents one side of the closed loop. Limitations of the operator's sensory and decision-making apparatus represent, perhaps, the first restrictions on the efficient working of the man–machine system.

Ensuring that the information is received and interpreted accurately, however, is only part of the problem; the loop will normally be completed only when the information has been responded to in some way. This means that appropriate actions have to be taken to transmit information back to the machine and these usually contain some motion component—pressing a button, throwing a switch, moving a lever, or even kicking the computer! In terms of the body's structure, therefore, the second set of limitations for the closed-loop system lies in the operator's ability to use the bones, joints and muscles that allow the body, or parts of it, to move appropriately.

One of the more obvious restrictions of movement that the operator could experience is likely to be in terms of his or her own physical size. A tall person in a small room, a large hand operating a small control, a small pair of legs trying to cover a large distance—each of these illustrates how the body dimensions themselves can restrict movement. The study of the operator's relevant body dimensions, often referred to as anthropometry, represents an essential aspect of any ergonomic study of a system.

Whereas the sizes of the bones and the body structure itself may restrict movement in the initial stages, complete mobility can only occur by using the system of joints and muscles which connect the limbs. When considering such aspects as, for example, the role of the back muscles and joints during lifting or sitting, or the range of arm movements during reaching and of leg movements during walking, ergonomists enter the territory of the physicist and applied mathematician. Because the actions of the bones and joints are analysed and interpreted in terms of complex systems of levers and motions, this aspect of body mobility is known as biomechanics.

This chapter will consider how people carry out and control their motor behaviour and the factors that limit motor performance.

BODY MOVEMENT: THE BONES, JOINTS AND MUSCLES

The 206 bones that make up the human skeleton perform one or both of two functions. A few, like those which comprise the skull or the breastbone, protect vital body organs from mechanical damage. But the majority do not fulfil a protectionist role; they give the body rigidity and enable it to perform its tasks—for example, the long bones of the arm and legs and the small long bones in the toes and fingers. There is a third group of bones of which the ribs are an example. They perform both a protectionist (of the lungs) and a working (aid to breathing) function.

In essence the body's bony skeleton consists of two lever systems, the arms and the legs, joined together by an articulated column, the spine. Since most bones in the body are designed to aid movement of the body parts, they are connected to each other at joints and are held together by ligaments and muscles. So the main role of the ligaments is to hold the joints tightly together and to resist any sideways movement which may damage them. By doing so, however, they also tend to limit movement when a muscle is fully stretched.

As well as being affected by how the muscles are distributed around the joints, the direction and degree of movement of body parts also depend on the shapes of the joint surfaces. At one end of the continuum are joints like those in the fingers, elbows and knees which have simple hinge actions and allow movement in just one plane. Movement in joints such as those in the wrist and ankle, however, can occur in two planes because their surfaces are less flat. At the other end of the scale are the hip and shoulder joints which are shaped as a ball and socket and permit a wide range of movement. The fact that the ball of the hip joint is almost completely enclosed in a deep socket provides great mechanical strength but also limits the range of movement. In the shoulder, where a much wider range of movement is needed, the socket is shallower—but a dislocated shoulder is fairly common as a result.

The joints in the spinal column are of a special type. Instead of the two smoothed surfaces of the joint moving against each other, they have between them a fibro-cartilage disc whose function is to act as a shock absorber and allow flexion—so providing a wide range of body movements.

The individual vertebrae in the spine are joined to each other by a series of elastic ligaments which help to maintain the normal curvature of the spine, and are probably the only ligaments to maintain a steady strain. The effect of the whole of this assembly (vertebrae, discs, ligaments) is that the body can bend forwards by about 180 degrees, but not very far backwards.

As well as bending, the spine also lets the body rotate—the degree of movement varying between 90 degrees in the neck vertebrae to about 30 degrees in the lumbar region. This range of rotational movements lets us scan the area surrounding our bodies. Thus the combined movement of the neck, the lumbar region and the eyes enables the full horizon of 360 degrees to be scanned, with the pelvis remaining in the same sitting position.

The importance of the spine for maintaining posture will be considered later, but it is useful to note here that an aching back may occur if undue strain is put on the mechanism. As will be seen later, more severe strain can cause damage to the muscles, to the elastic ligaments and, if the strain is sudden and prolonged, to the intervertebral discs. The result of this may be to cause part of the disc to be squeezed into the spinal canal producing the extremely painful back condition known as a 'slipped disc'.

Despite the perfect mechanical engineering of the body's bones and joints, no work could ever be done without an adequately functioning muscular system. Three kinds of muscles are present in the human body. The first, striated (also called skeletal) muscles, control the action of the main working bones. These muscles are composed of long, thin, cylindrical fibres which are connected in bundles and are attached to the bones via the tendons. They may be so short as to be invisible or quite long, like the tendons which operate the fingers.

About 40 per cent of the muscles in the body are striated and, except in some clinical conditions, their actions are under the operator's control. For this reason it is the striated muscle, and the way that it functions, that holds most interest to ergonomists. The second kind of muscle, whose action is not under voluntary control, has a smooth appearance and maintains the functioning of vital body organs like the stomach and intestines. Finally the heart is composed of a muscle system that is unique. Cardiac muscle is similar to a mixture of both striated (for work) and smooth (involuntary) fibres.

Muscles can contract only in one direction and, when they do, they become about half their original length. This limits the amount of limb movement to a function of the length of the limb's individual muscle fibres. On the other hand, the force which a muscle can exert is not related to its length but to the number of fibres it contains. Because of the way in which nerve impulses act, individual muscle fibres can only be in a state of contraction or non-contraction (a so-called 'all-or-none' functioning). Controlled, gradual movement, therefore, occurs by additional fibres successively being brought into operation so that as more force is required, more fibres have to be contracted. As was discussed in Chapter 2, such actions are monitored by kinaesthetic receptors in the muscles, which provide the feedback loop needed to give the operator relevant information about the speed, direction and force of contraction.

MUSCLE STRENGTH, ENDURANCE AND FATIGUE

The amount of work that a human operator has to perform must clearly be within physical as well as cognitive capabilities. This is why such aspects as anthropometry and biomechanics are being discussed in this chapter. However, it is often forgotten that the muscles themselves are constrained in their ability to carry out work. In the first place this is because of limits on their strength; secondly it is because their ability to maintain that strength (i.e. their endurance and their resistance to fatigue) is also limited.

When discussing any of these factors a clear distinction must be made between the kinds of work which the muscle may have to do (between static and dynamic work), because different kinds of work can lead to different kinds of fatigue patterns.

The distinction is normally made in terms of whether or not motion accompanies the muscular tension. The work is said to be static if no motion occurs, for example when holding a weight in the palm of the hand with the arm outstretched but not moving. If the arm moves up and down, however, then the upper arm and shoulder muscles will be doing dynamic work. The importance of this distinction will become clear when some of the antecedents of muscular fatigue are discussed.

Muscular Strength

Strictly defined, strength implies a situation in which static forces only are applied. For example, Kroemer (1970) has defined it as 'the maximal force muscles can exert isometrically in a single, voluntary effort'. Such a definition removes from consideration most forms of dynamic work. Restricting the definition to static situations, however, does ensure that the mechanics involved are easier to compute since, without movement, more complex considerations such as speed and velocity do not need to be considered. Furthermore, without movement the muscles do not change their shape (the movement is called isometric because the length of the muscle remains unchanged). Again, such a situation is more easily controlled and the effects more easily computed within a laboratory environment.

Information about isometric muscular strength is often needed to suggest appropriate control and movement systems; to determine maximum and optimum control resistances; to define the forces required in various manual tasks; and to ensure adequate arrangements for safe, efficient lifting or carrying. Levels of human strength are also relevant for the design of equipment that might have to be used under abnormal or special conditions such as space travel: because of area and weight restrictions, conventional sources of power may be logistically impractical or expensive. Finally it is important to remember that most muscular actions which interest ergonomists commonly require the integrated exertion of many muscle groups. For example, pushing on a pedal requires turning the ankle, extending the knee and the hip, and stabilising the pelvis and trunk on the seat. In these cases the maximum force that can be exerted in a complex action will be determined by the weakest link in the muscular chain.

Many factors are related to (and influence) muscular strength, perhaps the most obvious being age: tasks requiring strength that is easily exerted by young workers may exceed the capacity of older groups. Damon, Stoudt and McFarland (1971) suggest that strength increases rapidly in the teens, reaches a maximum in the mid to late twenties, and remains at this level for five to ten years.

Sex is another factor that is related to strength. Although skeletal muscle can produce the same force per unit area of muscle cross-section regardless of sex (O'Brien, 1985), since women generally have less developed musculature their overall strength tends to be lower than that of men. Indeed some authors, for example Hettinger (1961) and Lauback (1976), have estimated that the general strength of women is about two-thirds that of men, although they accept that such a figure depends on the muscle groups under consideration. The ratio also depends on age: data from Imrhan (1989), for example, shows that while this ratio holds for finger-pinch strengths of adult subjects, for children the female–male strength ratio increased to 89 per cent.

Assertions such as these, however, represent very broad generalisations. They imply both that the differences in muscle strength between the sexes are the same for all muscle groups and that men and women use their limbs in the same way. A number of authors have argued that no evidence exists to support such a suggestion (for example, Redgrove, 1979; Pheasant, 1983; O'Brien, 1985). Pheasant (1983), for example, has demonstrated wide strength variability within a population of women, with one of the most important variables being how strength was measured. Sex differences were also affected by the type of task—for example, using a handle gripping and turning task the sex differences in strength increased as the size of the handle was increased. Since there are sex differences in hand sizes, for example, such results imply the need to consider the nature of the task and the operator, as well as the strength required.

A further example of this need is supplied by Corlett and Bishop (1975). In a pedal pushing task, they showed that the optimum height of the pedal for both sexes was 25 cm below the chair seat. Although even at this height there was a male superiority of 9 per cent for exerting a force, this superiority increased by as much as 50 per cent at different pedal heights below the seat level. Ward (1984) urges that results such as these imply that greater care needs to be taken over placing controls for women if equality of effort is to be achieved.

Behavioural differences between the sexes might also account for strength variations. In children, for example, trunk and upper limb muscles are stronger in boys and this might reflect the fact that boys tend to participate more in throwing sports than girls do. Furthermore, in adults sex differences related to strength tend to decrease in the lower part of the body. O'Brien (1985) argues that this, again, may reflect usage—both sexes use their legs in habitual activities but in normal daily tasks men tend to use the upper body more than women. It may be, therefore, that some of the reported differences between the sexes in terms of their muscular strength simply reflect differences in patterns of activity, i.e. in the use and training of the muscles. (Wilmore, 1975, for example, has shown that trained female athletes are stronger than untrained males.)

Other factors that can account for strength differences, listed by Damon, Stoudt and McFarland (1966), include body position, fatigue, exercise, health, diet (hunger or inadequate diets decrease body strength), drugs, diurnal variation, environmental factors, motivation and occupation (although this may be related to the different amounts of exercise taken by people in various occupations). Additional factors include weight and height (Caldwell, 1963, obtained a correlation of 0.76 between pulling strength and height).

Muscular endurance

Endurance is the ability to continue to work, or in the static case to continue to exert force, even after fatigue has occurred. All of the data obtained in this area lead to the same conclusion: that the length of time for which a force can be maintained depends on the proportion of the available strength being exerted. Thus the smaller the force that is required, the longer it can be exerted. This relationship between required strength and endurance has been shown to be non-linear (for example, Caldwell, 1963, 1964; Carlson, 1969; Monod, 1985; Deeb, Drury and Pendergast, 1992) and this may be seen in Figure 3.1. This figure implies that while total strength may be maintained for only a very short time (total strength, here, is defined in

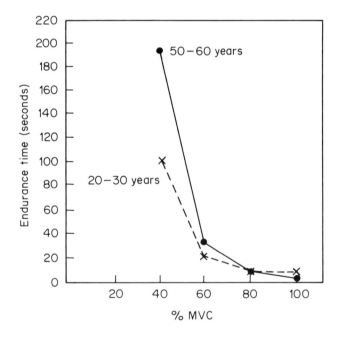

Figure 3.1 Muscular endurance for different age groups (after Deeb, Drury and Pendergast, 1992); reproduced from *Ergonomics*, **35**, 899–918, by permission of Taylor & Francis.

terms of maximum voluntary contraction, MVC), longer-term contractions will supply less than 20 per cent efficiency.

At this point a distinction should be made between individual and group strength. Although the function shown in Figure 3.1 indicates the relationship between endurance and the percentage of each person's individual strength, the curve was obtained by averaging across many different strengths. Carlson (1969) and others, however, have demonstrated that whereas the relationship between strength and endurance shown in Figure 3.1 remains the same over different groups, weaker people can maintain proportionately higher endurances than stronger people. In other words, the curve is shifted slightly up or down according to the individual's maximum strength. This is probably because stronger people, by definition of the term 'proportion of maximum strength', have to exert higher forces, so the muscles are working harder and require more oxygen-carrying blood. However, because the muscles are more contracted they tend to occlude the blood vessels, and this limits the length of time over which contractions can take place. (The importance of oxygen in reducing muscular fatigue is discussed below.) As evidence for this assertion, Monod (1985) has demonstrated that the ability to maintain isometric contractions deteriorates rapidly when the blood supply to the upper arm is occluded using an arterial cuff. While the normal 20–25 per cent strength shown in Figure 3.1 could be maintained after 10 minutes and longer with no occlusion, with the cuff inflated the strength dropped rapidly to zero after only six minutes.

Muscular Fatigue

Fatigue is an important aspect of any situation in which work (both dynamic and static) is done. Depending on the degree of the fatigue experienced it may cause discomfort, distraction and possibly reduced satisfaction and performance. In many cases such factors rapidly lead to accidents. Muscular fatigue can often be avoided, however, if the manner in which it arises is understood, so that the task is designed to avoid factors that induce it.

For a muscle to contract (i.e. to do work) an extremely complicated chemical reaction is set up in the muscle itself. Described in its simplest form, the energy for the contraction is supplied by a chemical in the muscles called adenosine triphosphate (ATP) breaking down to adenosine diphosphate (ADP). However, the ADP must be regenerated to ATP before further contractions can occur, and the energy for this reversing action is provided by the breakdown of glycogen.

Unfortunately a by-product of the glycogen breakdown is a substance called lactic acid which quickly accumulates in the muscles, causing the muscular pain so often associated with fatigue. This is removed by a reaction with oxygen and converted into carbon dioxide and water. The function of oxygen, therefore, is to convert the by-products of the energy-producing reaction—and this may continue for some time after muscular activity has taken place. The role of the blood is to transport oxygen to the muscles and to remove the carbon dioxide and water. The simplified reaction is shown in Figure 3.2.

It is interesting to note that the energy for muscular activity comes from a reaction which does not depend primarily on the presence of oxygen. Work can be done even if the immediate supply of oxygen is insufficient, and this allows the body to make a sudden, extreme effort which would be quite impossible if the energy had to be obtained from the oxidation of some substance in the muscle fibre. So the importance of understanding the mechanisms that cause fatigue lies in realising that the oxygen supplied by the blood, and the vascular system itself, are the sole agents for either reducing the level of fatigue or increasing the length of time before it occurs. Working conditions need to be designed, therefore, in which an efficient flow of blood to the muscles is maintained and even increased.

Blood flow can be increased during dynamic work simply as a result of the action set up by the muscles doing the work. Blood is pumped through the blood vessels which supply the muscles, so helping to break down lactic acid and remove the carbon dioxide and water. As long as the supplies of blood and oxygen can be maintained in sufficient quantities, therefore, and

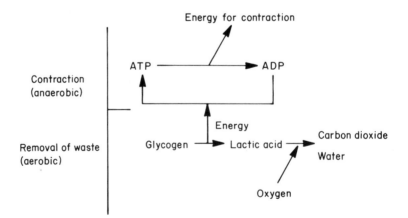

Figure 3.2 A simplified diagram of the process by which energy is obtained for muscle contraction

not exceeded by the production of lactic acid, muscular fatigue is likely to be kept at bay. Under conditions of static load, however, no such pumping action occurs and the muscles soon become starved of the oxygen that they require. In addition, the contracted muscles also help to occlude capillaries and thus further reduce the blood supply. When this occurs muscles are said to be in 'oxygen debt'. (Oxygen debt can also occur in dynamic work if there is an insufficient supply of blood and oxygen.) This effect can be demonstrated well if the arms are stretched even for a short period above the head. With the shoulder and arm muscles under static load, the effect of gravity and the lack of muscle contraction reduce blood flow to the muscles and create an oxygen debt. (Ulin *et al.*, 1993, demonstrated significant differences in muscular fatigue ratings when using a screwdriver at different locations with respect to the body itself; minimum fatigue was experienced at elbow height, maximum at shoulder height.)

The moral of the tale, therefore, is that work should be designed to avoid forces having to be applied over long periods. As far as possible all muscular activity should be intermittent so as to allow blood to flow through the muscle and reduce the possibility of any oxygen debt building up, or to facilitate paying back a debt which has been incurred.

When discussing fatigue, it is not commonly realised that the main group of muscles which do static work continuously are those in the back and shoulders, since they are involved in maintaining posture. Although they have more red muscle fibres than muscles which do dynamic work, they often run up an oxygen debt if a rigid posture is maintained for too long. This is particularly important to the seated operator. For example, a typist may develop back and shoulder pain unless adequate opportunity is given to relax and contract the muscles, perhaps by walking about or by doing other work.

In this respect changes in working practice caused by new technology can create problems. Word processors, for example, enable typing to be done more quickly and efficiently than is possible using manual or even electric typewriters. However, because the new task no longer includes the natural breaks and movements required by the older technology, such as to change paper or listen for auditory stimuli such as bells, etc., muscular fatigue often occurs more quickly and in different muscle groups. Winkel and Oxenburgh (1989) recommend relatively frequent posture changes between sitting and standing during prolonged VDU work. In addition, the design of the seat itself can help to reduce the degree of static load on the postural muscles, which will be considered in Chapter 9.

As well as the oxygen that it transports, the other role of the blood supply should not be forgotten—that of removing waste products from the lactic acid breakdown. Thus the same sensations of pain and fatigue may, in some cases, occur after long periods of continuous work even if an oxygen debt has not occurred. This is caused by the fluid produced after the breakdown building up between the muscle bundles and being unable to be carried away by the blood. This causes the muscles to swell, which may then press on the intramuscular blood vessels so further reducing the flow of blood to the muscles. In most cases this fluid will eventually be dissipated by rest after the activity has ended but, if insufficient rest is allowed, then further activity is likely to increase fluid level. Over time a muscle which is continuously used may become distended by intramuscular fluid and fibrous material can build up. This could ultimately interfere with the normal muscular contraction and may even cause permanent damage.

Heavy or repeated muscular exertion may have other consequences. For example, it is fairly common for frequently used muscles to become hypersensitive: they become more liable to contract than muscles which have not been exercised. Localised contractions or muscular spasms may result from such hypersensitivity, and perhaps a build-up of intramuscular fluid could cause local tender areas. In addition, whole groups of muscles may contract spontaneously to cause what is commonly called 'cramp'. This can occur when some muscles are used continuously to exert a static force or on repeated movements of a comparatively short range. 'Writer's cramp', for example, is a common affliction among authors and will be considered later.

BODY SIZE: ANTHROPOMETRY

For many hundreds of years humans have realised the importance of knowing something about their own body dimensions. Indeed, measuring units of the 'foot' and the 'hand' are still used today, having been derived from the dimensions of standard body parts.

The idea that the physical size of the person is somehow related to the ability to function in the world is so old that it is surprising how often the concept is neglected in everyday thought and design. Nevertheless many studies have demonstrated the reductions in performance that can occur if working environments are not matched to the individuals' body sizes. Within a military environment, for example, Lodge (1973) surveyed US Navy pilots and demonstrated that on average they were significantly taller than the non-Navy personnel whose measurement standards had been used to design the particular aircraft cockpit being studied. Analysis of 680 jet accidents suggested that pilots with heights that exceeded about 183 cm were disproportionately represented in accidents that could be attributed in whole or in part to 'pilot error'. Gregoire and Trimble (1986) demonstrated that performance using a 'head-up display' was significantly better when the display was positioned at a height that accommodated the pilot's own eye height, rather than one which required either additional body support or the pilot to adopt an erect posture to be able to perceive the display easily.

The term anthropometry is derived from two Greek words: *anthropo(s)*, human, and *metricos*, of or pertaining to measurement. Thus the subdiscipline is concerned with:

> The application of scientific physical methods to human subjects for the development of design standards and specific requirements and for the evaluation of engineering drawings, mock-ups, and manufactured products for the purpose of assuring the suitability of these products for the intended user population.   (Roebuck, Kroemer and Thompson, 1975)

The ergonomist, therefore, uses anthropometric data to ensure, quite literally, that the machine or the environment fits the person. Whenever the human operator has to interact with the environment it is important to have details of the dimensions of the appropriate body part. So overall stature is an important determinant of, for example, room size, door height or cockpit dimensions; the dimensions of the pelvis and buttocks limit the size of hatch openings or seats; the size of the hand influences the dimensions of controls and supportive stanchions; it is necessary to have details of arm reach to be able to position control consoles at appropriate distances. The list of possible examples is almost endless.

Until relatively recently the main source of anthropometric data has arisen primarily from military settings. This is possibly due to two reasons. First, in anthropometric surveys large numbers of subjects need to be measured so that representative dimensions of a population can be obtained. Military scientists have at their disposal many thousands of available men and women, particularly during wartime. Secondly, with the development of faster fighting machines (including tanks, boats, aircraft and space vehicles) physical space has increasingly been put at a premium. So the need effectively to build a machine around a single operator, but at the same time to build for a number of different operators, has meant that appropriate anthropometric data have been required. In addition anthropometric data are needed to design aspects of the individual's immediate working environment, such as efficient and specialist clothing for use in a number of different theatres of war.

Unfortunately, however, data obtained from military personnel tend to be misleading if civilian applications are envisaged (and vice versa, as Lodge

Table 3.1   Details of some anthropometric surveys of civilian populations

Author(s)	Date	Sample details	Population	Sex	Age
Kemsley	1950	27 515		Male	14–75
		33 562		Female	
Roberts	1960	78	Elderly	Female	Average 71.65
				Male	Average 81.62
Damon and Stoudt	1963	133		Male	?
Ward and Fleming	1964	70	African mine recruits	Male	?
Ward and Kirk	1967	100	Elderly	Female	?
Lewin	1969	87	Swedish	Male and female	25–49
Garrett	1971	26	The hand	Male	? (students)
		23		Female	
Andrew and Manoy	1972	323	British Rail footplate staff	Male	24–65
McClelland and Ward	1976	140		Male and female	18–30, 60+
Haslegrave	1979	1584	British drivers	Male	17–64
		416		Female	
Guillien and Rebiffáe	1980	8005	French bus drivers	Male	20–60
Gilbert et al.	1988	105	The thumb	Male and female	21–64
Buchholz and Armstrong	1991	30	The hand	Male and female	18–31
Fernandez and Uppugonduri	1992	128	Southern Indian	Male	25±4

(1973, above) demonstrated). For example, conscripts measured during or just after a war may have had an insufficient diet or may have been working in difficult surroundings. Over time, factors like these may affect the development of some body dimensions. In addition, as will be discussed later, the problem is further increased since anthropometric data obtained from members of one country, for example the United States of

America, may not apply to those of another country, for example Great Britain.

The anthropometric data which mainly interest ergonomists can be of two kinds:

- *Structural anthropometry* (often called static anthropometry) deals with simple dimensions of the stationary human being—for example, weight, stature and the lengths, breadths, depths and circumferences of particular body structures.

- *Functional anthropometry* (or dynamic anthropometry) deals with compound measurements of the moving human being—for example, reach and the angular ranges of various joints.

For both kinds of anthropometric measurements, comparative data are slowly becoming available on selected civilian populations. Some of the more easily obtainable reports are listed in Table 3.1. In addition, Barkala (1961) provides details of some earlier surveys undertaken to estimate body measurements in relation to seat design; and the results of the majority of studies up to 1971 have been collated and tabulated by Damon, Stoudt and McFarland (1971). However, these last two references deal mainly with data from military populations. A collection of papers edited by Easterby, Kroemer and Chaffin (1982) provides useful civilian data. Kroemer (1989a) discusses a range of techniques that can be used to measure different parts of the human body, and supplies a useful table of US civilian body dimensions for people in the age range 20–60 years.

Regarding functional anthropometry, the simplest forms of such data are those which indicate the ranges of motion of individual body articulations. In this respect the definitive study of joint ranges remains that of Dempster (1955).

Variability in Body Shapes and Sizes

Even to the least observant person one thing must be abundantly clear about body dimensions—there is wide variation between members of a population. Simply stand on any street corner and observe the differences in height, weight, shape, etc., of people that pass by. With such variability it should be readily apparent that anthropometric data need to be used very carefully if they are to be of value. Unfortunately, it is difficult to present such a wide variety of data in a simplified fashion—even the simplest of compound graphs, tables or slide-rules may serve only to mislead. Nevertheless Pheasant (1982a, b) provides very useful information about how anthropometric data can be estimated from available information concerning the heights of members of different populations.

Because the population exhibits such variability in body dimensions, it is the normal custom when reporting anthropometric data to indicate both some average figure and the extent of the variability within the population studied. It has become common practice, therefore, to specify anthropometric data in terms of statistical numbers called percentiles, which simply indicate the percentage of the population who have body dimensions up to a certain size (i.e. that size or smaller). For example, the value of a 95th percentile stature will indicate the height of 95 per cent of the population. Using these kinds of statistics, the 'average' is taken to be the 50th percentile (i.e. a value attained by 50 per cent of the population).

Before discussing why anthropometric data are so variable, it is important to consider the meaning of this variability and of the statistics that are used. In particular, it is necessary to question the concept of an 'average'.

Often an 'average' dimension is of little value when used alone—take, for example, the design of a desk. If its height was arranged so that a person having an 'average' lower leg length would fit into it then, by definition, only half of the population (those whose legs were of average length or shorter) would fit. So a feature like desk height needs to be designed to be larger than the average appropriate dimension. On the other hand, when dealing with a dimension such as reach, the distance used needs to be smaller than the average reach of a population. If it was larger then, again by definition, the smaller 50 per cent of the population would be unable to reach.

Just how much larger or smaller than average a particular dimension needs to be depends on the importance and function of the feature being designed. For example, a joystick is useless if it is placed outside the user's reach and so the reach dimension in this case would need to be related to the reach of the smallest member of a particular user population. At the other extreme, and taking a military example, an escape hatch in a submarine would need to be large enough to allow all (100 per cent) of the users through (with their clothes) in an emergency.

Other dimensions, however, may not be so critical. For example, as long as adjustable chairs are available a desk height does not need to be large enough to accommodate all users' heights and so could possibly be designed to accommodate, say, 90 or 95 per cent. For these reasons it is important to have details of the variability of the various body structures as well as the 'average'. For most purposes, a range of dimensions from the 5th to the 95th percentile (that is, from a dimension representing the smaller

5 per cent to one which represents 95 per cent of the population) is generally acceptable.

A further problem with the overuse of simple averages as statistical indicators should be pointed out. This is the fallacy of the 'average person'. Because the sizes of various body parts are not related in a constant ratio, it is not possible to describe accurately the dimensions of one part by reference to another. Thus it is not possible to say, for example, that a person who has an average height will also have an average arm length. Robinette and McConville (1981) have demonstrated this fact both statistically and by practical example and, as long ago as 1952, Daniels demonstrated the fallacy of this 'average man' concept. He considered the dimensions of 1055 subjects who had an average stature and found that only 302 (29 per cent) also had an average chest girth, 143 (14 per cent) had average chest girth and sleeve length, etc. Indeed, when only six body dimensions were added to the equation he found only six of the original sample who were 'average' in all six dimensions. (It should be noted that Daniels, conservatively, defined 'average' as falling in the central 25 per cent of the dimension distribution. Had he taken a true average of mean (± 0 s.d., far fewer subjects would have been average in all dimensions.)

Sources of anthropometric variability

The wide distribution of body dimensions and shapes which may be encountered in a population can often be due to slight genetic differences. However, other, more readily observable variables can also affect body dimensions and their variability, and these include age, sex, culture, occupation and even historical trends.

Age

The change in body dimensions from birth to maturity is well known and, indeed, the increases occur consistently although sometimes irregularly. For height, as for most other body lengths, full growth is attained for all practical purposes by the age of 20 in males and 17 in females (Damon, Stoudt and McFarland, 1971). Some 'shrinkage' of older people has also been noted, which is mainly due to biological changes that take place as a part of the normal ageing process—flattening of the discs between the vertebrae, general thinning of the weight-bearing cartilages, and so on. It can also be related to some of the secular trends discussed below. Stoudt (1981) provides data showing the decrease in a number of body dimensions between the ages of 18 and 74.

Sex

With the increasing observance of sexual equality in the workplace, designing for differences in body dimensions between the sexes will become an important aspect of the ergonomist's task. In this respect males are generally larger than females for most body dimensions, and the extent of the difference varies from one dimension to another. O'Brien (1985) details a number of specific anthropometric areas in which males and females differ.

Examples of sex differences in this respect may be seen in the various hand dimensions provided by Garrett (1971). In each of the 34 different dimensions (hand length, thickness and depth; hand, fist and wrist circumference; digit length and thickness, etc.), male sizes were larger than female sizes with the greatest differences occurring in the thickness dimensions (male dimensions being approximately 20 per cent larger than those of the females). For the length dimensions (hand, finger) males were approximately 10 per cent larger than females. Similar results were obtained by Buchholz and Armstrong (1991).

Women, however, are consistently larger than men in the four dimensions of chest depth, hip breadth, hip circumference and thigh circumference. Pregnancy markedly affects certain female dimensions, mainly in the abdomen and pelvic regions but also the breasts. Such changes begin to reach anthropometric significance about the fourth month of pregnancy, and Diffrient, Tilley and Bargady (1974) suggest that the average female abdominal girth increases from 6.5 to 11.7 inches during pregnancy.

Culture

The importance of national and cultural differences in anthropometry has been realised for some time, but until recently there has been little concerted effort to implement the relevant data in the production of new plant and machinery. As Chapanis (1974) suggests, until relatively recently ergonomics has been largely an American and Western European discipline—although reports of ergonomics studies that relate to populations other than American and Western European are beginning to emerge in the literature.

The variability in anthropometric dimensions due to national and cultural differences may not all be as dramatic as the difference between the Central African Pygmy tribes (average male height 144 cm) and the Northern Nitoles of Southern Sudan (average male height 183 cm) (Roberts, 1975). However, for design purposes the differences are important. Kennedy (1975) illustrates this point with data relating to the range of heights of seven military populations: United States, France, Germany, Italy, Japan, Thailand and Vietnam. Relating these statures to cockpit design, he points out that it is customary in the US Air Force to design for the central 90 per cent of the population (i.e. from the 5th to the 95th percentile). Whereas this range would accommodate essentially the same percentage of Germans, as far as height is concerned it would fit only the upper 80 per cent of the French, 69 per cent of Italians, 43 per cent of Japanese, 24 per cent of Thai and 14 per cent of Vietnamese users.

Variations also appear to exist between people in different areas within the same country. For example, Guillien and Rebiffé (1980) analysed the statures of a large number of bus drivers from east and west France. Their data, shown in Figure 3.3, illustrate a large difference between the statures

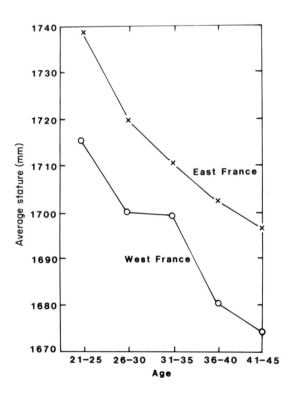

Figure 3.3 Variation in stature with age in people from two different areas of France (reproduced with permission from Guillien and Rebiffé, 1980, 'Anthropometric models of a population of bus drivers'. In D.J. Oborne and J. Levis (eds.), *Human Factors in Transport Research, Vol. I,* copyright by Academic Press Inc. (London) Ltd)

of subsamples, although the reduction in stature with age between the two samples is fairly similar.

For reference purposes White (1975) has collated anthropometric data for the weights, heights, sitting heights and chest circumferences of male, military samples from 19 countries.

Occupation

Differences in body size and proportion among occupational groups are common and are fairly well known. For example, many body dimensions of a manual labourer are on average larger than those of an academic. However, such differences may also be related to age, diet, exercise or many other factors, as well as the result of selection criteria designated by specific occupations. Whatever the reasons for the differences, however, anthropometric variability in different occupations must be realised so that appropriate environments can be designed for the particular occupation, and before anthropometric data obtained from members of one occupation can be used to design the environments of another.

Secular (historical) trends

Many people have observed that the equipment used in earlier years would be too small for effective use today. Suits of armour, the heights of doors and the lengths of graves suggest the stature of people in former times, and each measurement is smaller than its modern counterpart. Such observations imply that the average size of the population increases over time, perhaps because of better diet and living conditions. If true, the results would have important implications for the design of an environment that is to survive for some time. If we are getting taller, for example, then a design might need to take account of the statures of future generations as well as present-day users.

Some evidence exists to suggest that our body dimensions are increasing over shorter time periods than hundreds of years. For example, comparing the statures, weights, sitting heights and chest circumferences of demobilised US soldiers from the First and Second World Wars, it appears that Second World War soldiers were, on average, 3 cm taller, 6.4 kg heavier, sat 0.9 cm higher, and had a chest circumference of 3.9 cm greater than their First World War counterparts (data drawn from White, 1975). Unfortunately, however, such data are contaminated by the observation that the population's hygiene and diet have improved between the wars which could have provided more potential for growth. Thus, as Kroemer

(1983) points out, body heights of families that have been well off for generations no longer increase, while those of families still improving their socioeconomic status show gains in stature. With favourable living conditions for most people, the increase might then diminish and body height, for example, would possibly level out. That this might have happened is implied by comparing the reports of two surveys of schoolchildren produced by Tanner (1962, 1978). In 1962 Tanner felt that the evidence suggested an increasing secular trend and that puberty was occurring earlier. By 1978, however, he had pointed out that in some places, notably Oslo and London (for which data were available), the trend had appeared to have slowed down or stopped.

If the secular growth continues, the significance of any secular changes that might occur over a decade or so (the usual life expectancy of modern machinery) also has to be considered. This problem has been well illustrated in a study by Guillien and Rebiffé (1980). They were concerned with producing adequately sized cabs for bus drivers, particularly since the vehicles are designed to be in service for two or three decades. From an anthropometric survey of over 8000 male bus drivers they were able to predict that the height of their drivers would increase by about 3 cm in ten years although, with the reduction of height with age, this figure would reduce to an increase in height of 2.3 cm over 15 years. Although small changes like this may have little effect as far as the design of large systems like driving cabs is concerned, they may have important implications for other kinds of systems that are designed to be in use for many years.

BODY MOVEMENT: BIOMECHANICS

The human body has been built to move by the action of its bones, joints and muscles, and the movement may take many varied and complicated forms. Because of this a separate subdiscipline, biomechanics, has formed that considers the mechanics and range of human movement. Roebuck, Kroemer and Thompson (1975) define biomechanics as the:

> Interdisciplinary science (comprising mainly anthropometry, mechanics, physiology and engineering) of the mechanical structure and behaviour of biological materials. It concerns primarily the dimensions, composition and mass properties of body segments, the joints linking the body segments together, the mobility in the joints, the mechanical relations of the body to force fields, vibrations and impacts, the voluntary actions of the body in bringing about controlled movements in applying forces, torques, energy and power to external objects like controls, tools and other equipment.

It is beyond the capacity of this section to consider the total range of interest within biomechanics, but the important actions of the person at work, namely those of walking and lifting, will be discussed. The types of movements of the body segments and their respective angular limits may be obtained from reference texts (for example, Damon, Stoudt and MacFarland, 1971). However, it should be remembered when reading such figures that the ranges of joint motions vary from person to person due to anatomical differences, and as a result of other factors such as age, sex, race, body build, exercise, occupation, fatigue, disease, body position and the presence or absence of clothing.

LOCOMOTION

From an ergonomics standpoint, the mechanics of locomotion are important for a variety of reasons. First, locomotion can lead to fatigue; secondly, understanding how people walk may help in the design of suitable footwear; thirdly, many accidents are caused by slipping (i.e. inadequate locomotion); and finally understanding how normal legs work may help in the design of suitable prosthetic devices for the handicapped.

Walking from one place to another on two legs may seem to be a simple act. Actually it is the product of many complex interactions between the forces generated within the body and several external forces acting on it. These are coordinated in such a way as to produce not just any 'step' but rather a particular pattern of movement known as 'normal step'. This is accomplished by means of a control system that automatically integrates changing conditions in the force–motion–position picture at a number of joints within the body and the changing pattern of external gravitational forces. As discussed in the previous chapter, the vestibular apparatus in the ear plays a major part in this control system, which also corrects for changes in temperature, pressure, friction, loads being carried, obstacles, height, weight and orientation in space.

When considering how we walk, it is possible to make observations at two separate levels. The first is to observe the normal gait or movement of the leg and leg segments, while the second considers the more objective, but less easily observed, forces acting at the major joints.

To describe the biomechanics of gait, Peizer and Wright (1974) divide the cycle into two phases: stance and swing (see Figure 3.4). The stance phase begins when the heel of one leg strikes the ground and ends when the toe of the same leg lifts off. The swing phase represents the period between toe off on one foot and heel contact on the same foot. As we alternate from swing to stance on each leg there is a period when both feet are in contact with the ground simultaneously. This is called the period of 'double support' and

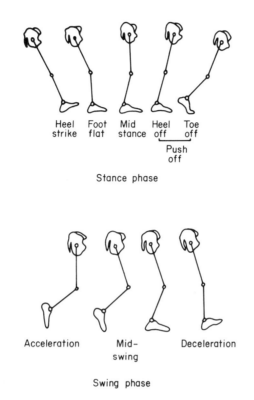

Heel   Foot   Mid   Heel   Toe
strike   flat   stance   off   off

Push
off

Stance phase

Acceleration   Mid–   Deceleration
                    swing

Swing phase

Figure 3.4 Diagrammatic representation of the stance and swing phases of human gait (after Peizer and Wright, 1974, and reprinted by permission of the Council of the Institution of Mechanical Engineers from *Human Locomotion Engineering*)

occurs between push off and toe off on one foot and heel strike and 'foot flat' on the other (the absence of double support indicates that a person is running rather than walking).

At ordinary speeds, a single leg is in its stance phase for approximately 65 per cent of the cycle and in swing for about 35 per cent. The period of double support occupies between 25 and 30 per cent of the gait cycle time.

The forces that cause locomotion result from those created by the muscles and from external forces, principally the influence of gravity on the body. When standing erect, the body's centre of gravity is in front of the hip, knee and ankle joints. This force tends to bend (flex) the hip, straighten (extend) the knee and bend (dorsiflex) the ankle. To begin walking we normally relax the muscles in one leg, allowing the body to fall forward to that side, and swing the leg forward at the hip.

Slipping and Tripping

The importance of analysing the normal gait and the motions which produce it may also be seen from Figure 3.4. The part of the gait producing the most instability is at the push off of one leg; at this point minimum contact is made with the ground. What contact there is occurs only through the toes of one foot. In addition, the pelvis is well forward of the contact point and stability is further reduced by the other leg being swung forward. It is at this point that most slips occur.

In relation to slipping Carlsoo (1972) suggests that there are two particularly critical phases of the normal gait. The first is at heel strike at the beginning of the stance phase. The weight of the body is then lying behind the contact ground, while the movement of the body's centre of gravity has just started the swing phase. The second critical instant is at the actual push off when the body's centre of gravity lies in front of the pushing foot. Such assertions have been confirmed by Strandberg (1983) who filmed over 100 laboratory 'skids'. It could well be said that the first of these two instances presents the greater danger since a person who slips when the centre of gravity is behind the foot is liable to fall backwards with little chance of using the hands to stop the fall. At least if the slip is during the second instant the body is bent forwards and is, therefore, likely to fall forwards.

Slips can take place on turning, and sideways slips of the forefoot can also occur. The likelihood of such turning slips can increase if the person is carrying a load. In the unladen state arm swing is used to offset some of the rhythmical acceleration and deceleration of the trunk caused by the leg movements, and also to damp out the rotational forces on the trunk from the same causes. Arm swing is not possible when holding objects and so increased rotational torques are needed at the foot–ground contact (Davis, 1983a).

Slipping is one of the most common causes of accidents at work, and Davis (1983b) estimates that injuries resulting from slipping, tripping and falling can account for up to 40 per cent of lost-time accidents. Manning (1983) provides further analyses of such accident data, although he points out that while data are readily available that describe the antecedents and results of falls, equivalent slipping data are elusive.

The extent to which slipping occurs depends largely on the static friction that exists between the foot and floor prior to the slip. Carlsoo suggests that slipping is highly likely to occur if the coefficient of friction between the foot and floor is less than that required for normal walking (about 0.4). Swensen et al. (1992) demonstrated that slipping occurs with coefficients of friction at around the value of 0.2.

Finally, it should be remembered that under relatively normal circumstances we can often walk on what would otherwise be slippery surfaces (for example, ice). This is because we adopt different postures and behaviours as a result of the environmental conditions. Thus the coefficient of friction depends on two forces which act normally and tangentially on the foot. For any given combination of floor surface and footwear the resultant coefficient of friction can be increased by using the ankle, leg and hip muscles to alter the forces that act on the foot—generally by shortening the stride. (Figure 3.5 illustrates the relationship between stride and the coefficient of friction necessary for stability.) If the muscles are used too frequently to overcome the tendency to slip, however, they will soon become fatigued. Once again, therefore, it is clear that the environment should be adapted to suit the operator, otherwise its poor design will soon become apparent.

LIFTING

Lifting is an action which is frequently required in work. However, it is one which, if carried out incorrectly, may result at the very least in strain injuries and discomfort or at the worst in permanent disability. Benn and Wood (1975), for example, have estimated that over 13 million days a year

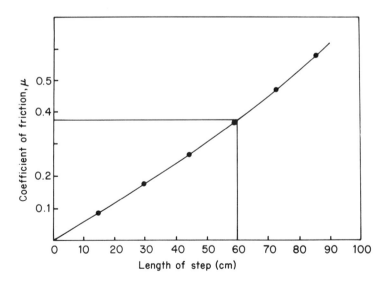

Figure 3.5 The calculated relationship between step length and coefficient of friction necessary for stability (after James, 1983; reproduced from *Ergonomics*, **26**, 83–9, by permission of Taylor & Francis)

are lost in industry due to painful back conditions. As they point out, this constitutes a greater loss of time even than strikes (between 6.8 and 11 million days in 1969 and 1970 respectively). Although these data may appear slightly dated, Pheasant (1991) points out that the proportion of accidents arising from manual handling activities has remained relatively stable at between 25 and 30 per cent (at least between 1945 and 1977).

Although it is clear that back complaints are a significant cause of time lost at work, as with slipping accidents it is difficult to gather industrial data about the precise relationship between materials handling and back injuries. David (1985a), for example, points to very general category descriptions being used in accident reports which vary between different industrial sectors and even within the same sector from year to year. Fully meaningful interpretations of such data, therefore, are very difficult to make.

Despite such pessimistic comments some conclusions can be drawn from accident statistics, and these imply a very strong relationship between inappropriate materials handling and the incidence of spinal injuries. For example, although Nicholson (1983) echoes David's comments regarding the quality of official accident reports, he used a confidential questionnaire that was administered to victims of accidents detailed in the official reports. Over a range of occupations his data suggest a very good relationship between the numbers of back injuries reported and those attributed by the victims to handling incidents. While a strong relationship does not imply a direct causal relationship, the data clearly demonstrate some link between handling and back injuries. They also show that approximately 25 per cent of all accidents gave rise to some form of back injury in the industries that Nicholson studied (telecommunications, electrical and construction workers).

Although such data should alert the ergonomist to considering the role of materials handling in accident causation, other features of the job should not be forgotten when considering the full relationship between lifting and back injuries. For example, Magora (1972) conducted a survey of over 3000 workers in Israel to determine the incidence of low back pain, and considered their occupational requirements in terms of sitting, standing and lifting. The results he obtained, shown in Table 3.2, are interesting from a number of points of view. First, more workers experienced pain symptoms who rarely or never sat, stood or lifted in their jobs than those who did so often. Secondly, the distributions of back pain for weight-lifting jobs were not significantly different from the sitters or standers. Thirdly, the results would suggest that the way to reduce the possibility of back pain is to introduce variability in the work.

Table 3.2 Proportions of workers complaining of lower back pain (LBP) having different occupational requirements for sitting, standing and lifting (from Magora, 1972)

Requirements	Proportion complaining of LBP (%)
Sitting	
Often	12.6
Sometimes	1.5
Rarely	25.9
Standing	
More than 4 hrs per day	13.8
Variable	2.5
Less than 4 hrs per day	24.9
Lifting	
Often	13.9
Variable	2.5
Rarely	28.1

Variables Affecting the Prevalence of Back Injury due to Lifting

As with many other factors at work, attempting to detail the precise effects of any particular factor is extremely difficult because no one variable acts alone and no one variable is a single factor. The effects of specific features are often confounded with behaviour. Take age as an example. Although this is simple to measure it is related to other factors: there is degeneration of the body, the rate of which is different for different people (Brinkmann, 1985), as well as a reduction in strength of the trunk muscles which resist internal pressures when lifting (Stubbs, 1985). Also, with age there is often an increase in skill—more skilled individuals might handle the material in a more appropriate manner. Sex is another variable often considered in relation to lifting, but any sex differences in lifting capacity can be attributed as much to experience as they can to structural differences of men's and women's bodies. Occupational differences may be confounded as much by the fact that people often choose different occupations because of their abilities as to the possibility that different tasks may contribute more or less to back injury, etc. Of course, the effects of task-related variables, for example the size, weight and carrying ability of the object, can greatly confound the effects of these individual (subject) variables.

Individual variables

With regard to age and occupation, in his questionnaire survey of workers in three types of industry Nicholson (1983) demonstrated the highest risk group to be aged somewhere in the thirties, although this was highly related to the type of work done. Thus in the construction industry the highest accident frequency occurred in the younger age groups (16–30), whereas in the telecommunications industry the problem was faced more by older workers (31–45 years).

A confounding factor that affects the extent to which age and occupation can be seen as important variables is training: different industries provide different degrees and qualities of training for their younger workers. For example, Nicholson (1983) points out that apprentices in the construction industry rarely receive any instruction in the prevention of back injury accidents; younger workers tend to take pride in physical strength rather than manual skill. Apprentices in the telecommunications and electrical industries, however, undergo an extensive four-year training period during which time they are instructed and supervised, and attention is paid to the skill aspect of their jobs. It could be argued, therefore, that the age distribution of injuries noted above for these two industries reflects both the training given to younger workers and the behaviours adopted.

Of course, when discussing the effects of individual variables such as age on the prevalence of back injury, the attitudes and practices of organisations need to be considered. For example, occupations in which heavy materials have to be lifted generally expect the younger workers to perform that task. In addition some occupations do not allow workers to perform heavy work if they have either had an injury previously or have a history of back disorders. The variable of age, therefore, is confounded by experience and occupation.

With regard to occupation *per se*, it is clear that different types of workers have different degrees of risk—even within the same profession. Again, this might relate to training and to learned behaviours. The nursing profession, for example, presents a particularly high-risk group, with 67 per cent of the back pain being attributed to patient handling. Stubbs *et al.* (1983) report identifying significant differences in the occurrence of back pain between nurses of different status, showing that auxiliary and student nurses were most at risk of back pain from patient handling. Subsequent analysis, however, demonstrated the multifactorial nature of this problem, in so far as sex, full- and part-time nursing, status and ward speciality were also shown to have some effect.

Regarding sex as an individual variable, mention has already been made of its potential as a contributing factor to the likelihood of back injury within the nursing profession. David (1985b) measured intratruncal pressures in women and demonstrated lower optimal levels than in men. On average, the female limits were between 45 and 60 per cent of those of men.

Task-related variables

In addition, of course, to the operator's ability actually to lift the material, the ways in which the material presents itself are likely to have implications for lifting quality and efficiency. In this respect, the object's size, weight (and weight distribution), as well as its position in relation to the lifter, are important features to consider—as also is the frequency with which the object is to be lifted.

Size was shown by Cirello and Snook (1983) to have important effects on the maximum acceptable lifting load, although they point out that the important size parameter is the object's width. It is this that determines the angles at which the lifter can grasp the object when the usual sidewise grasp is made. These conclusions are confirmed by Garg *et al.* (1983), who found that the maximum acceptable load decreases in a fairly linear fashion as the object width increases (they used widths between 30 and 65 cm).

Clearly, the extent to which an object can be lifted will depend on how well it can be grasped and thus the arm and hand postures that can be adopted. Grips and handles on the object can, therefore, influence its lifting abilities. In this respect, a survey by Drury *et al.* (1983) demonstrated that very few boxes had handles and, even when handles were provided, they were frequently not used. Often the lifter's behaviour was to grasp the boxes at the corners. This begs the question of whether the principles of Procrustes are being applied to handles: they may be provided but be of such a shape, position, design, etc. that they are difficult to use or cause more strain than if they had not been used at all.

Regarding handle design, Drury and Pitzella (1983) describe a number of variables, including shape, size and texture, that should be taken into account.

Handle position is a variable that is more difficult to define since it will be determined by the task to be performed. In this respect, and following from the results of the 1982 survey and subsequent studies, Drury (1985) argues that for most movements of box-like objects an asymmetrical, diagonal handle position is best with the left hand being higher than the right (presumably for right-handed lifters). Of course, the position of the handle on the box will also affect the angle that the wrist makes to the lifting plane. In this respect Drury *et al.* (1985) have demonstrated significant effects of wrist angle on the maximum amount able to be lifted, with some changes in wrist angle producing an equivalent load to a 16 per cent variation in object weight.

In respect to handle position, a further consideration is the extent to which the grasp points are placed so that the object's centre of gravity is also well positioned. For example, Mital and Manivasagan (1983) demonstrated that the maximum acceptable weight lift is significantly reduced when the load's centre of gravity is offset towards either of the two hands, although less so if the offset is towards the preferred hand. Offsetting the centre of gravity in the other plane, away from the body, means that the load distance from the body is increased, again causing reduced lifting capacity.

Finally, it should not be forgotten that sometimes lifting does not occur simply in a free environment. Often, environmental constraints are present with which the lifter has to contend: other machines, walls, even ceilings. Each can impose spatial restrictions that can interfere with lifting efficiency. For example, Ridd (1985) demonstrated performance reductions as soon as available headroom decreased below about 90 per cent of the lifter's stature. Barriers at both the front and side of the lifter also decreased lifting ability, although Ridd noted one beneficial effect of such barriers. When more than one barrier was present they sometimes combined to reduce the stress experienced, since subjects often used them to provide extra support during the lifting task. Although the experimental design did not include barriers at the back, rear barriers may be particularly beneficial in providing this supporting function for the lumbar region. If the environment is such that the lifter has to lift to one side, turning while lifting, then data from Mital and Fard (1986) suggest that the loads need to be at least 8.5 per cent lighter to be acceptable.

Lifting Methods

The evidence presented so far suggests that a number of variables, to do with both the lifter and what is being lifted, can interact to affect the extent to which lifting can take place with comparative safety. The final consideration must be the posture adopted by the lifter before and during the lift. Since the posture adopted can influence both the muscular stresses experienced and factors such as the object's centre of gravity and thus weight distribution, the lifting method employed can be crucially important.

Many authors, for example Davis and Troup (1964), have shown that manual activity is regularly accompanied by considerable increases in intra-abdominal pressure. This is due to the action which all the muscles around the abdomen (the diaphragm, pelvic floor and anterior abdominal wall) have on the fluid contents of the abdomen. These pressure increases are related to the force acting on the lower spine, and Davis and Stubbs (1977a) have demonstrated that occupations in which peak intra-truncal pressures of 100 mm Hg or more are induced, have an increased liability to report back injuries. (This was particularly so for the mining and construction industries.) After asking subjects to swallow a small pressure-sensitive radio pill, Davis and Stubbs (1977a, b; 1978) have produced a series of levels of the single loads or forces which can be lifted safely by fit young males, standing, sitting, kneeling and squatting with the back erect. Their data, however, were obtained from a military population and care must be taken if these are to be used for civilian applications. Nevertheless, Davis, Ridd and Stubbs (1980) have reported that a male industrial population produced very similar data up to the age of about 40, but the maximum loads which they could lift safely decreased to about 75 per cent of the military data after about age 50.

There are essentially two ways in which objects are lifted. The first, commonly known as the derrick action, derives its name from its general similarity to the action of a derrick crane. Throughout the lifting operation the knees are kept fully extended and the back and arms flexed forwards to grasp the object. Lifting is performed by extending, or attempting to extend, the lumbar region of the spine and hip joint. For this reason this type of posture is also called the stoop or back lift.

In the second method, known as the crouch or leg lift, the grasp is made by folding the legs as in squatting. In this technique the trunk is maintained quite erect and the lifting action occurs primarily as a result of extending the knee joint which, in turn, extends the hip joint. There are two variations to this technique: in the first, the heel is lifted from the ground so that the load is borne by the muscles in the upper leg. In the second, the heel of at least one foot remains in contact with the ground giving more stability and allowing some of the force to pass through more of the feet (Bendix and Eid, 1983)—see Figure 3.6.

Because the stresses resulting from different lifting postures will be borne by different parts of the anatomy, and because the postures will result in different positions of the body's centre of gravity (Bendix and Eid, 1983), it is clear that the lifting posture adopted is likely to have significant effects

Leg-lifting   Back-lifting

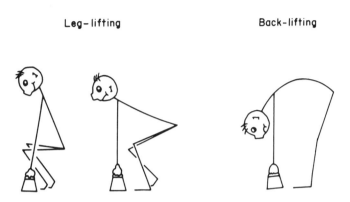

Figure 3.6   Three lifting techniques

on the intra-truncal pressures and the amount of muscular loads experienced. This has been found to be so by a number of authors, with the combined wisdom suggesting that the back lift method is hazardous to the lower back. Thus Ekholm, Arborelius and Náemeth (1982) measured the forces acting on the lumbar vertebrae during different kinds of lifting. They demonstrated significantly lower compressive forces during the leg lift rather than the back lift. These conclusions were confirmed by Leskinen *et al.* (1983). They also demonstrated that, during leg lift, significantly more of the force was conducted through the feet than in the back lift; during back lift the spinal discs (measured between the last lumbar and first sacral vertebrae—see Chapter 9) received significantly higher compressive forces.

With regard to the two forms of leg lifting technique (heel flat and heel off) Bendix and Eid (1983) have demonstrated that the heel off position allows the object to be lifted much closer to the body—so reducing the load placed on the lumbar vertebrae. Nevertheless, such a posture is possible only if the object can be lifted between the outstretched knees—for larger objects the arms will need to be extended and thus the knees kept together. In such a situation, it may be that the object passes the knees at a greater distance from the body with leg lifting than with back lifting. Again, the complex interactions of variables contributing to safe lifting are apparent.

Finally, it should be remembered that such conclusions are based solely on forces exerted using the different techniques and take little account of features of the body during lifting. For example, Davies (1972) emphasises that bending and twisting during a lift causes spinal injury and this is more likely to occur during a back lift. Furthermore, in addition to causing potential damage to the spine, the increased pressures in the truncal region predispose the operator to a hernia.

Pheasant and Stubbs (1991) provide a number of illustrations to emphasise 'good' lifting techniques in a variety of situations. Thus the 'classic good lift' urges lifters to 'keep the load close to the body, grip the object firmly with each hand, keep the back in a straight line from head to tail'. Lifting different kinds of objects generates different specific instructions, but the general missive of maintaining a straight back and keeping the load close to the body appears throughout.

Before concluding the discussion of lifting, it should be noted that Procrustes may well be starting to rear his head. One might well question whether, by instructing industrial man to adopt the knee action, one is attempting once again to fit man to the environment rather than make the environment fit the person. If the derrick action is the natural lifting posture, then the mere fact that heavier loads might be able to be lifted more safely by some other action should simply mean that reductions should be made in the maximum loads able to be lifted—not that man should be trained to adopt an unnatural posture. As was illustrated in Chapter 1, training may become ineffective under conditions of stress.

REPETITIVE STRAIN INJURIES

When discussing aspects of lifting it rapidly becomes clear that, because of the forces involved, frequent and inappropriate lifting can lead to disorders of the lower back and to chronic back pain. This is just one example of how the design of the total system, including the activities being undertaken within the system, needs careful consideration. However, it is also an example of how repeatedly adopting inappropriate postures while working, and repetitious overuse of particular muscle groups and other parts of the body, can lead to eventual body damage.

Although low back damage is recognised to occur as a result of overuse of part of the system, the general category of injuries known as repetitive strain injuries (RSI) is rather more difficult to identify—at least in terms of the causes (and, to a certain extent, the effects).

Concern relating to general tenderness, aches and pains resulting from the repeated use of specific muscle groups arose mainly in Australia in the late 1970s and early 1980s; the 'epidemic' peaked in 1985/1986 (see Pheasant, 1991, for details). Before then concern was mainly directed towards specifically identifiable injuries such as tenosynovitis, rather than the more diffuse collection of symptoms that have become known as RSI (Keisler and Finholt, 1988).

Thus RSI relates to a range of musculo-skeletal disorders that arise, in general, through overuse of particular parts of the body. They are characterised by the frequent absence of objective signs and where there is 'no agreement concerning the cause; the pathology is unknown; the clinical features are diffuse; there are no useful diagnostic investigations; and the prognosis is uncertain' (McDermott, 1986). The problems are caused or aggravated by repetitive motions including vibrations, sustained or constrained postures, and forceful movements at leisure or work (Kroemer, 1989b).

As well as the diffuse *nature* of the complaint, its case for acceptance as a recognised industrial injury is not aided by the fact that there exists considerable confusion over its definition and terminology. Thus, whereas the problem is known as 'repetitive strain injury' in the UK and Australia, it is recognised to be a collection of 'cumulative trauma disorders' (CTD) in the US. The Japanese and Scandinavians in turn prefer to talk about 'occupational cervico-brachial disorders' (OCD) when considering neck and upper limb problems. Other investigators also describe 'neck and limb disorders' (NLDs; Kuorinka and Viikari-Juntura, 1982) and 'neck and upper limb disorders' (Wallace and Buckle, 1987).

Wallace and Buckle (1987) point out that the range of symptoms that have been identified with these problems, and the variety of terms used to define them, have led some investigators to propose the existence of just two groups of issues. In the first fall problems that have objective signs and that can be measured, such as reduced grip strength, swelling, hardenings and tender spots in the muscles, and so on. Complaints in the second group are devoid of such signs and present more diffuse symptoms as vague pains in the neck and/or shoulder, constant feelings of stiffness and/or fatigue, and so on.

Stages of RSI

Whatever the terminology or diagnostic category, RSI problems demonstrate variable, often confusing symptoms. Although the onset of these symptoms can be gradual or sudden, Kroemer (1989b) points out that three stages can be identified:

- *Stage 1*: aches and tiredness during working hours but generally dissipating after a period from work (even overnight). Generally no reduction in work performance. The effects are reversible with rest.

- *Stage 2*: the symptoms persist even after an overnight period away from work. Sleep may be disturbed. Some reduction in work performance.

* *Stage 3*: the symptoms persist even at rest; pain occurs with repetitive movements; sleep is disturbed. Difficulty with performing work, sometimes incapacity.

Potential Injury Sites

There are many sites in the body at which repeated movement can occur, but repetitive strains injuries can generally be categorised in four main body areas:

* hand–wrist
* arm–elbow
* shoulder–neck
* leg–foot

Of these, the first three have received the most attention—probably because they are the areas that receive the highest load when working in a seated (generally office) environment. These three areas will be considered in more detail below, but first it is appropriate to consider what features of the body are susceptible.

Putz-Anderson (1988) discusses a range of body components that can be at risk, each of which can be categorised in two major groups: soft tissues, and nerves and blood vessels.

Soft tissue damage mainly concerns disorders arising in the muscles and tendons. The most likely result of overactivity of particular muscle groups is an increasing tendency towards strain or irritation, leading to temporary aching and/or swelling. This arises because as a load is applied to the soft tissues they change in shape, the amount of deformation being linearly related to the load applied. When the load is removed, owing to the inherent elasticity of the tissues they return to their original shape. If higher than appropriate loads are applied, however, the tissue becomes more plastic than elastic and more permanent swelling and deformation occur (Ayoub and Wittels, 1989). Even more serious are injuries that occur when the muscles are torn. Tendons can also be torn as a result of overextension, and the scar tissue that subsequently forms creates chronic tension and is easily reinjured. The sheath surrounding tendons, which contains the lubricant—synovial fluid—can also become inflamed and swollen, with the possibility of the synovial fluid in the sheath becoming diminished, allowing friction to occur between the tendon and its sheath.

Nerves and blood vessels can also be affected by repeated pressure, particularly if the part of the body through which the nerve travels becomes swollen. In these cases the result of the swelling will be either to increase pressure on the nerve or to compress the blood vessels and thus restrict blood flow.

Ranney (1993) presents a useful review of work-related injuries to the hand and forearm, with pointers for their diagnosis and methods of treatment.

Hand–wrist conditions

'Writer's cramp', a painful condition of the hand and wrist caused by adopting awkward writing postures and overexerting the wrist and fingers surrounding the pen, has been known to authors for many years. Indeed Pheasant (1991) traces reports of the condition back to the eighteenth century. It arises primarily as a disorder of the neural control of the voluntary muscles in the hand and wrist; Sheehy and Marsden (1982) suggest that it occurs as a result of a disruption to the motor program that controls the muscle patterns needed to create the characters on the page.

Carpal tunnel syndrome (CTS) is a special case of hand–wrist trauma that relates specifically to the median nerve of the wrist. This nerve passes through a 'tunnel' in the wrist composed of the metacarpal wrist bones on the outer rim of the wrist and the fleshy/muscular part of the inner wrist. It then branches out to the thumb and three larger fingers of the hand. CTS occurs as a result of a decrease in the effective cross-section of the tunnel— either by reducing the diameter of the tunnel or by swelling of the tunnel contents (which include hand–wrist tendons).

Early symptoms of CTS include numbness or tingling and burning sensations in the fingers. More advanced problems involve pain, wasting of the muscles at the base of the thumb, dry or shiny palms, and clumsiness (Konz and Mital, 1990).

Arm–elbow

Like writer's cramp, 'tennis elbow' (lateral epicondylitis) is a repetitive strain injury that has been known about for many years and which arises largely through overuse of the joints—often during professional activities. Lateral epicondylitis occurs as a result of inflammation of the tendon bundle that extends down the arm from the wrist and fingers and is attached to the lateral epicondyle of the humerus (the bony part of the elbow). Overuse of the muscles in this region leads to pain which may radiate down the forearm; the epicondyle region becomes tender and swollen. A related complaint, known as 'golfer's elbow' (median epicondylitis) occurs as a result of repeated wrist flexion and forearm rotation.

Tenosynovitis is a general term that applies to inflammation of the synovial sheaths surrounding the tendons, although it is generally applied to problems that arise in the tendons in the forearm. Pheasant (1991) points out that, in tenosynovitis proper, fluid exudate seeps into the tendon sheaths, fibrosis may occur and adhesions may form. The tendon may be thickened or frayed. Sommerich, McGlothlin and Marras (1993) describe a variety of complaints arising as a result of tendon inflammation, both as a result of synovial fluid seeping into the sheath (tenosynovitis) and inflammation of tendons where no sheath is present (tendinitis).

Shoulder–neck

Disorders of the shoulder–neck complex, as well as the upper limbs, present more of a problem as far as diagnosis and treatment are concerned. As Sommerich, McGlothlin and Marras (1993) point out, complainants often present themselves to the medical services with a range of concerns rather than specific aches or pains; the problem is often described, therefore, in general terms such as 'shoulder pain syndrome'. This set of complaints, however, has received much consideration in more recent years with the universal use of computer terminals in all parts of the workplace. Job characteristics identified by Sommerich, McGlothlin and Marras (1993) as increasing the risk associated with such disorders include activities which require awkward postures, static postures, heavy work, working at shoulder level and which lack sufficient rest. More will be said about this kind of RSI complaint when dealing with workspace features in Chapter 7.

Table 3.3 illustrates the kinds of disorders that can occur within the general heading of 'RSI' and the occupational factors that can give rise to them.

System Approaches to RSI

From the above discussion, it would appear that whatever the nature of the repetitive disorder, RSI arises largely as a result of overuse and overextension of the muscles and tendons in specific parts of the body. In this respect the term 'overuse' applies to frequent, intense, static and continuous use. Clearly, features of the environment need to be designed to ensure that body parts are not overused in these ways, and the information contained in this book should indicate how this goal can be achieved.

Table 3.3 Jobs with high risk of cumulative trauma disorders (from Ayoub and Wittels, 1989; reproduced from *International Reviews of Ergonomics*, **3**, 217–72, by permission of Taylor & Francis)

Type of job	Disorder	Occupational factors
Buffing and grinding	Tenosynovitis, thoracic outlet, carpal tunnel, Raynaud's, DeQuervain's, pronator teres	Repetitive wrist motions, prolonged flexed shoulders, vibration, wrist motion, forceful ulnar deviation, repetitive forearm pronation
Punch press	Tendinitis of wrist and shoulder	Repetitive forceful/flexion, repetitive shoulder abduction/flexion, forearm supination
	DeQuervain's	Repetitive ulnar deviation in pushing controls
Overhead assembly (welders, painters, car repairers)	Shoulder tendinitis	Sustained hyperextension of arms, hands above shoulder height
Belt conveyor assembly	Tendinitis of shoulder and wrist, carpal tunnel, thoracic outlet	Arms extended, abducted or flexed more than 60 degrees, repetitive forceful wrist motions
Typing, key-punch, cashier	Tension neck, thoracic outlet, carpal tunnel	Static, restricted posture, arms abducted/flexed, high speed finger movement, palmar base pressure, ulnar deviation
Sewers and cutters	Thoracic outlet, DeQuervain's carpal tunnel	Repetitive shoulder flexion, repetitive ulnar deviation, repetitive wrist flexion/extension, palmar base pressure
Small parts assembly (wiring, bandage wrap)	Tension neck, thoracic outlet, wrist tendinitis, epicondylitis	Prolonged restricted posture, forceful ulnar deviation and thumb pressure, repetitive wrist motion, forceful wrist extension and pronation
Musicians	Wrist tendinitis, carpal tunnel, thoracic outlet, epicondylitis	Repetitive forceful wrist motions, palmar base pressure, prolonged shoulder abduction/flexion, forceful wrist extension with forearm protination

Occupation	Disorder	Activity
Bench work (glass cutters, phone operators)	Ulnar nerve entrapment	Sustained elbow flexion with pressure on ulnar groove
Operating room personnel	Thoracic outlet, carpal tunnel, DeQuervain's	Prolonged shoulder flexion, repetitive wrist flexion, ulnar deviation
Packing	Tendinitis of shoulder and wrist, tension neck, carpal tunnel, DeQuervain's	Prolonged load on shoulders, repetitive wrist motions, overexertion, forceful ulnar deviation
Truck driving	Thoracic outlet	Prolonged shoulder abduction and flexion
Core making	Tendinitis of the wrist	Repetitive wrist motions
Housekeeping, cooking	DeQuervain's, carpal tunnel	Scrubbing, washing, rapid wrist rotational movements
Carpentry, bricklaying	Carpal tunnel, Guyon tunnel	Hammering, pressure on palmar base
Stockroom, shipping	Thoracic outlet, shoulder tendinitis	Reaching overhead, prolonged load on shoulder in unnatural position
Material, handling	Thoracic outlet, shoulder tendinitis	Carrying heavy load on shoulders
Lumber	Shoulder tendinitis, spicondylitis	Repetitive throwing of heavy load
Butchery and meat packing	DeQuervain's, carpal tunnel	Ulnar deviation, flexed wrist with exertion
Letter carrying	Shoulder problems, thoracic outlet	Carrying heavy load with shoulder strap

However, it is equally clear that the solution does not rest solely with appropriate equipment design. Again, it is the system that needs to be considered. Work schedules and operating postures play as important a role as reducing the loads placed on body parts by judicious design of equipment. Thus the first stage in RSI development is clearly schedule based; with appropriate rest the symptoms disappear as tissue swelling reduces. Managerial and other scheduling systems, therefore, need to be considered to ensure that the almost inevitable build-up of fatigue at work can be dissipated at regular and appropriate intervals.

Keisler and Finholt (1988), as well as other authors (for example Ayoub and Wittels, 1989), point also to the importance of the social and occupational environments in which the work takes place. Indeed they ascribe much of the Australian 'epidemic' to such features of the workplace, arguing that the suddenly high incidence of RSI in Australia in the mid-1980s was 'indicative of a larger social problem'. They suggest that 'this fundamental difficulty is rooted in dissatisfaction with the workplace that is revealed when new technology is introduced, and that this dissatisfaction is expressed in the form of "techno-illnesses", such as RSI' (p. 1010).

The suggestion is made, therefore, that RSI cannot be considered in isolation from the total working system. Whereas appropriate equipment design can alleviate many of the extreme loads that are placed on specific body parts at work, particularly during repetitive work, the total management of the work activity and the social situation in which it is carried out also need to be considered. This includes work-rest scheduling, the introduction of the work itself, social considerations at work, and even worker–management relationships.

SUMMARY

This chapter has considered some of the structures in the final link in the man–machine–man system, the bones, joints and muscles. No matter how efficiently a mechanical system has been designed—how fast it works, how reliable it is, how aesthetically pleasing it appears—if the operators cannot fit into it or around it, if they cannot pull the levers or push the buttons with sufficient force for a sufficient length of time, or if they cannot reach the controls in the first place, then the mechanical system is at the least effectively useless and at worst potentially dangerous.

4

MAN–MAN COMMUNICATION: WORDS AND SYMBOLS

The previous two chapters discussed in detail the physiological features of people that can affect their efficient interaction with an environment. It is now appropriate to turn towards psychological functioning and consider aspects of people's behaviour that can influence the efficiency of the complete system. Whatever approach is adopted, from a man–machine systems perspective to a person-centred view, underlying the interaction will always be the nature and quality of the information that is passed between actors within the system. That is, within and between people and machines.

In many respects information is the cornerstone of our civilisation. Without it governments could not govern, generals would have difficulty winning battles, and people in all kinds of work would be unable to function properly. We might well complain about the bad news we hear and see each day, but as individuals we would find it difficult to function adequately without constant, accurate, updated information about the state of the world and our interactions with it. The transmission of information between people, therefore, plays an extremely important, indeed a fundamental, role in everyday living and working.

As was outlined in Chapter 1, in some respects ergonomics itself can be viewed as the science of effective information communication between important parts of the system. However, this information does not appear simply as the written or spoken word—the concept of information implies an increase in knowledge and so can take any form. Thus you, the reader, are presently gathering information from this book, but at the same time you are also gaining knowledge about your body state (from, for example, proprioceptive receptors in your muscles), about the environment (from your ears, temperature receptors, etc.) and about people around you (from your ears, nose, and so on). Similarly, a person at work collects information from a variety of sources. For example, an operator will probably need information about how a machine works, how to operate it safely, what to do when it breaks down, and the like. Much of this will obviously be obtained from colleagues, supervisors, or manuals, but information is also transmitted from the machine via its displays and controls, by the environment, and so on.

So information is crucial to the effective working environment. But so too is the way in which the information is transmitted. Indeed, in many respects, the means of information transmission is as crucial as the message itself.

Put in its simplest terms, any communication system comprises just two components: a transmitter who (or which) communicates information through some medium to a receiver. Only if the receiver interprets the information in the way intended by the transmitter can proper communication be said to have occurred. The point may perhaps be illustrated by imagining a situation in which two people who speak different languages are trying to converse. The difficulties that are experienced arise largely from the receiver being unable to translate correctly the ideas conveyed by the transmitter. In such cases 'sign language' possibly helps the communication process by placing the message in a different medium—but one which can be understood by both. The communication problem, however, might be increased if one of the two can speak a smattering of the other's language but interprets the message incorrectly. In this case the communication system is likely to break down because of misunderstandings.

Because effective communication is so important for efficient working, and because inefficient communication can cause the man–machine system to break down, one of the ergonomist's primary functions is to design systems that will enhance the chances of the message being received and understood correctly. For this reason the present chapter, and the following two chapters, will consider different aspects of this communication process.

Since either a person or a machine can act as the transmitter or the receiver, four possible combinations of transmitter and receiver can be envisaged: a person communicating with another person; a machine communicating with a person; a person communicating with a machine; and a machine communicating with another machine. Since the first three of these options involve human beings interacting with the environment, they are within the realms of ergonomics and will be discussed in this and in the next two chapters. The fourth option (machine–machine communication) lies more in the domain of the cyberneticist or the engineer and will not be discussed here.

The present chapter will consider the problems presented by 'man' to 'man' communication—primarily those involved in the written communication of information and instructions. Detailed considerations of purely verbal interactions lie well outside the boundaries of this book, although indications of the importance of understanding verbal behaviour and some of the variables that influence efficient behaviour will appear in this chapter. Chapter 5 will continue the communication links by considering the question of communication between the machine and the operator, while the channels for reply (from the operator to the machine) will be discussed in Chapter 6.

MEANING, COMMUNICATION AND THE MESSAGE

The process underlying communication can perhaps best be understood when one realises that the linguistic origin of the word is the Latin *communis* meaning 'common'. One clear characteristic of meaning in human communication, therefore, is its 'commonness'—an essential prerequisite being a common understanding by those involved in the communication process. However, this quality of commonness does not necessarily mean that all participants in the communicative process have to have identical understanding of the symbols or thoughts transmitted, so long as some understanding is common to all. So communication can take place even if the transmitter and receiver do not 'speak the same language'—as long as the basic ideas being transmitted in the message are received accurately.

The role of ergonomics is to arrange a situation which enhances the chances of the transmitter and the receiver having a maximum common understanding. However, before looking at the ways in which this state of affairs may come about, it is interesting to consider briefly some of the reasons why the two may not display this commonness—why meanings and messages might be misinterpreted.

First, personalities might be involved. A receiver who dislikes or mistrusts the transmitter could be unreceptive to what is being said. Indeed, the receiver's understanding of the message could well be distorted by negative opinions of the transmitter or by imputed motives.

Secondly, even if the receiver is receptive to the message there may be distortion because of personal preconceptions (or 'set'). As Bartlett (1950) has argued, one of the chief functions of the active mind is to 'fill up gaps', that is constantly to try to link new material with older material to make it more meaningful. So a message might be distorted by the receiver placing it in a context in which it is not meant to be placed simply because of a 'set' to the message.

Thirdly, there is the problem of interest and attention. If the receiver is not attending to the message, perhaps because he or she is bored, part of it may easily be missed or misinterpreted. Finally, messages can become distorted because of our limited capacity to process the transmitted information. This concept has already been discussed briefly in relation to our ability to store different stimuli, but it also applies to the storage of complex, meaningful material such as ideas and concepts. If the message is too detailed or too long it may overload our memory system and become distorted, lost or simply unable to be retrieved. In summary, therefore, the common channel for communication may be distorted by social influences, by personal attitudes and expectations, by boredom and a lack of interest, or by information overload.

Messages which have to be transmitted between people take many forms, which Miller (1972) divides into three groups according to the physical appearance of the stimulus. These he terms verbal (including written words and signs), vocal (including spoken words and voice variations) and physical (including gestures and movements) stimuli. The remainder of this chapter will primarily consider the influence which ergonomics can have in facilitating the transmission of 'verbal' stimuli (including written communication). As the reader will become aware, many of the principles involved in verbal stimuli may also be applied to vocal stimuli but, because other aspects of the environment may possibly be important (for example environmental noise, or social and organisational factors), the specific problems of speech communication will be dealt with in Chapters 5 and 10. The role of non-verbal stimuli in the communication process (body signs, gestures, etc.) is one which is too wide for the scope of this book. However, texts such as those by Argyle and Cook (1976) or Morris (1977) may be interesting. Christie (1981) illustrates the extent to which such non-verbal cues can influence the efficiency of electronic communication between people.

PERCEPTUAL PROCESSES IN WRITTEN COMMUNICATION

Before considering how written communication (text, pictures, graphs, etc.) may be designed to enhance the communication process, it is appropriate to discuss aspects of the receiver's perceptual behaviour that might affect how the message could be perceived and recognised. Two features are important in this respect: first, the ways in which the eyes move over the presented information and thus begin the process of reception; second, how the observer integrates and organises the information. This is the process of perception.

Eye Movements

Whereas it is possible to hear speech and sounds quite passively, reading words and pictures is a very active process. Because the most acute part of the retina is towards the centre, near the fovea, the eyes constantly have to be moved to bring appropriate parts of the displayed material into clear view. Since a stable image is only formed when both the eyes and the object are stationary, however, visual scanning during reading is characterised by a succession of fast movements and stationary periods. The fast jerks are called saccades and the stationary points are termed fixations. (Even during these fixation periods the eye makes relatively small tremors.)

The existence of saccadic eye movements during reading has been known since the turn of the twentieth century and so there is a fair amount of experimental literature available on the subject (see Matin, 1974, for a historical review). However, it is only in more recent times that sophisticated equipment has enabled investigators to study these movements in detail and begin to understand the cognitive processes involved in reading and comprehension (see Young and Sheena, 1975, for a survey of the techniques). Rayner *et al.* (1989) present a comprehensive review of the relationship between eye movements and some of the underlying cognitive processes.

The two important parameters of saccadic movements that relate to reading efficiency are the duration of each fixation and the number of fixations required. In this respect, the average length of a saccade appears to be about two degrees of visual angle (which is about six ten-pitch or eight twelve-pitch character spaces) and, for skilled readers, the average fixation durations lie between 200 and 250 ms (Rayner, 1977). However, there is a great deal of individual variability in this matter. For example, Rayner (1978) reports that even for a single person reading a particular passage, saccade lengths often range from 2 to 18 character positions or more, and fixation durations range from 100 to over 500 ms. This variability in reading behaviour can be related to an individual's reading efficiency, and to the difficulty of the text (as the text increases in difficulty readers fixate for longer, move their eyes a shorter distance with each saccade, and make more regressions; Frazier and Rayner, 1982).

A simple exercise in introspection, of course, would indicate that saccadic eye movements do not simply take the form of continuous movement from, for European texts, left to right over the page. The eye's movements also include a third characteristic of saccadic movements: regressions. A regression is a movement in the opposite direction to the normal saccadic scan (that is, for English, in the right–left direction) and occurs approximately 10–20 per cent of the time in skilled readers (Rayner, 1978). As explained above, they are assumed to occur when the reader has difficulty understanding the text, misinterprets it and/or when the reader overshoots the next fixation target. They also occur, of course, when the reader reaches the end of one line and starts to process the text on the next (although Rayner, 1978, argues that these movements should be distinguished from a regression, both because they are necessary to continue the reading process and because there is some suggestion that they involve different cognitive control processes).

Discussing the relationship of line saccades to the reading process, Bouma (1980) points to the importance of typographical design:

> The horizontal extent of line saccades is controlled by visual information in the left visual field, concerning the far left-hand margin, which should therefore be in a straight vertical line ... with a sufficiently wide margin ... The vertical extent of line saccades is controlled by perceived inter-line distance. If this vertical component is inaccurate, the eye may mistakenly jump over two or perhaps even three lines.

The application of such information to the appropriate design and layout of text will be considered later. However, it is also important to realise that, although information about the position and quality of the left-hand margin is important for effective line regressions, information to the *right* of the fixation point is important for determining the quality of the saccadic process. Thus Rayner *et al.* (1989) point to evidence suggesting that *where* a reader looks next is very much influenced by the length of words to the right of the fixation point. (The decision of *when* to move the eyes—the other important parameter of reading skill—is a much more complex cognitive process.)

PERCEPTUAL ORGANISATION AND VISUAL SEARCHING

Thus how the eyes move over the printed material influences the extent to which the material will be received efficiently. However, it has been argued, for example by Rayner (1977), that eye movements are controlled by the observer's cognitive processes occurring at the time. This process monitoring hypothesis suggests some form of complex interplay between our perception and understanding of what is being read and eye movement control during reading. (Rayner and Morris, 1992, suggest that the important features of the text are 'low-level' aspects such as the length of the word to the right of the fixation point, rather than some 'higher-level' features such as its meaning.) Since there is such a clear relationship between our reading and comprehension ability and how we process the information, to ensure appropriate layout for ease and speed of perception it is as important to understand how we organise our perception as it is to understand how we control our scanning process when reading.

Perceptual Organisation

A number of models exist to explain how we organise our perceptual world (see, for example, Vickers, 1979), but one of the most enduring theories to have emerged over the years arose in the 1920s from the German Gestalt school of psychology. The Gestalt school's predictions regarding perceptual organisation provide some very simple suggestions as to how textual (and other) information ought to be arranged for easy perception.

The essential feature of this school of thought is grouping individual stimuli together during perception into wholes or *Gestalts*, which possess features of their own that are not obvious from an examination of their individual parts. Take, for example, the object that you are now observing: what you see is a book. This book is an entity in itself; it has meaning to you as a book. Although the book is composed of separate pages, each page containing printed words, each word being composed of individual letters, and each letter having different characteristics, you do not see the object in this way. You see it as a 'whole': the words, paragraphs or pages themselves do not imply the book, it is the whole book that implies the book.

One of the principal aims of Gestalt psychologists has been to specify the principles by which individual items are combined into larger, organised wholes. They also seek to find the principles by which these wholes are perceptually segregated and separated from other wholes: in other words, how the figure stands out from its background. Many of these principles are described by Wertheimer (1958) and are based on subjects' reactions to simple patterns of dots and line drawing. Examples of these principles are shown in Figure 4.1.

Perhaps one of the most important principles of Gestalt is *proximity*, which states that organisation of individual elements into groups occurs on the basis of distance: the nearer elements are to each other the more likely they are to be perceived as a whole, as a figure that stands out from the ground. As an example, simply flick through the pages of this book: small sections of text with headings stand out as being separate from the remainder of the text because of their grouped distance from the last line of the previous section.

In addition to proximity there is the principle of *similarity*. Similar features

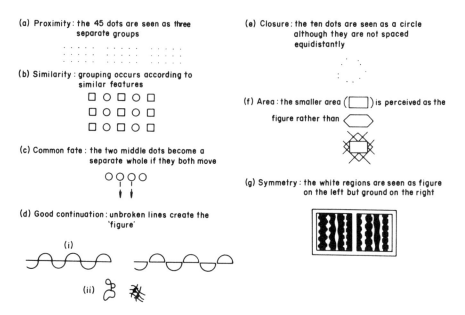

Figure 4.1 Examples of Gestalt principles for perceptual organisation

are likely to be grouped together so that, for example, the pictures in this book are seen to be different from the text—as in Figure 4.1 which is composed of small figures. Figure 4.1 is perceptually organised as a figure because the similar smaller figures are grouped together and are different from the surrounding text. Special highlighting features like colouring or underlining can help to create an appearance of similarity. If a particular pattern conforms to both the principles of proximity and similarity, Hochberg and Silverstein (1956) demonstrated that the principle of similarity is stronger than that of proximity.

Two elements will also be organised together if they share the same *common fate*. Thus if two portions of the text on a computer screen are flashing, or two areas or graphic symbols move in the same way, they will be treated as a whole—possibly as end points of an imaginary moving line.

This suggestion of an imagined continuation line between two common features is extended in the fourth Gestalt principle—*good continuation*. This states that elements will be organised into wholes if they produce few interruptions or changes in continuous lines. Of course, where interruptions do occur the principle of closure (described below) might be invoked to produce a set of smaller, individual 'wholes' (see Figure 4.ld(i)). This principle also explains why it is sometimes difficult to perceive a particular shape embedded in another. For example, the continuation lines on the number 5 in Figure 4.ld(ii) turn the whole shape into the 'figure' and the white paper surrounding it into the 'ground', rather than the '5' standing out as the figure and the remainder of the image being the ground.

Related to the principle of good continuation is the principle of *closure*. This states that we tend to organise elements so that they form simple, closed figures that are independent of other continuation, similarity or proximity properties. Such closed figures are often referred to as 'good figures'.

A major principle for determining whether or not a complete figure will be perceived as figure or ground is that of *area*: the smaller of two overlapping figures will be perceived as the figure and the other the ground. For example, in Figure 4.lf, the smaller square is seen as the figure against a grid background, rather than the hexagonal shape. A second principle of segregation, *symmetry*, states that the more symmetrical a figure is, the more likely it is to be seen as a closed figure, and this isolates it from the ground.

Finally there is the principle of *simplicity* which, as Hochberg and McAlister (1953) argue, probably underlies many of the other principles. They suggest that our perceptual processing system organises input into the simplest possible interpretation. Gestalt principles such as closure, good figure, etc. are simply statements about which elements of a stimulus are the simplest to group.

In summary, the importance of these Gestalt principles should be quite evident. Since we perceive stimuli in terms solely of how we arrange our perceptual world and since our understanding of the information presented is guided largely by such perceptual organisation, employing many of the Gestalt principles should make it possible to ensure that the operator perceives the material presented in the ways intended. This will be discussed in the next section but, before doing so, it is important to consider one further aspect of how we extract detail from the information presented—that is, how we organise our perceptual searching facilities. After all, when information is presented the operator generally has to perform some type of search task to perceive the relevant material: the eyes need to be directed towards the important part before the information can be processed.

Visual Scanning and Search

The available data relating to the visual search process can be divided, essentially, into studies that have considered the effects of different display arrangements on the task and those dealing with people themselves.

Display features

Perhaps one of the first important aspects to be considered is the position of the information in the material that is to be searched. Clearly, this can determine the part of the retina on which the stimuli fall and, because the retina is differentially sensitive, is likely to affect search performance.

A number of experimenters have shown this prediction to be true, both in terms of the probability of correctly identifying characters (for example, Bouma, 1973; Wolford and Hollingsworth, 1974a) and the time taken to identify characters (for example, Schiepers, 1980). In all cases the evidence suggests that the further a character is displaced from the gaze fixation position, the less likely it will be to be identified correctly and the longer it will take to be identified. Of course it should be remembered that the 'central point' in these studies implies the point at which the eye is fixated initially—not necessarily the centre of the material. The eye can be drawn to highlighted parts of the material, for example, so that these areas become the fixation point. This might then mean that information at the central part of the material falls on the periphery of the retina. Furthermore, eye movement studies in relation to the fixation points for words have revealed that the initial fixation in a word is about a quarter of the way into the word from the right (e.g. McConkie *et al.*, 1988). This 'preferred viewing location' (Rayner, 1978) is quite some distance to the left of the 'convenient' or 'optimal viewing location' (O'Regan and Levy-Schoen, 1987) which is the location where readers can obtain maximum information about the word.

Regarding the serial position of characters in a display, some evidence exists to suggest that identification is enhanced when gaps appear in the character string. Both Estes and Wolford (1971) and Wolford and Hollingsworth (1974b) have shown that a gap improves reporting accuracy for the letters that appear on either side of it. For example, take the following two arrangements of a character string:

A V F T Y U I O P L E

A V F   I O P L E

Accuracy for reporting the 'F' and the 'I' would be about 20 per cent better in the second than in the first string. This is possibly because, as the Gestalt school would argue, the gap enhances the principle of proximity. This creates the appearance of two substrings and allows attention to be directed to the letters on either side of it. As Gould (1976) suggests, 'people fixate on contours much more frequently than they fixate on homogeneous areas'. Furthermore, the evidence suggests that the letter preceding the gap (F) benefits more from the gap than the letter following the gap (I).

Appropriate spacing of displayed material, therefore, is likely to lead to increased detectability of individual items.

Detection efficiency is also related to the material that is displayed, particularly in terms of the display complexity and the distinguishability of the display items. In terms of material complexity, Teichener and Krebs (1974) have reviewed a number of laboratory studies and have shown that the detection time for stimuli presented as arrays (for example, a complex table) increases dramatically with array densities above about 200 stimuli.

Another feature of display complexity concerns the number of different types of elements that make up the displays, such as letters, numbers, pictures and highlighted material. In this case, the evidence suggests that if too much information of this type is presented, the reader's cognitive capacities are likely to be overloaded and thus search performance reduced. For example, although using colour can considerably reduce search time (Christ, 1975), Green and Anderson (1956) concluded that search time was slightly longer for multicoloured than for single-coloured displays.

The distinguishability of the displayed items is clearly likely to be an important factor in determining the efficiency of any search activity. In their literature survey, for example, Teichener and Krebs demonstrated that search efficiency was related to the extent to which the target stimulus stood out from the surrounding material. For example, when asked to detect squares in circles, subjects' performance deteriorated when only about 10 stimuli at a time were presented. The deterioration point for black triangles among black circles, however, was not until about 200 stimuli were presented. With even greater distinguishability between the array elements, for example detecting a large black circle among small black circles, very little deterioration occurred even with about 2000 display elements.

Subject features

Possibly the most important individual variable to affect processing performance concerns the information that the person wants to extract from the display. This is related, of course, to the reasons for looking. For example, Buswell (1935) demonstrated that faces and hands are the most fixated areas of pictures containing people among other things. (Kolers, 1976, describes in detail some of Buswell's findings regarding perceptual span in reading and looking at pictures.) Mackworth and Morandi (1967) showed that the parts of pictures rated as being most informative by one group of subjects were fixated most by another group of subjects.

Related to display meaning in terms of importance is the individual's motivation for viewing the display—thus people often search displays for meaning rather than to perceive specific targets. That observers can vary their search or scan patterns in relation to their intentions was demonstrated well by Yarbus (1967). He showed subjects pictures of different scenes, such as a group of individuals in a room, and asked them to infer different things from the pictures. For example, when asked to estimate the ages of the individuals, most eye fixations occurred around the facial regions; when asked to consider their social standing, most fixations related to the clothes and furniture, etc. Clearly, the observer's search and fixation pattern was related to the search intent.

TYPOGRAPHICAL FEATURES OF WRITTEN COMMUNICATION

How the eyes scan over the text and how we search for material within the text have clear implications for presenting material. For written information to be communicated efficiently, the message needs not only to be read (and interpreted) correctly but assimilated in the shortest time possible. Fast reading is important because of economy of time and, perhaps more importantly, it ensures that our long-term storage memory capacities are not overloaded. For example, the longer a reader needs to decipher a word or a symbol on a page (perhaps because of bad handwriting or because a faint photocopy is being used), the slower will be the comprehension rate.

Many experimenters have demonstrated a relationship between how material is presented and the subsequent efficiency of reading. For example, Bednall (1992) demonstrated that differences in screen design and layout affected the speed with which subjects could locate target material within lists of names. It also seems likely that such factors play quite a large part in determining whether the material will be read at all (McLaughlin, 1966). It is only comparatively recently, however, that those involved in presenting written information have considered, in any systematic way, the question of typographical factors such as the type and quality of the print and the page layout—despite the fact that it is these aspects that convey the message.

Print Features

Type size

Type size is conventionally specified in terms of the height of a line of print, the unit being the 'point' which is 0.0138in (about ⅓mm) high.

Using two measures of readability, the amount read and the degree of comprehension, Burt (1959) compared the readability of passages composed of different sizes of Times Roman print (designed in 1932) ranging from 8 to 14 pt. Unfortunately, he did not provide any data to support his claim, but was able to state that the 10 pt prose was the most legible. Most students found the 9 pt print equally as legible as the 10 pt, while older people often did best with 11 pt or even 12 pt. These results were replicated by Poulton (1969a) when he asked housewives to search for particular words in lists of ingredients printed in 10, 7.5, 6 and 4 pt lower-case type.

Tinker (1965a) investigated how type size affected eye movements during reading. His results are very similar to Burt's and Poulton's in so far as the 10 and 11 pt type were read faster with fewer fixations and longer saccades. Smaller and larger type sizes were read more slowly—mainly because fixations were more frequent. Smaller type sizes meant that the characters were harder to discriminate; larger sizes meant that the average saccade traversed fewer characters resulting in more fixations.

These conclusions, of course, are related to the number of characters on a line, which will be discussed below.

Upper and lower case

Irrespective of its size, alphabetic information can be presented in capitals, lower-case letters or a combination of both. The different modes, of course, affect both the character outline and distinctiveness, and the amount of space available between the lines. Lower-case ascenders and descenders (for example, the top parts of 'b', 'd' or the bottom parts of 'g', 'y') mean that the space available between lines of text varies. For example, more interline space is available when the letter 'a' is above 'c' than when it is above 'b' because of the ascender on 'b'. In the same way, just a glance at the characters on this page will show minimum space between, say, a 'p' and a 'b'. For these reasons it is important to consider the question of character case for ease and speed of reading.

Much of the earlier work in this area has been carried out using printed material—usually for the newspaper industry. For example, in 1946 Paterson and Tinker investigated the reading effectiveness of upper- and lower-case letters in newspaper headlines. At normal reading distances, their results indicated that on average more words were read when using lower-case letters than when using headlines printed in upper case in the same type face and point size (in this case 24 pt Cheltenham Extra Condensed). These results were replicated by Poulton (1967) who showed a 9 per cent advantage in reading ability of lower-case over upper-case headlines. A similar advantage was obtained by mixing upper- and lower-case letters, although they were not read any more reliably than headlines printed entirely in lower case. Poulton and Brown (1968) and Poulton (1969a) have also demonstrated a lower-case advantage, as did Fox (1963) who compared reading speeds and comprehension using 'gothic elite' (capitals) and 'standard elite' (lower-case) typefaces. Interestingly, however, this advantage occurred only when the standard elite text was read *before* the gothic elite text. When the results from the other group of subjects (those who read the gothic text before the standard) were added to the data, no case advantage was observed.

A number of authors, for example, Paterson and Tinker (1946) and Poulton (1969b), have suggested that the reason for any superiority of mixed over upper-case letters probably lies in the shape of the envelope surrounding the whole word (rather than the individual letters)—particularly for words that are used frequently (Haber and Haber, 1981). Words presented in capitals do not have a distinctive shape since all the letters are the same height. Word shapes using various lower-case letters, however, are more likely to be different because of the ascenders and descenders on different letters, and readers may well learn these shapes for high-frequency words. For example, the shape of the envelope surrounding the word 'dog' is different from that around 'cat' due to the extensions of the 'd' and 'g' in 'dog' and the 't' in 'cat'. The envelopes around 'DOG' and 'CAT', however, do not differ, and this lack of distinctive shape means that the reader has to examine some of the intermediate letters to identify the words, so increasing reading time.

A distinctive envelopes explanation for the lower-case advantage has been challenged by Phillips (1979), at least when a search task is employed. He compared subjects' abilities to search for place names on a map when the names were typed all in lower case, in lower case but with the initial letter a capital, all in upper case, and in smaller sized upper case with the initial letter larger. His results demonstrated that names set entirely in lower case took significantly longer to find than names in the other conditions; the shortest time was taken for names in capitals with the larger initial letter. On the basis of his results, Phillips suggests that, for search tasks at least, the important aspect of the word is not the overall shape but the initial letter and, by making this distinctive, the word should be found more quickly.

Unfortunately, even this straightforward explanation has been challenged more recently. Thus in a task in which subjects were asked to search for surnames in a database that were typed either in upper-case letters (BLOGGS) or in an upper/lower-case format (Bloggs), Bednall (1992) found no difference in search times between the two presentations. However, her presentation list (names from a telephone directory) may have had some effect on the outcome. Whereas the place names in Phillips' list generally had different first letters when names were in close proximity to each other on the map (for example, London, Croydon), Bednall's list of surnames were all similar (Beasley C., Beasley E., and so on). The first letter provided few cues as to the name.

Finally, two further exceptions to the lower-case advantage finding should be mentioned. Foster and Bruce (1982) asked subjects to read aloud text composed of 'nonsense' phrases written either in lower case with the first letter of the sentence in upper case, or all in upper case. Their data showed no significant advantage of lower- over upper-case letters, although there was a slight trend towards faster mixed-case reading. It is likely, however, that the task—reading aloud—may have reduced any advantage of using the lower-case arrangement. Thus the experiments described so far have asked subjects either to read to themselves or to read for comprehension. Silent reading can be performed more quickly than reading aloud since the processes involved in translating the (cognitive) words into vocal responses are not required. Thus, although perhaps lower-case letters and words may be perceived and 'registered' more quickly, it is possible that the speed advantage is reduced if a vocal response is required.

Second, Kember and Varley (1987) demonstrated that for viewing single letters, material presented in upper case was perceived more quickly and with fewer errors than single letters in lower case. For text-based material, however, the difference did not occur.

In summary, therefore, it would appear that for general comprehension and reading, text composed in both upper- and lower-case letters (as in this book) is superior both for reading speed and accuracy. The advantage is reduced, however, when the task includes components of search (particularly search through lists) and reading aloud.

Punctuation marks

Unfortunately, relatively little work has been done on the legibility of punctuation marks. Prince (1967) has reported on the difficulties of poor vision readers in distinguishing between the comma and the full stop. He suggests that the comma should be 55 per cent, and the full stop 30 per cent, of the height of the lower case letters used in the text. Reynolds (1983) argues that similar difficulties are often encountered with copies of text, where commas, semicolons and full stops may be virtually indistinguishable.

Layout Features

Sectioning prose

Dividing the text into meaningful sections has three advantages for the reader. First, it provides structure to the prose, informing the reader where one set of ideas ends and a new set begins. Secondly, through the Gestalt features discussed earlier, it allows the material's structure to be organised perceptually. Thirdly, it provides a chance for the reader to collect some thoughts and to prepare for the next section. Regarding the design aspects, Hartley and Burnhill (1976) have suggested that leaving an empty line between paragraphs is a more effective cue for the reader than simply indenting the first line of a new paragraph. Spacing between paragraphs helps the reader to group and separate those parts of the text which have similar content. In Gestalt terms, the paragraph is seen as a 'whole'.

Such assertions have been reinforced by recent studies which have used different kinds of prose sectioning techniques (for example, Grant and Davey, 1991; Krug *et al.*, 1991). The results suggest that the additional spatial cues created by sectioning prose in some way (by adding blank lines between significant paragraphs, using headings, or other typographic blocking techniques) can help readers organise how they process the information. Thus spatial features can affect how readers manipulate the text's schema.

As well as sectioning prose, Wright (1977a) suggests that colour can be used to create the appearance of blocks, colouring either the print or the background. Problems with the use of colour in the text have already been introduced, from the point of view of presenting too much information to the reader, but Wright's suggestions could be used to reduce the reader's burden. Thus she argues that a coloured background can provide supplementary indexing information, for example, as with a book appendix. It enables the reader to turn quickly from the text to the beginning of the appendix without having to look for page numbers.

Headings

A common way of sectioning prose is to use appropriate headings, and these serve a number of different purposes. Most obviously they assist readers who are searching through a display or printed material for particular sections. Perhaps less obviously they are extremely valuable to those who have to read the entire material, since they provide a structure that enables the information to be integrated as it is being read. Each of these factors may help to increase the reader's comprehension and retention of the information.

The available evidence in this respect, however, is rather more equivocal than intuition would suggest. As Krug *et al.* (1991) point out, some studies have demonstrated that the presence of headings can affect readers' comprehension and recall while others have shown no effect. The inconsistent pattern of conclusions, however, may be related to the kind of text and headings used in the studies, and to the tasks that the subjects were required to perform. Furthermore, as Grant and Davey (1991) have demonstrated, the effects of headings may not simply be to increase memory or comprehension of the text under consideration. They demonstrated, for example, that while headings had no effect on overall comprehension, subjects in the 'heading group' who answered items correctly were more able to use the material in other ways—in this case to locate parts of the text where the comprehension test answers appeared.

One aspect of headings that has received consideration concerns ways of numbering them. Numbering can serve two purposes: it may help to make clear to the reader how the sections are nested together (thus replacing, perhaps, the need for subheadings) and it enables the reader to refer to specific sections that are smaller than a page.

Perry (1952) has suggested that Arabic numbers are preferable to Roman numerals, although this is possibly so only for the smaller values—compare, for example, the ease of interpreting the sets of symbols iv (4), and xxviii (28). In addition, Wright (1977a) suggests that numbers are probably better for indexing than letters of the alphabet, and that the larger the sequence the greater the advantage for numbers. For example, people are more certain that 8 precedes 10 than that H precedes J.

The size of display area and line spacing

Whereas dividing text into distinct areas facilitates the reader's scanning and search behaviour, the question of the size of the text area relates more to the normal reading and comprehension processes. These involve saccadic eye movements and the need to divide words, phrases and sentences in a way that avoids them being frequently split in places that make comprehension difficult.

With regard to saccadic eye movements, it will be remembered that each saccade encompasses about 6–8 character spaces. As discussed above, the available evidence suggests that we do not sweep our eyes over the text in a rigid left–right direction, but often make recursive movements, perhaps to correct mistakes or to aid comprehension. Thus, although unfortunately no evidence is available to help decide on the optimum width of the text, it should be neither too small nor too large. If the width is too small, only a few saccades may be possible on any line, thus necessitating recursions to previous lines with the attendant problems of directing the eyes to the beginning of another line. If it is too large, too many saccades may be needed to scan the line. More importantly perhaps, it is necessary to ensure that when the eye is at the extreme right-hand end of one line it does not have too far to travel back to begin the next line (again, the ocular control mechanism can lead the eye to the beginning of the wrong line). In this context, Bouma (1980) relates the length of a line of text (i.e. the distance between the left- and right-hand margins) to the angle over which the eye travels to reach the next line. This, he suggests, should be approximately 2 degrees. Within reason, therefore, for long lines of text the interline spacing should be reduced.

The number of characters in a line needs to be related to the distance of the observer from the text. This determines the visual angle that each character presents to the eye.

Columns

Subsumed under the topic of display width lies the question of whether text is better presented as a single block or in a column format as appears, for example, in newspapers and magazines. Again, this concerns eye movement control between lines. With very long text lines (as would occur in a newspaper without a column format) the interline spacing would have to be extremely small to retain the optimal 2 degree recursive movement to the beginning of the next line. Columns help to keep the line length short.

The experimental evidence that has been produced to support such a contention suggests that column formats are advantageous, but only under certain circumstances. Thus, Tinker (1965b) demonstrated that both speed and comprehension are superior when text is arranged in a two-column layout compared with an arrangement in which it is spread across the page. However, Kak and Knight (1980) report that this column format was beneficial only for normal reading speeds. Subjects who had been taught to 'speed read' showed no advantage when using such a format, and even some disadvantage. It may be, of course, that the training that these subjects underwent during the speed reading course (for example, to control recursive eye movements, to scan efficiently) may have directly interfered with the eye movement patterns needed for column formats.

Text justification

Whenever characters at the left- or right-hand margin are vertically aligned with one another (as, for example, in this book) the respective margins are said to be justified. Whereas left justification clearly has advantages for the control of line recursive eye movements—the line always starts the same distance from the page edge—the advantages of right justified text are less tangible. Unless words are to be broken at sometimes inappropriate places (thus causing difficulties for word recognition), a constant line length can only exist with variable spacing between words. In lines which contain a fair number of words, of course, this will not be too noticeable, but for shorter lines the unpredictable interword spacing may cause problems for the reader. For this reason Burt (1959) recommended the use of the unjustified style in books for small children.

Gregory and Poulton (1970) performed a number of experiments designed to investigate this question, using both good and poorer readers. As stimuli they used three justification formats: right justified, not right justified, and not right justified but with words broken by hyphens in appropriate places. Their comprehension results demonstrated that the better readers neither benefited from nor were disadvantaged by the different formats. However, the poorer readers obtained lower comprehension scores for the justified than for the two non-justified formats. A second experiment, using the poorer readers, demonstrated that the non-justified format advantage no longer held when the line length was increased from about seven to twelve words. In this case, then, the disadvantage caused by the variable interword spacing was reduced.

Coding and cueing

One clear result which emerged from the discussion of visual search processes was that the more conspicuous the target area, the better the search performance. Clearly, highlighting important areas of the display, by increased display luminance, by typographical techniques such as underlining, italic, bold, capitals, etc. or by colouring different sections, can help the reader pick out salient parts of the display. With regard to written text, for example, Fowler and Barker (1974) found that library textbook readers had inserted some form of cueing such as underlining or asterisks in over 90 per cent of the books.

Emphasising parts of text can also provide readers with the visual analogue of the verbal emphasis that we use in everyday speech. Thus McAteer (1992) demonstrated that by emphasising words in text as they would be in speech, different reading times could be produced. In relation to *how* the words should be emphasised, she demonstrated that capital letters generally implied 'prominence' while italic highlighting was attributed to 'contrast' or 'connotation' effects.

As well as helping the observer's reading task, of course, many of these typographic techniques can also be used to code certain display areas or types of information. Colour coding, for example, is a well-known technique in many areas: a flashing red display is often used to indicate 'danger', green usually signifies safety, and so on.

The available research regarding the effectiveness of different typographical cueing techniques is inconclusive—primarily because of scarcity. The little evidence available, however, suggests that the occasional use of italics for emphasising significant points may be no better than plain text for comprehension, and a complex cueing system may actually impair study.

The research on underlining as a means of cueing is similarly inconclusive. For example, Cashen and Leicht (1970) showed that students who had received offprints with relevant passages underlined in red were better at answering questions both on the underlined statements and also (possibly because the underlining helped comprehension) on the adjacent, uncued passages. It would appear, however, that this advantage is only apparent if the reader is not under some time stress to complete the passage. For example, Crouse and Idstein (1972) found that cueing led to higher scores when the readers were given some time to study a 6000-word text, but not when they were given a shorter time. Furthermore, it may well be that underlining may actually make the text harder to read because it reduces the blank space between lines.

Foster and Coles (1977) considered the relative merits of using capital letters and bold type as cues. Their results indicated that bold type was a better all-round cueing technique. Although the capital letters led to higher scores on the cued material, when the subjects were tested on the uncued material they performed worse than those who had not had cueing. The authors suggest that when readers used the capital letter cueing technique it hindered their reading performance, perhaps by affecting their reading behaviour so that they had less time to perceive the uncued portions of the text.

Finally, the use of colour needs to be considered. Certainly for coding visual information, colour appears to be the most useful technique. For example, Hitt (1961) compared five types of code—numbers, shapes, letters, stimulus position and colour—and demonstrated that numerical and colour coding were equally the most efficient. Similar results were obtained by Smith and Thomas (1964) who demonstrated that a colour code consisting of five different colours was more effective than any geometric shape code that they used. In addition, Christ (1975) reviewed a number of similar experiments and showed that colour is superior to size, brightness and shape coding for identification tasks. However, in some instances the use of letters and digits was shown to be more efficient, which is not altogether surprising since the tasks used were essentially the identification of objects. When tasks which involved searching displays were reviewed, colour was superior in all cases. As far as coding is concerned, therefore, colour would appear to be the most useful 'all-round' method. However, it should be remembered that it does have its own limitations—particularly in environments containing coloured ambient illumination, and if the observers are 'colour blind'.

Regarding the effect of colour as a highlighting cue for text comprehension, Fowler and Barker (1974) found that subjects who were questioned a week after having read material were more likely to answer correctly questions concerning the highlighted parts of the text than the non-highlighted material.

In summary, although the evidence suggests that highlighting may have beneficial effects on reading performance and comprehension, caution should be taken about the overuse of such techniques. It has previously been pointed out that visual search times can be increased if the operator is presented with too much information (or, more specifically, too much uncertainty). Within the present discussion too much information implies, perhaps, too many cueing categories. Whereas using one or two colours may increase searching performance, using too many may actually degrade it. (Jones, 1962, suggests that the normal observer can identify about nine or ten surface colours, primarily varying in hue.)

A second caution relates to the possible distracting influence of cueing techniques and their deleterious effects on perceptual organisation. For example, Engel (1980) argues that, although colour can be a powerful means of improving the legibility of text displays, overuse (or non-optimal applications) can break up the display's Gestalt. Perhaps more insidiously, colour can create artificial groupings of material. This can happen particularly in displays which consist of non-prose information such as tables or menus. As a check to ensure that this does not happen, Engel suggests converting the alphanumeric characters in the display to rectangles of the same size and colour. In this way the influence of the colours on the layout will become apparent.

ALTERNATIVE WAYS OF PRESENTING INFORMATION AND INSTRUCTION

The millions of books, journals, magazines, manuals and newspapers available to us every day would seem to emphasise the fact that we crave for the printed word. Whenever a new product is marketed it needs to be advertised; a new machine also normally carries an instruction manual to tell the operator how it works and how to work it, and a maintenance manual giving details of what to do if it breaks down. In addition, the machine itself will probably carry small pieces of symbolic information to help the operator, such as small information labels saying 'danger', 'on/off', or 'position control'. Each of these communication media are aimed at reaching different audiences and will provide different kinds and levels of information. Although each will have its own features relating to how the information should be presented, some general points do apply and these will be discussed below. However, as with most design recommendations, it should be remembered that the most appropriate means of communication for one situation may not apply to another.

The first question to be answered is how the information should be presented. As Wright (1977a) points out, for example, people who keep information and refer to it when necessary (for example when using reference manuals) may have different requirements from those who, having studied the information, will be retrieving it from memory. Similarly, those who read a report from beginning to end will use the material differently from readers who wish only to understand specific information or answer particular queries and do not intend to read the entire document. Even among those who read all the information, there may be some who read it in order to take a decision but, once the decision is made, are no longer interested in the technical details.

Verhoef (1993), for example, presented subjects with tabular train and flight information that had been laid out in different ways. By arranging the material so that *destinations* were represented in the first column (rather than train times, for example), subjects provided 16 per cent more correct answers when tested, and the time needed to search the material for a train decreased by 42 per cent. In this case, therefore, it was the destination that was the most important feature of the information displayed; in other circumstances it might be the train time or the class of train.

A similar kind of study was carried out by White (1989) who considered the appropriate layout for calendars. His concern was whether people expect to read calendars with the days presented in rows or in columns—in other words, whether people search calendars in left–right fashion, reading across the table, or in a top-down way. His results demonstrated clear differences in search time (although not accuracy), with the horizontal arrangement producing shorter search times than the vertical arrangement. The question of which day started the week (Sunday or Monday) had no effect on performance.

Studies of alternative ways of presenting complex material have shown that some non-prose formats can increase the reader's ability to use the information. As an example, Dwyer (1967) provided subjects with information on the structure of the heart either orally or using simple line drawing. He showed that the line drawing was more effective when the subjects were subsequently tested on their memory of the heart's structure. However, for tests which examined the subjects' understanding of the heart's function, the oral presentation was most affective. Dwyer's results appear to suggest, therefore, that simple information is better presented visually, but when any action is to be taken, perhaps to integrate the information, it may be better to present it orally, with all of the different emphases that the voice can attain.

When deciding on the appropriate communication mode, as well as the use to which the information is to be put, it is also important to consider the type of information to be communicated. Booher (1975), for example, showed that if the information is 'static', that is merely informing the operator about, say, the location of controls on a machine, then it is better to present it as a series of pictures. 'Dynamic' information, on the other hand, for example informing the operator how to switch the machine on, is better presented as pictures and words.

The problem facing the ergonomist (or indeed the designer of any technical information), therefore, is to decide on the most appropriate way of presenting the information (or instructions) to the predicted audience. In doing so the first decision is to choose through which of the two senses, visual or auditory, to present the information. Even this choice can be limited, for example by environmental constraints. Thus spoken instructions may be more costly to produce and are certainly less affective in a noisy environment. Since more will be said in the next chapter about presenting auditory information, the remainder of this chapter will deal with the visual presentation of information and instructions. In this case the designer of the information channel is likely to have to choose between prose or some pictorial presentation such as graphs, bar charts, pictures, flowcharts and tables.

Graphs and Bar Charts

Graphs are used in a variety of situations to present numerical information. They have the distinct advantage that they give the reader both the numerical data itself and illustrate any apparent trends. This is particularly so if two or more functions are plotted on the same graph—variations in their relative trends can be seen easily. To this end Kosslyn (1989) analyses the constituent components of graphs (background, framework, specifier and labels) and considers their influence at syntactic, semantic and pragmatic levels of analyses of human information processing. Using this kind of analysis, he argues, it is possible to determine whether graph designs are more or less likely to lead to ambiguities and misinterpretations.

Although Kosslyn's analysis is somewhat detailed, some more readily available data are available to help the designer draw graphs to their best advantage. For example, Milroy and Poulton (1978) have shown that if more than one curve is drawn on the same graph, and each needs to be labelled, then labelling each curve directly (rather than putting labels elsewhere on the graph or even under the legend) results in the fastest reading without any loss of accuracy. This is probably because direct labelling requires the reader to make fewer visual scans of the graph and so puts less strain on short-term memory. The number of curves that can be included on the same graph without any loss of intelligibility will clearly depend on the degree to which the curves overlap each other. If there is a fair amount of overlap, Wright (1977a) suggests a simple rule of thumb: three curves may well be the maximum for clarity. Indeed it may also be advantageous to break graphs down into smaller units rather than have too much information presented on a single graph.

Finally, Wright reports other work which has indicated that presenting the axes of a graph as a square (i.e. extending the 'x' and 'y' axes on the top and right-hand side respectively) increases the ease with which the values of extreme points on the graph may be read. Such an arrangement, of course, follows Gestalt principles in so far as the squared axes help to produce the perspective of a 'whole' figure. Some of these suggestions are illustrated in Figure 4.2.

Despite the fact that they are used extensively, particularly in the advertising industry, little comparable work has been carried out regarding bar charts. Wright (1977a), however, has summarised their advantages and disadvantages in the following way:

> One of the *a priori* advantages of bar charts would seem to be the ease to which they can be used to present many differently related variables. Some alternative ways of doing this are shown in Figure 4.3. Experimental comparisons among these different formats are hard to find but some of the formats will be more suitable for a specific purpose than others. For example, Figure 4.3a conveys the most information in the least space and very clearly shows the growth in total expenditure over time; but comparisons may be error prone either between items in the same year (e.g. in 1951 more was spent on defence than on education, but this is not obvious in Figure 4.3a) or between different years for the same item (e.g. defence in 1968 and 1973). Indeed there may be two different ways of displaying the information to

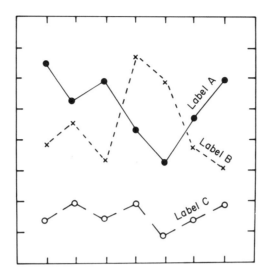

Figure 4.2 A hypothetical graph illustrating the principles of direct labelling and extending the axes

facilitate these two different comparisons. For example Figure 4.3c enables a comparison of items within the same year but comparisons between years are still very difficult; on the other hand, Figure 4.3b facilitates comparisons between the years but the distance between different items of expenditure may cause errors for these comparisons (e.g. education versus housing plus roads in 1968). Figure 4.3b makes it easier to compare the change in expenditure on particular items over time, whereas the lack of alignment between the different items makes this difficult in Figure 4.3a.

Flowcharts

The flowchart (sometimes called an 'algorithm' or 'logical tree') presents information to the reader as a set of choices and pathways and looks very similar to the computer programmer's flowcharts so much in evidence these days. On the surface at least, flowcharts appear to provide the reader with easily 'digestible' information, since the most complex textual structure is illustrated by the ways in which the pathways join the flowchart boxes. These routes give an overview of the various relationships between different aspects of the information.

Although a case has been made to consider flowcharts as means of presenting information, there is evidence to suggest that they may not be beneficial in all circumstances. If relatively simple information is transmitted, under some circumstances flowcharts may actually create

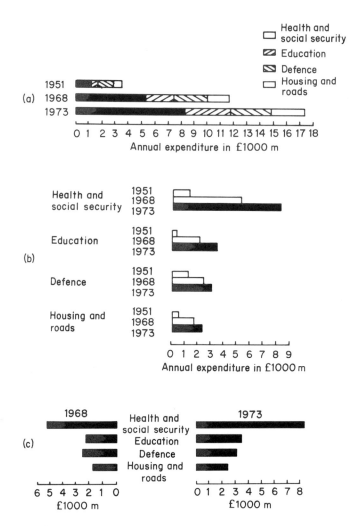

Figure 4.3 Alternative ways of displaying information using bar charts (from Wright, 1977a, reproduced with permission from *Instructional Science*)

problems. For example, although Wright and Reid (1973) have demonstrated that presenting difficult information in a flowchart format produced fewer subsequent errors when compared with prose, short sentences or tables, flowchart presentation of easy problems produced no advantage. Furthermore, if the material had to be remembered, the performance of subjects who had been presented with flowcharts deteriorated faster. It would appear, therefore, that flowcharts are more efficient if complicated information needs to be acted on immediately, but have little value (and may even be detrimental) if the information is otherwise easy to understand or needs to be retained.

A few research findings are available to help design an efficient flowchart. Kamman (1975) compared the efficiency of two kinds of flowchart for finding information in part of a telephone directory. The first design used essentially a vertical structure although horizontal pathways were included. A series of question boxes led, via arrows, to further question boxes or to 'action' boxes. The second consisted of a streamlined flow of short captions arranged horizontally only. Other layout changes included the pathways being made thicker and standing out against a grey background, each decision point could branch into three or even four pathways although more appropriate decision points were provided, and the number of words in the chart was reduced. Comparing these two forms Kamman showed that the second (streamlined) chart produced significantly fewer errors than the first. Both designs, however, produced more efficient performance (fewer errors, faster comprehension) than the standard telephone directory format.

The value of horizontally streaming the choice points has been emphasised subsequently by Krohn (1983) who compared horizontal (right–left and left–right) streaming with top-down. Whereas for simple problems there was little to choose between the three formats, streaming from right to left (i.e. against the normally accepted reading direction) produced significantly more errors and increased reading time when subjects were asked to use the flowchart to solve complex problems.

Although Kamman's study demonstrated the value of reducing the number of choice points within a flowchart, in some cases it may be neither practical nor desirable to do so. In such cases Gane, Horabin and Lewis (1966) have suggested producing small subcharts, each of which deals with separate sequences in the operation. A more radical solution has been advanced by Jones (1968) who suggests that the material can be rewritten in a 'branching list' structure so that the information is listed vertically and the reader has to jump to other questions. For example, the question might read 'Is the motor turning? If YES continue with question 2. If NO go to question 15.' Wright (1977b) argues that such a format may be useful in providing specific answers to specific questions, but it loses some of the other advantages of flowcharts—particularly the visual appearance of the decision-making structure emphasised earlier.

As well as reducing the number of choice points and words, Wright suggests other ways of increasing flowchart efficiency. First, it is often the case that the various outcomes are not equally likely to occur. The designer may, therefore, decide to produce a flowchart in which the most frequently used decision path is the shortest possible—rather than reducing the average path length. Secondly, there may be occasions when it makes better sense to emphasise particular aspects of the choice. For example, the fact that some of the outcomes may be more important than others might be an argument for putting the important decisions at the top of the tree; or different choices may have different levels of uncertainty attached to them, so making it reasonable for the decisions to be made in order from the highest to the lowest certainty.

Pictures

Illustrations are widely used in modern communication systems, for example with technical terms, and pictorial information is increasingly being employed to communicate instructions for using equipment. This is particularly so when the equipment is for use by people of different nationalities and literacy levels. Other advantages of pictures are that in some circumstances they produce better responses where viewing conditions are degraded (Ellis and Dewar, 1979) or viewing times are short (King, 1971). They can also be used during problem solving to answer specific questions which arise and can even influence the type of problem-solving strategy adopted. This, in turn, will determine the type of information sought (Szlichcinski, 1977a).

It must be emphasised, however, that pictures do have their limitations, particularly if the concepts being presented are too complex for the readers to understand. This was demonstrated well by Szlichcinski (1977b), for example, who found that his subjects had great difficulty in carrying out a fairly complex task when given only pictorial instructions.

Despite these negative points it is likely to be the case that pictures will be used increasingly more frequently to present both static and dynamic information. At the very least, the constant need to sell goods to people of different nationalities with different languages should ensure this. Furthermore, the observations that pictures may produce poorer performance under some circumstances must be tempered by the argument that such results will depend on the quality of the material used in the experiments. Poor pictures, for example, are likely to produce poor results. Indeed, Szlichcinski (1977c) showed that simply using three-dimensional pictures, rather than two-dimensional representations, tended to improve performance. It may be the case, therefore, that the pictures need to be designed well to produce better performance, and so it is up to ergonomists to produce guidelines for their efficient production.

In essence two types of pictures may be used: discrete symbols or more complex compilations of illustrations.

Discrete pictographic symbols, or icons, are already in widespread use on equipment, for example vehicle controls, and for public information and warning, for example road traffic signs. Unfortunately, despite their extensive use, it is only relatively recently that research has been carried out to consider their appropriate design (Zwaga and Easterby, 1983, for example, describe a series of evaluation procedures suggested by the International Standards Organisation). Two features need to be considered when designing a pictographic symbol to give a single piece of information: the content of the symbol and the extent to which it is perceptible.

Rogers (1989) provides detailed guidelines relating to the design of iconic symbols, in which she stresses the importance of the underlying referent that is employed in iconic depiction. Since it is the referent that enables the reader to 'link' the icon to the information it is intended to convey, it is important to understand, again, the reader's 'mental model' of what is being displayed.

Features that affect the picture's perceptibility can be gleaned from the discussion earlier relating to the principles expounded by the Gestalt school. Thus Easterby (1970) has suggested a number of factors, the more important of which are as follows:

- A *solid boundary* to the figure provides good contrast between the figure and its background (see Figure 4.4a).

- *Simplicity*: a simple shape is perceived more readily than one which contains too much detail (see Figure 4.4b).

- *Closure* of the figure helps to provide the 'whole' (it may be remembered that Wright advocated this principle for the production of graphs, suggesting that the axes should form a square) (see Figure 4.4c).

- *Stability*: because our perceptual system attempts to impose form on the incoming sensory information, some types of figures are inherently 'unstable'. For example, most people will know of the picture showing two faces in silhouette (Rubin's vase-profiles pattern). Depending on the observer's 'set' either two faces looking at each other or a Grecian vase against a dark background will be seen. Once both possibilities are seen the perception tends to keep changing from one to the other. The same effect can be seen in Figure 4.4d in which the arrow appears to be indicating, alternately, clockwise and anticlockwise movement. Because of this instability the picture becomes ambiguous, but removing part of the arrow reduces the ambiguity.

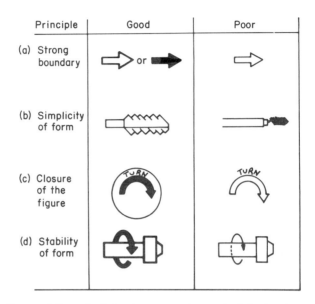

Principle	Good	Poor
(a) Strong boundary		
(b) Simplicity of form		
(c) Closure of the figure		
(d) Stability of form		

Figure 4.4 Some of the principles important in symbol design (reproduced from Easterby, 1970, *Ergonomics*, **13**, 149–58, by permission of Taylor & Francis Ltd.)

- *Symmetry*: to make recognition easier, the various elements in the picture should be as symmetrical as possible—as long as the production of a symmetrical figure does not mislead the observer. Szlichcinski (1979a), however, argues that there are some circumstances in which an asymmetrical figure may provide more information than one which is symmetrical—for example, his study mentioned earlier in which three-dimensional pictures (asymmetrical) produced better performance than the symmetrically drawn two-dimensional pictures.

Before concluding the discussion of pictogram appearance, the point made in Chapter 2, about increasing the dimensions (cues) present in information, should not be forgotten. The number of different dimensions able to be incorporated within simple pictograms is limited but can include shape, size and colour. Welford (1984), for example, points to the design of international road traffic signs which use the shape dimension as an initial identifier: circular signs are mandatory, triangular signs are advisory. In Great Britain colour is also used: green signs are used on major roads, blue signs are used on motorways. Such initial coding systems help the observer put the sign into 'perspective', i.e. it provides the 'set' from which the (hopefully correct) identification can be made.

The other important consideration is the kinds of pictures that should actually go into the pictogram. Welford (1984) argues strongly that designs need not be pictorially accurate, often more abstract symbols can do the job just as well. An arrow, for example, universally implies motion; a diagonal bar across a figure implies negation ('do not ride', 'do not cross'). However, Barnard and Marcel (1983) caution that the understanding of such abstract symbols is often culturally determined and they ought to be used carefully.

Cultural influences also appear when considering the actual picture to be used. Easterby and Hakiel (1981), for example, have demonstrated that the recognisability of a symbol is possibly the most important criterion for its comprehension: prior experience of the sign was found to increase the comprehension rate by 150 to 200 per cent. But prior experience does not mean simply having used the sign before—it also means having had 'experience' of the picture. For example, Barnard and Marcel (1983) point to the use of a penguin to imply frozen goods. This involves an inferential relationship between the picture (penguin) and what it is intended to signify (frozen goods). As long as the inference is made, then the connection should also be made. However, people who have never seen a penguin or do not know where it comes from may not understand the picture's meaning.

Although discrete symbols can be used to represent a great deal of information, their usefulness is mainly restricted to informing about specific features of the environment. When more complex information, such as instructions, needs to be conveyed then individual pictures may have to be combined in some way to form a sequential message. It is at this point that problems can emerge, since the sets of pictures have to fulfil many of the functions of natural language without having the benefit of some of the features that accompany language: voice intonation and stress, gestures, repetition, and so on. How the pictures are arranged, and the shapes from which they are formed, need to convey both their meaning and the message structure and logic in similar ways to those in which words and grammatical structure determine the meaning of simple sentences.

Barnard and Marcel (1976) carried out a fairly comprehensive study to determine how pictures should be designed and arranged to convey information. In essence they investigated:

- Part versus whole representation of equipment: whether each picture in the sequence should display the important part to be considered (for example, a dial or a switch), or whether it should represent the whole apparatus with the important part accentuated.

- The order of representing the status and actions: whether or not individual pictures should be linked—the first showing the action to be taken (for example, throwing a switch) and the second the consequences of the action (for example, a light illuminated).

- The use of insets to illustrate aspects of the actions.

Using subjects' reports of what they thought different sets of pictures were instructing them to do, Barnard and Marcel demonstrated the need to include details of the relevant parts of the machine in each picture (in other words the 'whole' representation). Surprisingly, however, the use of insets resulted in poorer understanding than using comparable instructions without insets. Overall, the action–state representation yielded the best results.

Tables

Tables are probably the most frequently used ways of presenting discrete pieces of information. However, perhaps because they *are* in such common use, little thought is generally given to their design.

A table is little more than a systematic arrangement of different items of information which can be numerical, as in timetables, or non-numerical, such as the table of chapters at the front of this book. A variety of ways is available to arrange the information. For example, the items could be listed alphabetically or in numerical order, or they could be grouped with reference to a common feature. Furthermore, as Wright and Fox (1970) point out, it is always possible to provide aids such as spatial cues by aligning items vertically or in rows, or to use typographical features such as variations in the size, style or colour of the print.

The many forms of table which can be seen in current usage differ, primarily, in the amount and kind of work that they require the user to perform. In this respect a distinction can be made between explicit and implicit tables. Explicit tables are those which give the reader all the information which may be needed, for example a bus timetable that lists each time of day the bus is due to arrive. An implicit table, on the other hand, gives some information only and leaves the reader to infer additional information. The bus timetable which tells the reader that the bus will arrive 'every 20 minutes after 11.00 a.m.' is an example of such a table.

For the designer, the main advantage of the implicit over the explicit table lies in the space saved. However, implicit tables can be disadvantageous since they demand further calculations, to which the wrong answer might be obtained.

With regard to the explicit type of table, Wright and Fox (1970) suggest that there are two main variants: linear and two (or more) dimensional (the latter are sometimes called matrices). In the linear version they argue that the reader searches through what is effectively one long list to find the information required—as in, for example, a tax code or a telephone directory. With the matrix version on the other hand, the reader has to make two or more searches for different parts of the information required, and then has to coordinate the results of this search in a particular way. For example, when reading a train timetable to determine the arrival time at a particular station, a passenger will first scan the rows to find the train, then scan the column to find the station. The arrival time is given at the intersection of the row and column. In many respects, of course, the linear type of explicit table may be viewed simply as an implicit version of a matrix table. Take the telephone directory as an example. To use it as a linear table to find the telephone number of a Mr H. K. Williams one could start at the beginning of the directory and work through until the required name is read. This is clearly not the way in which a directory is used—in fact a number of dimensions are (implicitly) imposed. Thus one first looks for the initial of the surname (dimension 1). The second dimension would be the second letter (or even the second couple of letters), and so on. In this way the search time is reduced considerably.

From the available research it is difficult to draw general guidelines as to which type of table should be chosen since, as was mentioned earlier, both users and the type of information to be conveyed differ markedly from situation to situation. However, from their studies Wright and Fox (1970) suggest that some people were completely unable to use matrices, difficulties which persisted even when the experimenter worked through examples with them. In addition conversions were made slightly more rapidly, but much more accurately, with the explicit than with the implicit table. Thus they argue that linear, explicit tables are generally better than either matrix or implicit tables, particularly if they are to be used by the general public.

Nevertheless many situations exist when a multidimensional table is more desirable, perhaps because of space limitations or because the user population is known to be more capable. In such cases guidelines regarding their design may be gleaned from understanding how people use tables. In this respect Wright (1980) points to three features of a table that require consideration: the table's logic, layout and function. Translated into the reader's behaviour, these relate to comprehension, searching for information and decision making on the basis of the interpreted information.

As far as the table's logic is concerned, Wright argues that one of the reader's first tasks is to understand the underlying principles on which the table was structured (as Verhoef, 1993, demonstrated with his train timetable study). The concept of compatibility has already been discussed (and will be discussed further in Chapter 7) and it should be apparent that it relates as much to written communication as it does to communication via other channels. Thus we expect tables to be arranged in certain ways— particularly two-dimensional ones. For example, the two main variables on the left and top sides with the 'answer' in the main body of the table. Arrangements that do not conform to these expectations are likely to lead to confusion and/or increased reading time.

The table's logic may also be emphasised by improved layouts, for example by reducing the number of dimensions in the table. In this respect Wright (1977a) has shown that subjects made fewer errors and performed more quickly when only two dimensions were used than when the table required four decisions. Thus arrangement 4.5(a) was preferred to 4.5(b). This is probably because, whereas the reader merely has to scan in one direction for each dimension in the first table, two directions need to be scanned in the second. To find alternative F2 in table 4.5(b), for example, the reader first has to scan horizontally to 2 then perform a vertical scan to F, so potentially increasing the time taken and the errors made.

Layout can also be improved by grouping sets of items together rather than having them equally spaced. Tinker (1960), for example, has shown that grouping items into blocks of five was more helpful to the reader than grouping by tens, but grouping by tens was better than no grouping at all. Spaces between items will also help to structure the table and provide a Gestalt, although thick ruled lines appear to be as effective as spaces for

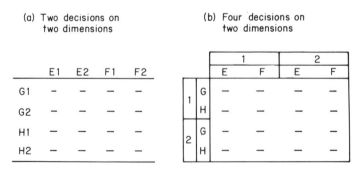

Figure 4.5 Two ways of arranging four alternatives along two dimensions used by Wright (1977b), *Ergonomics*, **20**, 91–6 (reproduced by permission of Taylor & Francis)

marking distinctions between rows and/or columns (Sprent, Crawshaw and Bartram, 1983). Wright and Fox (1970) make the following comment regarding the size of the gap between the grouped items:

> Although there seems to be no direct experimental evidence on the point, it is a common observation that when there is a large gap between the item that is looked up in the table, and the information which is as a consequence read off from the table, it is easy for the eye to misalign the two columns and so err by reading the information either directly below or above that required. Indeed, it was to the lessening of such difficulties that Tinker attributed the beneficial effect of grouping items within columns. Therefore it would seem advantageous to have the space between corresponding items within a table as small as possible ... even if lots of space within a table makes it easier on the eye, too much space in some places may make it harder on the user.

> (This material appeared in Vol 1, pp 234–242 of *Applied Ergonomics*, published by IPC Science and Technology Press Ltd., Guildford, Surrey, UK.)

With regard to arranging the table so that relevant items can be searched for quickly, this issue again returns to a question of layout, of making the relevant information 'stand out'. Typographic cues like bold type and colour can be valuable in this respect.

As far as the column and row headings are concerned, it would appear that it is not too critical where a heading is placed with respect to its column. Thus Hartley, Young and Burnhill (1975) have shown that column headings are as effective if they are aligned with the left-hand edge of the column as they are when centred. Column headings written horizontally, however, are easier to read than those which are written vertically. Tilting the heading by 45 degrees to the horizontal makes them easier to read than if they were vertical, but increases the risk that they will be thought to relate to an adjacent column.

Finally, Wright (1980) argues that the table's designer needs to know and to understand the use to which the tabular information is to be put. Often, for example, users may wish only to have approximate information rather than precise figures. It may be better, for example, to present train arrival times rounded to the nearest minute (or perhaps five minutes!) rather than to the second. This is because our use of time is often not more precise than this. Another use of tabulated information is often to compare information within parts of the same table or with information from another table. For example, a passenger may read a train timetable not only to find out the arrival time but also to see whether another train or a different route might be quicker. In these circumstances the table's layout and typography may serve to help or to hinder. Of course, if considerable comparisons need to be made—particularly in the form of trends—then graphs and bar charts may present the information more efficiently.

Forms

That form design is important from the viewpoints both of economy and efficiency can readily be seen by the number and range of forms that are in use today. Miller (1983), for example, points out that the United States government alone issues nearly 10 000 different kinds of forms and receives over 500 million responses per year. Furthermore, Wright and Barnard (1978) have reported that in at least one London borough several local authority staff were employed full time to assist people in completing their forms for benefits. As they point out, if to such staff costs are added the administration time and the postage that is normally involved in returning incomplete or wrongly completed forms, some idea can be obtained of the total cost and wasted time that can accompany poor design.

From the previous discussion it is clear that layout and typography are important when designing tables—structures that provide information for the reader but which the reader has to 'use' before the information becomes apparent. In this respect forms are very similar to tables: they interact with the user and they often look like tables. However, they differ from tables in one very important respect: the reader provides the information and the form determines how the information is provided. As with tables, however, some ways of asking the questions and laying out the form have been shown to be more efficient in obtaining the required information than others. Many of these features have been discussed already—structuring the form; using aspects like colour and lines; providing the reader with a logical flow and helping the respondent to move from one relevant question to the next; using typographical features such as cueing, letter size and shape to ensure adequate perceptibility of the questions, etc. Other aspects will be discussed in the next section when dealing with the prose that constitutes the instructions. This section will consider some of the problems specific to form design—that is, questions that relate both to the user's responses and to the administrator's interpretation of the responses.

Barnard and Wright (1977) investigated the effects of character spacers in the response boxes. As far as computerised forms are concerned, these vertical lines that separate the respondent's characters help to ensure that the maximum number of characters allowed by the computer program is not exceeded. However, Barnard and Wright demonstrated that the spacers break up the familiar shape of a word, impairing both writing and reading. Wing (1979), however, has demonstrated that the illegibility is not so great when the spacers occur as small marks at the top of the line, rather than at the bottom or as complete separators. This is probably because respondents will write with smaller letters and so form their letters below the marks. Wright (1983) also points out that using character spacers can make typing the responses, and reading typewritten responses, particularly difficult since the character spaces on the finished forms do not always match the usual 10- or 12-pitch character spacings.

Prose

The use of prose for instruction and information has been left until last to give the reader an opportunity to consider the value of alternatives such as tables or flowcharts. However, it is the case that most information transmitted between people is carried out by combining words (either verbal or visual) into (sometimes) meaningful sentences. Before considering appropriate ways of presenting information as prose, it is useful to discuss briefly some of the processes by which we comprehend text.

Comprehension can be considered to occur in three stages. First is the perceptual process by which the message is originally encoded. Second is the parsing stage in which the words are transformed into a mental representation of their combined meaning. Finally comes the utilisation stage, in which the reader actually uses the mental representation of the sentence's meaning to answer a question, to store information, to obey an instruction, etc. These three stages can occur sequentially or they can overlap. For example, while reading part of a sentence readers might make inferences about the meaning and implications of what has already been read.

Parsing

The way in which we break up sentences, known as parsing, can significantly affect both our reading efficiency and our understanding of the message being transmitted. This can be seen in a small illustration designed by Graf and Torrey (1966) (described by Anderson, 1980). They argued that a sentence would be more easily understood as its constituent structure becomes more identifiable. Thus they presented subjects with two forms of a sentence that had been split over a number of separate lines. In the first the break at the end of each line corresponded with a major constituent boundary; in the second it did not. For example:

Form A (split according to constituent boundaries)	Form B (split haphazardly)
During World War II,	During World War
even fantastic schemes	II, even fantastic
received consideration	schemes received
if they gave promise	consideration if they gave
of shortening the conflict.	promise of shortening the
	conflict.

As expected, their subjects showed better comprehension in Form A than in B. Such conclusions were also substantiated by Anglin and Miller (1968) who found that recall was higher when phrases in a prose passage were intact than if the phrases were broken, and by Cromer (1960) who reported similar findings for comprehension.

A number of other factors can influence this parsing procedure, each being related to how the text is constructed. These factors include the presence of ambiguity, the imagery contained in the sentence, the sentence length, the degree of activity or passivity implied by the sentence, whether or not it is couched positively or as a negative and, for instructions, the order of words used.

Ambiguity

Parsing so far has been discussed as a syntactic (rules-based) process. However, it must be remembered that the words themselves convey meaning and that parsing syntactically may not produce the understandings of a message that was intended by its transmitter. This can apply particularly when the sentence is ambiguous, that is when the semantic patterns do not necessarily relate to the syntactic ones. Because different interpretations can be placed on the same piece of text, ambiguity can cause major problems for the reader's comprehension and subsequent behaviour.

In essence, linguists distinguish between two main forms of ambiguity: structural and lexical ambiguity. *Structural ambiguity* arises when an entire phrase or sentence can have two or more meanings; *lexical ambiguity*, on the other hand, arises when only a word in the sentence can have two or more meanings—for example, the instruction 'light (meaning "set fire to" or "illuminate") the paper'. In addition it is useful to distinguish between permanent and transient ambiguity. Thus a sentence which contains permanently ambiguous information remains ambiguous even after the sentence has been completed. During transient ambiguity, however, the ambiguity is resolved by the words that make up the remainder of the sentence, before the sentence is completed; for example, 'the briefs were read by the lawyer'. Clearly, permanent ambiguity can lead to misunderstanding while transient ambiguity, depending on the extent of the ambiguity, can lead to increased reading and comprehension time. Such results were obtained by Bever, Garrett and Hartig (1973) who asked subjects to complete partial sentences having differing degrees of ambiguity. Interestingly, however, they also showed that once a reader has resolved the ambiguity of a constituent in a sentence, and has settled on a particular interpretation, the ambiguity has no further effect on processing the remainder of the sentence or text—providing that no further change in interpretation has to be made.

Both forms of ambiguity can arise in a number of ways. For example, if apparently redundant words are removed from the text, meaning can be affected by the various possibilities that result from alternative parsing. In addition, ambiguity can arise when prose written in one language is translated into another. Slight changes in the arrangement of translated words can radically alter the meaning or the comprehensibility of the message, as can subtle differences in the meaning of words in different cultures. For example, to an English car mechanic 'gas' implies the exhaust whereas an American counterpart would think of petrol; 'boot' in the United Kingdom is the same as 'trunk' in the United States, and so on.

As an example of this problem Sinaiko and Brislin (1973) asked Vietnamese airforce mechanics to perform various maintenance tasks using manuals which were written in either English (American), or in high quality, lesser quality or poor quality translations of the original. Although their Vietnamese subjects made many errors when using the American material (61 per cent), their error rate increased to 89 per cent when they were provided with the poor Vietnamese translations.

Finally, ambiguity can also arise if the information presented to the operator is incomplete, misleading or if it is too verbose. Chapanis (1965b) presents a number of examples to illustrate these points, in each of which the ambiguity results from the receiver having to restructure the information (often erroneously) into a message that can be understood.

Imagery

The effect of imagery on different cognitive processes has been studied extensively for many years. For example, high imagery words are recalled faster than those which do not easily conjure up an image (Paivio, 1971; Postman, 1975). Similar results have been obtained concerning the memorability of high imagery sentences (Marschark and Paivio, 1977). Furthermore, Ernest (1979) has shown that subjects with high imagery ability are able to recognise unfamiliar pictures more quickly and at lower threshold levels than subjects with low image ability.

If imagery is so important in these cognitive processes, it is reasonable to suggest that it also mediates sentence comprehension. Indeed, this was shown to be the case in a study by Eddy and Glass (1981), and Holmes and Lanford (1976) have also related comprehension to the concreteness or abstractness of sentences. As an explanation of these types of results, Begg and Paivio (1969) have suggested that we code abstract and concrete sentences differently in memory. Thus they proposed a dual coding hypothesis which suggested that concrete sentences can be coded in the form of non-verbal spatial imagery as well as in a verbal association form. Abstract sentences, however, can be coded using imagery only with difficulty.

The implications of such results, that picturable material is easier to understand than non-picturable material, are summarised thus by Paivio and Begg (1981):

> The thoughtful student can readily see some of the implications of this for such matters as the appreciation of literature. One reason why Shakespeare is so appealing, for example, may be the fact that his plays are unusually high in literature.

As an aid to choosing the most image-provoking words, Paivio, Yuile and Madigan (1968) produce data relating to the 'concreteness', 'imagery' and 'meaningfulness' of nearly 1000 nouns.

Sentence length

The end of a sentence enables the reader to take a short pause before considering further information. Since we have a limited capacity to process information, if the sentence is unduly long the reader will either begin to forget some of the earlier information in the sentence or will impose an individual structure. In this case readers will break up the long sentence themselves, perhaps in the wrong places, and obtain a slightly different meaning to the one intended. The problem appears to be particularly prevalent in government, legal and even military circles, as the following example given by Chapanis (1965b) illustrates:

> This radio uses a long life pilot lamp that may stay on for a short time if radio is turned off before radio warms up and starts to play.

As Chapanis suggests, this 29-word statement could have been more explicitly put as 'the pilot lamp stays on for a while after you turn the radio off' (16 words). Wright and Barnard (1978) suggest that to be readily understood each sentence should contain only one clause. To implement this they suggest that writers should scrutinise sentences with more than one verb, looking for alternative ways of expressing the information.

Sentence activity

It is often possible to convey the same message in different forms, one distinction being along an activity dimension. Thus a sentence can often take the form simply of a passive statement or can be made in an active or an imperative fashion. For example, a passive instruction could be 'The button is pressed' while its active counterpart would take the form 'Press the button'. The available evidence suggests that comprehension time is reduced for the active form of the text. Olsen and Filby (1972), however, showed that the relationship is a strong function of the focus of the sentence. Thus the active sentence advantage is maintained only when the receiver of the sentences can identify with the active part of the sentence. When the event described by the sentence was coded in terms of the receiver of the *action*, passive sentences were more easily verified. The same results were found for answering (rather than simply identifying) active and passive sentences.

Finally, there is also evidence to suggest that the active advantage holds only for text in which a sensible active–passive transformation can be made. For example, Slobin (1966) measured the verification time for reversible sentences such as 'The boy is being hit by the girl' (in which the subject and object can be interchanged to the active form 'The girl hits the boy'), and non-reversible ones such as 'The boy is raking the leaves'. He found that active reversible sentences were verified more quickly than passives, but that the verification time did not differ for active and passive non-reversible sentences. Paivio and Begg (1981) suggest that such results arise because in non-reversible sentences it is easy to determine which noun is the logical subject so that passives do not cause any problem. With reversible sentences, however, it is more difficult to determine the subject, so that passives are more difficult.

Positives and negatives

Just as a sentence can be couched in terms of different degrees of activity, so it can also be arranged along a dimension of positive to negative. For example, the positive instruction 'Press button A' could also be put into its negative form 'Do not press button B'. Words like 'not', 'except', 'unless' have negative elements as, in some circumstances, do words like 'reduce' or 'decrease'.

Again, the evidence appears to suggest an advantage of one form over the other—in this case the positive form of a sentence is generally comprehended more quickly than its negative counterpart (for example, Gough, 1965; Greene, 1970).

Despite this general conclusion, however, it would appear that contextual aspects can, again, affect the positive form's advantage. Thus Wason (1965) has argued that if the negative form carries with it more information than its positive counterpart—if it is both plausible and performs its natural

function of contrasting and distinguishing the exception from the norm—
then the positive form is no easier to comprehend than the negative. This he
calls the plausible denial hypothesis. For example, since most people go to
work in the morning, saying 'I went to work yesterday' carries very little
information. The statement 'I didn't go to work yesterday', however, tells
us something new. In such cases Wason found that the reaction time to
plausible negatives was significantly shorter than to both positive and
negative implausible forms of the sentence. Nevertheless, it was still the
case the plausible, positive sentences were reacted to most quickly. These
results have been confirmed by Arroyo (1982).

Temporal order of words

If a series of actions is either to be described or performed, it is better if they
are written or spoken in the order in which they are to be carried out.
Broadbent (1977) illustrates this point with the following example: if an
action involved pushing in the carburettor control and then starting the
engine, it is better to write the instruction 'depress the carburettor plunger
before starting the engine' than 'before starting the engine depress the
carburettor plunger'. In the first case the words are matched to the actions,
in much the same way as, in ergonomics philosophy, the environment is
matched to the person.

READABILITY

Having decided on the appropriate wording of instructions and
information, a designer may wish to check that the prose produced is the
most readable that is able to be devised. In many respects, readability is
largely subjective, with individual styles of writing being able to be
discerned in different pieces of work. As Klare (1963) points out, however,
although there are rules for efficient writing, careful adherence to them
does not guarantee good writing. Writing is an art not a science. However,
he points to three general principles which the writer must bear in mind.
First, to know something of the type of reader—educational level,
motivation and experience. Secondly, the writer's own purpose for writing
should be considered—what is intended; perhaps to help the reader read
more efficiently; to judge whether the material is acceptable; to read for
comprehension, learning and retention; to understand orally presented
material; or to accomplish some combination of these and other purposes.
Thirdly, as emphasised above words should be selected carefully. It is the
words used and their construction into sentences which make the prose
readable.

To produce some standard in the readability of material, various readability formulae have been proposed which operate by analysing the words used in selected passages in the prose. Klare (1963) describes many such formulae, but perhaps the most popular was produced by Flesch in 1948.

To compute Flesch's 'Reading Ease' score, first a 100-word sample passage of the prose to be analysed is chosen. Then the number of syllables (wl) in those 100 words is counted in the way in which they are read aloud. For example, 1980 will have four syllables ('nine-teen-eigh-ty'). Secondly, the formula requires the average number of words per sentence (sl) to be computed. With this data reading ease can be calculated as:

$$206.835 - 0.846wl - 1.015sl$$

This score puts the piece of writing on a scale between 0 (practically unreadable) and 100 (easy for any literate person). As a more detailed guideline, however, Flesch produces a table of typical scores for different types of prose, as shown in Table 4.1.

As with all kinds of statistics, however, such scores—from whatever formula—should be used with caution. As Wagenaar, Schreuder and Wijlhuizen (1987) point out, simple rules cannot represent such complex factors as logical content and organisation of material. Indeed, they argue that proper readability analyses should deal with such 'macro' units of analysis as well as the 'micro' aspects such as average word length, or whatever.

Again, therefore, the person-centred movement is seen to emerge in ergonomics. Whereas mechanistic formulations can provide valuable first

Table 4.1 The range of Flesch 'reading ease' scores

Score	Description of style	Typical outlet	Syllables per 100 words in words	Average sentence length
0–30	Very difficult	Scientific	192+	29+
30–50	Difficult	Academic	167	25
50–60	Fairly difficult	Quality	155	21
60–70	Standard	Digests	147	17
70–80	Fairly easy	Slick fiction	139	14
80–90	Easy	Pulp fiction	131	11
90–100	Very easy	Comics	123 or less	8 or less

principle suggestions for good practice and design, a complete ergonomic analysis will be made only when the individual's own feelings, preconceptions and humanity are realised.

SUMMARY

This chapter has considered communication in its most basic sense—the transmission of information and meaning from one person to another. After considering the meaning of meaning, and the ways in which the communication system may be corrupted, the remainder of the chapter discussed the various processes involved in transmitting information using the printed page: typographical aspects and the use of various communication media such as tables, graphs and pictures. Finally, some of the problems involved in the efficient communication of prose were considered.

5

MACHINE–MAN COMMUNICATION: DISPLAYS

Chapter 4 showed how important information is to us, and how it can be presented in different ways with varying degrees of effectiveness. The person at the centre of the man–machine system thrives on information; he or she needs it to understand past events, determine current details, and anticipate and predict future progress. Without information the whole working system will soon degrade and, as importantly, if poor information is provided then poor outcomes will probably occur. Communicating information and instructions from one person to another, therefore, can be considered to be the first link in the working chain.

For any simple system, however, once the initial instructions have been given much of the information that the operator subsequently receives is likely to arise not from another human being, who can perhaps be questioned further in the case of misunderstandings, nor from written instructions which can be re-read for better understanding, but from single or composite instruments which display information about the state of the system. Since an appropriate response can only be made on the basis of the operator's interpretation of the information provided by the display, it is clear that this aspect of the system needs to receive careful consideration.

In practice the 'best' display is normally chosen by trading off the criteria of speed, accuracy and sensitivity in communicating the information. Since the act of communication requires the receiver to interpret correctly the transmitter's message, however, these criteria refer just as much to the operator's performance as they do to that of the machine. It is for this reason that the requirements of the task and the operator must be made explicit. In some cases it may be that the speed of assimilating the information is more important than other criteria, for example when a pilot reads the rapidly changing height information from the altimeter on take-off or landing. In other cases accuracy may be as important—avoiding errors or ambiguity. It is of little value, for example, for the pilot to read the altimeter quickly if it is either inaccurate or read inaccurately. In other situations the display may need to be very sensitive (i.e. able to detect the slightest change in the variable being measured). For example, a heart-rate monitor in an intensive care unit should respond immediately to any change that occurs in the patient's condition. It would be a useless machine if the nurse was able to read (quickly) the fact that the patient's heart had stopped beating (accurate) three minutes ago (insensitive).

This last point emphasises that although speed, accuracy and sensitivity are the primary criteria on which a display's value is judged, they are not independent. A display that can be read quickly is valueless if its readings (either the readings which it gives or the interpretation of the readings) are inaccurate; a display which communicates slight changes in machine state is worthless if it takes a long time to read; and so on. For this reason it must again be emphasised that both the operator's and the system's requirements should be considered before the appropriate display is chosen.

Displays, therefore, represent the sole means by which a system can communicate information about its internal state to the operator. As Rolfe and Allnutt (1967) put it, 'The display translates what is at first imperceptible to us into perceptible terms.' As such it can only function in one of the operator's five sensory modes: vision, hearing, touch, taste or smell. Under normal circumstances only the first two (or sometimes three) of these senses are used.

To understand fully the ways in which the display's requirements can be matched to the operator's capabilities, therefore, much of the information regarding the human sensory system which was discussed in Chapter 2 needs to be remembered.

Before discussing visual and auditory displays in more detail it is useful to compare the two types and to consider briefly situations in which each is more usefully employed. In general, *visual* displays are more appropriate when:

- The information is presented in a noisy environment. Under such conditions auditory displays may not be perceived.

- The message is long and complex. Compare, for example, a written sentence on a computer screen (visual) with the same information presented from a tape-recorder (auditory). Because the eyes can scan the visual material more than once, short-term memory capacities are less likely to be overloaded. Unless the (auditory) taped message is translated into written material, the decoded words somehow have to be stored in memory while other words in the message are being decoded.

- The message needs to be referred to later. Visual information can produce a permanent record; unless auditory recording equipment is used, acoustic information is stored only in memory.

- The auditory system is overburdened—perhaps because of too many auditory displays or (as in the first point) in a noisy environment.

- The message does not require an immediate response.

Visual displays are more appropriate, therefore, for providing continuous information to the operator. On the other hand, *auditory* displays are more useful when:

- The message requires an immediate response—they are more attention getting. It is for this reason that warning messages are normally presented using a klaxon or a bell.

- The visual system is overburdened—perhaps because of too many visual displays or in glaring conditions.

- The information needs to be presented irrespective of the direction in which the operator is facing. The drawback of visual displays lies in the fact that the operator needs to be looking at them before they are able to communicate the information. Auditory displays do not have such restrictions. This is another reason why they make such acceptable warning indicators.

- Vision is limited—for example in darkness, at night, or when it is likely that the operator will not have had time to adapt to the light or dark conditions.

VISUAL DISPLAYS

Types of Display: Digital and Analogue

Visual displays are the most commonly used instruments for communicating information from the machine to the operator, whether they take the form of unitary displays such as dials or the composite presentations seen in modern computer displays. However, they are frequently badly designed, with sometimes disastrous results, and the increasing complexity of displays adds to the chances of poor display design and the opportunities for negative interactions between the display components. For example, Fitts and Jones (1947a) analysed 270 errors made by pilots in reading and interpreting their instruments, each of which could have led to an accident. Their results suggested that there were a number of different ways in which visual displays could be misread. These include 'simple' misinterpretations of the instruments (for example, misreading the altimeter by 1000 feet); reversal errors (for example, interpreting the bank indicator as showing a left bank when, in fact, the aeroplane was banking to the right); misinterpreting visual warning signals; substitution errors (confusing one instrument with another) and illusory errors (for example, misreading the altimeter because of an illusory connection between body sensations and the instrument indication). Clearly, a display which can be misinterpreted is effectively worse than useless (particularly if the misinterpreted information leads to a totally inappropriate control action).

Individual visual displays are generally of one of two kinds: digital and analogue. Digital displays, like those found on calculators and digital watches, present numerical information directly as numbers. With the analogue display, on the other hand, the operator has to interpret the information from a pointer's position on a scale, from the shape, position or inclination of a picture on the screen, or from some other kind of indicator, the state of which is analogous to the real state of the machine. For example, a conventional clock face is an analogue display since if the minute hand points to '9' it has travelled three-quarters of the way around the face and indicates a position which is analogous to being three-quarters of the way through the hour. The pilot's pictorial artificial horizon display (which indicates the attitude of the aircraft relative to the horizon) is also an analogue display since the relative positions of the 'aircraft' and 'horizon' indicators in the display are analogous to the respective positions of the aircraft and ground in the real world. Finally, a warning light is an analogue display since the state of the light (on or off) is analogous to the state of the machine (danger/safe) in the real world.

Using Visual Displays

In many respects, how a display is to be used determines the type that should be chosen although, of course, exceptions to this rule exist as will be discussed later. Displays may be used:

- To make quantitative readings—to read the state of the machine in numerical terms: the temperature in degrees centigrade, the height in feet, the speed in miles per hour, etc.

- To make qualitative readings—to infer the 'quality' of the machine state. For example, whether it is 'cold', 'warm' or 'hot', rather than its precise temperature; whether the aircraft is banking 'shallowly' or 'steeply' to the right or to the left, rather than its precise angle, etc. Also subsumed under this heading is the use of displays to make check readings—i.e. to compare the state indicated by one display with that shown by another.

- In combination with controls to set the machine, or to track (maintain) a steady machine state.

- To enable the operator to predict or anticipate the state of the system at some time in the future.

- To warn the operator of danger, or that a specified machine state has been reached.

When deciding on the type of display to be used and its characteristics, Murrell (1971) points out that it is important to consider the nature of the information that the operator needs in order to do the job effectively, and then to question how this can be presented quickly and unambiguously. Sometimes the same kind of display might be used in different ways. Take, for example, a voltmeter: sometimes this might be used to indicate whether the machine is on or off; at other times a direct numerical (voltage) reading may be required; in other cases the operator may wish simply to compare the information with that obtained from other displays. It is only possible to decide on the appropriate type of display when it is known what proportion of time the display is used in each case, and this information is 'weighted' in terms of the importance of each operation in the particular situation.

Quantitative readings

Both digital and analogue displays may be used for making quantitative readings, although it is only with increased electronic sophistication that digital displays have become a viable alternative to analogue displays. A mechanical type of digital display which is operated by a system of reels (as may be seen, for example, in the milometers of most types of car) has two major drawbacks: first, a number may not always be fully visible as it moves around a continuously revolving wheel; instances can occur when only the bottom half of one number and the top half of the next are visible. Clearly this can lead either to misreadings or to increased reading times. Secondly, because the number is actually moving the image will not be in the same place on the retina, and may be blurred if the values change too quickly.

Given that it is now relatively easy to produce digital displays which do not contravene these basic principles, the important question is the circumstances under which the analogue or digital display should be used. In this respect, much of the comparative work was carried out some time ago and concerned the design of suitable aircraft displays (usually the altimeter). However, the principles that evolved can still be extrapolated to any situation in which people need to interact with machines.

The results of early experiments to resolve the question tended to suggest that digital displays produce fewer reading errors and faster reading times than do analogue displays. For example, Murrell and Kingston (1966) describe results from an experiment with skilled journeymen using graduated and digital micrometers. Whereas about 3 per cent of the readings were in error using the graduated micrometer, the same men made only 0.05 per cent errors when they used a digital micrometer. Similarly, Zeff (1965) compared conventional and digital clock faces for reading speed and errors. He showed that the digital clock face was read faster than the conventional clock, with only 10 per cent of the errors.

One of the earliest investigators to compare the effectiveness of dials and counters was Grether (1949), who recorded the reading time and errors made by trained pilots and college students. He presented photographs of altimeters bound into booklets, each photograph showing a different height on one of eight analogue arrangements or a counter (see Figure 5.1). His results indicated that the standard (analogue) three-pointer altimeter used extensively in aircraft at the time (one pointer indicates ten thousands of feet, another thousands of feet, and the third hundreds of feet) caused the highest error rate and longest reading times. The digital display, on the other hand, was associated with the lowest error rate and fastest reading times.

It is perhaps useful at this point to emphasise the implications of making reading errors in these types of circumstances. For example, the skilled journeymen in Murrell and Kingston's experiment misread their graduated micrometers by up to one hundred thousandths of an inch, a significant amount in precision engineering terms. Perhaps a more sobering example is provided by Rolfe (1969a), who quotes the reports of investigations into two airline crashes, of which the following is an example:

> On the evening of 28th April 1958, a BEA Viscount airliner fitted with modified three-point altimeters was making a final approach to land at Prestwick Airport at the end of a flight from London. The captain reported to the ground that he was 14,500 feet and descending. As he descended he reported he had passed through 12,500 feet. Soon after the last report the aircraft struck the ground. The subsequent investigation ... showed that the captain had misread his altitude by 10,000 feet and had perpetuated his misreading error until the aircraft struck the ground and crashed.
>
> (This material appeared in Vol. 1, pp. 16–24 of *Applied Ergonomics*, published by IPC Science and Technology Press Ltd, Guildford, Surrey, UK.)

This report has more than simply historical interest. It illustrates a further aspect when making quantitative reading—a misreading error from a badly

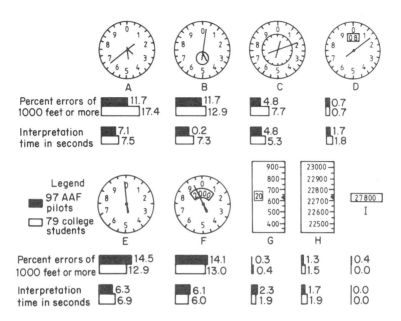

Figure 5.1 Speed and accuracy in reading altitude from different types of instruments (from Grether, 1949)

designed display may not necessarily be a one-off event. Often a 'set' is introduced that causes the error to be perpetuated on subsequent readings. Thus, not only did the captain misread his altimeter once, he continued to misread it by the same amount until he hit the ground.

Although the kind of evidence presented above suggests that numerical information should always be presented digitally, digital displays do have their drawbacks, particularly in dynamic situations when the information is often changing rapidly. In addition, digital displays are often not the most effective when the display is used as a predictor as well as providing numerical information or, as discussed earlier, when mechanical digital displays are used. Finally, tasks in which displays are used to compare values (check reading) are often better served by analogue rather than digital presentations.

Fast-changing information and blurring. Many of the earlier experiments that compared the efficiency of digital and analogue scales for quantitative reading presented the stimuli as static pieces of information: each stimulus was either shown to subjects for a specific short period or the subject was timed reading the display. Under these circumstances the results demonstrate quite conclusively that digital displays produce fewer reading errors and faster reading times than do analogue displays.

In the dynamic (real life) situation, however, values indicated by the display will often be constantly changing, sometimes very quickly. In this case the image may become blurred and this can have serious consequences if the numbers have to be read with some precision. As anyone who has tried to read the fast-changing times provided by a digital clock at a sports meeting will know, the blurred image makes reading the information practically impossible.

Fast-changing information does not appear to affect the efficiency of analogue displays to such a large extent, however. This is because the pointer that is lacking in digital displays itself provides some additional cues for the operator. Thus spatial (the direction in which the pointer is moving) and rate of change (how fast it is moving) information gives the reader further data and helps to interpret the reading.

Using spatial cues for prediction. It is very rare for an operator simply to read the values indicated on a display. In many cases, although possibly it is not immediately obvious, operators use the information received to make predictions—perhaps about the state of the machine or about the machine's future behaviour.

This unconscious prediction can be illustrated by the following example: an operator knows that the machine is likely to explode when the display indicates 10 units; although the display indicates only $9^1/_2$ units, the pointer is moving upwards. At this point the understandable reactions (possibly of panic) will be due to predictions of the machine's future state!

A second example concerns the conventional (analogue) watch face: the large (minute) hand may point at 7 and the small (hour) hand somewhere between 11 and 12, indicating that the time is 11.35. Within the same glance, however, the position of the minute hand also provides spatial cues to enable the reader to predict, quickly, that 25 minutes are left of the hour. Digital displays do not give this information so readily—the operator has to carry out fast numerical computations (with attendant problems of accuracy) to achieve the same result.

The efficiency of analogue displays in providing spatial cues was demonstrated by Simon and Roscoe (1956). They presented subjects with display information intended to represent an aircraft's present altitude, the predicted altitude after one minute, and the final altitude to be reached. One of four types of display was presented: (*a*) a vertical (strip) display incorporating three pointers; (*b*) a circular (dial) display with three pointers (similar to the three-pointer altimeter); (c) three separate five-digit counters; and (d) three separate circular, single-pointer displays. From this information subjects had to decide:

- whether they were diving, climbing or flying level;

- in order to reach and/or maintain their final altitude, whether they should climb, dive or continue flying level;

- if they should climb or dive, whether they should increase, decrease or maintain their present rate;

- whether they should eject!

In terms of the time taken to complete the task, the results showed that the vertical displays produced the lowest average time in a series of ten problems (56.3s). The combined circular display came second (64.2s), the digital displays third (74.6s) and the separated circular displays fourth (79.7s). In terms of errors, however, the digital displays had the highest (approximately 7 per cent) and the vertical strip displays the lowest proportion (approximately 3 per cent). Discussing their results Simon and Roscoe argue that the digital display's poor showing, both for speed and accuracy, was related to its failure to provide any direct spatial cues.

Similar kinds of evidence have been provided by Koonce, Gold and Moroze (1986). They demonstrated that analogue displays enabled novice pilots to acquire and retain basic flying skills better than did digital displays, and created lower 'cognitive load' on the novices (measured by a secondary task). Clearly, therefore, the kind of task being carried out has an important bearing on the choice of display type.

Thus it would appear that for recording quantitative information, digital displays make the task easier for the operator (faster reading time and fewer errors) than do analogue displays. The superiority of digital displays is reduced, however, in situations where the values change quickly, where the operator might need to predict the future 'conditions' of the machine, and, as will be discussed below, where some sort of check reading is required.

Qualitative readings

In some situations an operator may use the display not to record precise readings but to register the machine's qualitative state. For example, rather than needing to know the temperature in degrees centigrade, it may simply be necessary to know whether it is 'hot', 'neutral' or 'cold', or whether it is 'safe', 'dangerous' or 'critical'. In these circumstances numerical values are not recorded and so the digital display's advantage may be reduced. Indeed, analogue displays may be more effective than digital displays.

Visual coding. As McCormick (1976) points out, the ideal display designs for qualitative readings depend on what needs to be read. If the whole range of machine states can be divided into a limited number of 'levels', then the best way of representing these levels is to code different areas separately on the display face. Many visual cueing methods are available that enable different features of a display to be distinguished, and some of the coding methods listed by Morgan *et al.* (1963) include colours, shapes (both numbers, letters and geometric shapes), and brightnesses.

The efficiency of various coding techniques was discussed previously in Chapter 4. At this point, however, it is pertinent to emphasise the cautions expressed regarding the overuse of colour as a coding system for qualitative displays—particularly if coloured ambient illumination is used or if there is a chance of normal light being reflected from a coloured surface. Since colour is perceived because of a specific wavelength of light being reflected from a surface, it is clear that if a coloured light is used to illuminate a coloured patch the resultant colour perceived will not be what would be expected under daylight illumination. (This problem may occur even when fluorescent illumination is used—fluorescent lights are not normally white: they contain high proportions of light in the yellow part of the spectrum.) These effects may cause the colour coding system either to be lost entirely or to be altered.

A further limitation of colour coding systems is if 'colour-blind' operators are employed. As was discussed in Chapter 2, about six per cent of healthy adult males have marked reduced sensitivity to colours, most having difficulty in distinguishing between red, green or blue colours.

Pictorial displays. Pictorial displays are a particular kind of qualitative display which, as the name suggests, present the operator with a pictorial representation of the machine state. Examples of this type of display may be found in many large process industries that provide information about such aspects as the stage of the process reached. Large panels give the operator a 'picture' (usually a representational picture in terms of interconnecting lines) of the system and its operation: parts of the display may be colour coded and/or illuminated to indicate special features. In some respects these may be considered to be large kinds of flowchart.

Another example of a pictorial display is the artificial horizon seen on most pilots' control panels, which indicates the aeroplane's position with respect to the horizon. The relationship between the aeroplane and the horizon is generally shown by the relative positions of a horizontal bar and an outline symbol of an aeroplane.

The overriding principle in pictorial display design is to ensure that the picture that they present is as realistic to the true life situation as possible. For example, if a section of railway track is represented pictorially by a series of interconnecting lines on a signalman's panel, the length of the lines should, as near as possible, be in proportion to the relative lengths of the track sections, the points should be in their relative correct positions, and the speed of the 'train' (perhaps indicated by a moving light) should be proportional to the real train speed. If principles such as these are adhered to, a pictorial display will provide the operator with both useful and readily available information.

In some cases, however, it may be difficult to decide what is a 'real life' representation. For example, with the artificial horizon in the pilot's cockpit the question has arisen in the past whether it is more true to life for the aeroplane symbol to move and the horizon bar to remain static, or vice versa. From the viewpoint of someone standing on the ground watching an aeroplane bank, there is no doubt that the plane moves with respect to the horizon. From the pilot's position looking out of the aircraft, however, the horizon appears to move while the world (the aeroplane) remains 'stationary'. The dilemma is whether the pilot relates to the aeroplane in terms of the 'view' from the cockpit or from the ground.

The many studies that have been carried out to investigate this specific type of pictorial display have concluded that the moving aeroplane type of pictorial display is interpreted more quickly and with fewer errors than the moving horizon display (Johnson and Roscoe, 1972). This may be explained if one considers that the pictorial display represents a figure–ground configuration, with the figure being whatever is the moving part of the display and the ground the stationary part. When a pilot is looking out of the cockpit window the horizon, normally accepted as a stable frame of reference, is the ground against which the moving aircraft is a figure. However, when the pilot's eyes move to accommodate on the panel containing the artificial horizon display, the panel itself becomes the ground with the moving horizon bar becoming the figure. In this way it is quite possible to misinterpret the display elements and make a control movement that aggravates the condition. As with the symbols discussed in the last chapter, therefore, it is important to determine the figure–ground relationships of the various elements before an adequate pictorial display can be designed.

Check reading. This will be discussed in more detail in Chapter 7 when ways of grouping displays are considered. In the meantime it is useful to remember that displays are often used not only to obtain precise, quantitative information: they are also used to compare readings or to check that a certain value is or is not being indicated. For example, Murrell (1971) discusses data from a survey of naval ships in 1952 which indicated that, on electrical and steam equipment, only 18 per cent of the dials were used for quantitative reading whereas over 75 per cent were used for some form of checking. Similar conclusions were reached by White, Warrick and Grether (1953) who report that pilots flying on instruments fixate on their instruments on average for only 0.5s, suggesting that aircraft instruments are typically used in a check reading manner.

For check reading, the available evidence suggests strongly that some kind of analogue display produces more efficient performance. This is probably because of additional spatial cues that the pointer provides (for example, the angle between the pointer and 'north', or the angular difference between two pointers). Digital displays lack this information and so the operator has to compare numbers before any check reading can be made. For this type of task, therefore, digital displays may increase both the time needed to read the instruments and the number of errors made.

Setting and tracking.   Little work has been carried out to find the optimum type of display for use when settings have to be made. Comparing the merits of analogue and digital displays for this type of task, it would appear that analogue displays are easier to use. For example, Benson, Huddleston and Rolfe (1965) asked subjects to maintain a constantly changing display reading at a steady position (i.e. to carry out a tracking task). At the same time they were required to react to a light that was illuminated at irregular intervals. (This use of a secondary task ensured that the subject's total attention store was used.) Two types of display were presented: a combined analogue and digital display, and a single digital display. Whereas the subjects' performance on the two displays was not significantly different, their performance on the secondary task was worse when the digital display alone was presented than when they were presented with the combined analogue and digital display. This, coupled with the fact that the subjects' heart rate, sweat rate, muscle activity and respiration rate all increased when the digital display alone was used, suggests that the digital display made the subjects work harder to maintain their performance.

The possibility that analogue and digital displays may differentially affect the quality (rather than accuracy) of an operator's performance on a setting task was also considered by Rolfe (1969b). His subjects were asked to alter the 'altitude' using either a digital or a combined analogue/digital (counter/pointer) display. Again, no significant differences in either speed or accuracy were reported between the two types of display when the experiment was carried out in the presence of a secondary task. Differences in the type of error were apparent, however. Using the combined display, 62 per cent of the 21 errors made were caused by the operator 'levelling out' too early (for example, levelling at 25 000 ft when being asked to ascend to 26 000 ft). Using the numerical display, however, the majority of the 26 errors (69 per cent) were caused by the subject 'overshooting' the required setting (i.e. exceeding it by more than 150 ft and then returning to the correct setting). Again, therefore, it would appear that adding the analogue component to the display alters the operator's behaviour, to create a more 'conservative' and, perhaps, cautious setting. Table 5.1 summarises the relative advantages and disadvantages of analogue and digital displays as discussed above.

Visual Display Design

By now the importance of choosing the correct type of display should be clear, if the system's efficiency is to be maximised. To do this one needs a full analysis of the task that the operator has to undertake, and this can then be matched against the display's abilities to carry out these requirements. Unfortunately, however, knowing which type of display is useful in which circumstance is only half a solution to the problem. Just as the previous chapter showed how communication between people can go very wrong if, for example, the words are not put together in a suitable fashion, so the right type of display can give a wrong (or misleading) communication if it is poorly designed. The purpose of this section is to consider the second half of the problem—visual display design. Naturally very few people will be in a situation to design suitable displays, but many are in a position to

Table 5.1 The respective merits of analogue and digital displays

Quantitative readings	Best if a precise reading is not required, or if the task contains predictive or checking components	Best for accurate reading of slowly changing values; poor if the task includes predictive or checking components
Qualitative readings	Best for warnings, checking and prediction; useful to have visually coded areas	Poor
Setting and tracking	Best	Poor

buy them. This section, therefore, should provide some guidelines for making a sensible choice.

Display design for quantitative reading

Analogue displays (dials). The design aspects of a dial simply to take readings of the machine state have been investigated from most possible aspects. Such studies were carried out in the early years of ergonomics, with some of the recommendations being embodied in national standards (for example, British Standards: BS 3693 Parts 1 and 2 (1964, 1969) which have been discussed at length by Murrell, 1971). Possibly the two most important criteria to consider when choosing a dial are the ease and the accuracy of making a reading which, translated into design features, implies simple, uncluttered, bold design.

The first requirement is that the dial should be large enough to be read comfortably by an observer positioned some distance (the reading distance) away. This distance, of course, may change with the dial's position on the console. For example, a dial placed above the operator (not a recommended position, as will be discussed in Chapter 7) will be further from the eyes than one directly in front.

Second, since most of the required information will be obtained from the scale itself, the size and length of the scale play a large part in determining the dial size. For all practical purposes, the British Standards Institute (1964, Parts I and II) has suggested that the length of the scale (L) is related to the reading distance (D) by the formula $D = 14.4L$. So, for example, if the dial is placed one metre from the operator the scale base length (the distance around the scale between 'minimum' and 'maximum') should be at least 7 cm.

Having chosen an appropriately sized dial, the next question to be asked by a potential purchaser concerns the scale divisions and markers: their number and size.

The distance between the scale markers represents possibly one of the most fundamental factors affecting the readability of the scale. For any particular scale base this will be a function of the number of markers used. Thus, as the space between two successive markers is reduced, while the distance between the dial and observer is maintained, the visual angle which the space subtends at the eye will also decrease proportionately. If this visual angle falls below a critical value then the observer will begin to make reading errors, and the frequency of such errors increases linearly with the logarithm of the decreasing visual angle. Murrell (1958) has demonstrated that, for most reading applications, a visual angle of 2 minutes of arc is the critical point. It should be remembered, however, that Murrell's studies were carried out under ideal viewing conditions. Under poor illumination, for example, the critical visual angle would be increased and so require a larger scale gap. Practice and poor vision also play important roles in acuity tasks of this nature. For these and other reasons, McCormick (1976) recommends minimum scale gaps of between 1.25 and 1.75 mm.

The desirable length and thickness of scale markers have also been the subject of many studies. These have generally indicated that within limits some variations can be accepted without influencing reading ability to any large extent. However, it is obvious that the major scale markers (i.e. those associated with particular values) should be emphasised, and the British Standards Institute (1964) suggests that each major marker should be twice the length of the minor markers. Regarding the thickness of the markers, Morgan *et al.* (1963) suggest that the major markers should be between 0.125 and 0.875 mm for good to poor illumination conditions, and McCormick (1976) appears to agree with these dimensions.

As far as the arrangement of scale markers is concerned, the body of opinion appears to suggest that a system that progresses in 1s or 10s (1 ... 2 ... 3 ..., or 10 ... 20 ... 30, etc.) is the easiest to use. A system increasing in 2s would appear to be slightly less effective, whereas progressions of 4s, 8s, 25s or decimals are not recommended. (It may be postulated, of course, that these results simply reflect our practice of counting in tens rather than in fours.) The minor markers should assist the observer's accuracy in interpolating between major markers and for this reason the divisions need to be sensible. Since people can be fairly accurate in interpolating into fifths or even tenths of a scale division (Cohen and Follert, 1970), however, the number of minor markers may not be too critical.

No readings could be made without some kind of pointer, and details are available concerning appropriate pointer design (Spencer, 1963). In summary, the pointer should be pointed rather than blunt and the tip should meet, but not overlap, the base of the scale markers. If the pointer is placed away from the dial surface, parallax problems may occur. These can perhaps be demonstrated by envisaging reading a dial first from the left, then in front and then to the right. In each case a slightly different reading will be made because of different sight lines between the dial number, the pointer and the eye. To minimise the chance of parallax errors some dials have a small, thin mirror positioned behind the pointer. Only when the pointer obscures its reflection in the mirror will the observer be positioned in front of the dial and a true reading made.

Finally, of course, there is the question of the design of the numbers presented on the dial face. In this case the two important features are the character shape and size. Regarding the shape, two criteria apply— confusability and readability. Unfortunately, as was demonstrated by Smith (1978), these two requirements sometimes conflict in that shapes designed to reduce confusability may also lead to reduced readability. Confusability is often a function of the extent to which characters are composed of the same basic shapes. For example, the numbers 0, 3, 6, 8 and 9 are sometimes confused since they usually have curved or rounded outlines. This dilemma can be increased when letters are introduced, for example B, 8 and 3 are commonly confused. The effect of different number shapes on readability does not appear to be too great. Most conventional alphanumeric fonts can be read with reasonable accuracy under normal conditions where size, contrast, illumination and time permit. For this reason the only recommendation which Buckler (1977) makes is that font styles are kept clear and simple.

Although the character's shape may not be too important to legibility, its size certainly does matter: characters that are too small may be difficult to read; too large and they waste space. This depends on such factors as the reading distance, contrast, illumination and time allowed for viewing. After reviewing the relevant literature and performing an experiment of his own, Smith (1979) demonstrated the range of readability to lie between a visual angle of 7 and 24 minutes of arc. This means that a dial placed 1 metre from the observer requires character heights of at least 2.5 mm for readability (7 min). Using Smith's data, 90 per cent readability will be obtained with characters 3.5 mm high (10.5 min), and 100 per cent with 7 mm high characters (24.5 min).

In summary, therefore, a potential purchaser should pose the following questions:

- Is the scale base length large enough to be read at a 'normal' reading distance?

- Is the gap between scale markers at least 1 mm?

- Are the major markers able to be differentiated easily from the minor markers?

- Is the numbering system in 1s or 10s?

- Is the pointer designed adequately?

- Do the characters subtend a visual angle of at least 10 min of arc?

- Are the characters legible and non-confusable?

• Does the dial as a whole look uncluttered and easy to use?

Digital displays (counters). Digital displays may appear as any of three forms: mechanical, electronic and computer generated using cathode-ray tube (CRT) or liquid crystal displays. In the mechanical kind of display, the numbers are printed on either a revolving drum or on pieces of metal which 'flip' over. However, with the discovery of crystals and diodes which become illuminated when a current is passed through them, mass-produced and very cheap electronic digital displays became available. Computer-generated displays are, of course, also a form of electronic display, but their advantage lies in the easy generation of letters as well as numbers. Ergonomists, therefore, should also consider the production of alphanumeric displays.

Mechanical counters. Two aspects of the counter are important: how the numbers change, and the design of the numbers themselves. If the numbers do not change in a 'snap' action, but revolve around a drum, an undesirable situation will sometimes arise in which only parts of the number are shown in the display window, for example the bottom half of the number 8 and the top half of 9. Naturally this will increase the time required to read the number and may possibly lead to errors.

Electronic displays. Electronic displays now play an important part in the working environment. They include computer-linked visual display units (VDUs), light-emitting diodes (LEDs) that illuminate when a current is passed through them, and liquid crystal displays (LCDs) that turn black when exposed to a current (modern LCDs can also produce 'colours' other than black). Because VDUs have some ergonomic issues associated with them that are additional to those relating to the crystal displays, they will be discussed later in this chapter.

The advantages of electronic displays are fourfold: first, because information is produced by different display 'segments' being illuminated, the character is always in the same part of the observer's retinal field. There are no problems with numbers 'flicking' or rolling over. Secondly, the LED display generates its own illumination, enabling it to be read in the dark without additional light sources. This is not the case with LCD displays: the segments appear black and so background illumination is required for adequate contrast. Thirdly, both LED and LCD displays can be computer driven and this provides greater flexibility in terms of both the design and the content of the displayed information. Finally, multicolour LCDs enable products to be colour coded if necessary (for example, the numbers may change from green to red if the machine state changes from 'safe' to 'danger' or the bank balance changes from being in the 'black' to negative cash flows in the 'red').

Many of the design considerations discussed earlier also apply to electronic displays. However, the segmented characters produced by LEDs or LCDs do have further problems: because they are composed of segments (usually 7) the character's appearance differs from that of a drawn number, so that the normal curves are lost. A secondary problem can sometimes concern the spacing between different numbers: because the character is formed by illuminating different segments the spacing between numbers varies, depending on the number combinations that are to be read. For these reasons, Plath (1970) has cautioned against the overuse of segmented numbers, although the modern computer-generated display panels can generally overcome the problem by using higher resolution characters than those with seven segments.

As far as the ubiquitous seven-segmented characters are concerned, Plath's cautions are also reflected in terms of the character's readability. The available evidence suggests that seven-segment displays using either LCDs or LEDs produce worse performance (that is, more errors—usually errors of confusion—and slower reading) than both conventional (printed) characters (Plath, 1970) and dot matrix produced characters (Orth, Weckerle and Wendt, 1976). Ellis and Hill (1978), however, have demonstrated that reading segmented numbers is as efficient as reading conventional ones where reading time is not critical. Furthermore, even with time-stressed reading, appropriate training helped to overcome difficulties in reading segmented numbers. Unfortunately, without the opportunity for continued practice the skills acquired decreased significantly within a month.

Combined analogue and digital displays.   The earlier discussion of the relative merits of analogue and digital displays for making quantitative readings showed that each has advantages and disadvantages in different situations. For example, analogue displays are more valuable for recording fast changes while digital displays are more appropriate for making static readings; digital displays, on the other hand, are more useful when it is necessary to read precise values, etc. A sensible compromise, therefore, would seem to be to produce displays that have both analogue and digital components.

Only one detailed study reported in the literature has considered this compromise. After producing such a display Rolfe (1969a) carried out both a pilot opinion survey and a laboratory experiment to investigate whether the digital display should be separate from (that is, above) or an integral part of (that is, inside) an analogue altimeter display. Using static trials (subjects were presented with photographs of each altimeter showing different readings), no difference was obtained between either of these two combined forms, although a significant difference was shown to occur between these two displays and an analogue only display: the average reading time for both counter–pointer displays was consistently about 30 per cent faster than for the analogue display. No errors were made on either of the counter–pointer displays, while 20 per cent of the readings made on the analogue display were in error by 100 'feet' or more.

Dynamic trials, on the other hand, pointed to the 'counter-inside' display being more valuable than the 'counter-outside' display. This was also reflected in the pilots' opinion survey which suggested that the counter-outside display tended to appear as two independent displays demanding an alternation of attention. Remembering the Gestalt principle of closure— that a solid boundary leads to more efficient perception because it gives the appearance of a 'whole'—it is not surprising that the counter-inside display was read more efficiently.

Display design for qualitative readings

The evidence discussed earlier suggests that an analogue (dial) display represents the most efficient means of presenting qualitative information to the operator. The pointer position, its movement speed and its direction, provide the operator with relatively low-level information about the machine state which, coupled with coded areas on the dial, enable fast qualitative judgements to be made.

Colour coding.   When discussing the various kinds of coding available to the designer (p. 104) it was apparent that colour produces the most effective coding system. This is possibly reflected in the fact that most indicators used for qualitative readings include colour coding. However, two important questions have to be answered before an appropriately colour-coded display can be produced. These are: how many colours should be used overall, and which colour should represent which type of machine state?

The maximum number of colours that should be used in the coding system would appear to be around ten. For example, Jones (1962) suggests that normal observers can identify about nine or ten surface colours, primarily varying in hue. On the other hand, Morgan *et al.* (1963) suggest a maximum of 11 different colours. It is possible to increase the optimum number quite significantly if stimuli vary along several different dimensions, for example size, luminance levels, hue and colour purity (Jones, 1962).

Having decided on the number of colours the next question relates to which colours should be used. In this respect it was pointed out earlier that many colours are already associated with different moods or conditions, so it is important that the colours chosen should be compatible with the operator's own (often stereotyped) ideas of what they represent. Unfortunately, little research has been carried out to answer this problem, so most of the colours used in modern displays are chosen on the basis of 'common sense'. In this respect Morgan *et al.* (1963) have suggested the meanings and uses of a number of different colours (Table 5.2). Umbers and Collier (1990) provide a helpful overview of the use of colour, and other techniques, for various coding outcomes.

Finally Poulton (1975) has pointed out that colour coding can often be used to indicate sizes. For example, some stores code cloth sizes according to colour, and electrical resistor values have been colour coded for some years (black = 0 ... white = 9). On the basis of a small survey in which he asked people to say what colour they thought represented the largest size etc., Poulton was able to recommend an 'ergonomic colour code' for sizes in which red represents the largest size and white the smallest. Intermediate sizes should be represented by colours arranged in rainbow order.

Table 5.2   The suggested meanings of different colours

Colour	Meaning	Use
Red	Hazard	Fire: alarms, extinguishers, hoses
		Danger: symbols
		Stop: signs on machinery, road signs
		Emergency
	Hot	
Orange	Possible danger (but not immediate hazard)	Dangerous parts of machines and guards
Yellow	Caution	
Green	Safety	First-aid equipment
Blue	Caution	
	Cold	
Purple	Radiation hazards	

After Morgan *et al.*, 1963; reproduced by permission of McGraw-Hill.

Pictorial qualitative displays. Pictorial displays which illustrate the state of the machine were discussed above. In this respect it was shown that the overriding design principle is that the display should be as 'true to life' as possible.

Display design for check reading

Although comparing two readings (comparison) or checking whether a value has or has not been reached (checking) are frequent tasks, very little research has been carried out to help design appropriate check reading displays. This is possibly because colour coding is generally used to differentiate the important areas of the dial for check reading, although this may not be the most useful way of helping the operator. For making comparison readings, for example, the most useful technique is to arrange the actual displays rather than to make particular changes to the display's appearance; this will be discussed in detail in Chapter 7.

An interesting design for a dial face that is to be used mainly for check reading was suggested by Kurke (1956) who produced a dial face in which a high-contrast wedge-shaped 'flag' appears when the pointer reaches a predetermined level such as 'danger'. The flag is not visible when the machine is operating in 'safe and 'normal' conditions. Kurke demonstrated significantly reduced errors and operation times when using this type of dial compared to one which had a colour-coded (red) area permanently on the dial face or one which had no obvious aids (Figure 5.2).

With Kurke's display, therefore, the operator has only to perceive the presence or absence of the flag. A display with colour-coded portions, on the other hand, requires the operator first to find the pointer and then to decide whether or not it is in the red area; a display without aids requires the additional load of having to decide on the meaning of the reading. Clearly, having only to decide whether a flag is present or not is likely to be a considerably easier task.

Thus the important feature of a display to be used for check reading is that the display's appearance should change and present a new coding system when significant states are reached. Colour, shape, position and so on can all be used to indicate this new state, particularly when using computer-generated displays (see, for example, Spiker, Rogers and Cicinelli, 1986).

Cathode-ray Tube and Visual Display Units

The cathode-ray tube (CRT) and its relative, the visual display unit (VDU), offer the designer a more flexible man–machine communication system

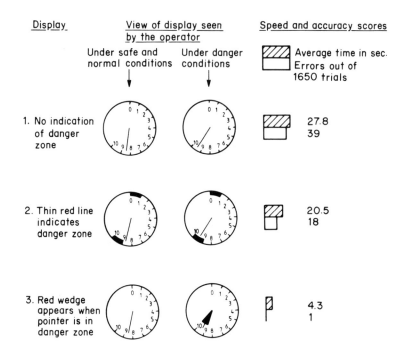

Figure 5.2   The value of a warning flag appearing on a display to indicate 'danger' (from Kurke, 1956, copyright 1956 by the American Psychological Association. Reprinted with permission)

than either analogue or digital displays alone. Being computer linked, in many respects they represent an amalgam of all cases of display, enabling alphabetic characters, numbers and pictures to be displayed. Furthermore, it is also possible to produce some kind of time-sharing display when there is limited panel space and increased amounts of information to be shown. Thus by using appropriate software the electronic display's versatility allows flexibility of formats—such as the order in which information is presented (emergency signals can be programmed to override normal communications, for example) and how different information is emphasised. Another benefit of VDUs, of course, is that they generate their own illumination and so can be used in the dark.

The operating principles of VDUs have not changed significantly since the times of early television sets; both have as their basic mechanism the cathode-ray tube. This is essentially an evacuated glass tube with a 'gun' at one end and a phosphor-coated 'screen' at the other. The gun fires a stream of electrons at the phosphorescent screen which interact with the phosphor and cause it to glow at each point of impact. An observer viewing the face of the screen perceives, at each point of impact, a bright spot of light which dims as soon as the beam has moved. Since the glow decays rapidly once the beam has passed, the screen needs continually to be refreshed to present a stable, flicker-free image. The speed with which this happens is called the 'refresh' or 'regeneration' rate, which is also determined by the way the beam of electrons is moved over the screen.

When the scanning control circuitry sweeps the electron beam across the surface of the screen, character images are 'written' by switching the beam 'on' and 'off as it travels through its scanning pattern. These scanning lines are generally made horizontally, as on a television, and it is their density which determines the display's resolution and thus the character size and clarity. Jones (1976) and Cakir, Hart and Stewart (1980) describe the various ways in which scan lines are produced on the screen and the ways by which distortion due to the screen curvature is eliminated.

The most common procedure for producing text on VDUs is the dot matrix method in which each character is composed of a series of bright dots ('pixels'). The required dot positions for each character are stored in a dot matrix memory in the computer. The matrix resolution is defined by the number of horizontal and vertical dots and the character is written to the screen in a 'sliced' form. Thus the tops of all characters in the line are written first, followed by successive horizontal slices until the bottoms are reached some seven or so lines later.

Radiation

Before discussing the design of VDUs and their displays in more detail it is appropriate briefly to consider the question of the radiation which they emit. For a VDU to operate it must produce a considerable amount of radiated energy—otherwise the characters would be invisible. Although this kind of radiation (electromagnetic radiation in the visible spectrum) is quite safe, many operators fear the possibility of other radiation wavelengths being produced by the cathode-ray tube—radiation that cannot be perceived through our normal, biological sensors. All of the available evidence, however, strongly suggests that both ionising and non-ionising radiation levels produced by commercial cathode-ray tubes fall far short of any levels set for maximum occupational exposure to such radiation. Indeed, measurements of ionising radiation from a number of terminals have consistently shown that the levels produced are often no higher than the normal background radiation to which we are constantly exposed (for example, Terrana, Merluzzi and Giudici, 1980). After reviewing the literature concerning radiation issues and VDUs, Smith

(1987) concludes that 'most experts agree that the biological effects of VDT radiation are inconsequential to health' (p. 245).

VDU Design and Use

Two aspects will be considered: first the user's requirements with respect to the physical characteristics of the display—its brightness, colour, etc; and secondly the requirements from the point of view of the information displayed—in a sense the 'software' aspects.

Physical aspects of the display

Illumination and luminance. From the earlier discussion of how the eye operates, and from experience, it is obvious that we can only see objects when light enters the eye, either directly from the object or reflected from it. The light that falls on an object is termed the illumination, and that which enters the eye from an object is known as the luminance. (The object's brightness refers to the subjective experience of luminance.) These terms will be discussed more fully in Chapter 11.

Regarding the luminance of visual display units, Gould (1968) points out that the amount of light reflected from the normal paper pages under ambient house and office illumination is around 160 cd m^{-2}. He therefore suggests that this level may be used to estimate the recommended luminance for symbols on VDUs. Comparing different VDUs of the time, Gould considered that most fell within this loose specification. More recently Läaubli, Häunting and Grandjean (1981) measured the luminances arising from terminals in more modern offices and recorded similar values: average (median) luminance of 163 cd m^{-2} on terminals used for data entry, and 108 cd m^{-2} on 'conversational' terminals. (The main difference between the two types of terminals was in the task performed: with data-entry terminals the operator had to keep moving the eyes from the terminal to the source document on which the data were recorded and back again. Conversational terminal use, however, was typified by the operator interacting only with the screen.)

Schmidtke (1980) points out that the range of display luminance is a function also of the overall illumination levels in which the screen is to be used. Thus in normal office environments with illumination levels between 100 and 1000 lux, a range of symbol luminances between 10 and 150 cd m^{-2} would be required. However, in much darker environments, such as some kinds of control rooms, the range must be able to be extended downwards or else the symbols will appear too bright. On the basis of his own

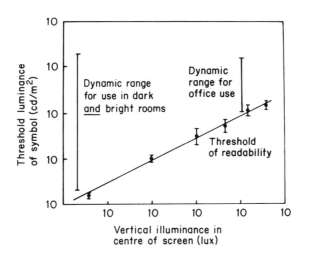

Figure 5.3 Suggested ranges of display luminances in different environments (Schmidtke, 1980), reproduced by permission of Taylor & Francis

experiments Schmidtke suggests a range of 0.2 to 200 cd m^{-2}. The data from which these suggestions were made are shown in Figure 5.3.

Finally, as Schmidtke points out, the symbol luminance is controlled by a potentiometer. If its control resistance characteristics are linear, a small deflection of the potentiometer will brighten the screen to such an extent that the operator's adaptation level may be disturbed when the display is used under dark conditions. He suggests, therefore, that a non-linear control resistance is used as the dimmer. The same control detection will then lead to a small increase of symbol luminance under dark conditions, with larger increases under daylight conditions.

Contrast. Coupled with overall luminance is the factor of luminance contrast between the characters and the background. Too low a contrast level will prevent the characters from being readily and accurately identified; too high a contrast, however, can cause glare problems.

It is generally accepted that the minimum acceptable object : background contrast ratio for information presented on a visual display unit is about 3 : 1, with preferences for ratios in the range 6:1 to 15:1 (see, for example, Knave, 1983). Timmers, van Nes and Blommaert (1980) demonstrated that there was no significant performance increase as the ratio increased (to 30 : 1 in their study).

The contrast problem is further exacerbated when a dot matrix type of character generation is used since the luminance levels of the dots that make up the character are not uniform. Whereas, for example, the luminance from any one of the characters on this page is constant, a symbol (or light spot) produced on a VDU is composed of a spread of illumination levels with the brightest part in the centre where the electron beam strikes and gradually becoming dimmer towards the edges. This means, of course, that the contrast between the edge of the symbol and its background is not as high as between its centre and the background, resulting in a slightly 'hazy' symbol. Fellman *et al.* (1982) have demonstrated wide variations in character sharpness between different makes of VDUs. To overcome the slight blurring effect from dot matrix displays Gould (1968) suggests both reducing the level of ambient illumination (and thus the amount of illumination reflected from the background) and adding a darkened filter to the screen.

Polarity.   The question of whether light symbols should be viewed against a dark background (negative polarity) or dark characters on a light background (positive polarity) has been posed by a number of investigators. The evidence which has emerged is equivocal in so far as some studies have shown increased performance when using a positive polarity display (dark characters on a light background), while others have shown no significant performance differences between the two.

For example, Bauer and Cavonius (1980) found that changing the polarity from the normal negative view to positive (by setting the letters to be as dark as possible and increasing the background illumination), the success rate for recognising nonsense words increased by 23 per cent and the speed of recognition increased by eight per cent. Gould *et al.* (1987) showed no such advantage.

After reviewing the field Haubner (1986) and Pawlak (1986) both reached the conclusion that image polarity by itself does not have a significant effect on display readability. Any differences that may occur could be the result of display characteristics when the two different kinds of polarities are used. For example, Cushman and Rosenberg (1991) argue that dark characters should have about 20 per cent greater stroke width than light ones.

Despite the inconclusive findings, anecdotal evidence and simple observation show that users appear to prefer positive to negative polarity images. Radl (1980) suggests that the reason for the positive polarity advantage lies in the type of task which a VDU operator has to perform: moving the eyes from the VDU to a printed sheet which itself has positive polarity (i.e. black letters on white paper); the screen and data sheet, therefore, appear the same. Furthermore, having a light background reduces the possibility of glaring reflections on the screen which might mask the displayed symbols (see Chapter 11).

Tapagaporn and Saito (1990) pose an additional explanation for preferring positive polarity. They demonstrated that positive polarity displays increased the tendency to dilate the pupils, so that the smaller pupil diameter allowed less light to fall on the retina (presumably because the overall illumination level of a positive polarity display is brighter than the negative display). They point out that this also enables operators to attain greater depths of field (and focus) and thus not to have to rely so much on frequent accommodation changes to focus the image. The narrower pupil diameter is also beneficial in environments with fluctuating illumination levels, such as near windows with varying light levels arising from the sun and sky. Under such conditions, there is less need for the papillary response to be activated frequently if the pupil is already somewhat dilated.

Resolution. As was discussed earlier, the usual way of producing characters on the VDU screen is to build them up as a sequence of bright dots. Each character is composed of a number of scan lines and the size and definition of the character (the resolution) will be related to the number of scan lines used. In this respect, an important parameter involved in perceiving an object correctly is its size or, more accurately, the size of its image on the retina. For this reason the minimum acceptable character size for VDUs has been determined by some experimenters in terms of both the number of raster lines and the visual angle (i.e. the angle subtended at the eye by the object). Essentially, the research has indicated that about ten raster lines per character height are required for accurate detection of individual characters, and somewhat fewer to detect words. Elias, Snadowski and Rizy (1965) reported fairly good performance with alphanumeric symbols composed of as few as 5 lines per character, although reading speed increased progressively from 5 to 11 lines. These figures, however, are averaged over all alphanumeric characters—the authors also found quite high variability in performance with different characters. For example, when using 4 scan lines approximately 90 per cent of the subjects recognised the letter *L* correctly, whereas only about 30 per cent recognised the number *8*.

Hemingway and Erickson (1969) discuss a number of studies which have investigated the effects of resolution on the recognition of geometric symbols. From such data, they conclude that about ten lines per symbol are required for good (80 per cent) identification with about twelve lines being required for 90 per cent identification, although the results of their own

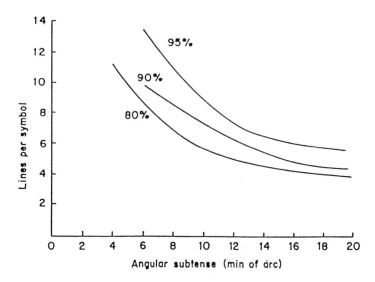

Figure 5.4   The relationship between the number of VDU raster lines and the angle between the lines subtended at the eye for 80, 90 and 95 per cent correct detection (from Hemingway and Erickson, 1969, and reproduced by permission of the Human Factors Society)

study showed that at least eight raster lines and a visual angle of at least 10 minutes of arc are required per geometric symbol. With an average viewing distance of 66 cm (Grandjean *et al.*, 1982) this would imply a minimum character height of about 2 mm. This is slightly smaller than one suggested by Giddings (1972) of approximately 4 mm for words and 4.6 mm for digits. Hemingway and Erickson have produced a family of curves relating lines per symbol and the angle which has to be subtended at the eye for 80, 90 and 95 per cent correct detection (see Figure 5.4).

Flicker and regeneration.   As was discussed previously, when the electron beam has passed a particular spot on the screen the phosphor glow declines and, unless it is regenerated on the next scan, it will disappear. If the regeneration rate is too slow characters appear to flicker and this could lead to the eye muscles having to work more to keep the image in focus, causing operator fatigue. As will be discussed later, excessive flicker can cause other physiological problems such as epilepsy. In a survey of VDU users Stammerjohn, Smith and Cohen (1981) found that 68 per cent of the operators complained of flicker from the screens. To ensure that this does not happen, relevant information about an observer's ability to perceive flicker is important.

If a light is repeatedly turned on and off at a fairly slow rate, then it appears to flicker. As the frequency of reversals is increased, however, there comes a point at which the flickering appears to stop and the light appears to fuse. To ensure that the characters do not appear to flicker, therefore, it is important that the screen regeneration rate is faster than this critical fusion frequency (c.f.f.).

Harwood and Foley (1987) compared the visual fatigue response of subjects presented with a three-hour search task using either a VDU or a backlit projection display. Other than the means of presentation, all other work-based variables were the same in both conditions, even to the extent of the two kinds of displays having the same luminance levels. The only difference between the conditions, therefore, was the fact that the illumination levels of VDUs vary because of flickering. Over the longer periods subjects reported increased task difficulty, difficulty in concentrating, tired eyes, and the need to shut the eyes more frequently when using the VDU than with the back projection method. In addition, when the subjects' c.f.f.s were tested at various points throughout the experiment, while the fusion frequency did not change for the back projection condition, it fell by significant levels for the VDU condition. This suggests that the flicker aspects of the VDU placed greater demands on the visual system. Similar conclusions were reached by Watten and Lie (1992) who demonstrated (temporary) changes in visual acuity and ciliary muscle convergence ability after two hours of continuous VDU work.

As discussed in Chapter 2, because flicker depends on so many variables it is not possible to provide precise regeneration rates to ensure that flicker is overcome. However, Gould (1968) suggests that the normal electric mains regeneration rates that are used (50 Hz in the UK and 60 Hz in the USA) are probably sufficient to prevent the perception of disturbing flicker. Furthermore, the regeneration rate can be reduced if screen phosphors having longer persistence are used.

Flicker and photosensitive epilepsy.   One consequence of flicker that should be considered is its potential for inducing minor epileptic seizures. A small proportion of the population (estimated to be about 1 in 10 000; Jeavons and Harding, 1975) suffer recurrent convulsions in the presence of flickering light stimuli. Of course, the most common 'natural' cause of such stimuli at work is likely to be the VDU. The probability of an adult VDU operator reacting to the screen in this way, however, is in fact likely to be much lower.

Using complex striped patterns to affect the brain's responses (measured by electroencephalography—EEG) Wilkins (1978) studied aspects of the display which were likely to trigger an epileptic onset, without actually inducing seizures in his patients. His results suggest that the primary correlate of such seizures is the number and intensity of retinal cells stimulated. In particular his data suggest that the epileptogenic attributes of VDU screens can be reduced, first by reducing the area of the retina stimulated. This can be achieved by using a small screen, by displaying light characters on a dark background, by limiting the amount of text on the screen, and by seating the operator further from the screen.

Secondly, the tendency can be reduced by reducing the overall luminance of the display, perhaps by the observer wearing dark glasses (Wilkins notes that this is quite common among TV studio managers who have to watch TV displays for long periods). However, the glasses would have to have a transmission rate of only 10 per cent or so to be effective. Another technique, suggested by Isensee and Bennett (1983), is to ensure that the screens are not placed in an offset position to the viewer's central viewing area. As discussed in Chapter 2, images that fall on the periphery of the retina are decoded primarily by the rods which have lower acuity thresholds. Thus moving or flickering objects are perceived more effectively in this region.

Finally, work by Wilkins, Darby and Binnie (1979) suggests that reducing the screen–surround contrast will also reduce the potential for seizures. Thus with a contrast ratio of 0.2 the probability of seizures was about 25 per cent of that when the ratio was 0.3.

Colour.   For some years technological advances have enabled colour to be used on VDU screens. This section will discuss only the use of colour for character presentation and the screen background. The use of colour for highlighting, coding or making specific parts of the displayed information more interesting was discussed in Chapter 4.

Despite the widespread use of colour in modern computer-generated VDUs, there has been comparatively little work published to suggest which colours should be used. Radl (1980) investigated operator performance and preference for different coloured phosphors and filters (white (monochrome), green, two types of orange and three types of yellow). His results indicate that both performance (a letter-transcribing task) and preference were maximum for the yellow phosphors. Of the yellows, the true yellow phosphor produced maximum performance and preference, although a monochrome screen with a yellow filter was nearly as 'good'. The reason for this discrepancy is probably related to the luminances of the screen: whereas the yellow phosphor transformed the full energy of the electron beam into the yellow colour, the yellow filter is likely to have removed some of the luminous energy.

Radl also considered the combined effects of different coloured characters and backgrounds. Using five character colours (red, blue, green, yellow and violet) and seven background 'colours' (red, blue, green, yellow, violet, grey, and grey with 'noise'), he showed that the different colour combinations produced combined error rates (wrongly named colour and character not detected) which varied between 4 and 95 per cent. As is shown in Figure 5.5, not unreasonably the maximum error rate occurred when the character and background colours had wavelengths close to each other (for example, violet on blue, yellow on green). This is in line with the results of experimenters, such as McLean (1965) and Ohlsson, Nilsson and Ronnberg (1981), who have shown that legibility and text-scanning speed increase with increased colour contrast. However, Radl's results also showed that minimum overall error was obtained when coloured characters were presented on a grey background.

Finally, in addition to the phosphor's colour, consideration also needs to be given to its purity (that is, the proportion of white contained within the colour; Umbers and Collier, 1990). In this respect Fukuzimi and Hayashi (1989) have demonstrated that for each dominant wavelength there is an optimal stimulus purity that ranges in value from 0.2 to 0.5. The optimum varies in terms of individual users' preferences and also affects readability (Fukuzimi, Yamamoto and Hayashi, 1987).

Aspects of the software

As well as the hardware aspects of visual display design, it is also important to consider the actual characters which are displayed and the

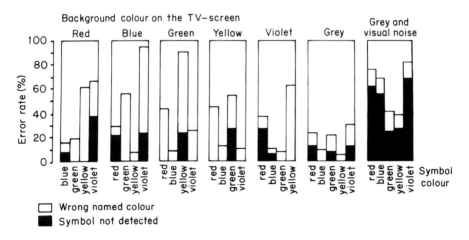

Figure 5.5 Error rate for the different VDU symbol/background colour combinations (Radl, 1980), reproduced by permission of Taylor & Francis

ways in which they are produced; for example, whether or not characters should be presented in lower case and whether lower-case characters should be produced with their descenders. The relative value of mixed case over simply upper-case characters was discussed in Chapter 4.

Character shape and design. Vartabedian (1971) reported a study in which he compared recognition speed and the numbers of errors made for different CRT displays. In essence, two forms of display were used—four forms of dot matrix and two types of stroke display (in which the electron beam traces the character shape on the screen). The dot matrix display was either a 5 × 7 matrix, using circular or elongated 'dots', or a 7 × 9 matrix, using circular or slanting 'dots'. The stroke displays were either upright or slanted.

The results indicated, fairly conclusively, that the 7 × 9 circular dots produced fewer errors and faster reaction times than the other forms. Whereas the 5 × 9 circular dots produced roughly similar numbers of errors to the 7 × 9 matrix, the characters took rather longer to recognise. The two slanted displays (7 × 9 elongated and stroke) produced a higher proportion of errors and slower reaction times than the upright counterparts. Finally, Vartabedian also demonstrated that elongating the 'dot' also affected legibility.

On the basis of this work Vartabedian (1973) produced a set of alphanumeric characters for a 7 × 9 dot display. A similar matrix was used by Huddleston (1974), although his display was composed of square rather than circular dots. In addition Maddox, Burnette and Gutman (1977) have produced recommendations for a 5 × 7 dot matrix display.

Pastoor, Schwarz and Beldie (1983) considered the efficiency of larger dot matrices, including 9 × 11 and 11 × 15. Their results demonstrated greater efficiency with both the 9 × 11 and the 11 × 15 matrices, although the difference in both performance and suitability ratings between the two were not significant. On the basis of these data, since the 9 × 11 matrix requires less room than one which is 11 × 15, the authors suggest that a 9 × 11 matrix should be used.

Another dimension of character shape relates to the character's height : width ratio. In this respect, Beldie, Pastoor and Schwarz (1983) demonstrated that character sets which are composed of variable width characters—as in proportional spacing, for example—produced faster reading times and fewer errors than fixed-width character sets.

The cursor. The cursor is a very important aspect of a visual display which performs two main functions: first, it acts in the same manner as the carriage position on a conventional typewriter and indicates where the next character is to be placed; secondly, it directs the operator's attention to specific parts or features of the display. Its twin roles, therefore, are an information presenter and an attention seeker.

Cakir, Hart and Stewart (1980) suggest that cursor types can be divided into three categories, defined by their effect on the character they are meant to be indicating. They describe these categories as 'superimposing', 'replacing' and 'enhancing'. Superimposing cursors do not affect the character at all; the cursor, for example a box, simply adds to the character. A replacing cursor is one that actually replaces the character, although it perhaps alternates with the character. Finally, an enhancing cursor highlights the character in some way, perhaps by intensifying the character or by colouring it.

Unfortunately, there is very little published work regarding cursor design to assist either in choosing between the types outlined above or in determining their parameters (size, speed of flashing, brightness, shape, etc.). However, it is well known that we orientate our eyes towards a novel stimulus and so a flashing cursor is likely to prove most effective for the attention-seeking aspects of its task. With regard to the frequency of flashing, Cakir, Hart and Stewart suggest that a blink rate of between 3 and 5 Hz minimises both search and tracking times. Although it may be effective as an attention seeker, however, a flashing cursor can be distracting to the operator who is, say, simply typing data at the keyboard (particularly if the operator has to think while doing so—for example when composing text). For this reason they suggest that facilities should be provided for turning off the blinking cursor to provide a steady symbol.

AUDITORY DISPLAYS

Although the visual modality is the most extensively used medium for presenting information to the operator, auditory displays do have their value, particularly if the visual system is already overloaded or if the operator needs to have the information irrespective of the head's position at the time. In addition, as Colquhoun (1975a) has pointed out, combined auditory and visual displays can often make monitoring performance superior to that given by using visual displays alone. Auditory displays, therefore, are suitable primarily for presenting qualitative information—as warning devices—although they are used in some circumstances to display information about the machine state. These aspects will be discussed below, but it should also be remembered that in some cases quantitative information can be displayed in the auditory mode. The hourly chimes of a clock or Morse code dots and dashes are examples of such uses.

Warning Displays

A warning sound is probably the simplest type of auditory display since it conveys information of an 'on–off' nature. Either the system is 'safe' or 'unsafe' and its state is indicated by the absence or presence of the sound. To be effective, therefore, a warning sound should be both perceptible and attention getting. Unfortunately, however, little scientific data exists to guide the designer in choosing suitable warning displays, and a variety of surveys have demonstrated that insufficient thought has generally gone into the design, placement and even need for many warning displays in the workplace (for example, Patterson, 1985; Edworthy, Loxley and Dennis, 1991).

Murrell (1971) suggests that to be effective the sound intensity should be at least 10 dB higher than the background noise, although he offers no supporting evidence for this assertion. As will become clearer in Chapter 10, because of masking effects the warning sound should be louder than the background noise, but by how much is not clear since significance levels depend on such factors as the signal's frequency and duration. Unfortunately, no authors other than Murrell suggest a minimum level.

As long as it can be heard, possibly a more important criterion is the need for the warning display to be attention getting. Again, few design data are available although it would appear sensible to use a sound to which the ear is maximally sensitive—i.e. in the range 500 to 3000 Hz. McCormick (1976) has drawn together most of the available evidence regarding the qualities of the sounds which are suitable for auditory warning signals. In addition to using signals in the 500 to 3000 Hz range, he suggests that if the sound has to travel far then frequencies below 1000 Hz should be used. If signals have to 'bend' around major obstacles or pass through partitions, then the frequency should be reduced to below 500 Hz. He also suggests that a modulated signal (1–8 beats per second or warbling sounds warning from 1–3 times per second) are different enough from normal sounds to demand attention.

Related to the concept of attention is that of perceived urgency. Thus the main feature of a warning sound is that it should communicate a need for action, sometimes immediate (such as a fire alarm) and at other times less urgent (like a reminder timer on a cooker). As Edworthy, Loxley and Dennis (1991) point out, there is often a serious mismatch between the perceived urgency implied by the warning sound and the degree of urgency that the operator has learned to associate with the warning in terms of the situation itself. In a series of experiments, these authors showed that many common acoustic parameters, including frequency, harmonic series, amplitude envelope shape, speed, melodic structure and harmonics, can directly affect perceptions of the urgency of the sound.

Finally, McCormick (1976) argues that 'high intensity', sudden onset signals are often desirable for alerting an operator, and these could be presented dichotically (alternating the signal from one ear to the other) if earphones are used. Overriding all these considerations, however, is the requirement that the quality of the warning sounds should differ from any other sound which the operator is likely to experience in the workplace. Fidell (1978), for example, demonstrated that signals that were equally detectable were equally efficient in producing an effective response to an emergency. Table 5.3 describes the relative advantages and disadvantages of different types of auditory warning displays.

Speech as an auditory warning display

The development of computer-generated speech has provided the opportunity for more sophisticated warning displays than a 'simple' sound. Thus operators can now be told the state of the system in a language with

Table 5.3   Types of auditory alarm—their characteristics and special features

Alarm	Intensity	Frequency	Attention-getting ability	Noise-penetration ability
Diaphone	Very high	Very low	Good	Poor in low frequency noise Good in high frequency noise
Horn	High	Low to high	Good	Good
Whistle	High	Low to high	Good if intermittent	Good if frequency is properly chosen
Siren	High	Low to high	Very good if pitch rises and falls	Very good with rising and falling frequency
Bell	Medium	Medium to high	Good	Good in low frequency noise
Chimes and gong	Low to medium	Low to medium	Fair	Fair if spectrum is suited to background noise
Oscillator	Low to high	Medium to high	Good if intermittent	Good if frequency is properly chosen

After Morgan *et al.*, 1963; reproduced by permission of McGraw-Hill which they are familiar, rather than having to interpret the meaning of a warning sound. In many respects, therefore, warning speech can be viewed in the same way as digital visual displays, while warning sounds are similar to analogue displays.

Unfortunately, however, information relating to the ergonomic design of speech-based warning signals is lacking—probably because the area itself generates a number of problems and issues relating to speech intelligibility (often in the presence of noise), message meaning, and so on. In this respect, many of the points and principles adduced in Chapter 4 dealing with meaning, communication and the message are important when considering the use of speech as a kind of auditory display.

Simpson and Marchionda-Frost (1984) considered the effects of speech rate and voice 'pitch' (of synthesised speech) on pilot recognition accuracy and response time within a relatively noisy, cockpit-type environment. They demonstrated that although the pitch had no effect on intelligibility, performance fell with faster rates of speech—above 178 words per minute. On the basis of their data, and taking cognisance of the fact that faster speech rates convey the message in shorter times, they recommend that a speech rate of about 156 words per minute should be used.

A second feature of speech warning displays that has been considered relates to the use of alerting cues such as a tone or a bell. Licklider (1961), for example, argued that a non-verbal sound presented immediately before the speech itself would help to gain the attention of the operator and act as a primer for the warning speech to come. Taking the opportunities further, Hakkinen and Williges (1984) considered the effect of such an alerting cue on different kinds of synthesised speech. They showed that when synthesised speech was used *only* in emergency situations, the presence of an alerting cue led to greater response times than when there was no cue. However, when the speech was used within a multi-function mode (that is, when it provided other kinds of information as well as emergency functions), more emergency messages were detected with than without the alerting cue. Clearly, therefore, periodic use of the cue tended to confuse the subjects, while with regular use they became used to its appearance and could benefit from its alerting features.

Other Qualitative Auditory Displays

Just as a visual display can present the observer with relatively low-level qualitative information—for example, whether the machine is 'hot', 'cool' or 'cold'—so too can auditory displays. In this case the coding is usually made in terms either of the tonal pitch or some other quality. The modern telephone provides an ideal example of this use. As soon as the receiver is raised a tone is heard which indicates that the system is working and is ready to be used. On dialling or keying a number a different tone is presented, depending on the new state of the system: number ringing, engaged or unobtainable. Other examples of the use of auditory information in this way can be conceived but, in all cases, it is essential that the tones indicating the different machine states are easily distinguishable.

Tracking displays

Auditory tracking aids have been used for some time to help pilots maintain a steady course, perhaps the simplest of which was the A/N signal system. This consisted of a continuous 1020 Hz tone being heard when the pilot was flying on course. Deviations to the left caused the tone to become more of a Morse 'A' (dot-dash) signal, whereas an 'N' (dash-dot) signal (which interleaves with the 'A' signal to form the continuous 'on course' tone) would become apparent with deviations to the right. Although some success was claimed with this system, it does again depend on the distinguishability of the two codes (A and N). As McCormick (1976) points out, under adverse noise conditions the difference between the two signals may not be properly identified.

Hoffman and Heimstra (1972) report an auditory tracking system that proved to be superior to a visual display. In this case the subject was required to maintain a particular random course using a hand-wheel, in which no noise was heard if the pointer remained on target. Deviations of more then 5 per cent, however, caused a noise signal to be heard in either the right or left ear, depending on the side of the track towards which the deviations occurred. Using this system, more time was spent on target using the auditory than the visual display. From these two examples, therefore, it is clear that acoustic displays can be used to provide simple, one-dimensional tracking information, although great care needs to be taken to ensure that the various displayed states are easily distinguished.

SUMMARY

This chapter has discussed various ways by which the machine can present information to the operator through its displays. Although many types of display are available, it is readily apparent that the most appropriate display depends to a considerable extent on the nature of the task for which the information is to be used. In the visual modality the choice is essentially between an analogue and a digital display, although a number of different ways of presenting these two basic types were discussed. In the auditory modality, the designer's choice is more restricted.

The following chapter will consider the third main sensory system which is used at work—the sense of touch. Although the main theme of the chapter will be to discuss ways of enhancing the information flow in the other direction, from the operator to the machine via controls, it should not be forgotten that each time the operator operates a control, for example using a push-button, the control shape, dimensions and movement, etc., are also passing information from the machine to the operator.

6

MAN–MACHINE COMMUNICATION: CONTROLS

By enabling the operator to return information to the environment, controls represent the return link in the man–machine closed loop system and are very much the complement of displays. Indeed, the value of a well-designed display (reduced reading errors; faster reading time) could be seriously affected if the many features important in operating its associated control are not considered. Display design was discussed in Chapter 5, and so the present chapter will consider factors that are important when designing the operator's controls and tools.

That poorly designed controls alone may lead to inefficiency and breakdown in the man–machine system is well illustrated in a survey carried out by Fitts and Jones (1947b). In a complementary study to their investigation of aircraft display reading errors, they analysed 460 'pilot error' experiences in operating aircraft controls. Of these errors, 68 per cent were related to poor control design. The remainder were owing either to mistakes occurring because of a lack of compatibility between the display and the control (6 per cent) or to poor control placement on the cockpit panel (26 per cent). (Chapter 7 will discuss these points.)

Inappropriate use of controls and control design were also found to be important factors in aircraft accidents in a factor analytic study by Gerbert and Kemmler (1986). They considered over 60 different possible causes for accidents and, from this list, distilled 27 errors that were most frequently involved in incidents. Factor analysis of these errors led to four primary factors emerging: vigilance errors, information processing errors, perception errors, and sensorimotor/handling errors. The component 'poor coordination of controls' was placed firmly within the last factor, and was related to such pilot variables as 'tension', 'nervousness', 'excessive motivation to succeed', and 'lack of confidence'. Clearly, therefore, the implication is reinforced that control, and other handling activities, are affected as much by the operator's ability to interact with them as they are with the design of the components themselves.

Controls, therefore, are important components in the system. However, a number of factors need to be considered before an effective control system can be designed that will match the operator's expectations, abilities and behaviour. The operator's task needs to be understood to determine the degree of accuracy, force, precision and manipulation required to operate the system, and these features have to be compared with the operator's abilities to carry out such tasks. As always, if abilities do not match requirements then changes in the mechanical part of the system should be considered—perhaps involving different types or designs of controls and control systems.

This chapter will first consider the kinds of controls available for different kinds of operations. Secondly, some of the factors important in control design and aspects of the system which could affect control effectiveness will be examined. Finally, the discussion will consider the extent to which such factors are incorporated into different types of control.

TYPES OF CONTROL

Controls are commonly classified into two groups according to their function. The first group includes those controls used to make discrete changes in the machine state, for example switching it 'on' or 'off', or switching to different levels of activity. Second are controls that are used for making continuous settings. For example, a radio volume control allows the user to increase the volume gradually, and to stop at any of an infinite number of intensities within its operating range. McCormick (1976) further subdivides these two functions into discrete and continuous:

Discrete

- Activation—for example, turning a machine on or off.

- Data entry—as on a keyboard to enter either a letter or a number.

- Setting—switching to a specific machine state.

Continuous

- Quantitative setting—setting the machine to a particular value along a continuum, for example turning a radio frequency control to receive a specific radio station.

- Continuous control—continuously altering the machine state, usually to maintain a particular level of activity (commonly known as tracking). For example, steering a vehicle using the steering wheel.

Different controls will be more appropriate for some of these activities than for others. The respective advantages of controls for different activities are shown in Table 6.1.

Table 6.1   Types of controls and their functions

	Discrete			Continuous	
Control type	Activation	Discrete setting	Data entry	Quantitative setting	Continuous control
Hand push-button	Excellent	Can be used, will need as many buttons as settings — not recommended	Good	Not applicable	Not applicable
Foot push-button	Good	Not recommended	N/A	N/A	N/A
Toggle switch	Good, but prone to accidental activation	Fair, but poor if more than three possible settings to be made	N/A	N/A	N/A
Rotary selector switch	Can be used, but on/off position may be confused with other positions	Excellent, provided settings are well marked	N/A	N/A	N/A
Knob	N/A	Poor	N/A	Good	Fair
Crank	Only applicable if large forces are needed to activate — e.g. open/close hatch	N/A	N/A	Fair	Good
Handwheel	N/A	N/A	N/A	Good	Excellent
Level	Good	Good, provided there are not too many settings	N/A	Good	Good
Pedal	Fair	N/A	N/A	Good	Fair

Of course, no single control is appropriate in all circumstances. Take the case of the ubiquitous push-button as an example. After reviewing the literature dealing with different kinds of switches, Chambers and Stockbridge (1970) showed that in terms of operating speeds the most efficient activation control was the push-button followed by the rocker switch, the slide switch and the toggle switch. The order for accuracy was the reverse of that for speed, however, because the push-button is usually associated with a 'ballistic-like movement which produces increased speed but reduced accuracy'.

Finally, the usefulness of any control can be limited by such features (if relevant) as the ease to which it can be identified, its location and size, its relationship to the appropriate display, and the type of feedback which it gives to the operator. The next section will consider some of these factors.

FACTORS IMPORTANT IN CONTROL DESIGN

Feedback

Feedback has been discussed already in previous chapters. It refers to the information received, from both outside and inside the body, which helps the operator to assess his or her performance, body position, etc. In relation to hand controls, for example, information that is fed back from the eyes, shoulders, arms, wrists and fingers informs the operator by how much a control has been moved, its speed of movement, and its final position. In addition, feedback from the more sensitive pressure receptors in the skin provides information about the nature of the control being operated: its size, texture and any tactile coding characteristic. In many respects, therefore, this kind of feedback relates to the control's 'feel'.

Burrows (1965) points out that control 'feel' arises from two separate sources. First, as just discussed, it occurs as kinaesthetic feedback from the muscles, for example telling the operator where the arm is at the time and the speed with which it is moving through space. As was discussed in Chapter 2, this is a very efficient form of feedback, particularly for learning different skills. Secondly, 'feel' is determined by the control itself in terms of the amount of resistance to movement which is built into it, its looseness, etc. Of course, to these sources should be added any tactile, visual or auditory feedback loops which may help the operator (for example 'clicks' or marks on the control surface).

Control Resistance

The control's resistance to movement is possibly the most frequently used feedback cue. In most cases, particularly when continuous settings are to be made, some inbuilt resistance is desirable since it helps the operator to make settings with some degree of precision. Resistance can also help to guard against accidentally activating the control. However, if too much resistance is incorporated into the control, or the wrong kind of resistance is experienced, the operator could become susceptible to fatigue and performance may be reduced. Understanding the nature of different types of resistance, therefore, should enable appropriate controls to be chosen with characteristics that will minimise any possible negative effects while at the same time maximising performance.

Control resistance takes four main forms, and their advantages and disadvantages are shown in Table 6.2. Thus it would appear that static friction is most appropriate for discrete setting controls since it reduces the possibility of accidental operation. For continuous setting controls, however, elastic or viscous resistance will allow greater precision owing to the nature of the kinaesthetic feedback which it provides.

Regarding the level of resistance to be introduced, it is difficult to suggest specific figures since they will be related to the kind of operator, control location, and the frequency, duration, direction and amount of control movement required. Clearly, however, the maximum level set should lie within the range of abilities of the operating population, for which texts such as those of Damon, Stoudt and McFarland (1971) and Roebuck, Kroemer and Thompson (1975) should be consulted. For minimum levels Morgan *et al.* (1963) suggest that, for all hand controls except push-buttons, resistance should not be less than 2–5 lb, since below this level the hand's pressure sensitivity is very poor. If the full weight of the arm and hand rest on the control the minimum resistance should be 10–12 lb. Table 6.3 summarises some of the data available for maximum resistances for different kinds of control.

Size

Control sizes and dimensions clearly need to be related to the anthropometric dimensions of the limbs used. Thus the diameter of a push-button should be at least that of the fingertip (approximately 16 mm); the size of a knob on a lever equal to the breadth of grip (49 mm); and so on. Garrett (1971) provides a set of these various dimensions for the human hand, but it should be remembered that these dimensions will be altered, sometimes considerably, if the operator is wearing gloves.

Not only is it important to relate the size of the control to the dimensions of the limb which operates it, it is also necessary to consider the kind of action that the control requires. All controls need some degree of manipulation.

Table 6.2 Characteristics of static, coloumbic, viscous and intertial control resistances

Type of resistance	Example of incidence	Characteristics	Advantages	Disadvantages
Static and coloumbic	1. On/off switch 2. 'Stuck control'	Resistance is maximal at the start of the movement but falls considerably with further force (i.e. the control slips)	Reduced chances of accidental activation	Little precision control once the control has begun to move
Elastic	Spring-loaded control	Resistance is proportional to control displacement	1. Kinaesthetic cues may be maximally effective 2. Control returns to null position	Because control returns to neutral, operator needs to maintain constant force
Viscous	Plunger	Resistance is proportional to the velocity of the control movement	1. Good control precision — particularly rate of movement 2. Reduced chance of accidental operation 3. Operator can remove limb and control remains in position	
Inertia	Large crank	Resistance is caused by the mass of the control	1. Allows smooth movement 2. Reduced chance of accidental operation owing to high force required	1. May cause operator fatigue 2. Does not allow precise movement because of danger of overshooting

Table 6.3 Minimum resistances required for different controls (adapted from Morgan *et al.*, 1963; by permission of McGraw-Hill)

Control	Minimum resistance
Hand push-button	10 oz (2.8 N)
Foot push-button	4 lb (17.8 N) if foot does not rest on control; 1.25 lb (5.6 N) if foot rests on control
Toggle switch	10 oz (2.8 N)
Rotary selector switch	12 oz (3.3 N)
Knob	0–6 oz (0–1.7 N) depending on function
Crank	2–5 lb (9–22 N) depending on size
Handwheel	5 lb (22 N)
Lever	2 lb (9 N)
Pedal	4 lb (17.8 N) if foot does not rest on control; 10 lb (44.5 N) if foot rests on control

For hand controls, therefore, different kinds of manipulative tasks will require different control dimensions, depending on the part of the hand that is used to operate the control.

Most manipulative tasks can be placed along a continuum of 'gripping' to 'non-gripping' activities. In gripping activities the fingers and parts of the palm form a closed chain and act in opposition to each other to exert compressive force on the object to be gripped. In non-gripping actions the forces are exerted either through all of the hand or through the fingertips in an open chain. As well as the amount to which the fingers are closed, a second manipulative dimension concerns the degree of hand/object contact. From such a two-dimensional classification it is possible to determine the anthropometric dimensions required for any particular task, and also the forces and torques needed. Some of these dimensions, with examples, are illustrated in Figure 6.1.

Again, however, when considering the amount of limb/object contact that needs to be accommodated in relation to the control dimensions, the kind of task being carried out should also be taken into account. Catovic *et al.* (1989) demonstrated that the posture adopted when operating small hand controls significantly affects the kind of gripping behaviour and forces able to be adopted. For example, grip forces were found to be higher in the standing than in the sitting posture, and appropriate handle design (to allow all fingers to be spread during a pinch—closed-chain—grip) enabled forces up to 50 per cent higher to be applied (with concomitant reductions in fatigue potential) than with just thumb and forefinger grip devices.

Freivalds (1987) provides a comprehensive review of the general principles involved in control design, particularly the design of tools and the

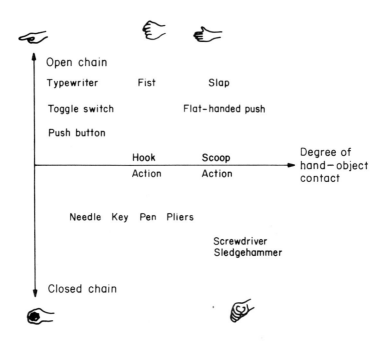

Figure 6.1 A classification of hand control functions (adapted from Grieve and Pheasant, 1981, reproduced by permission of Cambridge University Press)

relationship between handle size and shape and the resultant forces that can be applied. Mital (1991) has also summarised the research relating to tool dimensions for different kinds of grip.

Weight

The weight of many controls becomes important only when there is sufficient inertia to cause undue resistance (for example as with a crank handle), otherwise the weight will be supported by the machine itself. However, some controls are used away from a machine (particularly as hand tools) and in these cases the tool's weight may obviously play an important part in its effectiveness.

As well as the overall tool weight, its weight distribution is an important feature. For example, a rod held in the hand which is in a relaxed, neutral position makes an obtuse angle of approximately 102 degrees to the forearm. Significant deviations from this will cause the wrist muscles to be under static load. If most of the weight is distributed towards the front or the back of the tool so that the wrist needs to work to maintain its natural posture, the static load will soon cause fatigue. The ideal weight distribution, then, will be one which places the maximum weight over the place where the tool is held and maintains the 102 degree angle.

Kadefors *et al.* (1993) describe various techniques available to measure the amount of hand/wrist deviation that occurs from using different kinds of hand tools.

Texture

Since the control acts as the interface of information flowing between the operator and the machine, it might be thought to be an obvious point that the quality of the control action will depend largely on the extent to which the operator's limb is able to remain in contact with it. As with many aspects of the working situation, however, ensuring that this occurs is not so simple. For example, it is obvious that the surface of hand-held controls should not be so smooth as to cause difficulties in making a firm grip. This is particularly important if the hands are likely to be moist from sweat. In addition, a highly polished surface may cause glare, perhaps adversely affecting the operator's performance on a visual task. On the other hand, surfaces that are to be grasped or which may be rubbed against should be free of any abrasive properties (rough surfaces are often contaminated with sand or dirt, etc. and so it is likely that an abraded wound could eventually become infected). A balance must be struck, therefore, between the two extremes and so the question becomes to what extent the control should be textured. Many of these problems are solved by using a non-reflective, rippled coating, but the ripples should not be raised so much that they cause painful pressure spots.

When the operator applies a force to a hand control, the direction of the force may act either transversely across the palm, as in the case of a steering wheel, or longitudinally as with a lever. (Feet also exert longitudinal forces along a pedal.) In both cases the rippled texture described above may help the designer to minimise the possibility of the hand slipping. However, the two kinds of force suggest that the ripples should be at right angles to the likely direction of force.

Finally, in relation to hand controls, Kadefors *et al.* (1993) point out that it is not always an asset to have a very high level of friction between the hand and tool, particularly when the grip needs to be changed frequently—as when turning a screwdriver, for example. They also emphasise that, in the absence of adequate information concerning optimal friction values, the designer will generally have to resort to subjective methods of assessing the textural suitability of controls.

Coding

The value of highlighting different aspects or areas of the machines to ease identification was discussed in the last chapter. For qualitative displays colour coding different areas was shown to increase performance and reduce errors.

It is also possible to colour code controls, of course, particularly when the coding is used to aid the operator's selection of relevant actions. However, because they are usually operated by a limb it is probably more appropriate to code controls along some tactile dimension. This releases the eyes to deal with other, visual information. Unfortunately, however, touch is a less accurate sensory mode than vision for perceiving differences, and this may lead to uncertainties in the operator's actions and probably slows down discrimination time. For this reason Moore (1976) recommends that tactile identification of controls should only be used as a final check on the control's identity, rather than as the primary coding method. Adequate labelling, he suggests, is probably as efficient. Like colour coding, however, labelling also needs to be seen to be effective and, as was discussed in Chapter 4, requires careful design.

In many cases controls may have to be put in places where labels or colours are not easily seen and in such cases shape, texture, size and location coding, or any combination of these, may be used. With each of these techniques, the aim is to produce groups of controls such that the controls within each group are rarely confused with each other.

Coding by shape

We distinguish different shapes mainly by pressure differences over the hand tissue caused by various protrusions in the shape. For this reason shape coding is normally useful only to ungloved operators.

A number of sets of unconfusable shapes have been produced by different investigators over the years (e.g. Hunt, 1953; Jenkins, 1947; Moore, 1974). In general the work has shown that simple forms are easier to discriminate than more complicated ones. Furthermore, learning their use can be simplified and made more efficient if the controls also have shapes which, either by design or by convention, look similar to the part of the machine which they operate.

Coding by texture

As well as its shape the control's texture may also be coded, for example the edge may be differentially rippled or knurled. As Bradley (1967) demonstrated, as long as the textures are distinct enough confusions will not occur. He produced smooth, fluted and knurled textured control-wheel edges which would not be confused. Furthermore, appropriate training and practice may significantly improve an operator's ability to distinguish between textures (Eckstrand and Morgan, 1956)—although the cautions expressed in Chapter 1 concerning the value of training alone should be remembered.

Like shape coding, but perhaps to a lesser extent, the stimulus perceived from using textured controls is related to different patterns of fingertip deformation. This is what the operator learns to recognise and any impediment to the perfect transmission of this information from the control to the operator could result in errors being made. Gloves provide a good example of this problem. Even if the gloves are thin enough to let the operator manipulate controls under normal circumstances, they may impair (or perhaps more importantly distort) perception of the surface texture. Dirt and grime collecting in the textured surface may cause similar problems.

Since the important stimulus is the amount and the pattern of skin and tissue deformation, texture coding does not need to be confined solely to 'smoothness', 'rippledness', or 'knurledness'. Moore (1974), for example, describes an experiment designed to investigate ability to discriminate between different raised surface shapes on push-buttons. By asking subjects to feel (blindly) the surface of different push-buttons and to compare them with pictures, he was able to produce a set of six discriminatable surface textures.

As far as tactile shape coding is concerned, Moore recommends the following five principles:

- Shapes to be distinguished by touch should have as gross a shape as possible, covering an area which can be touched by one finger.

- Geometric shapes, numbers or letters should be formed from outlines rather than from solids.

- Shapes should be made to vary along as many tactile dimensions as possible.

- If at all possible, the buttons should be designed or chosen to ensure that the shapes remain in the same orientation at all times and do not revolve.

- The shapes should not be uncomfortable or difficult to use.

Coding by size

The size of the control itself may provide useful visual or tactile cues, but size alone generally is not as useful for coding as is shape or texture. Again the different sizes used should be such that they are discriminatable from one another. In this respect, Moore (1976) suggests that the dimensions should follow a logarithmic progression with at least a 20 per cent difference between each.

Coding by colour

Colour coding has previously been discussed in relation to visual displays, and similar principles exist for coding controls. Unlike visual displays, however, the prime function of controls is not to present visual information and so they may not be in a position which can easily be seen by the operator. Indeed, they are often put in places which enable them to be operated while the operator is looking elsewhere, perhaps at the display. In these circumstances colour coding—a visual aid—is often of little value for controls which have mainly manual and tactile features.

FACTORS THAT CAN AFFECT CONTROL EFFECTIVENESS

In many respects most topics discussed in this book will affect control effectiveness: the quality of the information reaching the operator; the operator's position with respect to the control; environmental factors (both social and physical); fatigue; stress, and so on. However, this section will consider aspects of the interaction which are not discussed elsewhere and which are specific to control design: operator handedness, wearing clothing (in particular gloves and shoes), control shape, and how the control is used.

Handedness

For everyday use, an individual's handedness (or, more accurately, hand preference) may be classified as being 'left' or 'right' simply on the basis of the writing hand. For complex tasks, however, this simple dichotomy clearly becomes insufficient; an individual may have different hand preferences for various actions and this could cause problems from the viewpoint of determining which hand should operate which control. Take the action of tightening a screw as a very simple example. A right-handed person would need to rotate the wrist with a movement of the palm upwards, i.e. twisting the wrist away from the body (supination). The operator with a left-hand preference will need to protinate the wrist (palm moved downwards, wrist twisted towards the body). Unfortunately for the left-handed person, however, supination allows a greater torque and range of movement than protination (Damon, Stoudt and MacFarland, 1971).

The problem of left-handed operators, however, does not simply rest with considering the strengths and types of left- and right-hand movement. Controls, particularly tool handles, are often designed for use by right-handed operators. Left-handed operators frequently find them difficult or uncomfortable to use and this may lead to fatigue and possibly accidents.

A solution to the problem caused by hand preference, however, is not simple. A number of estimates of the incidence of left-handedness have been made and vary from 2 per cent to 29 per cent (Hardyck and Petrinovich, 1977), although generally less than 10 per cent of any large national population is left-handed (or at least has a left-hand preference for most activities) (Kimura and Vanderwolf, 1970). Since ambidexterity, in the sense of equal preference, is extremely rare, the question must be posed whether it is possible to accommodate fully the requirements of the left-handed operator. Naturally, sometimes right- and left-handed tools may be available, when the different handle shapes and directions of movement will need to be considered. In other cases, however (for example, the question of control placement with respect to the operator's own position), it may not be possible (or economical) to produce both right- and left-handed versions. In such cases it is even more crucial to assess the requirements of the job and to match them to the operator's capabilities.

Clothing and Protective Clothing

The types of clothing most likely to interfere with efficient control action are gloves covering the hands and shoes on the feet. Both may affect relevant control dimensions and both are likely to alter the operator's ability to use the control adequately.

Although gloves are designed to protect the operator's hands they may have a number of undesirable consequences, particularly in relation to manipulating the control and obtaining feedback from it. As an example, the normal sensation of 'grip' probably results from the pressure perceived when the flexed fingers around the gripped object press against each other. A working glove which is too thick in these regions can cause high pressures to be generated between the fingers before the hand is firmly closed around the tool handle or equipment control, and this may result in an insecure grasp. A thick glove can also interfere with the fingers and stop them from wrapping around the handle sufficiently for a firm grip. Alternatively, of course, an operator who is aware of these problems may grip the control unnecessarily tightly so increasing fatigue in the finger and other muscles.

Cochran *et al.* (1986) considered the effects of gloves on grasp force by measuring pressure while using a leather glove, a leather glove with cotton backing, a cotton glove, a nylon–stainless steel glove, a steel mesh over cotton glove, and no glove at all. All of the gloves used were shown to degrade maximum grasp force by a minimum of 7.3 per cent to a maximum of 16.8 per cent. Similarly, Weidman (1970) considered the effects of wearing gloves on manual performance. He demonstrated that neoprene gloves slowed performance times by 12.5 per cent over bare-hand performance, leather by 45 per cent, and PVC by 64 per cent. Reasons for such effects may be found in a study by Bellingar and Slocum (1993) who used high-speed photographic techniques to demonstrate that protective gloves have the effect of reducing the manipulative abilities of the wrist/hand complex.

After carrying out a series of experiments to determine the degree to which gloves interfere with control manipulation and operation speeds, Bradley (1969a) concluded that the efficiency with which instrument controls may be operated by a gloved hand depends on the glove characteristics, the physical characteristics of the control, and the type of control operation. Specifically, snugness of fit and resistance to slipping were shown to be the two most important glove parameters, and under some circumstances a snug glove which did not slip over the controls actually improved performance. In many cases, however, gloves are worn for protection against injury, and snugness and even resistance to slipping may be absent. In such cases the control size needs to be increased to allow adequate manipulation and, as discussed earlier, the control ought to be textured to reduce slipping.

As well as interfering with grip, gloves can often impede the perception of any coded texture differences on various controls. As was discussed earlier, such texture differences cause different pressure patterns on the observer's skin and these could be occluded by the gloves.

In a similar fashion to gloves interfering with the operation of hand-held controls, shoes sometimes affect the efficiency of foot-pedal operation. Heavy, protective footwear, for example, may not allow the feet to be moved with the required precision since the necessary feedback may be either missing or of poor quality.

A second interfering feature of shoes which is often forgotten is the height of the heels. As will be discussed later, most foot pedals are designed for the forces and angles produced by a foot having 'average' dimensions, and the presence of high heels can alter these parameters. For example, Warner and Mace (1974) demonstrated that the average brake response time of female drivers was increased by 0.1s when wearing platform (with a heel higher than 2 in and a sole ½ in thick) as opposed to 'normal' shoes— despite that fact that the subjects were used to wearing platform shoes.

(This is simply a further example of training being unable to overcome the effects of poor equipment design.) Translated into vehicle stopping distances, this represents an increase of 1.42 ft for each 10 m.p.h. speed increase, which could mean the difference between safe and unsafe stopping.

Control Shapes

Control shapes can have an important influence how an operator uses the control which, in turn, may affect the posture. Awkward postures can put undue stress on the musculoskeletal system causing fatigue over long periods.

Many tools are used which, under normal operational conditions, require the wrist to be bent either downwards or upwards. This causes the tendons connecting the finger muscles to the forearm bones in the elbow region to bend and to become subject to mechanical stress. Whereas infrequent use of such a tool and posture is unlikely to lead to any ill effects, under continuous operation the effect will be to cause muscular fatigue and thus loss of efficiency. As Tichauer (1978) points out, it is much safer to bend the tool than to bend the wrist.

Shape is also important when considering the cross-sectional configuration of a hand tool. If high grip forces are required, the handle should distribute the forces to as large a pressure-bearing area on the fingers and palm as possible, while still being small enough to allow the fingers to wrap round the handle. To this end, Pheasant and O'Neill (1975) have demonstrated that muscular strength is minimal when using handles around 5 cm diameter. Below 3–4 cm and above 5–6 cm both the amount of hand contact with the handle and the amount of torque able to be exerted fell dramatically. Fellows and Freivalds (1991), however, have shown that if the increased diameter is created by using foam, which compresses easily when gripped, the resultant pressure distribution over the tool handle is more uniform.

Movements Required for Different Controls

As mentioned previously, different types of controls require different postures to be adopted and different kinds of operation, and this can significantly affect the effectiveness with which the control is operated.

As an example, consider the types of control operation described earlier in terms of open and closed chain operation. The movement required to operate a keyboard is characterised by an 'open chain' approach, with the hand having little contact with the control. Thus the operation is performed using more of a 'pointing' movement which has a ballistic nature (Chambers and Stockbridge, 1970). Essentially, therefore, the problems facing the operator are considerations of speed and accuracy: to place the fingers accurately over the appropriate keys, and to strike the keys as quickly as possible. The muscles involved include those in the shoulder, arm and wrist, in addition to the muscles needed to operate the appropriate fingers.

The operations required to use controls such as a pen, however, are different. These involve rather more hand–object contact, particularly because more than one finger has to hold and operate this type of control. Thus, more muscles are used and, because of the nature of the controlling task, they are maintained under tension for longer. Inevitably this will lead to more static load and to a higher risk of muscle fatigue.

A further biomechanical problem associated with controls occurs when they have to be positioned or operated at some distance from the body. Since more stability occurs as the operation is carried out nearer to the body, it follows that operations like touching a pen to a computer screen at arm's length, or turning a valve above the head, may be less accurately performed than pressing a key on a keyboard near to the operator. The reason for this is twofold. First, as the arm is extended forces on the shoulder muscles are increased because the centre of gravity of the hand–arm complex moves away from the body. More work will be required from the muscles, therefore, to maintain a stable position—to counteract the force of gravity. Indeed, this was demonstrated well by Mead and Sampson (1972) who measured hand steadiness while subjects performed various types of movements. The amount of tremor was considerably reduced, and thus accuracy increased, when subjects made ballistic-like 'in–out' movements than when they were required to move a stylus 'up–down'. Secondly, as the arm is extended the wrist orientation has to change. This means that the degree of finger–control contact tends to be reduced—unless the operator takes specific steps to counteract this tendency. Doing so, of course, will increase the amount of static load on the finger muscles.

THE DESIGN OF SPECIFIC TOOLS AND CONTROLS

When discussing the development of modern ergonomics, many sceptics describe the era of the 1950s and early 1960s as being the period of 'knobs and dials' investigations. By this they imply that ergonomists were interested mainly in the design aspects of specific kinds of displays or controls—rather than considering how these pieces of equipment function as parts of the total working system. Although a cursory examination of the published literature of this period tends to support this observation, it could well be argued that basic research of this nature needed to be carried out before the advantages of different types of display or control in the system could be considered. Because it is important to be able to recognise good 'ergonomic' control designs, this section will provide a very basic description of the design recommendations for different types of control as elucidated by the research of the period. Chapter 7 will consider the use of such controls within the total system. When discussing these recommendations, however, it should be realised that some of the data are based on experiments using comparatively small numbers of subjects. Given the wide variability of performance abilities shown by individuals, therefore, it is not possible to provide figures for diameters, loads and so on with absolute certainty. Nevertheless, as Murrell (1971) points out:

> At the best [the figures] have a reasonable estimate of the design parameters concerned, at the worst they are better than guesswork on the part of the designer who, if he follows them, may rest assured that the equipment which he is producing is being designed in accordance with the best knowledge available at present.

Hand Controls

Naturally the basic considerations of all hand controls concern the anthropometric and biomechanical capabilities of the operator's fingers, hands and wrists.

Knobs

The knob is a cylindrical control which is operated by gripping the thumb and forefinger around its circumference and moving them in opposition. Knobs may be used for making fine, continuous adjustments or as rotary selector switches.

It is important that the diameter of this type of control is not too small to prevent it from being gripped and turned easily. On the other hand, panel space should not be wasted by using controls which are larger than those required for efficient operation. For this reason Bradley (1969b) asked subjects to make various clockwise and anticlockwise 'standard' operations, using knobs with diameters ranging from 0.5 to 3.25 in (1.2 to 8 cm), in 0.25 in (0.6 cm) increments. Two levels of shaft friction (torque) were used: normal (77–85 inch grams; 0.5–0.6 N) and heavy (171–181 inch grams; 1.2–1.3 N). Using turning time as his main measure, Bradley demonstrated that a knob diameter of approximately 5 cm was optimum for both normal and heavy friction. When the shaft friction increased the turning time was magnified significantly as the knob diameter deviated from the optimum.

As control panels increase in complexity, more instruments may have to be crowded into a limited panel space. One way of accomplishing this is by grouping controls together. In the case of concentric controls, this would mean ganging several control knobs perpendicular to the panel by mounting them on concentric shafts. Unfortunately, however, ganging control knobs probably increases the chances of inadvertently operating adjacent knobs. While turning one of the knobs the operator's fingertips or knuckles might scrape against the face of the knob immediately behind it, or the fingers or palm may rub against one of the knobs in front of it, so altering the setting of the knob which was inadvertently operated.

Bradley (1969c) investigated the optimum dimensions for such controls. In a similar experiment to his determination of optimum knob diameters he demonstrated that, for three-ganged controls, if the diameter of the centre knob is 5 cm (optimum knob diameter) the diameter of the front knob should be less than 2.5 cm and that of the rear knob about 8 cm. His results also indicated that the front and middle knobs should each be 8 cm thick, whereas the back knob could be as thin as 0.6 cm. Bradley further argues that concentrically ganged knobs should only be used if enough shaft friction is present to prevent accidental operation.

Push-buttons

Push-buttons are small, single-action controls which operate in one direction only. They are usually activated by the fingers but sometimes by the foot. They range in size from comparatively large 'on' or 'off' buttons for heavy machine tools to small, individual finger-controlled buttons of which modern electric keyboards are examples. Three kinds of push-button are commonly available: 'latching' (push on, lock on), 'momentary' (push on, release off) and 'alternate action' (push on, push off). All three modes are found in hand-operated buttons, but the latching mode is seldom found in foot-operated buttons.

The important physical parameters of push-buttons are their size, separation, shape, operating force, the provision of feedback, and the separation between the buttons. Of these factors the shape of the button has already been discussed and the separation between buttons will be discussed in the following chapter, particularly in relation to grouping buttons together to form a keyboard.

Regarding button size, the limiting factor must be the dimensions of the fingers that are to operate the controls. In this respect, a minimum diameter of 13 mm is often suggested for finger-operated controls and 19 mm for those operated by the base of the thumb (for example, an emergency stop button). Unfortunately few data are presently available to enable comparisons between these dimensions and the size of the average fingertip.

As an indication of the importance of ensuring that the size of the keys is optimum, Deininger (1960) reports a study which investigated button size as a variable in different keyboard arrangements. By increasing the dimensions of a square button from 9.5 to 17.4 mm, he was able to show a reduction in keying times from 6.35 to 5.83 s, and reduced errors from 7.1 to 1.3 per cent.

For use when designing key sizes and spacing to fit the operator's hand, Garrett (1971) provides a number of anthropometric dimensions for different parts of the adult human hand. His data suggest that the top of the finger joints have an average breadth of approximately 1.7 cm for males and 1.5 cm for females. Ninety per cent of the male population falls into a range of from 1.6 to 1.9 cm, and of the female population 1.3 to 1.6 cm. Naturally, the width of this joint is not the same as that of the fingertip, since fingers tend to taper, but data such as these are still currently the nearest available.

As was discussed earlier, key resistance performs two functions: first, it provides the operator with kinaesthetic feedback relating to the extent to which a key has been pressed; secondly, by requiring force to depress the key, resistance can prevent accidental operation. Because of its properties of acting against movement, however, resistance is likely to increase muscular fatigue and reduce fast performance and so needs to be set to a type and level that are optimum.

Moore (1975) suggests a range of push-button resistances from 283–1133 grams if one finger is used, 140–560 grams if different fingers are used, and 283–2272 grams for large, thumb-operated controls. Chambers and Stockbridge (1970) emphasise, however, that caution must be sounded against reducing the resistance by too much since it becomes easier to operate the button inadvertently. A hair-trigger on a gun, for example, requires a safety catch to prevent accidents.

With regard to the maximum force able to be exerted, Alden, Daniels and Kanarick (1972) report a study performed by Haaland, Wingert and Olsen (1963) in which the maximum pushing force for each finger of the adult male hand was measured. As can be seen from Table 6.4, quite wide variations occur over the five fingers, and Haaland, Wingert and Olsen attribute this to differences in the finger musculature. Furthermore, they observe that individuals whose fingers bend back when pushing

Table 6.4 Maximum finger pushing force in grams (Haaland, Wingert and Olsen, 1963)

Finger	Thumb	Index	Middle	Ring	Little
Mean	1055	684	657	513	342
Range	855–1226	485–884	485–741	342–627	171–542

perpendicularly could not apply as much pushing force as those whose fingers remain rigid.

Of course, the maximum force able to be pushed will not necessarily be the ideal force required for a keyboard. It is, therefore, important to consider what is the optimum force for maximum speed and minimum fatigue. For example, Droege and Hill (1961) demonstrated that variations in key resistance can have important implications for performance.

In his experiment investigating different key arrangements, Deininger (1960) found that varying the key force from 3.5 to 14.1 oz (100 to 403 g) or varying the maximum displacement from 0.03 to 0.19 in (0.08 to 0.48 cm) produced insignificant differences in his subjects' keying performances. However, later reports from the subjects indicated a general preference for the light touch keys and a definite dislike for the keys requiring greater displacement. Unfortunately as Alden, Daniels and Kanarick (1972) point out, many of Deininger's results are questionable given his lack of experimental controls. Nevertheless, the subjective reports have some use and the results do relate favourably to other studies in the area.

For example, Bergenthal (1971) reports a study in which subjects were required to push buttons having a range of forces from 3–48 oz (86–1371 g). His results demonstrate a strong preference for buttons having a resistance of approximately 10 oz (286 g). Preference fell significantly as resistances departed from this value. It should be pointed out, however, that Bergenthal's study was performed with subjects pressing the buttons sequentially with a 'stiff' finger and this may not be an appropriate type of action for all forms of push-button operations. Typing, for example, is performed using the fingers in a bent posture, the control being operated by the finger-pad rather than the fingertip.

Finally, as has already been discussed, effective feedback is essential if the control is to be operated efficiently; thus the operator needs to know that the control has functioned correctly. Although this feedback may be visual, in the case of push-buttons it is most usefully given by feel or by an audible click. The eyes can then be released for other work. However, the resistance needed to produce such a click should not exceed the maximum resistance suggested above or fatigue may occur after continued use (users of some calculator keyboards will have experienced this fatigue). Modern control panels often use indicator lights as feedback devices but, as Moore (1975) rightly points out, they are only useful if they can be seen by the operator. He also emphasises that the value of indicator lights usually bears an inverse relationship to the number alight at any one time; the more alight, the less that each new one will mean to the operator.

Switches

Switches have one or other of two shapes: either rotary selector switches, which look like knobs but which are used to make discrete settings, or a toggle type of switch which has the appearance of a miniature lever. These switches generally have two positions—'on' or 'off'; speed and ease of operation may be sacrificed with additional settings.

Few data are available on which to base the design of toggle switches, although Morgan *et al.* (1963) suggest that the maximum length should be 2.5 cm with a minimum of 3 mm. Murrell (1971), however, would allow toggles up to 5 cm long but agrees with the minimum dimensions. Both agree that the switch should 'snap' into position and should not allow the possibility of intermediate positions.

The advantage of a rotary selector switch lies in the increased number of positions which may be used (Chapanis, 1951, suggests between 3 and 24). Most of the dimensions discussed for rotary control knobs are relevant to selector switches, apart from the resistance. As with the toggle switch, the resistance should be applied to enable the switch to 'snap' into position— i.e. it should be reduced at each position.

Perhaps the most important design consideration for rotary selector switches is the way in which the settings are indicated. This is usually done by moulding either the whole switch or the top part of it into a pointed shape, or by marking the switch surface. Whatever method is employed it is essential that no ambiguity can exist regarding the position selected (see Figure 6.2).

Levers and joysticks

The difference between levers and joysticks is simply that joysticks operate in two dimensions whereas levers only operate in one. For this reason, joysticks are used more often for complex tracking or positioning tasks (for example, vehicle guidance), while levers are used in situations in which only one dimension is altered (for example, changing vehicle speed or direction).

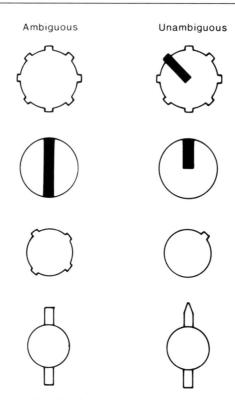

Figure 6.2   Some examples of ambiguous and unambiguous switch shapes and markings

Because joysticks are used when precision adjustments are made, it is desirable that only the hand and fingers are used, since these muscles are more densely supplied with nerves than are, for example, those in the arm. For this reason, joysticks will generally be smaller than levers. To aid precision they should have resistance in all directions with, perhaps, a return to centre position if the hand is removed. Morgan *et al.* (1963) further suggest that the joystick should be designed to enable the operator to rest the wrist while making the movements, and that the pivot point should be positioned under the point at which the wrist is rested. As will be discussed in Chapter 10, however, the value of resting the wrist when making tracking movements may be reduced considerably if the joystick is to be used under vibrating conditions.

Few data are available for choosing the optimum length of either lever or joystick handles, perhaps because the important consideration relates more to the extent to which the display alters in relation to the control movement.

This factor, the control–display ratio, will be discussed more fully in the next chapter.

Hand-operated Computer Input Controls

With the advent of computers a number of new types of hand-operated controls have appeared which are used essentially to move a cursor about the screen. These are controls which operate as discrete entry controls or for continuous movement.

Touch displays

Touch displays let the user control the machine's operation simply by touching an appropriate part of the computer screen or some representation of the screen. In this way the computer screen becomes, essentially, a bi-directional instrument in that it both presents information to and receives information from the operator. With appropriate software, different parts of the screen can represent different responses as different displays are presented to the operator. For example, a screen may first present a list of actions available to the operator, who chooses a particular action by touching, say, the centre of the screen. The centre of the screen for the next display, however, may represent a totally different choice.

Both Hopkin (1971) and McEwing (1977) discuss the advantages of screen-based displays, which can be summarised thus:

- *They are easy to use.* Such displays present a direct, 1:1 relationship between the information presented to the operator and the response required. Indeed, the two are the same. Because they are easy to use, training time is reduced (Usher, 1982) so that the need for careful selection of operators is also reduced.

- *They are fast to use.* In a small pilot study, McEwing (1977) compared the speed of inputting information using typewriters and touch displays. Touch displays took about one-third of the time taken when using typewriters.

- *They minimise errors.* Because they limit the choices available to the operator and because of the close proximity of the responses to the choices, touch displays minimise the occurrence of keying errors (Hopkin, 1971).

- *They are flexible.* Because touch displays are under software control they are extremely flexible, both in the variety of ways in which sequences can be arranged and in the comparative ease with which modifications and additions to sequences can be made.

- *Operator reaction is generally favourable.* Usher (1982), for example, describes an experiment carried out to compare the efficiency of a touch-sensitive screen with a conventional keypad. Nearly five times as many subjects preferred the touch display and, for emergency operation, this ratio increased to ten times as many. Hopkin (1971) also reports that 'operators enjoyed using the touch display and immediately formed favourable attitudes towards it'.

Against these advantages, however, Pfauth and Priest (1981) suggest a number of disadvantages of touch displays. These include an initial high cost for the system, increased programmer time, reduced flexibility for some types of input, possible screen glare, physical fatigue from reaching to the screen, and the finger and hand blocking the operator's line of sight to important areas of the screen. Some of these points have been discussed already when considering control effectiveness in relation to operating posture.

An alternative type of touch pad to the screen-based display is one which is (topographically) associated with, but not actually situated on, the screen. The advantage of this type of touch display is its increased mobility. Like a remote keyboard it can be moved around to suit the operator's posture. For example, as Bird (1977) and Pfauth and Priest (1981) emphasise, over time continuous pointing to a vertical, or near vertical, screen is likely to cause fatigue since the ideal angles of the surface for vision and for touching may not be the same. Also, in the act of touching the screen, the fingers or part of the hand may obscure the rest of the display. An 'off-display' touch panel mounted on a desk surface below the screen may reduce some of these potential problems. Unfortunately, although it may be biomechanically more convenient, such a display lacks the immediate visual feedback on finger position in relation to the displayed information. Operators, therefore, have to translate information presented from the screen in the vertical plane to responses made in the horizontal plane.

Nevertheless, the evidence appears to demonstrate that off-display types of touch pad do not carry any performance penalties. For example, Hopkin (1971) reports a study in which performance on a touch-wire display was compared with that on a 'remote labelled keyboard'. Using these two variations of the touch input concept, Hopkin reported no significant differences between the devices. Furthermore, when subjects trained on one type of device were asked to transfer to the other, complete transfer of training resulted; the subjects showed no marked preference for either device. Whitfield, Ball and Bird (1983) have also demonstrated no significant performance penalty using off-display touch pads for three types of task: menu selection, tabular display and target acquisition.

Similarly Wolf (1992) demonstrated very similar efficiency rates for gestural data inputting (in which the user 'scribbles' commands over parts of the tablet) when using touch-type displays and off-display keypads with the computer screen superimposed.

Light-pens

Like touch displays, light-pens are fully interactive control devices. They can be used effectively to position the cursor on the screen or to select responses from a 'menu' displayed to the operator. The user simply touches the appropriate part of the screen with the 'pen' and, through the photosensitive diode situated in the end, the computer is able to compute the pen's position on the screen. The operation of the pen, therefore, is very similar to that of the finger on a touch display. Indeed, Goodwin (1975) demonstrated that for selecting particular words or characters from a text display as, for example, in text editing, a light-pen appears to be much faster than using keyboard cursor controls.

Despite the positive features of light-pens, however, if the task requires the operator to mix modes of data entry (say, to type using the keyboard but, on occasions, to use a light-pen to respond to questions) then using the light-pen can be quite detrimental (Earl and Goff, 1965). Thus the operator needs to stop using the keyboard, re-orientate the hands (to pick up and to operate the light-pen), and then return to using the keyboard.

Although little information is available for designing the pen itself, it should be possible to predict some of the problems which constant light-pen users might face—in particular those to do with muscular fatigue in both the arm and the wrist. Thus, as argued earlier, as the arm is extended the hand's prehensile grip on the pen varies so that higher forces are required to maintain the pen support. Secondly, continuous working of the hand both away from the body and high up causes the upper arm and shoulder muscles to be under static muscular load. Thirdly, the pen's weight distribution is important to ensure that undue forces are not placed on the wrist. A relatively 'heavy' cable connecting the end of the pen to the computer, which is needed to transmit information from the pen to the computer, could detrimentally affect the weight distribution and thus increase static muscular load on the wrist. Finally, when operating any pen the forces acting on the pen itself are in an apposite direction to that in which the pen is pointing, i.e. from the screen towards the operator. This being so, to stop the fingers slipping down to the tip of the pen the operator has to grip hard with the fingers. Any design which will increase the finger/pen resistance, such as using a non-slippery surface or by putting grooves around the barrel (i.e. opposite to the direction of slipping) will help reduce the amount of grip required and thus the amount of static load.

Bar-code scanners

Bar-code scanners are devices which both look and operate like light-pens, although they are not used interactively with the computer screen. Instead, they are passed over alternate black and white bars, the composition of which contains the information to be entered. In some installations, in many supermarkets for example, the 'pen' remains stationary and the operator passes the code over it.

As with light-pens, little work has been published that considers the appropriate design and operating characteristics of a bar-code reading system. However, the increased use of such devices in all aspects of work seems to attest to their perceived usefulness. Thus Gilchrest and Shenkin (1981) report that the obvious saving for one large US supermarket chain through using bar-code scanners arose in the following way: 37 per cent increased checker productivity; 21 per cent easier cash register checking and balancing; 21 per cent automatic produce weighing and pricing; and 14 per cent eliminating pricing, reading or keying errors. It is not certain from their figures, however, whether the increased productivity arose from the reduced keying errors and so on, or whether it occurred because data entry using a scanner is faster.

Supermarket checkout customers also see advantages using scanners. Wilson and Grey (1984), for example, argue that a faster through-flow of customers can be accomplished, with itemised till receipts and lower prices as a result of more efficient stock control. Another advantage emphasised by Hoffman and Cramer (1981) is that the system reduces the operators' cognitive and motor workload—although Wilson and Grey question whether further reducing the load of an otherwise boring job is really an advance.

As far as the operator's performance is concerned, bar scanners do have a major advantage over light-pens in that their operating postures are not constrained by the computer system itself. Thus, the arm and hand do not need to be maintained under static load to enable the pen to touch the screen. The code on the product can be read at any angle desired by the operator. However, Wilson and Grey (1984) point out that the fixed 'pen' system of scanners, in which the material to be read is passed over the scanner, can create postural difficulties for the operator. In their study of supermarket scanners, they demonstrated that the fixed nature of the device and the amount of reach required created problems for operators with smaller stature. However, these are problems associated with the workplace rather than with the device itself.

Roller ball and mouse

As the name suggests, 'roller balls' are spherical objects which the operator can rotate in any direction. Their distinctive characteristic is that they rotate within a socket; thus they are fixed pieces of equipment. The 'mouse', on the other hand, operates in a similar fashion to the roller ball but is not fixed; the operator is able to move it around, much like a pen is moved around paper to form characters. In most other aspects, however, the two devices are similar.

Card, English and Burr (1978) demonstrated the superiority of these input devices over the conventional keyboard when used to move a cursor around the screen. Despite their apparent superiority in this type of situation, however, little research appears to have been carried out to determine their optimum parameters.

Roller balls can be manipulated in a number of ways. As Jackson (1982) illustrates, the fingers can be placed on the surface and moved, so drawing the ball surface along in continuous contact, or the ball can be flicked into ballistic motion by the fingers, with further flicks for additional motion. Friction pressure is then used to halt the ball abruptly. The palm of the hand can also be used in the same way as the fingers.

From these descriptions, it would appear that an important parameter in the ball design is the amount of surface area exposed to the operator, since this determines the extent to which displacement can occur without relocating the fingers, for example. The surface area, of course, is a function of the ball diameter. The size of the ball is also related to the friction and inertia that it presents to the operator; these will increase with ball dimensions. Unfortunately, information is not available on the sensitivity of operator performance to such variables as inertia and friction, although Bahrick (1957) has suggested that operators quickly learn the physical 'feel' of a control. They balance its friction and inertia against the amount that they want it to move, and gauge their manual input by this 'feeling'. The result is that each control movement takes a roughly similar time to accomplish. In a study performed in 1963, Rogers used a 3½ in (8¼ cm) ball to determine the optimum velocity at which the ball could travel for correct placement of the cursor on the screen. From his results, he recommended a maximum surface velocity of 28 in/s (0.71 m/s). When considering these recommendations it is important to remember that the velocities used by his subjects were related to the distance of the target from the cursor. Thus an inertial system which allowed this velocity would produce the fastest and most accurate responses.

Foot Controls

Pedals

Pedals are frequently used when large forces need to be applied with relative speed, but they are rarely used for the primary control process—this is usually reserved for hand controls. Historically this situation has arisen because it has been felt that the feet are slower and have less precision than the hands. However, as Kroemer (1974) points out, such assertions are based on very little data. Indeed, his own experiments suggest that an operator can be trained to use the feet with almost as much effectiveness as the hands (consider, for example, the precision with which an experienced motorist can control the speed of an accelerator pedal). Since the hands always appear to be the overloaded control channel (like the visual system and displays), efficient use of the feet may reduce operator overload.

Apart from the pedal size, which is clearly related to the amount of space available, the important parameters of foot pedals are the position and angle of the fulcrum (if the pedal is hinged) and the maximum force required to operate the pedal. These factors are clearly interrelated, as was demonstrated by Hertzberg and Burke (1971). They measured the force able to be exerted by 100 subjects using pedals set at different angles to the floor. As may be seen from Figure 6.3, an optimum angle of between 25 and 35 degrees produced the highest forces. This was verified by asking the subjects to rate their ankle comfort at each angle. Eighty per cent preferred angles between 25 and 35 degrees.

The angles suggested by Hertzberg and Burke are the initial pedal–floor angles—not the operating angles of the pedal. This should be related to the possible range of movement at the ankle, otherwise fatigue is likely to occur very quickly. In this respect, Damon, Stoudt and MacFarland (1971) suggest that 95 per cent of the population can attain an ankle angle of 20 degrees, and so it would appear sensible not to exceed this angle by any large amount.

In their experiment Hertzberg and Burke used fit, male aircraft personnel as their subjects, who were asked to push their feet against the pedal as hard as possible. As can be seen from Figure 6.3, under these circumstances forces of approximately 140 lb (623 N) were obtained with a 'neutral' leg position. Mortimer (1974), however, has demonstrated that although 95 per cent of his male subjects were able to attain these forces, a similar proportion of his female subjects were able to press with a force of only 70 lb (311 N). Once again, therefore, this demonstrates the need for the design of the equipment to take account of the type of operator who is to use it.

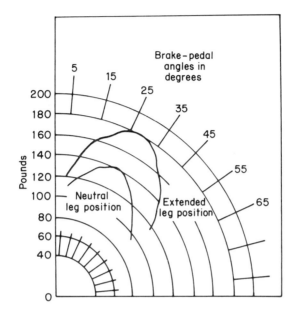

Figure 6.3 Maximum pedal forces able to be exerted in various leg and foot positions (from Hertzberg and Burke, 1971, reproduced by permission of the Human Factors Society, Inc.)

SUMMARY

With the efficient transmission of information to the machine via controls, the communication link is completed. However, as this chapter has demonstrated, the choice and design of appropriate controls are not independent considerations, they are highly related to the type of task, operator and clothing. Only when all aspects of the system have been considered can the information be transmitted from the machine to the person and back again in an unimpeded fashion.

7

WORKSPACE DESIGN

The discussion so far has concerned principles relating to particular aspects of the operator's immediate work environment, especially various machine components. According to this view the operator receives information (perhaps instruction) about the task or the machine from a colleague or a manual (Chapter 4) or from the machine itself (Chapter 5). Chapter 6 then considered ways in which the operator communicates with the machine via controls. However such features, although extremely important for effective information communication, are unfortunately not the only aspects that need to be considered. Any advances gained from an appropriately ergonomic design of displays and controls, for example, may be negated entirely if these individual components are inappropriately arranged 'in front of' the operator. This immediate area is often called the workspace—a term which should not be confused with the workplace, which refers to the arrangement of different workspaces. This latter aspect will be discussed in the next chapter.

This chapter will consider the principles governing how controls and displays should be arranged around the operator to ensure their most efficient use, i.e.:

- The position of controls with respect to other controls

- The position of displays with respect to other displays

- The position of controls with respect to displays, and vice versa

- The shape and dimensions of the operator's workspace

Although much of the discussion will centre around the relatively concrete concepts of a 'panel' that contains displays and particular controls, the wider workspace concept should always be remembered. For example, included in a car driver's immediate workspace will obviously be the dashboard (which includes both displays and controls), a steering wheel and foot pedals (controls). Taking the extended concept of a display as any feature that provides information, however, the car windscreen can also be considered to be part of the driver's display system. It displays a considerable amount of information regarding the machine's (the car's) operation *vis-à-vis* the road. Other displays are also present outside the vehicle, for example signals, road signs and even other vehicles. In the future discussion, therefore, notions such as 'display', 'control' and 'panel' should be taken in their widest sense—primarily in terms of the direction in which information is transmitted and arrangements used to aid this transmission.

Determining where controls and displays should be placed within the operator's workspace is not a simple problem. Not only do aesthetics and styling need to be considered, but also such factors as the operator's comfort and safety, the closeness of controls for ease of use, control separation for avoiding mistakes, the balance of work between limbs, avoiding operator overload, the need to satisfy a wide range of operator sizes, the layout of components to help operator understanding, and many other factors which are possibly not quantifiable. Because the problem is so complex, computer-aided design packages have been developed that enable the user to simulate practical situations on the computer screen and to test out various arrangements. Despite the apparent sophistication of such programs, however, the final decisions still rest with the human designer and will have to be made in terms of practical criteria based on ergonomic, person-centred principles.

GENERAL PRINCIPLES OF WORKSPACE DESIGN

When deciding how controls and displays should be arranged in front of the operator, the overriding considerations are that they should be able to be used quickly, accurately and without fatigue. For this reason an attempt is normally made to ensure that complementary sets of components are arranged so that they suggest to the operator how they should be used. Groups of displays and controls are arranged, therefore, in terms of the sequence in which they would normally be used, their frequency of use, and their importance. However, superordinate to these considerations is the basic requirement that the components should be accessible to the operator when they are needed. So relevant data concerning anthropometry and the positions adopted by operators performing the task must be obtained. In addition, as discussed in previous chapters, any restrictions placed on the operator's movements, by clothing or by other equipment, will affect these considerations.

Sequence of Use Principle

Time sequence

This principle suggests that if controls or displays are normally operated in some sequence—for example switching on a lathe, increasing its speed, moving spindles together, etc.—then they should be arranged in that sequence. All that the operator then has to do is to follow the arrangement provided, rather than work in an apparently random fashion.

A slight variation to arranging components according to a temporal sequence was described by Shackel (1962). In this case the temporal sequence related to reading the setting made by five rotary switches (note that this is an example of a component acting as both a control and a display: the switch is used as a control to make the setting and as a display to read the setting). In an original prototype, five switches arranged on a console in front of the operator were used to make a five-digit setting (see Figure 7.1). Unfortunately, however, the position of the switches did not suggest to the operator the order in which they should be used or read to generate the final setting value. The correct sequence was executed in the form of a capital letter W with the top left switch setting tens of thousands, the bottom left setting thousands, the top middle hundreds, and so on. When faced with such an arrangement the 'natural' setting sequence would be to set the first three digits using the top trio of controls and the last two using the bottom pair, so errors were clearly likely to occur. For his redesigned console, illustrated in Figure 7.1, Shackel simply rearranged the controls in a linear, sequential order.

Functional sequence

Having arranged the panel components according to a temporal sequence, it is also possible to arrange them also in terms of their function—either within the temporal sequence or in terms of a temporal sequence of different functions. For example, the workspace around a pilot may include components concerning altitude, attitude, speed, radio contact, and so on. It is common sense to suggest that all the controls and displays that are related to any one of these functions should be grouped together. However, it may also be the case that the different functions are used in a temporal sequence—for example first the radio, then the speed, then altitude, and then the attitude, etc. In such circumstances it is sensible not only to group the components according to their function (perhaps in terms of a sequence of usage order within each group), but to arrange the groups in the order in which they are to be used.

(a) Original W pattern

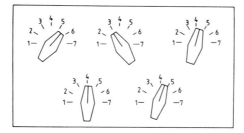

(b) Redesigned sequential pattern

Figure 7.1 Rearranging five switches to be used in temporal sequence (both settings read 54345) (reproduced from Shackel, 1962, *Ergonomics*, **5**, 229–41, by permission of Taylor & Francis)

Frequency of Use Principle

As its name implies this principle suggests that controls and displays should be arranged in terms of how frequently they are used by the operator. Thus the more frequently used components should be placed within easy sight and reach (directly in front) of the operator.

Importance

The frequency of use principle provides a useful guide to design, but, if it is taken to extremes, situations might arise in which a rarely used but nevertheless very important component might be positioned well outside the operator's effective area. Obvious examples include emergency controls. By their nature these are operated infrequently, but when they are required they have to be operated quickly and accurately. The frequency of usage principle, therefore, must be tempered by considerations of importance.

POSITIONING CONTROLS WITH RESPECT TO OTHER CONTROLS

Spacing

Once the controls have been placed in the optimum area in front of the operator (that is, having regard to sequence and frequency of use, function and importance), the next consideration relates to the specific position of each control. In this respect the amount of space allowed between each control can be very important. Too much space is likely to make the operator move the limbs unnecessarily or, if a large number of controls are to be arranged, will result in a less than optimum spatial arrangement. Too little space, on the other hand, may cause the wrong control to be activated accidentally.

The minimum spacing required between each control is determined largely by the kind of control to be operated (and thus the limb to be used), how it is operated (sequentially, simultaneously or randomly), and the presence or absence of protective clothing.

The necessity to design controls that fit the limb or part of the limb that operates them should be clear. For example, controls such as push-buttons which are operated by the fingertips will require less inter-control space than pedals operated by the feet. Similar 'common sense' can be applied to the manner by which the control is to be operated. Using levers as an example: if two levers have to be operated simultaneously the space between them will need to accommodate two hands (or at least the parts of two hands which overlap the lever handles). Sequential operation, however, is likely to be carried out using one hand only and this would require less inter-control space. Again, if more than one lever is to be operated at once and by the same hand, the inter-control space should be reduced sufficiently to allow the fingers to spread easily to each control.

Similar arguments may be advanced for other controls. For example, Bradley (1969d) measured the time taken to reach and turn four concentric controls arranged about a central point. He varied the spacing between the knobs (0.5 in to 1.75 in (1–4 cm)), the knob diameter (0.5 in to 1.5 in (1–3.5 cm)) and the knob configuration, and recorded the number of inadvertent touchings of adjacent controls.

Bradley's results indicated that performance increased rapidly with increasing distances between the knobs up to 1 in (2.5 cm), after which it continued to increase but at a much slower rate. Interestingly, his results also indicated that 'inadvertent touching' of knobs depended on their

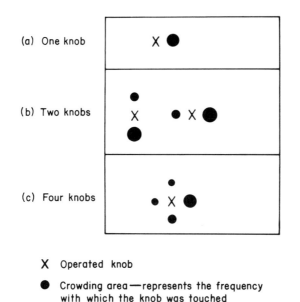

X   Operated knob

●   Crowding area—represents the frequency
    with which the knob was touched

Figure 7.2 The effect of the number and orientation of adjacent knobs on the likelihood that they will be inadvertently touched (from Bradley, 1969d, and reproduced by permission of the Human Factors Society, Inc.)

position. Figure 7.2 illustrates the frequency of touching when one, two or four other knobs were arranged around the knob to be operated. Whenever any knob was arranged horizontally to the one that had to be operated, the right-hand knob was always the one to be touched inadvertently. With a vertical arrangement, however, the lower knob was most vulnerable. These results, of course, might have been predicted since right-handed subjects were used. Thus, when using the right hand the right control knob would normally have to be passed over to operate the central knob. Similarly, with a vertical orientation an upward movement of the hand is likely to be used. The results are interesting, however, in so far as they illustrate that the position and direction of movement of the operating limb need to be considered as well as the position of controls on the panel. Table 7.1 indicates the desirable separation between different controls.

Accidental Operation

The problem of accidental operation has already been introduced when discussing the spacing between controls. For example, the 'wrong' control

Table 7.1 Desirable separations between different kinds of controls (in cm) (adapted from Morgan *et al.*, 1963; by permission of McGraw-Hill)

Type of operation		Finger		Hand			Foot	
		Push-button	Toggle switch	Lever	Crank	Knob	Between pedals	Between centres
Simultaneous		—	—	12.5	12.5	12.5	—	—
One finger/	Sequential	2.5	2.5	—	—	—	10	20
hand/foot	Random	5	5	10	10	5	15	25
Different fingers/ hands/feet		1	1.5	—	—	—	—	—

may be activated if too little space is provided between adjacent controls or if the controls are arranged so that the operator's limb movements will be such that they pass over (with the danger of touching) another control.

Even if controls are in ideal positions, however, they can still sometimes be activated accidentally. These mishaps need to be guarded against, and a number of techniques are available:

- Recessing the control.

- Orientating the control so that the normal direction from which any accidental activation may occur will not cause it to be operated. For example, if the operator needs to reach over a lever (so that the arms move in a vertical direction) orienting the lever to operate horizontally may reduce the possibility of an accident.

- Covering the control with a hinged cover.

- Locking the control.

- Operationally sequencing a set of controls. If controls need to be operated in sequence it is often possible to ensure that control 2 cannot be operated until control 1 has been activated.

- Increasing control resistance.

Control Position on the Console

Even if the controls have been arranged with an ideal spacing between them and all necessary guards against accidental operation have been incorporated, one further consideration still remains—locating the controls on the console for optimum reach and performance.

Reach is clearly a problem which relates to the operator's anthropometric dimensions, and this will be discussed further in the next chapter. Overall 'performance', however, depends on a number of factors including speed and accuracy. One of these factors, speed, was investigated by Sharp and Hornseth (1965). They placed three types of control (knob, toggle switch and push-button) in different positions on a console situated about 30 in (76 cm) from the seated operator. Their results, shown in Figure 7.3, demonstrate different performance 'maps' for the three different types of control. Thus the knob, for example, can be placed in a much wider range of positions than the toggle switch can before the same decrease in performance is observed, implying that the location of the toggle switch is more critical than that of the knob. Other, similar kinds of conclusions may also be drawn from Figure 7.3.

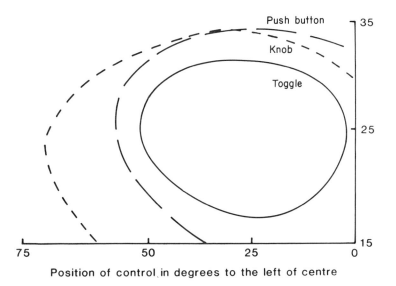

Figure 7.3 Ten per cent reduced performance contours for the toggle, knob and push-button controls placed in front of and to the left of the operator (from Sharp and Hornseth, 1965)

SPECIALISED GROUPS OF CONTROLS—THE KEYBOARD

Although controls are often thought of as being single units, or sometimes pairs of units, used by the operator to alter a machine state (for example, a switch to turn the machine on or off, or a knob to increase speed), these single units are sometimes used for fast, sequential operations, presenting information in bursts. The typewriter, data entry and digital telephone keyboards are instances in which controls are used in this way. Because the operator works with groups of either letters or digits, the key arrangement has to take account not only of the control spacing but of optimum control groupings. If the arrangement is not ideal, since a full-time typist may press up to 75 000 keys each day (Klemmer, 1971), fatigue may occur in both the finger muscles and in the muscles maintaining posture in the back.

Ferguson and Duncan (1974), for example, have demonstrated that the finger loads using a standard keyboard layout are maldistributed, with the ring and little finger being overloaded relative to their strength—see Figure 7.4. Rose (1991) has argued that the conventional keyboard requires the hands to be held with the forearms fully protinated so that the palms are flat down, a posture that exceeds the 20 degrees anatomical limits of most people. Protination is further increased if the operator needs to flex the elbow to less than the recommended 90 degrees between the upper and lower arm.

In essence three kinds of keyboard are available. First, alphanumeric keyboards, containing alphabetic, punctuation and numeric keys. These are mainly used for processing text. Secondly, numeric keyboards (sometimes called key-pads) which contain only the numeric keys with associated function keys (plus, minus, etc.) for entering numeric data. Finally, chord keyboards which are used to input both alphabetic and numeric information. Their characteristic lies in the fact that each letter or number is 'composed' by pressing groups of keys—rather than separate keys as with the alphanumeric boards and key-pads.

Alphanumeric Keyboards

The normal typewriter keyboard (often called the QWERTY board because these letters occur at the beginning of the top line) has been in existence since before the beginning of the twentieth century. It was designed by C.L. Scholes and his colleagues in 1874 (patented in 1878) to conform to the mechanical constraints of contemporary typewriters. The problem was that typists were able to press keys at a faster rate than that at which the machines, with their mechanical links and reliance on gravity to return the

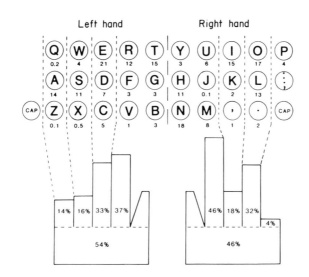

Figure 7.4 Distribution of finger strokes of each hand on individual keys using the QWERTY keyboard (Ferguson and Duncan, 1974; reproduced from *Ergonomics*, **17**, 731–44, by permission of Taylor & Francis)—the figures below each key represent the percentage of times the key was pressed when the particular hand was used

keyhead, were able to respond. The resulting key jamming was overcome by an apparently haphazard arrangement of the letters. The QWERTY board, therefore, was designed originally to slow down the typists of the day. Commenting on the continued use of this antiquated arrangement, Papert (1980) argues:

> There is a tendency for the first usable, but still primitive, product of a new technology to dig itself in. I have called this the QWERTY phenomenon. The top row of alphabetic keys on the standard keyboard reads QWERTY. For me this symbolises the way in which technology can all too often serve not only as a force for progress but for keeping things stuck. The QWERTY arrangement has no rational explanation, only a historical one.   (pp 32–3)

Various authors have suggested different reasons for the QWERTY arrangement. The first is a machine-based argument. For example, Norman and Fisher (1982) suggest that the arrangement is such that the keys are typed successively as far apart on the keyboard as possible, so that the type bars approach each other at relatively sharp angles with minimal chances of jamming. Hackmeister (1979) supports this argument but adds one further observation: the top row contains all of the letters in the word 'typewriter', and it was Scholes who designed the first 'Typewriting Machine'!

Second is an operator-performance explanation that supports the 'slow down' hypothesis. For example, Martin (1972) argues that the arrangement is such that the letter most likely to be typed next is obscured by the operator's hand. Biegel (1934) has suggested that the QWERTY keyboard produces less efficient performances because of anthropometric, biomechanical and perceptual factors:

- The ring (third) finger and little fingers have to be stretched when moving from the home keys to the third and fourth rows. This reduces the strength of the stroke and leads to the edge of the fingertip rather than the centre being used to hit the keys.

- Dividing the keys into parallel but oblique vertical 'strips' for the different fingers means that the strips for the fingers of the right hand present the same shape as those for the left. This is despite the fact that the hands are not congruent, but are inverse images of each other.

- Tracks from the home keys are difficult to follow so that often the wrong key is struck.

One positive feature of the QWERTY board suggested by a number of authors (for example, Kinkead, 1975; Cakir, Hart and Stewart, 1980; Noyes, 1983a) concerns the workload that it places on each hand—rather than on each finger. Thus, when typing English text almost all keystrokes alternate from one hand to the other. Noyes (1983a), for example, argues that common letter sequences typed on the QWERTY board involve either alternate hands being used, the whole hand being moved over the keyboard, or non-adjacent fingers being moved sequentially. The implications for well-distributed hand and wrist muscle loads are thus clear.

Despite this positive aspect of the QWERTY arrangement, and despite (or possibly because of) the fact that many millions of typewriters have been produced using the arrangement, a number of alternative keyboard arrangements have been proposed. All are based on the frequencies with which letters and letter pairs occur in the English language. The two which have captured most experimental time are the Dvorak and the Alphabetic boards.

The Dvorak board (patented by A. Dvorak in 1932) was produced as a result of a decade of physiological and language research. The main principles behind the arrangement are:

- Layout is arranged on the basis of the frequency of usage of letters and the frequency of letter patterns and sequences in the English language.

- All vowels and most used consonants are on the second (or 'home') row, so that about 70 per cent of common words are typed on this row alone.

- Faster operation is possible by tapping with fingers on alternate hands (particularly the most used index fingers) than by repetitive tapping with one finger. Since the probability of vowels and consonants alternating is very high, all vowels are typed with the left hand and frequent (home row) consonants with the right hand.

- Finger travel and consequent fatigue are thus greatly reduced.

The arrangement shown in Figure 7.5 was produced using such principles and Dvorak claims that this letter sequence provides a more even distribution of finger movements and a bias towards the right hand. This is also shown in Figure 7.5 (compare these figures with the finger analyses for the QWERTY board shown in Figure 7.4). Dvorak also claimed that this arrangement reduces between-rows movement by 90 per cent, and allows 35 per cent of all words normally used to be typed on the middle row.

There is continuing controversy over the relative merits of the QWERTY and the Dvorak keyboards. For example, a US government-sponsored study in 1956 demonstrated little difference between the advantages of each arrangement (Alden, Daniels and Kanarick, 1972). Martin (1972), however,

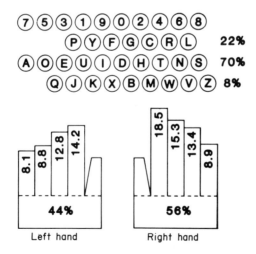

Figure 7.5 The Dvorak keyboard layout and workload distribution in typing English text—the row figures relate to the proportion of times the keys in each row are used

discusses (unreported) novice training experiments carried out in Great Britain which demonstrated a 10 per cent saving in training time using the Dvorak board. Furthermore, Dunn (1971) argues that the Dvorak board is superior in terms of ease of learning, reduced likelihood of error and fatigue, and increased speed of data entry.

In the alphabetic board, keys are arranged as the name suggests: from A to Z. The argument behind the use of this arrangement is, quite simply, that an alphabetical ordering of the keys makes logical sense, particularly to inexperienced typists who currently need to spend considerable time learning the QWERTY arrangement.

Despite the apparent logic of using an alphabetically arranged board, Norman and Fisher (1982) point out that the available studies do not support the view that inexperienced typists find the alphabetic board easier to use. Indeed both Hirsch (1970) and Michaels (1971) have shown that for semi-skilled typists, keying rates and error correction are better using the QWERTY board, and the performance on the two boards is essentially the same for novices. Norman and Fisher have also shown that typing speed is faster with the QWERTY board. They suggest two reasons for these apparently paradoxical findings. First, an experimental one in that it is difficult to find subjects who have not had some exposure to the QWERTY arrangement. (When they used schoolchildren as their subjects, Nicolson and Gardner (1985) demonstrated a distinct superiority of the alphabetic keyboard over the QWERTY arrangement.) Secondly, although logically superior, the alphabetic keyboard still requires considerable visual search and mental processing (to remember, for example, that m appears after k). At the novice stage at least, therefore, all keyboard layouts are equivalent. Once the skill has been learned, visual feedback gives way to kinaesthetic feedback so that the different board arrangements are likely to be equally efficient.

In summary, it would appear that, from the point of view of key arrangement alone, it makes little difference which type of board is used. Since the high cost of converting machines and of retraining typists to use the alternative boards is likely to ensure the continuation of the QWERTY arrangement, more valuable time could possibly be spent in redesigning the physical arrangement of the board to make it fit more closely the anthropometric and biomechanical properties of the user.

Before concluding the discussion of alphabetic input, however, one final point should be emphasised. The discussion has so far has centred around the arrangement for entering Roman characters into the computer (Cakir, Hart and Stewart (1980) describe some experimental boards for Spanish and German languages). However, as Chapanis (1974) points out, there are large numbers of different languages and forms of script, and the problems outlined above increase markedly when languages that do not use the Roman alphabet are considered—Japanese, for example, uses between 2000 and 4000 characters. To this end Brown (1974) describes the development of a Japanese card-punch machine which, as with the Dvorak concept, puts the most frequently used characters on a special high-usage region of the board. For example, about 70 per cent of ordinary Japanese can be written with 600 of the most frequently used characters. Grouping these characters together decreased the search time and the average distance which had to be reached when keying in ordinary text. Using these principles Brown was able to show that skilled Japanese operators could key about the same average number of words per minute, and almost as accurately, as skilled American card-punch operators working in English.

Numeric Keyboards

Compared with those investigating alphanumeric arrangements, fewer studies have been carried out to determine the optimum arrangement of numeric keys. This is possibly because, with only ten keys (0–9), there are fewer sensible key arrangements.

A number of these arrangements were investigated by Deininger (1960) in a study of push-button telephone sets. Four designs, shown in Figure 7.6, were shown to be roughly equally acceptable on criteria such as keying time, errors and 'voting' for and against. For 'engineering' reasons, however, Deininger suggests that either arrangement 1 or 2 be used for telephones. Indeed, the 'standard' telephone arrangement has now become that shown in arrangement 1; i.e. a 3+3+3+1 matrix starting with 1, 2, 3 on the top row and ending with 0 below the third row.

Although this arrangement has become standard for telephone key-pads, it is not currently used for numerical input on keyboards such as calculators. This is normally the reverse of the telephone arrangement, the keys on the 3+3+3+1 matrix having the order 7, 8, 9; 4, 5, 6; 1, 2, 3; and 0.

Conrad and Hull (1968) compared the keying efficiency of these two types of arrangement. No significant differences were obtained in terms of the speed of data entry, but they did obtain significantly fewer errors using the telephone key-pad (1, 2, 3; 4, 5, 6; etc.) than with the calculator pad arrangement (7, 8, 9; 4, 5, 6; etc.) (6.4 per cent versus 8.2 per cent).

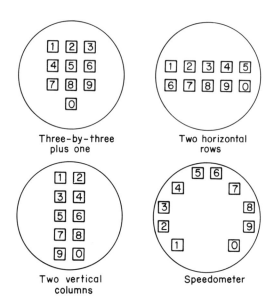

Figure 7.6   Four efficient numeric key arrangements found by Deininger (1960)

Chord Keyboards

In the search for improved ways of keying data, particularly alphabetic data, the possibility of reducing the number of keys by requiring the operator to press more than one key at a time has often been suggested. Such key arrangements are called chord keyboards and they appear in many different forms. Some are operated by one hand only (usually with five keys—one for each finger), while others are operated by both hands (with 10 keys). (Litterick (1981) describes some of these boards, and Noyes (1983b) describes the history and development of chord keying.) Some boards use groups of keys to form different letters while others, usually the larger boards, also enable words or parts of words to be created. By pressing combinations of keys, a large number of characters can be formed. In fact with N keys 2^N-1 sensible combinations can be made (one combination—no keys pressed—is not sensible in this context), while Eilam (1989) points out that if some of the 31 combinations serve as shift keys, 'an almost unlimited number of signs can be obtained by means of a small number of keys'.

The main impetus to reduce the number of keys arises from a wish to reduce the amount of time that fingers travel over the keyboard and the possibility of errors being made. If the fingers are hovering over chord keys (as they appear to do during 'normal' typing), the argument goes, the time taken to form characters and the number of errors should both be reduced.

Very few experiments have been performed to compare directly keying performance using a typewriter and a keyboard. As Conrad and Longman (1965) point out, this is probably because of difficulties in obtaining matched groups of subjects and being able to train them for very long periods using the same instructor.

Bowen and Guiness (1965) compared performance on a semi-automatic mail-sorting task using either a typewriter, a small (12-key) chord board, or a large (24-key) chord board. Both chord boards resulted in more items being sorted correctly per minute than the typewriter, with the small board proving superior. McCormick (1976) attributes this observation to the fact that the small keyboard did not require such difficult finger patterns as the large board. The superiority of chord keyboards over typewriters has also been established by Conrad and Longman (1965) who, like Bowen and Guiness, used a letter-sorting task. However, they continued the experiment for nearly a month. Their subjects used either a two-handed, 10-key chord board (with some associated control keys) or a typewriter. The results suggested that subjects trained on the chord board learned the key arrangement quicker than those on the typewriter (with an average of 12½ days rather then 20½ days) and, once learned, operated the machine faster. It should be pointed out, however, that most of the letter and number sequences used by Conrad and Longman were postcodes—apparently random pairs of letters and numbers. Whether or not the typewriter would maintain its inferiority with recognisable chunks of English is a question that remains unanswered.

Finally, the impression should not be gained that chord keyboards will automatically be more efficient than standard keyboards. Thus, as McCormick (1976) has pointed out, much is likely to depend on the combinations of keys which have to be pressed to produce particular letters. In this respect data from Seibel (1962) are important in that they demonstrate how different combinations of keys can lead to varying keying times and errors. Furthermore, the time required to learn particular key combinations is likely to be a strong function of the ease of remembering the logical arrangement of the keys to be used, and this is determined by the quality of the system employed to code combinations of keystrokes (Seibel, 1964).

POSITIONING VISUAL DISPLAYS WITH RESPECT TO OTHER DISPLAYS

The main consideration when placing visual displays on the operator's console is the physical relationship between the display and its associated control(s). This will be discussed in more detail in the next section. However, two features peculiar to displays should be considered. These are the display's visibility, and how the pointers are aligned when groups of analogue displays are used for check-reading purposes.

Visibility Requirements

Since the value of a visual display depends entirely on the operator's ability to perceive it, ensuring that displays are within the line of sight is an extremely important aspect of panel design. However, it is one which is sometimes overlooked because the problem can take two forms. First, visibility might be impaired because the display is obscured (either fully or partially) by another component on the console. This can happen quite frequently, particularly when controls and displays are placed close together. For example, a display located towards the periphery of a console may be partially obscured by part of a nearby control, simply because of the operator's position with respect to the control and the display. This aspect will be considered in more detail in the next chapter. Less obvious, perhaps, is the case when reaching out to operate a control can easily cause a display to be obscured by the hand or arm.

The response to a display can also be impaired because, although the operator's visual field may be quite wide, response speed and accuracy depend largely on the stimulus position in the visual field. Within a narrow range of positions, for example, it was shown in Chapter 2 how foveal perception is both faster and more accurate than image perception towards the retinal periphery; that is, towards the parafovea. Haines and Gilliland (1973) measured the response speed of seven subjects to separate lights placed in different areas of their visual field. Figure 7.7 illustrates their results and shows the various boundaries of equal reaction time over the visual field. The fastest response was obtained within an area bounded by about 8 degrees above and below the central sight line, up to 40 degrees to the right, but only 10 degrees to the left of the mid-point. This general 'oval but skewed to the right' trend can be seen in the other equi-response time boundaries—although the right side superiority reduces towards the edge of the visual field.

Haines and Gilliland suggest that Figure 7.7 can be used to aid the designer when placing important displays (particularly warning displays) in front of the operator. By superimposing the contours over a scaled-down model, the positions for the various displays can be pinpointed.

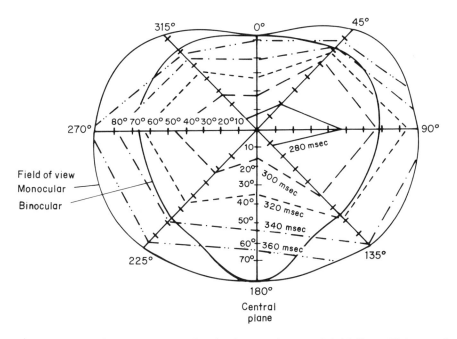

Figure 7.7 Equal response times for displays in the visual field (from Haines and Gilliland, 1973, copyright 1973 by the American Psychological Association. Reprinted with permission)

Grouping Displays

For check reading

As was discussed in Chapter 5, displays are not only used for making quantitative readings but also for simply checking that the machine state is within certain (perhaps safe) boundaries. Since the operator makes readings largely in terms of the amount by which the pointer deviates from a particular position, rather than from the precise dial reading, the task would appear to contain a significant memory component. Using coloured 'danger' areas on the dial helps to reduce the operator's load, as does the arrangement of the dial so that when showing a normal state the pointer is orientated to, say, 9 o'clock (White, Warrick and Grether, 1953).

If a number of displays are used for check reading, however, they may be arranged so that each facilitates the reading of the other. Johnsgard (1953), for example, has demonstrated that pointer symmetry (i.e. arranging the pointers to form a pattern) is possibly better than pointer alignment (arranging the pointers to point in one direction) for check reading. He compared four arrangements of a bank of 16 dials for check-reading accuracy. In the first arrangement the dials were each rotated so that, under 'normal' conditions, all pointers were aligned at the 9 o'clock position. For the other conditions the dials were rotated so that the pointers produced different patterns under 'normal' conditions (see Figure 7.8). Any deviation of a pointer would thus be highlighted by a break in the pattern.

Johnsgard's results clearly demonstrated that the configuration in which the pointers were arranged to point to the centres of groups of four dials (configuration number 4 in Figure 7.8) was less effective than any of the other three. However, arranging the dials so that the pointers were vertically symmetrical (configuration 3) produced significantly more correct responses than the simply horizontal alignment shown in configurations 1 and 2. Similar results were obtained by Ross, Katchmar and Bell (1955), although they could not support the contention that a symmetrical (patterned) alignment produces more correct responses than a simple, uniform alignment.

The use of patterns like these was taken one step further by Dashevsky (1964) who extended the lines made by the pointers under 'normal' conditions by drawing on the console (see Figure 7.9). Comparing these

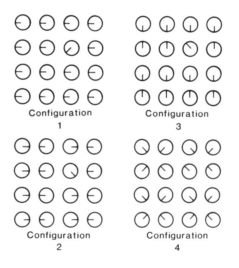

Figure 7.8 Four pointer configurations used by Johnsgard, 1953 (one pointer in each case is indicating 'non-normal') (copyright 1953 by the American Psychological Association. Reprinted with permission)

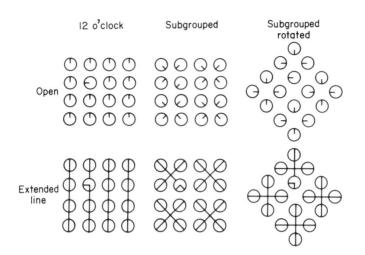

Figure 7.9 Groups of displays used by Dashevsky (1964) to investigate whether extensor lines between displays aid check reading (copyright 1964 by the American Psychological Association. Reprinted with permission)

extension lines with the open (no line) arrangement, he produced an 85 per cent reduction in error rate over a uniform alignment, and a 92 per cent error reduction when the dials were rotated as in Johnsgard's condition 4.

For flow diagrams

Different displays can often be grouped to provide the user with a 'working model', or flow diagram, of the process or machine, illustrating parts of the working system from which the information is arriving. For example, large panels are commonly found in modern railway signal boxes which graphically depict the rail sector under the signalman's control, the position of the points, and the movement of the train through the sector. Such displays help the operator to integrate different aspects of the total system which are displayed, and allows speedy location of faults or delays. Although such composite displays are very frequently used in large process industries, Morgan *et al.* (1963) caution that they are limited in terms of the additional space required for the connecting lines between displays. In addition, much of the value of the display is lost if too much information is presented in too complex a form. Nevertheless, flow diagrams allow the operator to feel that he or she has some involvement with the system being controlled.

POSITIONING DISPLAYS AND CONTROLS

A theme that has been emphasised throughout this book is that the information which flows from the machine to the operator and back can be seriously disrupted if any part of the chain is deficient (for example the display, the operator's processing capacities, or the control). However, even if each separate component is operated at its peak efficiency, the process may still be interrupted if the information received from one component does not 'fit' the expectations or requirements of the next link in the chain. For example, information displayed too quickly may overload the operator's perceptual and decision-making capabilities; a control with an inappropriate type or amount of in-built resistance may be difficult to operate because the operator lacks sufficient strength, and so on.

Taking this argument further it is apparent that, for information flowing in the display–operator–control direction, workload may be further reduced if a display is compatible with its associated control(s). Then, just as a well-considered display or control will help the operator because it 'fits' his or her capacities, components that are compatible with each other will require less work to complete the display–operator–control link. Of course, it is just as important to ensure that links in the opposite (control–display) direction are also compatible.

Before considering in detail the concept of display and control compatibility, as was emphasised earlier it is important to remember that the term 'display' must be taken in its widest sense. Thus any aspect of the operator's environment may display information about the machine and its state. The way that the machine itself behaves (for example, the speed at which a drill moves into a piece of wood or metal) is information that is displayed, as is the machine's behaviour with respect to the rest of the environment. For example, how a car moves along a road is displayed to the driver through the windscreen. In this case, both the windscreen and the car's movements represent the display.

CONTROL–DISPLAY COMPATIBILITY

In effect, a display and a control may be said to be compatible if one suggests how the other should be 'operated'. Compatibility effects can possibly best be exemplified by a simple experiment carried out by Crossman (1956) (described by Welford, 1976). Crossman presented his subjects with up to eight stimulus lights, to any one of which they had to respond as quickly as possible by pressing the appropriately numbered key. Two conditions were presented. In the first (high compatibility) each button was located below its light, and in the second (low compatibility) the buttons were arranged randomly. The results demonstrated, not unreasonably, that faster response times were produced when the lights (displays) and keys (controls) were compatible than when they were incompatible. As Welford explains it:

> presumably in the first [condition], once the light was identified the key was also, whereas in the second arrangement the light had to be identified first and then its number used to locate the corresponding key. In other words, in the second condition the data had to be recoded from digital to spatial form before a response could be chosen, so that the translation mechanism had more 'work' to do than when each light was located above its corresponding key.

In other words, in the low compatibility condition the display did not 'suggest' the appropriate key response. This implies, therefore, that people operate systems according to some 'internal mental model' of how the system should work.

As well as an increased response speed from using compatible displays and controls, Murrell (1971) suggests two further reasons why compatibility should be the goal. First, learning time for operating equipment on which controls and displays are compatible will be much shorter than if they are incompatible. In Crossman's experiment, for example, the subjects had to learn the new (random) arrangement before they could respond quickly. Secondly, under stress an operator's performance on equipment with incompatible display–control relationships will deteriorate as he or she reverts to the expected relationship. The example has already been given of a press operated by a lever that had to be lifted to make it fall. Whereas under 'normal' circumstances this incompatible operation was carried out efficiently, when a stressful situation occurred and the operator needed to raise the press quickly the 'natural' reaction was to lift the lever—thus compounding the problem by making it fall.

Fitts and Seeger (1953) suggest that this happens because a person's response can be considered to be a function of two sets of probabilities:

- the probabilities (uncertainties) appropriate to the specific situation in which the operator works—training, instructions, past experience, successes, failures, etc.; and

- the more general and more stable experiences or habits based on the operator's experiences in many other situations.

They suggest that training will nearly always lead to changes in the former but will have relatively little effect on the latter. Loveless (1962) takes this argument a little further by suggesting that the new (trained) behaviours do not replace the old behaviours which were learned as a result of past experiences and expectations—they merely overlay them. Certain situations may then arise in which the old behaviours may be stronger:

> During training the old response is weakened sufficiently to allow the new response to appear, and the latter is then strengthened by further practice; but the old habit has been suppressed rather than eliminated. The suppression is likely to be in part temporary, so the old response may reappear after a period away from the task.

He further suggests that 'it can also be predicted on theoretical grounds that habit regression will occur when the operator's motivation is decreased, when he is fatigued and when he is subjected to any novel change in the working situation'.

The implication, therefore, is that compatibility arrangements are learned, that there are more examples of compatible relationships in everyday living than there are incompatible ones, and that the more that one is exposed to these relationships the more likely they are to be expected. This begs the question of whether there are developmental trends in the learning and durability of compatible relationships, but unfortunately few data are available about this.

In the mechanical environment there are two main ways of arranging compatibility between control and display. First, spatial compatibility, in which the two components are compatible if the position of one on the console suggests that of the other. Crossman's lights and buttons in the first condition had high spatial compatibility. Second, movement compatibility, in which the control's movement suggests how its associated display is likely to move, and vice versa. For example, by turning a knob clockwise an operator would expect its associated display to indicate an increased reading. Such movement relationships which are expected by the majority of the population are described as 'population stereotypes'. (Petropoulos and Brebner (1981) point out that the 'clockwise = increase' stereotype does not apply when the control releases material which is stored or contained under pressure of force—taps that control water or gas flow, for example, are turned anticlockwise to increase the flow.)

Although spatial and movement compatibility are applied to physical controls and displays, the advent of computers and other forms of information technology has helped to bring the question of compatibility between 'controls' and 'displays' back to a cognitive/information type kind of concept. With computers, for example, a display may be considered to be as much a kind of result (say storing data on disk) as a piece of hardware such as a screen. Similarly, a computer command like PUT may be considered to be as much a control as the keys on the QWERTY keyboard. In these cases, the third type of compatibility that needs to be considered between display and control represents more one of cognitive compatibility.

Spatial Compatibility

As evidence that the need for spatial compatibility exists on all kinds of equipment, Chapanis and Lindenbaum (1959) investigated different control/display positions using four-burner gas and electric cookers. In this case the burners represent the displays. Four arrangements were investigated and the results indicated fewer errors as the control's position matched more that of the displays' (see Figure 7.10). Thus, in arrangement 1, when the burners were staggered to be in the same sequential order as the controls, no operating errors were detected. The same sequence of controls but with non-staggered burners produced some errors, but far fewer than incompatible arrangements. Similar results were produced later by Ray and Ray (1979). Chapanis and Mankin (1967) followed this study with an investigation of ten control—display relationships. In this case, however, the controls were in the same plane as the burners (displays), an arrangement commonly used with 'split-level' cookers.

Whereas population stereotypes exist for control—display movement relationships, as will be discussed later no such stereotypes seem to exist for spatial relationships. Thus Shinar and Acton (1978) asked over 200 subjects which sequence of controls they considered most appropriate using the burner arrangement described by Chapanis and Lindenbaum. Of the four most obvious arrangements (ABCD, ABDC, BADC, BACD) the first three were suggested by very similar numbers of respondents.

For these kinds of situations, it would appear that some further aid to spatial compatibility would be appropriate. Two suggestions have been made: first, to use linking 'sensor lines' between controls and displays (Chapanis and Lockhead, 1965); and second, to colour code the display and its appropriate control (Pook, 1969). In both cases the experimental results were remarkably similar in so far as the aids produced no increase in performance when the display and control had maximum spatial

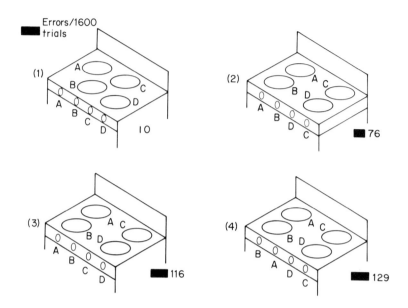

Figure 7.10 Four control–display arrangements used by Chapanis and Lindenbaum (1959) (reproduced by permission of the Human Factors Society, Inc.)

compatibility. When they were arranged incompatibly, however, large improvements in accuracy and response times were obtained (up to 95 per cent reduction of errors on large panels using sensor lines, and approximately 40 per cent faster response using colour coding).

Although the discussion of spatial compatibility has so far centred on visual displays, displays that use other sensory modalities may also be arranged to be 'spatially' compatible. For example, Simon and Rudell (1967) demonstrated that information presented to the right ear was reacted to faster by the right hand, while a left-hand advantage was obtained for information presented to the left ear. Since we have fairly accurate abilities to localise sounds, particularly at the lower frequencies used for warning klaxons, for example, these data suggest that the emergency controls associated with auditory displays should be located in the same direction as the display. Wickens, Vidulich and Sandry-Garza (1984) discuss the need for maintaining mode compatibility in this respect.

Movement Compatibility

Controls and displays are composed of moving (or in the case of digital or auditory displays, apparently moving) parts. Since the two components are related both in the machine and in the operator's 'mental model' it is important to ensure that the directions of their moving parts are compatible with each other and conform to the operator's movement expectations. Again it should be stressed that the display represents the means from which the operator receives information. A windscreen, for example, will generally display as much information as a dial.

The commonly expected control–display relationships which might arise have been fairly extensively researched and documented and can be divided into two subsets. The first group includes relationships in which the control and display are in the same plane—perhaps on a console. In these cases the general movement rule, using either linear (for example, a lever) or rotary (for example, knob or switch) controls, is 'up or clockwise' for an increased or right-moving reading, and 'anticlockwise or down' for a left or falling reading. In addition, to make the operator's task easier it has often been suggested that the controls and their displays should have the same appearance—that strip displays are associated with linear controls and dial displays with rotary controls.

If the types of control and display are mixed, for example a rotary control and a strip display, curious effects which sometimes deviate from these generalisations may be noted. This was first documented by Warrick (1947) (and is discussed by Brebner and Sandow, 1976) who pointed out that the indicator is expected to move in the same direction as the point on the control closest to the display. Whereas the expected movements of vertical controls and displays may simply conform to Warrick's principle, if the display is vertical and the control rotary then Warrick's principle implies that the side of the display on which the control is situated is important. Thus a clockwise movement on the left of the display would be expected to produce a reduced reading since the part of the control next to the display is moving downwards. The same control on the right, however, would need an anticlockwise movement to produce an expected fall in the reading (see Figure 7.11). Brebner and Sandow (1976) note that this effect is enhanced if the scale values are placed on the side of the vertical display which is opposite that of the control.

The second control–display relationship occurs when the two components are situated in different planes, perhaps with the display positioned in one plane with the control on the other side of a horizontal console. Using this type of arrangement the appropriate movement relationship becomes that which would occur if the two planes were imagined as being one simple plane, in which case Warrick's principle is invoked (see Figure 7. 12).

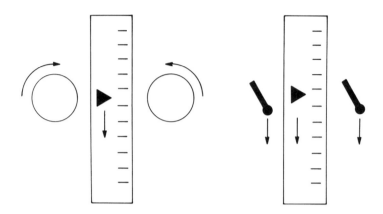

Figure 7.11 The different control actions required according to Warrick's principle, when the control is on the left and right sides of the display

Control–display ratio

When discussing movement compatibility, it is also important to consider the amount by which the 'moving' part of the control and the display actually move. This has implications for the sensitivity with which the control is to be adjusted. A small control movement which is associated with a large display 'deflection' means that the operator interacts with a highly sensitive system; like a 'hair-trigger' on a gun, a small movement produces a large response. At the other end of the continuum lies the low sensitivity system in which a large control movement is needed to produce a small movement on the corresponding display. (Like the terms 'control' and 'display', the concept of 'movement' must also be taken in its widest sense. This includes not only linear distances but, perhaps, degree of turn, number of revolutions, or even, as with the gun analogy earlier, the intensity of a reaction.) The ratio between the control and display movements is, naturally, known as the control/display ratio and is an index of the system sensitivity. Thus a low C/D ratio (small control:high display movement) indicates a highly sensitive system, whereas a high C/D ratio suggests the reverse.

The optimum ratio for a control–display system depends entirely on the system requirements and properties, and so there is no general formula that exists to help decide on an appropriate ratio. However, the optimum ratio for a particular system can be determined experimentally, as was demonstrated by Jenkins and Connor (1949).

Whenever a continuous control is used, the operator effectively performs two kinds of movement. First is a relatively crude, gross motor movement

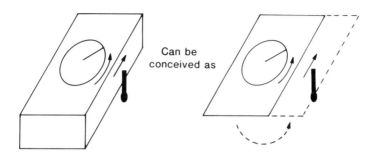

Figure 7.12 The application of Warrick's principle to cases in which the control and display are in different planes

to position the control in the vicinity of the final setting. Jenkins and Connor describe this as the travel phase. Second there appears a much finer movement, the 'adjustment' phase, in which the operator regulates his or her motor control to bring about the final control setting. The optimum control/display ratio, Jenkins and Connor argue, will be when both of these movements occur in the shortest time.

Figure 7.13 illustrates these relationships. Taking, for example, a system which has a low C/D ratio (small control : high display movement), the proportion of the control time used for adjustment will be higher than that for travel. However, as the amount of control movement required to produce a corresponding display movement increases (i.e. as the C/D ratio increases or the system sensitivity decreases), the time spent travelling will also increase. At some point the two times will intersect, and Jenkins and Connor argue that this will be at the optimum C/D ratio for that system.

Cognitive Compatibility

Just as it is necessary to ensure physical compatibility between the user and the system, through controls and displays, so it is important that they are compatible at a cognitive level. This means that the machine's 'conception' of what the user can do needs to be compatible with what the user actually can do—and vice versa.

The importance of such cognitive compatibility generally makes itself known when dealing with computer systems, particularly in relation to the concept of computer-centricity. This refers to the effects that occur when those who program the computer's operating system work to a model of the world in which the computer is at the centre of events. Unfortunately,

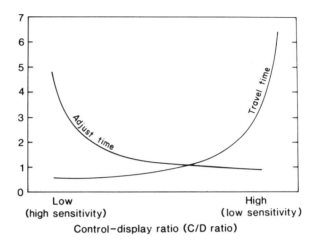

Figure 7.13 The relationship between adjustments and travel time for varying control–display ratios (from Jenkins and Connor, 1949)

when it comes to those who use the system, such a model might not be compatible with their expectations.

In essence, three forms of cognitive incompatibility can arise: linguistic, memory and perceptual. Linguistic incompatibility can occur at both a syntactic and a semantic level. As an example of the syntactic level, consider interactive commands that are often used by computer systems such as DELETE (to delete an entry or a file), MOVE (usually to move one piece of a file to another area), INSERT (to insert information into a file), etc. Accompanying each of these commands are usually two further pieces of information: the information to be deleted, moved or inserted and the file or memory area from which or to which the information is deleted, moved or inserted.

The incompatibility often arises because the information following the commands often has to be used in abbreviated forms, such as DELETE X, Y; MOVE X, Y; INSERT X, Y. In 'natural' language, the operator's own language, the above abbreviated commands might well be interpreted as DELETE (information X) from (file Y), or MOVE (information X) to (file Y), or INSERT (information X) into (area Y). If this is how the computer programmer or system designer intended the actions to take place, then there is no syntactic incompatibility. Often, however, commands of the form such as DELETE X, Y imply the reverse of what is expected in natural language, so that the command's syntax is intended to suggest DELETE Y from file X. Such incompatibility is likely to lead to disastrous results.

Semantic linguistic incompatibility can occur in a similar way, in so far as the system designer's view of the user's behaviour is at variance with the user's expectations. In this case, however, the problem concerns command meanings—particularly when the commands are computer-centric. Carroll (1982) discusses some of these semantic incompatibility problems. Examples might include the terms PUT and GET or LOAD and DUMP. Both pairs of operators are often used to transfer information from the computer to some storage medium and vice versa. However, the direction of the transfer is only immediately obvious if the user has already accepted that the computer is at the centre of the operation. Then PUT, for example, implies putting information onto the storage medium and GET suggests retrieving it. However, if the operator shifts attention from the computer towards the storage medium itself, so that this is viewed temporarily as the centre of operations, then the actions of PUT and GET become cognitively incompatible. Similar problems also exist with the commands LOAD and DUMP. Although a computer-centric user would possibly understand that information is DUMPed to a file, the word LOAD does not immediately imply that the information is LOADed from the file to the computer.

The second form of cognitive incompatibility that has been suggested is a memory incompatibility. In this case, the machine's requirements of the user's memory capabilities can be incompatible with the user's actual abilities. Again, linguistically incompatible terms can increase the memory load needed because they require the user to remember, for each command, the relationship between the variables X and Y.

Finally, there is proposed perceptual incompatibility. This relates primarily to the presentation of information as displayed on the computer screen and its relationship to the operations required of the user. As such this returns more to the spatial and movement compatibility concepts discussed earlier.

THE WORKSPACE SHAPE

By this point the reader should have a good idea of where individual components of the workspace (principally its controls and displays) should be placed. The final consideration is how the machine, the panel, the console should be arranged around the operator.

Regarding the complete console, again few experimental data are available to guide the designer in a choice of shapes. This is probably because 'sense' and 'aesthetic' principles (which are by no means complementary) have arisen over the years.

The 'common-sense' approach to shaping the workspace argues that an appropriate shape is one that allows the operator to reach all the controls easily and to see each of the displays. Thus full details are needed about the anthropometric dimensions of the user population: arm reach, hand sizes, sitting height, eye height, etc.

As Morgan *et al.* (1963) point out, the most appropriate shape to ensure that the operator can reach all controls easily is one with a continuously curved surface which effectively wraps around in front of the operator. However, this is often difficult to produce, particularly if large, flat displays need to be mounted on the console face. To overcome this problem, therefore, a sectioned console may offer the next best alternative, having angled side panels which can, again, be located around the operator. For this type of design, Siegel and Brown (1958) demonstrated that side panels at 50–55 degree angles produced the fewest operator body movements.

The problem is not so under-researched, however, when smaller panels are considered—particularly the size and shape of keyboards. This is understandable, of course, since the keyboard is one of the most prominent features of modern computer systems.

The physical dimensions of alphanumeric and numeric keyboards are clearly determined by the dimensions and arrangements of the keys which they contain. In this respect, the anthropometric dimensions of the fingers and hands discussed earlier are important. So, too, are the ways in which the keys need to be pressed—sequentially or in groups. This will determine the minimal inter-key spacing.

With respect to keyboard angle, or tilt, both Alden, Daniels and Kanarick (1972) and Cooper (1976) point out that there is a relatively small literature on the question of typing performance as a function of keyboard tilt. Furthermore, the few studies that are available suggest that, providing the board does not deviate too far from the optimum tilt, performance is not greatly disrupted. For example, Alden, Daniels and Kanarick report a study by Galitz (1965) who investigated the effect of a computer keyboard tilt on typing performance. He used slopes of 9, 21 and 33 degrees to the horizontal, and found no significant performance differences between them. However, his subjects did appear to prefer the 21 degree slope. This 'idealised' slope of about 20 degrees is substantiated in a study by Scales and Chapanis (1954). They used keyboard slopes of between 0 and 40 degrees to the horizontal, and their subjects were asked to perform a task of keying ten-character alphanumeric characters. Although no significant differences were obtained in either typing speed or errors, the 'operator preference data' suggested that some slope was desirable. Half the preferences occurred between 15 and 25 degrees.

Regarding numeric keying, as opposed to alphanumeric, Alden, Daniels and Kanarick point to studies by Creamer and Trumbo (1960). They used a key-tapping task in which subjects were required to tap keys in a particular sequence, alternating fingers and hands. Five tilt angles were used (0, 22, 44, 66 and 88 degrees). Although the maximum number of errors were made at 0 degrees, the variation in errors after 22 degrees was only very slight. Using an actual number keying task (telephone numbers) Cooper (1976) again showed that the 'best' key-pad angle appears to be around 25 degrees to the horizontal, since this produced least keying time and errors. However, he also points out that his data indicate that the effects of a deviation either way from this angle was quite small.

In summary, therefore, the optimum keyboard angle appears to lie between 20 and 30 degrees to the horizontal.

As an extension of the idea of tilting the keyboard, and taking account of biomechanical data relating to the ways in which the wrist and forearm have to be extended during typing, Kroemer (1972) describes a new type of alphanumeric keyboard (called the K-board) which is split at the centre and hinged backwards at angles of either 30 or 50 degrees—each half being operated by each hand. The main feature of the K-board is that the keys are arranged in straight columns (rather than offset as on a conventional board) and in curved rows. The space bars, one for each sectional keyboard, are bent from the inside of the keyboard to below the bottom row. Such an arrangement reduces the tendency to twist the forearm into the body noted by Ferguson and Duncan (1974) and prevents operating the wrists in the 'abnormal' (protinating) posture.

Kroemer (1965) reports that normal keyboard tilts of 15 degrees proved significantly slower and more fatiguing than the experimental K-board. With regard to the K-board itself, Kroemer (1972) reports an investigation in which four angular tilts (0, 30, 60 and 90 degrees) were used. Inclinations of 30 or 60 degrees produced significantly faster and less fatiguing stroking performance than either the 0 or 90 degree inclination. Nakaseko et al. (1985) describe an extension of this split board concept, with variations in both lateral and horizontal angle. Results from both biomechanical observations and subjects' reports indicate strong preferences towards this type of arrangement when compared with the normal, flat type of keyboard. Thus preferences tended towards a system of two half keyboards with an opening angle of 25 degrees and angled laterally (that is, lifted at the centre) by 10 degrees.

Results of studies by Zipp *et al.* (1983) support these conclusions. Their data suggest that horizontal rotations of the keyboard split by 26 degrees reduced different muscle activities by between 5 per cent and 60 per cent, while lateral inclination reduced muscle activities by up to 100 per cent.

SUMMARY

Having decided on the appropriate controls and displays, this chapter considered how they should be arranged around the operator—within the workspace. The overriding principles to consider are the arrangement of the components in terms of their sequence and frequency of use, and their importance. Having estimated these parameters, however, careful consideration needs to be given to where displays should be placed with respect to other displays, controls with respect to other controls and, finally, displays with respect to controls (and vice versa). Only when these aspects have been assessed will the link between the operator and the machine be able to work to its best advantage.

8

WORKPLACE DESIGN

When the operator's immediate workspace has been designed—displays, controls and consoles—the final part of the man–machine systems jigsaw concerns ways in which the various components (including both people and machines) should be arranged around the operator within the workplace. Just as the efficiency of a display or a control can be reduced by an inadequately designed console, so can the usefulness of different machines if they are poorly positioned. In this case, the concept of 'usefulness' probably reflects more the ease of use than speed or accuracy. If speed is a factor, its importance lies more in terms of the operator's mobility around the environment than in the faster reaction times which have been considered so far.

When discussing placing people and machines in the workplace the social relationships of operators themselves should also be examined, an aspect which so far has not been considered. As was discussed in Chapter 4, the kinds of communication link that are set up between individuals and between groups of individuals may facilitate or hinder activity. Existing social relationships can easily influence these communication links. Needs for privacy, peace and territory are different aspects of the social environment which will be discussed later in this chapter.

Perhaps the first decision that needs to be made when designing the workplace, however, is whether or not the operator is to be seated. Specific aspects of seating design will be discussed in the next chapter, but suffice it to say at this stage that although a seated operator will experience less fatigue, mobility will also be reduced. This chapter considers first the physical aspects, and then discusses some of the social factors, which are important when considering where people and machines should be placed within the environment.

PHYSICAL REQUIREMENTS IN THE WORKPLACE

Anthropometric Considerations

The need to design the environment to fit the operator's anthropometric dimensions has been stressed throughout this book. They are, perhaps literally, the most basic considerations for ensuring that a person is able to fit into the working situation.

Passageways

Anthropometric details are very important when considering the ideal arrangement of machines in the system. For example, if people have to walk down passageways or between machines, the space available has to be at least wider than the shoulder breadth so that both arms can be accommodated, as well as any clothing which the operator will be wearing. For 99 per cent of the population, Damon, Stoudt and McFarland (1971) suggest the following minimum dimensions for various kinds of passageways (including corridors, aisles and tunnels):

Height: at least 195 cm, or 160 cm if stooping is permitted
            (although this is undesirable).

Width: at least 63 cm.

If space is at a premium the passageway can be trapezoidal in shape, 63 cm wide at shoulder level and 30 cm at the feet. For gangways in which two or more people may pass, Damon, Stoudt and McFarland suggest the same height but increasing the width by approximately 50 cm for each extra person likely to walk abreast.

While these figures apply specifically to passageways that are bounded on each side by walls, it is likely that similar dimensions will also be required for gangways between machines. Indeed, a case might be made for increasing the width since, unlike walls, machines often have protruding controls which could possibly be knocked by a passing operator, resulting in injury or accidental activation of the machine.

Stairs and ramps

Anthropometric and biomechanical considerations are also important when the operator needs to move between different levels—using either stairs, ramps or ladders.

Corlett *et al.* (1972) compared the average energy required to climb either stairs or ramps which had slopes ranging from 10 to 30 degrees. Using oxygen consumption, heart rate and maximum knee joint angles as their comparison measures, they demonstrated that the physiological cost of stairs was always less than that of a ramp of equal slope. However, they also point out that stairs impose a particular gait on the user which causes increased knee-bending. For old or infirm people (and even those carrying loads which sometimes create an awkward gait) this makes ramps easier to use—regardless of the energy cost. In addition it should be remembered that ramps allow the operator to push or pull large loads between levels (within the constraints discussed in Chapter 3). Stairs make this activity more difficult and, if the operator is carrying goods, ramps are likely to be safer than stairs.

Although for normal purposes stairs require less effort than ramps, they still need to be designed to fit the user. Four aspects of the stair geometry are important in determining their ease and safety: first, the riser height (the vertical distance between one step and another); second, the tread depth (the distance between the front and the back of the step); third, the steepness (slope) of the stairs; and finally, the tread texture. The first three factors determine the amount of energy required, and the fourth affects the likelihood of slipping.

Regarding the riser height and tread depth, many architectural codes of practice still embody an eighteenth-century formula derived in about 1792 by François Blondel, Director of the Royal Academy of Architecture in Paris. From personal observation he concluded that the normal pace in level walking (said to be about 60 cm or 24 in) must be decreased by a regular and fixed amount to allow the foot to be raised in climbing stairs. His formula stated that the pace should be decreased by 5 cm (2 in) for every inch of riser. In other words, the tread depth should be 60 cm (24 in) minus twice the height of the riser.

Fitch, Templer and Corcoran (1974) point out that this formula has been passed down almost unaltered through generations of architects. This is despite the fact that in stairways which span either larger or smaller gaps than usual the rule produces either extremely narrow or extremely wide treads, corresponding to the higher or smaller risers. In addition, as was discussed in Chapter 3, anthropometric dimensions are generally bigger now than in the eighteenth century, and today's inch is shorter than that used by Blondel in his calculations.

As Corlett et al. (1972) and Fitch, Templer and Corcoran (1974) demonstrate, all stairs impose an individual gait on the user because of the knee and pelvic angles required. As a result of proprioceptive feedback this gait soon becomes learned as a person moves up or down the stairs, so that any irregularity in either riser height or tread depth might cause a misstep to occur. (This was well understood by castle builders in the Middle Ages who added an irregularly spaced 'trip step' near to the bottom of the stairs to catch the unwary intruder.) In this respect a worn step caused by continued use may be enough to make the climber stumble.

Although the gait adopted when climbing or descending stairs can provide useful feedback cues to the user, if it is irregular or accentuated it can also cause discomfort and increase the energy expenditure. Corlett *et al.* (1972), for example, demonstrated that subjects used less oxygen when climbing stairs with a 6 in (152 mm) riser than with a 4 in (102 mm) riser and, naturally, climbed the stairs faster. A larger riser height was also suggested by Fitch, Templer and Corcoran (1974) whose data suggested that increasing the height from 6 to nearly 9 in (15 to 22 cm) reduced the number of missteps. Biomechanical data from Mital, Fard and Khaledi (1987) support these findings in that they showed that a riser height of 102 mm, along with a tread depth of 305 mm, were required to produce the least movement at the ankle, knee and hip joints.

Finally, work by Irvine, Snook and Sparshatt (1990) considered the user's preferences rather than their biomechanical and biological efficiencies. Using a series of stair dimensions (risers, heights and slopes) they demonstrated that the optimum riser was 7.2 in (183 mm) high, with a depth of 11–12 in (279–300 mm). These dimensions were acceptable to all kinds of subjects, of both sexes, and varying ages and heights. Subject height became a very important consideration when the stair dimensions departed from the optimum, with larger subjects disliking the smaller dimensions and vice versa for the subjects with smaller heights.

The ideal tread depth is clearly related to the user's foot size since, as Ward and Bealding (1970) have noted, as the size of the tread decreases a point is reached where the shod foot can no longer fit on the step without being twisted sideways. This awkward movement induces a crab-like gait and a poorly balanced posture. If stairs are to be adequate for the largest people, therefore, Fitch, Templer and Corcoran (1974) support Irvine, Snook and Sparshatt's (1990) results and suggest that the tread will need to be 11.5 in (27 cm) deep. This allows a nominal 0.5 in (0.25 cm) between the heel and the riser, and the toe of the shoe can overhang the step by 1.75 in (1.5 cm) (on descent). Finally, all authors appear to support the contention that the steeper stairs cause less energy to be expended. Corlett *et al.*'s (1972) results, for example, showed that almost twice as much oxygen was used on a 30-degree slope than on a 10-degree slope.

Although the dimensions of a stairway may be designed to fit the eventual user, accidents can still occur if the tread texture is too smooth. This was illustrated in Chapter 3 when discussing how reduced friction between the walker and the floor can result in slipping. Kroemer's (1974) data, for example, illustrate how different combinations of shoe and floor material can aid or hinder slipping.

Finally, accidents when using stairs may be reduced if handrails are provided which facilitate a more stable movement, as well as helping to provide extra movement forces. In this respect, two factors would seem to be important: handrail diameter and shape, and handrail height. The first will determine the amount of grip able to be exerted on the handrail; the second affects the forces able to be generated and thus the stability in moving up the stairs.

Maki, Bartlett and Fernie (1985) investigated the optimum height of handrails for generating stabilising forces and movements when moving up and down stairs. Their results indicate a fairly linear relationship between forward and backward force generation and handrail height, although an optimum height of about 90 cm was demonstrated from both biomechanical and preference data. In a subsequent study the authors demonstrated that, within bounds, this optimum height was fairly independent of stair pitch.

Ladders

Rather than using lifts, which are space consuming and extremely costly to install, the other practical means by which an operator can move from one floor to another is by ladders. These are particularly useful when slopes greater than the 20 to 30 degrees discussed above are employed.

Ladders, however, are more dangerous to use than stairs. Data are not available comparing the probability of accidents occurring when using ladders rather than stairs, but the Royal Society for the Prevention of Accidents (1977) suggests that about 10 per cent of all falls from a height in industry involve ladders. Buck and Coleman (1985) claim that 17 per cent of the nearly 46 000 industrial accidents reported in 1982 which resulted in a fracture were classed as 'falls from a height'. Clearly such a category includes sites other than ladders, but the figures do support the contention that falling represents a significant feature of the accident data.

Dewar (1977) describes an analysis of one set of 248 ladder accident reports. Of these accidents 66 per cent occurred when the ladder slipped, either during climbing or when working on the ladder. A large proportion of the remaining 34 per cent were attributed to misplacing the feet or otherwise stumbling when climbing. It would appear, therefore, that two aspects of the interaction between the user and the ladder are important: first, the forces which restrain the ladder on the lower level, and second, a person's climbing action. For this second factor Dewar suggests two further influences: the ladder angle, which affects the awkwardness of the climbing action; and the climber's stature, which alters the knee and pelvic angles required to move up the ladder.

As far as the climber's behaviour is concerned, simple observation would suggest that all the limbs are involved. Ladder climbing is characterised by both the hands and the feet being used, the hands helping both to propel and to stabilise. Using films of climbers ascending ladders with different inclinations, McIntyre and Bates (1982) demonstrated four distinct climbing patterns: in the lateral gait, the arm that is on the same side as the moving foot is used both for propulsion and stability and is moved at the same time as the foot. The four-beat lateral gait is similar except that the hand moves slightly later than the foot. Less frequently used were the two diagonal gait patterns which operated in a similar way to the lateral gaits but the arm opposite to the moving foot was used. Clearly, therefore, since the hands are used to such a great extent in all types of ladder ascent, sufficient attention should be given to the design of the part of the ladder that the hands use—either the rungs or the ladder side. Unfortunately no data are available to make recommendations in this respect.

For an environment with fixed machinery it is likely that the ends of the ladder would also be fixed, thus ruling out any ladder slippage. For situations without fixed or secured ladders, however, Hepburn (1958) suggests that the 'quarter length' rule should be used: that is, the horizontal distance from the foot of the ladder to a point vertically below its top should be one-quarter of the ladder length. This represents a gradient of 4 in 1 or approximately 75 degrees.

This suggestion has been challenged by Dewar (1977). After recording the hip and knee-joint angles of both tall (average height 181 cm) and short (average height, 167 cm) men climbing ladders set at 70.4 and 75.2 degrees (representing gradients of 3 in 1 and 4 in 1 respectively), he demonstrated that the steeper (75-degree) ladder caused the body's centre of gravity to be further back from the ladder than was the case for the 70-degree ladder. This means that more reliance has to be placed on the hands for support. Under such circumstances, therefore, he argues that if the hands slip there is less chance for the person to regain his or her balance.

With regard to stature, Dewar's data indicated a slight, although non-significant, increase in the amount of leg movement associated with the shorter subjects. In other words, taller subjects ascended the ladder with a less natural, 'stiff-legged' posture. This difference increased with the steeper ladder. Since a forced and unnatural posture may result in increased errors, Dewar's data suggest that taller people are more at risk as the angle of a ladder becomes steeper. Hepburn's suggestion of adopting the quarter length rule, therefore, might require slight revision.

COMMUNICATION CONSIDERATIONS

As has been stressed continually, the operator's communication requirements consist of links in all directions with the machine and with other operators. These may occur via any of the operator's sensory systems, although the visual (for example, displays), auditory (for example, speech) and tactile (for example, controls) systems will most often be used. This means that the operator must be able to see the machines, move around and operate them quickly, and be in a position to hear and communicate with other operators and the machines within the system. The anthropometric and biomechanical requirements for moving around machines have already been discussed, so this section will consider the operator's visibility and auditory requirements, and the importance of arranging machines so that movement from one to another is reduced.

Movement Considerations

To reduce movement time between components, the principles governing the arrangement of people and machines in the workplace are similar to those suggested for arranging controls and displays in the operator's immediate working area. These are that the most important machines are placed within easy access of the operator, as are those which are used most frequently. Machines or workplace areas should be grouped according to function and, whenever possible, operator movement from machine to machine should follow some sequence of use.

Unfortunately, few data exist to enable these guidelines to be evaluated. However, an experiment carried out by Fowler *et al.* (1968) (discussed by McCormick, 1976) indicates that when controls and displays are arranged on the operator's console according to one of these principles, the average time for carrying out a task was lowest for the sequentially arranged components. The 'functional', 'importance' and, finally, the 'frequency' arrangements respectively took progressively longer. Translating these results into the gross body movement time of an operator moving between machines, however, is difficult and no comparative data exist. Nevertheless, without any evidence to suggest the contrary, it would appear sensible to arrange machines as far as possible according to these principles.

Visual Considerations

After it is ensured that the operator can move safely and quickly between machines, a further consideration is to ensure that visibility is not impaired—in terms of both machines for which the operator is responsible and other operators who may need to be consulted. Such visibility requirements could be hindered in two ways: first, if the illumination level is too low to be able to see accurately (this is discussed in more detail in Chapter 11); second, if lines of sight are obstructed by other equipment or by other operators, a problem that concerns placement of both machine and operators.

The problem may be overcome during the design process by very simple procedures which involve mapping the operator's sight lines. Usually this takes the form of running pieces of cotton or string from where the operator's eyes would normally be to the machines (and to the important parts of the machines) which are to be under his or her control. (Scaled models are often used for this purpose.) As long as the cotton can run in a straight line, the operator's visibility requirements will be unimpaired. Bends in the cotton indicate features of the workplace that will be in the way.

Sell (1977) employed a very similar procedure to design the structure of a moving crane cab used to transport steel in a mill. The shadow thrown by a small illuminated light bulb, placed at the position of the operator's eye in a scaled-down model of the cab, provided a preliminary idea of the directions in which obstructions to vision (caused by, for example, girders) would occur. He was then able to obtain more detailed information by running threads from the place where the operator's head would be to the various points that had to be viewed. Using these threads, it was easy to measure the sight line angles and thus to design the cab structure on this basis.

Finally, rather than providing for maximum visibility to as many parts of the operator's environment as is feasible, in some cases (or in some sight directions) it may be more sensible to ensure that visibility is obscured—perhaps by erecting screens. This is particularly useful in two cases: first, when requirements for privacy override communication needs (this is discussed in more detail below when landscaped offices are considered); secondly, machines might be sited to shield the operator from too high a glare source, such as a furnace.

VISUAL STRAIN AND FATIGUE FROM CLOSE WORK

A feature of the visual workplace that has received some considerable attention in recent years, particularly with the advent of computer workstations, is the relationship of the workplace to the visual load experienced by the operator. In some respects, of course, this relates as much to the workspace as to the workplace, but it is considered here because the problem involves as much the arrangement of workspaces as the workspaces themselves.

Dainoff (1982) presents a comprehensive review of studies investigating the effects of both short and prolonged use of VDUs on visual fatigue. All the studies he considered reported significant fatiguing effects, although it should be pointed out that many of the earlier studies lacked good control groups against which the results could be compared (groups of equivalent workers who did not use VDUs), and some studies simply asked operators what effect they felt VDUs had (this is not the same as asking what effects they actually had).

With regard to the nature of the complaint Läubli, Hünting and Grandjean (1981) asked a number of VDU operators to provide details of the visual impairments they felt were caused by VDU operation. From the responses they were able to extract two eye impairment factors, as shown in Table 8.1. The main group is composed of a 'discomfort' dimension, while the minor group of factors comprises, essentially, a visual impairment dimension.

As far as the effects of the task are concerned, Dainoff (1982) provides an excellent description of some of the work in this area. In particular he describes an extensive series of studies carried out in New Zealand by Coe et al. (1980) who sampled nearly 400 employees from 19 different firms. Their results demonstrated a significant difference occurring between the VDU users and the controls (50 versus 33 per cent)—but only for the fatigue-like symptoms. Creative workers (such as computer programmers) reported fewer symptoms than any other category of operators. Furthermore, full-time operators were significantly more likely to report asthenopic complaints (both fatigue and irritation) than were part-time operators.

This task duration effect has also been reported by other investigators. For example, Rey and Meyer (1980), in their study of VDU users in a Swiss watch-making factory, found that VDU operators who worked 6–9 hours per day at their terminals were significantly more likely to have visual complaints (73 per cent) than those who used their terminals for less than 4 hours per day. These patterns of complaints appeared to be the same for both young and old operators. Ghiringhelli (1980) also found that complaints of eye irritations increased for workers who used terminals for more than 3 hours per day, and they were significantly higher than for control (clerical) workers.

One reason for the relationship between eye strain complaints and the type of task probably lies with the amount of work which the eye muscles are called on to do—particularly the ciliary muscles which control the lens

Table 8.1 Factor analysis of eye impairments of VDU users (Läubli, Hünting and Grandjean, 1981; reproduced from *Ergonomics*, **24**, 933–44, by permission of Taylor & Francis)

Factor	Proportion of variance	Name	Symptoms
1	81	Visual discomfort	Pains
			Burning
			Fatigue
			Shooting pain
			Headaches
2	19	Visual impairment	Blurring of near sight
			Flicker vision
			Blurring of far sight
			Double images

shape. To perceive near and far objects, the lens shape constantly has to be altered to focus the image on the retina—a process known as accommodation. For practical purposes all objects further than 6 m from the normal eye are sharply in focus and the nearer the object is to the eye the greater the amount of muscular effort required to maintain the correct lens curvature. With 'normal' visual work, then, the ciliary muscles are continually varying in the level of contraction and, because they are performing dynamic work, can pump blood to maintain their oxygen supply, etc. For the type of work normally done at a computer terminal, however, this does not necessarily happen. The copy and the screen are generally placed close to each other and the operator's eyes rarely have a chance to vary the accommodation level from one which requires the ciliary muscle to be under constant static load. This argument is supported by findings of Starr, Thompson and Shute (1982) who showed that if operators wear correctly prescribed glasses, the incidence of complaints from VDU users is no greater than that from other workers.

Finally, Läubli, Hünting and Grandjean (1981) investigated how different aspects of the display affected these complaints. In particular, they considered the effects of luminance contrasts between the screen and the surround (arising from, say, windows and reflections off the copy) and the quality of the displayed characters.

With regard to contrast, their data suggest that it is the high-contrast displays which cause more eye complaints. Indeed, significantly more members of the high-contrast group reported that the complaints continued after work and even until the next morning. In addition, the extent of reflections off the screen correlated well with operator annoyance, although there was no relationship between measured reflection luminance and actual eye complaints. Regarding the characters themselves, the authors measured the extent to which the character luminances oscillated in brightness. Complaints of eye irritations and red eyes were more frequent from operators who had used displays with strongly oscillating luminances. Character luminance oscillation was also related to performance—with high oscillation leading to reduced visual acuity.

AUDITORY CONSIDERATIONS

Whereas the operator's communication channels from machines will be mainly in the visual mode, apart from the case of non-verbal information, communication with other operators usually occurs in the auditory mode. For this reason, assessing the levels of environmental noise and attempting to reduce the noise levels is important, as will be discussed in Chapter 10.

Noise is usually reduced at source by some methods of noise absorption—for example, by placing padding around the noisy machinery or by using sound-absorbing wall and floor materials. However, it is also possible to reduce noise levels by a few decibels simply by appropriate arrangements of the equipment. For example, Corlett, Morcombe and Chanda (1970) suggest that altering the positions of movable pieces of equipment produces both screening and reduced levels of reflected sound. They demonstrated a drop in sound level of 5 to 10 dB by judiciously arranging storage of work-in-progress material. Although this appears to be a small amount when compared with much larger reductions from sound-deadening materials, the authors suggest that small reductions can be beneficial by permitting considerable increases in tolerance and speech communication. However, they concede that the siting of such storage areas (or, in the context of the present discussion, other machines) should not override the other considerations discussed elsewhere in this chapter.

SOCIAL REQUIREMENTS IN THE WORKPLACE

So far, the discussion has centred around the concept of physical aspects of the working environment which may interfere directly with the operator's ability to carry out the task. However, it is important to remember that the environment contains other operators who will probably interact with each other, and these interactions can also affect performance. The physical arrangement of both men and machines, therefore, may inhibit or facilitate these more social interactions and can have important

implications—with consequent effects on the behavioural effects of the complete system design. Unfortunately, despite the fact that the operator's environment includes other men and women, little attention has been given to the influence of social environmental parameters on performance, safety or comfort. Two important aspects of the social space requirements are personal space and territoriality, and these are discussed below.

Personal Space

Personal space has been defined as an area with invisible boundaries surrounding a person's body into which intruders may not enter (Sommer, 1969). It may be considered as a series of concentric globes of space, each defining a region in which certain kinds of interaction can occur. The regions, however, are not necessarily spherical; sometimes they extend unequally in different directions. Savinar (1975), for example, has shown that people have space requirements in both vertical and lateral directions. If the available space is limited in one dimension (for example, by reducing the ceiling height), then a person's spatial needs will increase in the other directions.

Hall (1976) broadly divides the social space areas surrounding a person into four distance zones from the centre: intimate, personal, social and public distance (Figure 8.1), each zone having both a close and a far phase. However, as discussed below, the boundaries of each zone are not necessarily constant—they sometimes fluctuate under different conditions. The importance of these distances to the present discussion lies in the observation that only certain classes of people are allowed to enter each space area. The behaviour of a person whose space is violated may change considerably if the 'wrong' person infringes.

At intimate distance (close phase 0–15 cm; far phase 15–45 cm) the presence of the other person is unmistakable and may sometimes be overwhelming because of increased sensory stimulation. The close phase is typified by actual physical contact which, in many cultures, is considered taboo between strangers. Within the far phase the degree of physical contact is slightly reduced but increased visual awareness of the other person is maintained. As Hall describes it:

> The head is seen as enlarged in size, and its features are distorted ... The iris of the other person's eye seen at only 6–9 in is enlarged to more than life size. Small blood vessels in the sclera are clearly perceived, pores are enlarged.

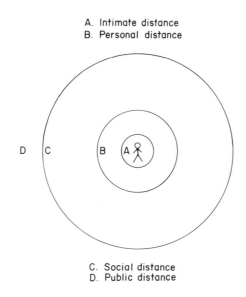

Figure 8.1   Personal space zones (to scale)

Although, as its name suggests, personal distance is concerned with friendly contact, fairly large differences may exist between behaviours associated with the close and far phases (45 to 76 cm and 76 to 120 cm, respectively). The close phase is reserved for 'well-known' friends, since a stranger moving into this distance may imply a threatening situation. The far phase begins at about arm's length and is the area in which normal social contact is made. The personal distance, therefore, may be conceived as a buffer zone between an area reserved for intimate acquaintances and one in which less personal contact takes place. Perhaps because physical violence may be perpetrated, only well-known friends are allowed to enter.

Interpersonal business is normally conducted within social distance (close phase 1–2 m; far phase 2–3.5 m). People who work together tend to use close social distance. It is also a common business distance for people who are attending a casual social gathering. If business is conducted at the far phase it has a more formal nature. Hall suggests that a feature of the far phase of social distance is that it may be used to insulate or screen people from each other: 'The distance makes it possible for them to continue to work in the presence of another person without appearing to be rude'.

Public distance (close phase 3.5 to 7.5 m; far phase 7.5+ m) is well outside the circle of social involvement. At this distance other communication problems may occur similar to those discussed in Chapter 4.

A stranger who violates a person's space (that is, enters a zone that is not reserved for the invader) may cause tension, discomfort and flight. For example, Sommer (1969) intruded mental patients' space by sitting too close to them on benches. The patients' typical reaction was to face away, become rigid, and pull in the shoulders. Within two minutes, 33 per cent of the victims departed while none of the control patients whose space had not been violated did so. Within nine minutes, 50 per cent of the experimental subjects and only 8 per cent of the control subjects had departed. In another study reported by Sommer (1969) female students working alone at a table in a library departed much faster than control subjects when another female subject occupied the adjacent chair and moved it closer to the subject. Interestingly, the 'defence behaviour' is typified by a lack of verbal response to the invasion. Only two of the 69 mental patients and only one of the 80 students asked the invader to move over. As Sommer suggests, this provides support for Hall's (1959) contention that 'we treat space somewhat as we treat sex. It is there but we don't talk about it'.

Flight is an extreme reaction to personal space invasion. McBride, King and James (1965), however, showed that subjects' arousal (measured by skin resistance—GSR) rose more sharply when they were approached from the front compared with a lateral approach. Both of these directions produced greater GSR changes than invasion from behind. Other less extreme reactions were recorded by Patterson, Mullens and Romano (1971) who describe both 'leaning away' and 'blocking out' responses, both of which were designed to 'exclude' the intruder. These responses increased in frequency as the intruder seated himself closer to his victim. Mahoney (1974), however, was unable to replicate the increased 'leaning' and 'blocking' responses when using control subjects whose space was not violated. This was primarily due to their subjects 'tensing up' and 'fleeing' rather than actively moving to block out the violator. Consistent with this interpretation are the findings of Mehrabian and Diamond (1971) who showed that relaxation decreased as chairs were located so as to increase immediacy.

Another study which demonstrated the arousal that can result from personal space invasion was reported by Lundberg (1976). He measured the level of catecholamine (a pharmacological stress indicator) in the urine of selected passengers both before and after crowded or empty train journeys. Significant increases were obtained under crowded conditions, and his findings were supported by subjective responses of increased feelings of discomfort as the number of passengers increased.

As an example of how the discomfort and stress that might result from personal space invasion could affect performance, Middlemist, Knowles and Matter (1976) recorded performance in a men's lavatory. In a three-urinal lavatory a confederate stood either immediately adjacent to a subject, one urinal removed, or was absent. They showed that both the onset and persistence of micturation was delayed significantly in the adjacent condition compared with the other conditions. Leaving aside the ethical questions of privacy which such a study raises, the results do indicate that personal space invasion may cause reduced performance, probably because the space invasion causes the individual's arousal level to rise higher than is optimum. As was discussed in Chapter 1, for example, over-arousal is likely to lead to reduced performance.

A study that investigated the effects of personal space infringements on tasks that are more appropriate to the workplace was carried out by Sinha and Sinha (1991). They considered the effects of spatial infringements on subjects performing either simple or complex cognitive tasks. Whereas infringement did not affect performance on the easy tasks, significant performance reductions were shown to occur when the subjects were asked to carry out the more complex tasks.

It is clear, therefore, that the invasion of a personal space zone by someone who should not normally enter causes a complex series of behavioural responses. The purpose of these responses would appear to be to 'distance' the intruder by the victim leaning away, turning, or more simply 'withdrawing' from the situation. In this way, an individual may temporarily shrink his or her personal space zone so that invasion is not perceived. For example, Sommer (1969) observed that people in a very crowded situation (such as a crowded train) seemed to control their potential discomfort from the overcrowding by behaviours such as staring at the floor or into space, thus relating to those close by as if they were 'non-persons'. The importance of such invasion, therefore, lies in increased feelings of unease, discomfort and stress with a possible loss of performance.

Many variables affect the distance of these different space zones and include personality, sex, age, culture, the status of the individuals involved, and environmental conditions.

Personality

Many studies suggest that subjects with personality abnormalities need more personal space, although findings are not totally conclusive (Evans and Howard, 1973). Several studies have also been carried out to examine the relationship between personal space and personality types. Patterson and Sechrest (1970), for example, found that extraverts have smaller personal space zones than introverts, but Meisels and Canter (1970) found no such relationship.

Sex

An examination of sex differences in the way we use space indicates that females have smaller personal space zones, and hence can tolerate closer interpersonal contacts than males (Liebman, 1970). When opposite sex pairs are mutually attracted it is not surprising to find that the magnitude of such buffer zones decreases considerably (Allgeier and Byrne, 1973). One striking difference between the sexes is in the positions which each adopts: research on attraction indicates that males prefer to position themselves across from liked others while females prefer to position themselves adjacent to liked others (Byrne, Baskett and Hodges, 1971).

Age

Very little research has been reported which explores the developmental aspects of personal space. Willis (1966) studied three age groups: older, younger and peer (within 10 years) and found that peers approached one another more closely than they approached those who were older. Age differences, however, are often confounded with status differences, the effects of which are discussed below.

Culture

Clear differences appear to exist in the spatial behaviours of members of different cultures. For example, Hall (1976) observed that Germans have larger personal space areas and are less flexible in their spatial behaviour than are Americans. Latin Americans, French and, particularly, Arabs, on the other hand, were found to have smaller personal space zones than Americans. Sommer (1968) found no significant differences in personal space between English, Americans and Swedes, but showed that Dutch have slightly larger, and Pakistanis slightly smaller, personal space areas. Sommer does suggest, however, that such studies are difficult to interpret fully because of language barriers which sometimes make it difficult for subjects to understand the purpose of the experiment.

Status and familiarity

In general, studies support the contention that external sources of threat (for example, meeting a higher status individual or one who is not known) lead to increased personal distance. Correspondingly, those who wish to convey a friendly impression or a positive attitude choose smaller interpersonal distances than neutral or unfriendly communicators (Patterson and Sechrest, 1970).

Environmental conditions

Mention has already been made of the effect of ceiling and wall constraints on the shape of the personal space 'bubble'. Adams and Zuckerman (1991) have also shown that environmental considerations such as the quality of the lighting and the direction of approach (which will be influenced by the position of doors in a room) can affect personal space requirements. Thus spatial requirements were lower in brightly lit rather than dim rooms, and increased as the approach angle varied from directly in front to directly behind the 'victim'.

Territoriality

Like personal space, territoriality is a concept that invokes social, unwritten rules of behaviour, with infringement causing discomfort and/or other behavioural reactions. It is a concept which is widely understood in the animal world but has only been considered comparatively recently in relation to humans. Territoriality differs from personal space, however, in that territories have fixed locations and do not move around with the person. Furthermore, the boundaries are often quite visible, being marked by recognised stimuli which may either be personal (like a coat) or impersonal (like a fence).

Although different societies and political systems have different rules governing territoriality, there exists a commonly shared distinction between territory (or property) which is private and territory which is public. Private territory (for example, a house) may be occupied or owned in absentia by a single person who has the authority to decide who may or may not physically enter it. Public territory (for example, status, streets, workplaces, etc.) is accessible to many different kinds of people and cannot be owned by a single person other than on a temporary basis.

Of interest to designers are the cases when a semi-private territory is set up in what is otherwise public territory: for example, reserving seats in a canteen, marking seat boundaries in transport, or the 'ownership' of machines and office areas.

Fried and DeFazio (1974) observed the territorial behaviour of commuters in a New York City underground train. The seating accommodation in each car consisted of four long benches (two on each side of the car), each of which seated up to eight passengers, and 2 two-passenger seats. No armrests or other means of delineating territory were present. The authors' interest centred on the use of the two-passenger seats. Under low-density conditions (up to 15 passengers) it was observed that only one passenger ever sat on a two-passenger seat, and the other seats were used in such a way as to provide a large degree of separation between passengers. Clearly, therefore, the two-passenger seat was regarded as 'territory' which remained sacrosanct even under medium-density conditions (16–40 passengers). Indeed, many passengers were observed to prefer to stand rather than to sit in the 'free' space on the two-passenger seats.

Territorial boundaries broke down under high densities (40+), however, with all seats being occupied and distances between passengers, both sitting and standing, being minimal.

From their study Fried and DeFazio concluded that certain implicit by-laws exist with respect to territory which can be applied to other situations:

- Seated passengers may not be challenged or deprived of their territory except under very special circumstances. Such circumstances include very high-density or other extreme conditions when a person may be asked to 'move over'.

- There shall be little verbal interaction between passengers. This explains the success of the many territorial markers which are used: coats or bags on the adjacent seat and books on a desk all indicate temporary territorial control. Another person who wishes to sit at the seat has either to ask for the marker to be moved (contravening this rule) or move it, which breaks other accepted behavioural standards.

No matter how well the physical environment has been designed to match a person's behaviour, therefore, social constraints may intervene to reduce the system's efficiency. So the value of the perfect seat (in terms of comfort and reduced backache) may be reduced if it is placed so close to another that the two occupants' personal space requirements are infringed. A well-designed seminar or boardroom (in terms of noise level, temperature, ventilation, etc.) may be rendered ineffective if the seating arrangements are such that either the occupants are unable to mark their territories (for example, not enough desk space is provided to 'spread out' their papers) or no account is taken of personal space requirements, with the result that the participants may tend to withdraw into themselves to maintain 'distance'.

At this point it would be pertinent to ask how these social space requirements may be accommodated within the confines of a modern work environment. The obvious answer, clearly, would be to increase the space available to individuals in a potentially crowded condition. This would result in a lower density of people, and territorial and personal space requirements would be met. In many cases, however, such propositions are not feasible. Indeed, sometimes the space available may not be able to be increased by a single inch. In such cases territorial requirements may be accommodated by providing fixed markers, for example individual armrests to delineate seats, or small, individual tables. Structures such as armrests might help to segregate sitters enough to avoid actual physical contact.

Finally, although physical space may not be increased, it may be possible to increase apparent space using appropriate interior design. Thus, it is well known that broad horizontal stripes make an object appear wider than is actually the case, whereas vertical stripes have the reverse effect. Interior designers know of other perceptual 'tricks' for altering the appearance of shape, depth, etc. Little (1965) has demonstrated that people take account of their background surroundings when considering their personal space requirements. Although the surroundings used in his study were the interior of a living-room, an office and a street corner, his results suggests that a background which makes the distance between two people appear to be greater than it actually is would help to reduce perceived space infringement.

THE LANDSCAPED OFFICE CONCEPT

A further practical solution to individuals' need for space is to allow them freedom to arrange their workplaces as they wish, thus allowing individual territories to be set up and ensuring that infringements do not occur unwittingly. The arrangement of both people and equipment in this freer way is embodied in the 'landscaped office' concept, said to have been proposed originally by West German furniture manufacturer Ebehard and Wolfgang Schnelle in the early 1960s (Brookes, 1972).

The important feature of the landscaped office lies in its lack of boundaries, so providing spatial flexibility to both employees and employers. Whereas a conventional office system might take the form of one floor of a building which has been further divided into smaller offices by fixed walls and doors, a landscaped office will use the same floor space but the different work groups are scattered around without being restricted by walls. Spatial needs of privacy and territory are meant to be accommodated by providing low, movable screens and allowing users, within limits, to arrange desks (boundaries) as they feel fit. The geometry of the workgroups, therefore, is supposed to reflect the pattern of the work process and is arranged by the individuals rather than being superimposed as a rectilinear plan. Furthermore, it allows workgroups to adjust work areas to the changing needs of their business. Brookes and Kaplan (1972) also point out that the concept insists that all staff participate—not just clerical staff and a few supervisors. Among the many advantages which were claimed for this type of spatial organisation were that group cohesiveness would be enhanced by the mixture of executives, management, supervisors and clerical staff, and that productivity would be enhanced.

The few controlled studies which have been carried out to substantiate or refute these claims do not lead to any firm conclusions. Brookes (1972) has reviewed much of the literature which suggests that information flow between workgroups and a perception of group cohesiveness might increase in a landscaped office, and that employees prefer the brighter, more colourful and friendlier design that a landscaped office provides.

On the other hand, this type of office arrangement produces a greater loss of privacy, increased noise, distractions and interruptions and, paradoxically, a perceived loss of control of the space around workplaces (Nemecek and Grandjean, 1973). In terms of the loss of privacy, this occurs at both a visual and an acoustic level. Thus, as Parsons (1976) points out:

> In the open-plan office, even with head height partitions, everyone can see whether or not someone is at work, present or absent, writing a report or reading the newspaper, thinking, catching forty winks, typing or with feet on the desk. Everyone can see who is talking (directly) with whom.

This last problem is interesting in so far as it suggests that allowing employees to have physical control over the size and arrangement of the immediate space is not enough to overcome territorial requirements— employees must actually feel that they have control. Whereas the landscaped office concept allows some physical control, because of the lack of privacy it does not allow users to have subjective control.

Brookes (1972), therefore, concludes that there is no strong body of evidence to support the claims of the landscapers. However, he also points out that evaluations so far carried out have been of a survey nature on existing designs rather than a systematic attempt to investigate variables which could be beneficial to the concept.

SUMMARY

When considering how the operator's workplace should be arranged, two factors need to be assessed. The first concerns communication requirements—communication with colleagues and machines (mobility, and visual and auditory needs). The second relates to feelings of ease and comfort with respect to the position of other people in the immediate environment. In this case concepts such as personal space and territoriality may help to explain how the presence of others might affect performance.

9

SEATING AND POSTURE

As we progress through this book it becomes increasingly clear that slight changes to components within the system, slight variations in the load that the system places on the individual, the expectations and experiences that the individual brings to the system, and how the system is composed from its components, can have significant influences on the effectiveness of the system and the operator's activities within it. As was indicated in Chapter 8, such principles even extend to the otherwise simple question of whether or not the operator is seated at the task.

A seated posture has many advantages, indeed Grandjean (1973) describes sitting down as being 'a natural human posture'. For example, because sitting relieves us of the need to maintain an upright posture it reduces the overall static muscular workload required to 'lock' the joints of the foot, knee, hip and spine. So sitting reduces energy consumption. Grandjean also points out that sitting is better than standing for the circulation. The blood and tissue fluids in a standing person tend to accumulate in the legs—a tendency that is reduced when seated; the relaxed musculature and lowered hydrostatic pressure in the veins of the legs offer less resistance to blood returning to the heart. Seating also helps the operator to adopt a more stable posture which might help when performing tasks that require fine or precise movements, and it produces a better posture for foot control operations.

Although seats offer these physiological advantages, seated operators are possibly disadvantaged in other respects—perhaps the most important being that mobility is severely restricted. As will be discussed later, a 'good' seat is one that helps the sitter to stabilise the body joints and maintain a comfortable posture. A person who has to move around the workplace will need to make radical changes to this stability to move from a sitting to a standing posture; if this is repeated too frequently fatigue will almost certainly occur.

A further aspect of sitting relates to the task to be performed. Because it aids stability a seated posture is often ideally suited for performing fine manipulative jobs. However, it is unlikely to be useful when hand controls have to be operated with large forces or torques. In such cases the operator's normal behaviour will be to rise from the seat to adopt an appropriate posture for carrying out the task—an activity which, in itself, is also likely to induce fatigue if repeated too often. Operators who remain seated at their tasks while carrying out heavy manual activities place themselves open to risks of low back injuries (see, for example, Boudrifa and Davies, 1987).

A third disadvantage of being seated becomes apparent in a vibrating environment, particularly if it is vibrating sufficiently strongly for the vibrations to be transmitted through the seat. As will be discussed in Chapter 10, the seat backrest, armrests and even harness may cause vibrations to be transmitted to the controlling limb—with the likelihood of reduced manipulative performance. Finally, although sitting is healthier in terms of spinal loads and short-term vascular circulation, prolonged sitting can cause health problems. For example, a sitting posture causes abdominal muscles to slacken and curves the spine, as well as impairing the function of some internal organs—particularly those of digestion and respiration. Furthermore, Pottier, Dubreuil and Mond (1969) have demonstrated that prolonged sitting for more than 60 minutes produces swelling in the lower legs, caused by increased hydrostatic pressure in the veins and by compressing the thighs resulting in obstructions to the returned blood flow.

Clearly, therefore, although a seated posture is generally less fatiguing and is likely to aid body stability when working, a number of factors should be taken into account before a decision is made about whether an operator needs to sit to perform a task.

Finally, as has become clear throughout this book, the design of any aspect of the environment has to be considered in relation to all other aspects; and sitting is no exception to this principle. Thus, as Corlett (1989) urges:

> It's [seating] design and functioning that will be influenced by the tasks to be done, the other equipment to be used, the environment and, of course, the individual human differences. It will be evident that there is unlikely to be one seat suitable for all jobs and the concept of the 'ergonomic chair' independent of the task is not possible.

This chapter considers three primary aspects of maintaining a seated posture. From each, guidelines may be derived relating to appropriate seat design: first, orthopaedic considerations which relate to possible damage to the sitter's health caused by poor design; secondly, muscular aspects; and thirdly, features of the behaviour of the sitter, who may be viewed as a 'comfort seeker' or as a 'discomfort avoider'. Finally, optimum seat dimensions which arise as a result of these considerations are discussed.

ORTHOPAEDIC ASPECTS OF SITTING

When seated, the body's main support structures are the spine, the pelvis and the legs and feet.

The spine consists of 33 vertebrae joined together by multiple ligaments and intervening cartilages, the functions of which were discussed in Chapter 3. For descriptive purposes the vertebrae are divided into four areas which correspond roughly to the areas in which the spine changes shape. These are the top-most seven cervical, then twelve thoracic and five lumbar vertebrae, followed by five fused sacral and four fused coccygeal vertebrae. From the viewpoint of seating design, the orientation of the lumbar and sacral vertebrae are important since it is these vertebrae and their respective discs and muscles that take most of the spinal load of a seated person.

Although when viewed from the front or back the normal, relaxed spine appears vertical, when viewed from the side its curved nature can be seen (Figure 9.1). The top, cervical curve bends forwards leading into a convex backward bend throughout the thoracic region. The lumbar region bends forward again, ending in the sacrum which is positioned on the pelvis.

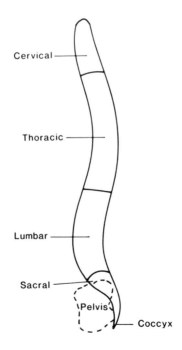

Figure 9.1   The shape of the normal spine viewed from the left side

When standing, the natural curved shape of the spine enables the body's centre of gravity (CG) to pass through the trunk and the feet, so requiring only minimal muscular activity to maintain a posture. Reduced trunk muscle activity is aided by the lumbar outward curve of the spine (lordosis) which brings the lumbar vertebrae close to or over the CG of the trunk, arms and head. However, sitting upsets this vertebral arrangement. Sitting with a 90-degree angle between the trunk and thighs, for example, causes the pelvis to rotate backwards which reduces the natural lumbar lordosis. This requires increased tension in the muscles and ligaments in the lumbar region to compensate for the movement of the CG towards the anterior of the body, leading to increased loads on the spine and the intervertebral discs. An appropriate chair design from the viewpoint of reducing spinal load, therefore, will pay particular attention to the seat pan/backrest angle; that is, to the amount of pelvic rotation.

Since the spine has evolved in this way it seems reasonable to suggest that this is a 'natural' shape and is also one that produces both the optimum pressure distribution over the cervical discs and static load on the intervertebral muscles. It follows, therefore, that a seat which causes a sitter to adopt a different posture will be likely to cause maldistributions in disc pressures and will result, over time, in lumbar complaints.

A number of studies have investigated the pressures between vertebrae when adopting various seat angles and postures. All arrive at similar conclusions and suggest that intradiscal pressure gradually falls when the angle is increased to above 110–120 degrees. Figure 9.2 illustrates data from Andersson (1980), which also demonstrate the importance of a backrest that provides support to the lumbar region. Andersson and Örtengren (1974) have also shown that a slumped posture produces *less* intradiscal pressure than does one that is upright—as adopted during typing, for example.

Regarding the actual spinal shape, Branton (1984) has collated data from anthropometric surveys that illustrates the general spinal shape of 114 people. Although very wide variability in measurements was reported, the shape finally produced does provide a starting point from which appropriate backrests may be designed. For example, in general the lumbar area extends to about 20 per cent of the full sitting height. This is the area which requires most support from the backrest since it receives the full weight of the rest of the body. The top of the thoracic curve, the area at which most 'back' pains are reported, extends to a position about 75 per cent of sitting height. It must be emphasised, however, that these are static measurements; sitting is very much a dynamic activity, as will be discussed later.

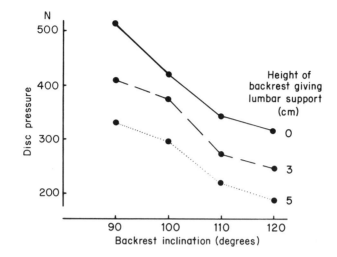

Figure 9.2 Relationship between disc pressure and backrest inclination with different levels of lumbar support (reproduced with permission from Andersson, 1980, copyright Academic Press Inc. (London) Ltd)

Using X-rays to study the spinal shape during different postures, Keegan and Radke (1964) suggest that the normal, relaxed spine shape is produced when a person is lying comfortably on his or her side with the thighs and legs moderately flexed—giving a thigh–trunk angle of about 135 degrees. Comparing the lumbar curve produced in this position with those in 10 other seated positions, wide variations in curve shapes can be seen (Figure 9.3). Keegan and Radke's data suggest that a sitting posture which produces the nearest approximation to the 'normal' lumbar shape is one in which the trunk–thigh angle is about 115 degrees and the lumbar position of the spine is supported. Their figures also suggest that a 'sitting up straight' position produces a great deal of spinal distortion. In this position the compressive weight from the upper part of the body is harmful to the lower lumbar vertebrae, and this is the cause of the discomfort and sometimes pain experienced when sitting in chairs which have this 90-degree backrest angle.

As may be seen from Figure 9.3 a forward posture causes the normally forwards-bent lumbar area to be straightened and, eventually, to bend backwards. Continuing up the spine this also affects the angles of the thoracic and cervical areas causing a 'hunchback' posture. If such a posture is maintained for long periods it increases the loads on the musculature supporting the head and produces both neck and back fatigue.

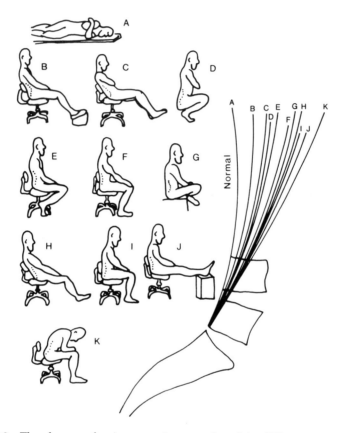

Figure 9.3 The degree of spine curvature produced in different postures (from Keegan and Radke, 1964, reprinted by permission; copyright 1964 Society of Automotive Engineers Inc.)

As the back moves from an upright to a hunched position, the pelvis makes a corresponding backward rotation because it is attached to the sacral area. Grandjean (1973) suggests, therefore, that seats should be designed so that in both the forward and backward sitting postures they provide support to the upper edge of the pelvis in an attempt to arrest this trend to rotate.

MUSCULAR ASPECTS OF SITTING

Because the positions of vertebrae are maintained by muscles and tendons, any alteration to a 'natural' spinal shape will produce corresponding stresses on the associated musculature. This increase in muscle activity can be demonstrated and measured by recording the electrical potentials (myoelectric activity) produced by the different muscles, a technique known as electromyography or EMG.

This kind of study was carried out by Floyd and Ward (1969) who recorded the activity of four groups of muscles (in the neck, on the collarbone, on the back just below the shoulder blades, and in the lumbar region) when the sitter adopted various positions. Their results fully support the conclusions from orthopaedic studies. Thus, again, 'sitting up straight' without any backrest produced fair amounts of activity in the lumbar region—presumably because this posture attempts to straighten the lumbar curve. However, the activity ceased as soon as a backrest was provided. A forward, hunchback posture caused most activity to occur in the upper back and shoulder regions, again substantiating the orthopaedic observations. Finally, of interest to all who write for a living, Floyd and Ward's data indicate that providing a table support on which the author can rest the arms does not reduce muscle activity. Indeed, shoulder muscle activity on the side of the writer's preferred hand increased dramatically. Similar findings were obtained by Andersson *et al.* (1975) from both EMG recordings and pressure recording in the lumbar discs.

Evidence from electromyographic studies, therefore, supports the orthopaedic studies in arguing for a backrest angle of at least 110–120 degrees. In fact, Andersson *et al.* (1975) found that backrest angle was the main seat feature that influences myoelectric activity. Again, however, such statements need to be tempered by the real-life situation. Thus Burton's (1984) EMG studies demonstrated that although backrest use is very important in reducing muscular activity, the technique adopted by the operator during a typing task had more effect on muscular activity than did the design of the chair.

An interesting use of muscle recording data was made by Mandal (1981) to suggest that working chairs should have their seat-pan tilted forwards rather than backwards. He measured the extent of sitters' muscle elongation in various chairs with both forwards and backwards tilting seat-pans, and demonstrated less muscle elongation and a more even pressure distribution over the seat using a forwards-tilting (by 15 degrees) rather than a backwards-tilting seat. He supports these conclusions with observations of people actually sitting.

Although this suggestion of a forwards-tilting seat will be discussed in more detail later, it should be noted that other authors have pointed to the importance of designing both the chair and the workspace to suit the anthropometric and muscular requirements of the sitter. Thus Freudenthal *et al.* (1991), for example, demonstrated that a desk that has a 10-degree incline in its work surface produced more upright postures with reduced lumbar load than did a flat surfaced desk. In a similar kind of study, De Wall *et al.* (1991) demonstrated that a 10-degree incline on the desk surface produced a posture in which the head was, on average, 6 degrees more erect and the trunk 7 degrees more erect. Clearly, therefore, an inclined desk surface helps to maintain a more appropriate posture, and such conclusions can be related to the discussion in Chapter 7 concerning the angle of the keyboard within the workplace itself.

In summary, therefore, both orthopaedic and muscular evidence suggest that:

- an upright and a forward leaning posture will cause fatigue;

- supplying a backrest will reduce some of the lumbar fatigue; as will

- an obtuse-angled backrest which helps to stabilise pelvic rotation.

BEHAVIOURAL ASPECTS OF SITTING

The Concept of Comfort

The discussion so far has concerned the effects of different seating positions on the body's stature, but it will now turn to consider postural evidence gained from the person who is sitting. At this point, a subtle change occurs in the criteria used to judge 'success'. Previously the criteria for successful design have been discussed in terms of the operator's response speed, accuracy and ability to cope with the incoming information. Fatigue and poor anthropometric fit have been emphasised as contributing factors that help to reduce performance effectiveness. In seating, however, the criteria are more in terms of reduced fatigue and excessive postural strain on parts of the spinal column. Muscular fatigue and spinal deformation reduce comfort and increase operator stress, and this, in turn, is likely to reduce performance.

The emphasis, therefore, has shifted to consider the user's physical requirements rather than cognitive and motor performance abilities. Since it is comfort rather than ability which is the main consideration with aspect to sitting behaviour, it follows that the term 'comfort' needs to be defined. (An accurate measuring tool can only be developed when the properties of the subject-matter being measured are understood.) Unfortunately, however, this concept is extremely difficult to define, primarily because it is such an entirely subjective concept; the features of a seat which one individual looks for in helping to adopt a comfortable posture may be different from those chosen by another. As Branton (1972) has suggested 'the problem is ... to relate measurements of a physical nature to subjective and essentially private experiences of feeling'.

The problem is increased further by the possibility that one cannot define or measure comfort as such—rather, we tend to think in terms of levels of 'discomfort'. Indeed, Hertzberg (1958) first operationally defined comfort as 'the absence of discomfort'. As an analogy Branton (1972) uses the definition of health: it is only possible to declare a person to be healthy when there is no evidence of illness. Branton further suggests that the absence of discomfort does not mean the presence of a positive feeling but merely the presence of no feeling at all:

> There appears to be no continuum of feeling, from maximum pleasure to maximum pain, along which any momentary state of feeling might be placed, but there appears to be a continuum from a point of indifference or absence of discomfort, to another point of intolerance or unbearable pain.

This argument suggests, therefore, that the ideal seat is one in which the sitter loses all awareness of the seat and the sitting posture. When in this state a person can give undivided attention to whatever activities may need to be pursued.

This concept of comfort leads to another aspect which deserves consideration—the reason for sitting in the seat; in other words, the sitter's motivation to sit. If an ideal seat is one which lets the operator pursue activities that have to be carried out, it is reasonable to suggest that a soft, low, easy chair, for example, will be unsuitable for a task that requires fine, manipulative work at a console. Branton (1969), therefore, has suggested strongly that a seat may be 'inefficient' in terms of the extent to which it interferes with the primary activity. So the assessment of 'comfort' sometimes needs to give way to consider the operator's 'efficiency', since it is unlikely that one can exist without the other.

A factor closely related to the motivation for sitting is the duration for which the sitter is sitting. Prolonged periods of sitting, for example, have been shown by some to lead to higher risks of back damage (e.g. Wood and McLeish, 1974), although others have failed to confirm these effects (e.g. Frymoyer et al., 1980). If sitting comfort changes over time, a chair that is designed for ease, comfort and long-term sitting would need to be assessed according to different criteria to one which is to be used for only a few minutes at a time.

The few data available on this point suggest that chair comfort is not affected significantly by the length of time for which the sitter is seated.

Grandjean (1973), for example, cites an experiment in which 38 subjects were asked to assess the degree of discomfort in different parts of their body after both 5 and 60 minutes of sitting. No significant difference was observed between the responses. This is not to say, however, that the duration of sitting has no effects at all on sitting comfort—it is simply that for the durations studied it had no effect.

The Behavioural Dynamics of Sitting

The discussion of seats and sitting so far has emphasised the fact that it is important always to consider the behaviours adopted by the sitter. For example, Mandal's (1976) observation that the front edge of a seat often assumes importance for seated workers illustrates the value of examining behaviour under natural settings. In addition, Grandjean, Hünting and Hedernann (1983) have demonstrated that people adopt different postures at computer workstations and that these can create different types of pain complaints. Finally, in their study of the effects of an inclined desktop on muscle and spinal load, Freudenthal et al. (1991) place great stress on the fact that the effects of the sloping desktop varied considerably between individuals. Individual behaviour, therefore, can often interact with the environment to affect the efficiency of a design.

As well as the spine, the main structures used by the sitter during sitting are the pelvis, legs and feet. These take the form of a simple mechanical lever system that helps to stabilise the body.

The hip portion of the sitting body—the pelvis—can be likened to an inverted pyramid. In fact, the main contact with the seat is made by only two rounded bones, the ischial tuberosities. Although this part of the buttocks is covered with very little flesh, because of the pressures placed on this area by the sitting person the blood supply to the buttocks can still be restricted. Indeed, Dempsey (1963) has pointed out that the human body supports approximately 75 per cent of the total body weight on 25 sq cm of the ischial tuberosities and the surrounding flesh (this is illustrated in Figure 9.4). He also suggests that this load is sufficient to produce 'compression fatigue', which varies according to the compressive load of the body and the duration of loading. 'In physiological terms, compression fatigue is the reduction of blood circulation through the capillaries, which affects the local nerve endings and results in sensations of ache, numbness and pain.' Branton (1966) further adds that, although the findings illustrated in Figure 9.4 relate to hard seats, they are not altered drastically when sitting on a cushion:

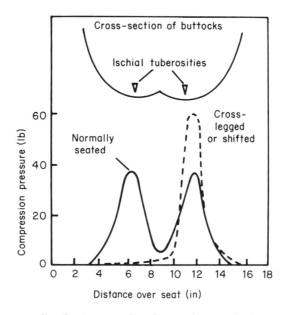

Figure 9.4 Pressure distributions produced over the seat during normal and cross-legged positions (from Dempsey, 1963, reproduced by permission of McGraw-Hill)

If the cushion is soft, it give as little support to the flabby muscle or fatty tissue; if it is compressed to the point of being solid, i.e. if 'bottoming' occurs, the cushion is no different from a hard seat.

The use of modern upholstery, however, may alter Branton's position slightly. Thus Diebschlag and Müller-Limroth (1980) recorded the pressure distributions of subjects sitting on either a hard seat or on one which was padded using polyurethane foam. As a result of the foam, the pressure values under the buttocks were reduced by nearly 400 per cent and the supportive area of contact between buttocks and seat was increased from approximately 900 to 1050 sq cm.

Similar conclusions were arrived at when the backrest was also changed. With the mass of the body suspended over what is essentially a two-point suspension system on the seat-pan, the system is mechanically unstable. This instability occurs because the body's centre of gravity is not situated vertically over the tuberosities when sitting upright, but about 2½ cm in front of the navel. This system is only made stable by the addition of levers provided by the legs and feet. Crossing the legs, for example, is a normal way of locking the system, as is resting the arms on a table or the head on the arms. The whole forms a most complex mechanical system which allows movement in both the horizontal and vertical planes.

Over long periods, blood circulation to the capillaries in the buttocks is also reduced if the body cannot move at regular intervals. If the body is confined in a relatively fixed seating position for more than four hours, the physiological functions that control the flow of body fluids slow down. This action, coupled with continuous pressure loading on the flesh, accelerates the rate of compression fatigue. Fatigue can be delayed, however, by periodic movements of all the major body segments. This results in changes in the loading conditions and allows muscular relaxation and contraction for adapting to new weight conditions.

For this reason, the sitter's behavioural repertoire is likely to include activities such as fidgeting which alter the pressure distribution on parts of the body caused by the compression fatigue. Indeed, the degree of fidgeting can act as an indicator of seat discomfort, as was demonstrated by Branton and Grayson (1967). They recorded the changes in sitting posture of 18 subjects during a five-hour train journey while sitting in one of two types of seats. On the basis of the significant increase in the number of fidgets produced in one seat over the other, the authors were able to recommend which seat should be adopted.

Any summary of these considerations (orthopaedic and muscular on the one hand, and behavioural on the other) must lead to antagonistic requirements for seat design. Thus, the orthopaedic and muscular considerations suggest strongly that the sitter should be supported as much as possible; that the intervertebral discs and muscles should be constrained so that the pressures they experience should not be excessive. The behavioural evidence, however, suggests that the seat should allow the sitter to move body parts; that the sitter often needs to fidget to reduce compression fatigue. Unfortunately, a seat that allows movement is unlikely to be one which provides a great deal of support.

To accommodate these two requirements from the viewpoint of the sitter's behaviour, Branton (1966) has formulated a theory of postural homeostasis. Homeostasis is widely understood in physiology and concerns the self-regulation of body functions. A common example is body temperature regulation: if the body temperature rises, sweat is produced which, when it evaporates, has a cooling effect. If the body becomes cold, however, blood is routed away from the skin to warmer, central parts of the body (thus giving cold skin its characteristic bluish appearance).

One of the characteristics of such homeostatic activities is that they are automatic; they are not under deliberate, conscious control. Awareness only comes with drastic changes of conditions and then only after the event has occurred. Branton argues that postural activity falls into the same category of autonomic regulation and that postural homeostasis is a process by which the sitter strikes a compromise between needs for stability and variety. Sitting behaviour, therefore, is characterised by cycles of inactivity and activity and so an efficient and comfortable chair needs to be able to accommodate these homeostatic requirements and allow both stability and flexibility.

SEAT DESIGN

A number of principles for seat design can be extracted from the above discussion. These include:

- The type and dimensions of the seat are related to the reason for sitting.

- The seat dimensions should fit appropriate anthropometric dimensions of the sitter.

- The chair should be designed to provide support and stability for the sitter.

- The chair should be designed to allow the sitter to vary posture, but the fabric should resist slipping when there is fidgeting.

- Backrests, particularly those prominent in the lumbar region, will reduce the stresses on this part of the spinal column.

- The seat-pan requires sufficient padding and firmness to help distribute body weight pressures from the ischial tuberosities.

Regarding the motivation for sitting, seats may be divided simply into three groups. First are the easy, comfortable chairs used for relaxation. In these the criterion for an effective chair should be, in Branton's terms, lost awareness of the seat and minimal discomfort of any part of the body's supporting structure. The second group includes chairs that are used for work. In these cases stability is an important consideration, requiring adequate lumbar support and body weight distribution over the seat-pan. The final group includes the kind of chairs that Grandjean (1973) describes as 'multipurpose' chairs. These may be used for a variety of different purposes, for example they could be used at a table, occasionally for working, or as spare chairs that frequently have to be stacked.

Regardless of the seat function its linear dimensions must fit those of the likely user population. This by now is axiomatic and appropriate anthropometric data exist. Normally these figures all relate to an unclothed sitter, so the presence of clothing and footwear will increase the dimensions by a proportional amount. The dimensions indicated below will take account of this factor.

Seat height: easy chair 38 to 45cm; workchair 43 to 50 cm.   The seat height is adjusted correctly when the sitter's thighs are horizontal, the lower legs vertical, and the feet flat on the floor. This is because the soft underside of the thighs is not suitable for sustained compression, and pressure from the front edge of the seat-pan can become uncomfortable. For this reason, the limiting case for the seat height is that of the short-legged person who would be prevented from resting his or her feet on the floor.

The reason for the different recommended seat heights between easy and working or multipurpose chairs is because of the way in which they are likely to be used. The height of an easy chair should allow the legs to be stretched forward since this is one of the preferred relaxing postures, as well as to helping to stabilise the body. For a working chair, however, the sitter is likely to be in a more upright posture with feet flat on the floor.

Many authors recommend that working chairs should be designed to enable height adjustment to accommodate the wide range of workers who may have to use them. If the chair has to be higher than the recommended dimensions (perhaps because of a tall machine or high workbench) an adjustable footrest is also recommended. Grandjean (1973) also argues that the optimal height for a work seat can only be decided in relation to the height of the working surface. This optimal height, he suggests, should be between 24 and 30 cm below the working surface.

Finally, Arborelius, Wretenberg and Lindberg (1992) point to circumstances where the seat might need to be much higher than any of the above criteria would suggest. They considered the heights of work stools and demonstrated that the effort involved in rising from a low stool or an 'ordinary' seat without armrests is much higher than from a high stool. They thus recommend that high stools are valuable alternatives for people who frequently have to change between sitting and standing postures.

Seat width: 40–43 cm.   In this case the largest person needs to be accommodated. Since the appropriate dimension is the hip width, and since there are significant sex differences in this dimension, the limiting case should be the upper range of the female sitter.

Seat depth: easy chair 43 to 45 cm; workchair 35 to 40 cm.   An appropriate seat depth ensures that all potential sitters find support in the lumbar area from the backrest. Seats deeper than the thigh length of the shortest person will mean that the front edge of the seat will restrain the sitter, causing the lumbar area to curve to reach the backrest. In addition, pressure-sensitive areas at the back of the knee will be pressed against the seat. For a workchair that will be used by a large proportion of the population, the recommendation is to make the seat depth accommodate even shorter people, since the only consequence of taller members sitting in such a seat will be that knees protrude slightly at the front. As long as the seat height is adequate and the feet can be placed flat on the floor, this is unlikely to induce compression fatigue in the thighs.

Seat angle: easy chair 19 to 20 degrees; workchair less than 3 degrees.   This refers to the angle of the seat-pan to the horizontal. A seat-pan that is tilted backwards has two advantages. First, because of gravity the sitter is moved towards the backrest, so supporting the back and reducing static load on the back muscles. Secondly, the slight seat-pan inclination at the front helps to prevent the gradual slippage from the seat that was observed to occur over long periods in the sitting study by Branton and Grayson (1967). The 20-degree optimal inclination is supported by Andersson (1980) who measured the amount of EMG activity in the back muscles at different backrest angles. His results, shown in Figure 9.5, illustrate well the value of the sloping backrest.

There seems, however, to be a large divergence in the recommendations

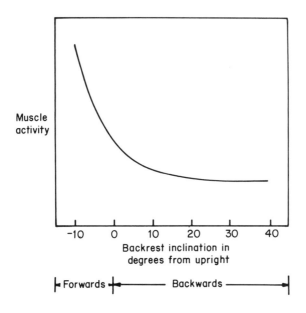

Figure 9.5 The relationship between back muscle activity and backrest inclination (reproduced with permission from Andersson (1980), 'The load on the lumbar spine during sitting postures'. In D.J. Oborne and J.A. Levis (eds.), *Human Factors in Transport Research, Vol. II.* Copyright by Academic Press Inc. (London) Ltd)

proposed for easy chairs and those suggested for workchairs. These relate to the chair's function and to the motivation for sitting. In an easy chair the sitter wishes to relax, the most relaxing position, of course, being horizontal. A backwards-sloping seat-pan helps to attain this. In a working chair, however, the requirements are to be positioned for easy access to a work area in front. A backwards-tilting seat would mean that an operator would have to bend forwards and would curve the spine unnecessarily.

Mandal (1976) has taken this further to argue that since most work is carried out in a forward-bending posture, a forwards-sloping seat is more appropriate. He suggests that a backwards-sloping seated work chair of even 5 degrees will cause straightening of the lumbar area and thus discomfort. For this reason, he suggests that a sitter will gradually tend to sit on the front edge of a seat, pivoted at the thighs. 'That this position really is one of the most frequently used can quite clearly be seen as only the front part of the seat covers of old office chairs is worn; the rear part being almost untouched.' (This is a good example of an unobtrusive investigation, as discussed in Chapter 14.)

As was discussed earlier, Mandal measured the amount of muscle elongation of sitters in various chairs with both forwards- and backwards-tilting seat-pans, and demonstrated less muscle elongation and a more even pressure distribution over the seat using a forwards-tilting (by 15 degrees) rather than a backwards-tilting seat. Data from Bridger (1988) reinforces this observation in that postures exhibited less trunk flexion when a sloping chair was used (which sloped forwards by 25 degrees; subjects almost 'kneeled' on a knee-pad that had a 45-degree angle) than when sitting in a 'normal' chair. When this chair was used in conjunction with a sloping desk (by 15 degrees) less neck flexion and a more upright trunk were also observed.

This suggestion of a forwards-tilting seat should only be considered in relation to appropriate seat coverings, however, which will increase the sitter/seat friction. Otherwise, the tendency to slip forward out of the seat (Branton and Grayson, 1967) will be exacerbated and will have to be counteracted either by muscular activity, particularly in the legs, or by increased pressure on the knees resting on the knee-pad.

As well as reducing muscular activity, a forwards-tilting seat may have another advantage: helping the sitter rise from the seat. Rising from a chair places quite considerable loads on both the spine and the knees. For example, Andersson, Örtengren and Nachemson (1982) demonstrated that intra-discal pressures doubled during the act of rising from a seat. Using armrests reduced this effect. Similarly, Ellis *et al.* (1979) demonstrated knee joint forces almost seven times the body weight when rising. A motorised chair, in which the seat-pan lifts and tilts forwards to aid the person in rising, considerably reduced these forces. Mandal's forwards-tilting seat, therefore, could also help in this respect.

Backrest height and width: up to 48 to 63 cm high; 35 to 48 cm wide. Proposed backrest dimensions relate, quite simply, to the distance from the shoulder to the underside of the buttocks (height) and to the shoulder width (width). The height dimension, of course, extends from the compressed seat if padding is present.

As has become apparent, however, the linear dimensions of the backrest are only part of the consideration. Since its function is concerned as much with maintaining a relaxed (that is, non-fatiguing) spinal posture, the backrest shape and the angle it makes with the seat-pan are extremely important. In addition, since spinal curvature varies considerably from one person to another, a complex relation between height and shape arises. In this respect, data concerning spinal shapes discussed in Chapter 3 and earlier in this chapter are important (e.g. Branton, 1984).

So that the sacrum and fleshy part of the buttocks which protrude behind a sitter can be accommodated, while at the same time allowing the lumbar region to fit firmly into the backrest, many authors suggest that the backrest should have an open area or should recede just above the seat-pan. A space of at least 12½ to 20 cm is needed to accommodate the buttocks in this way.

Finally, a high backrest might prevent full mobility of the arms and shoulders in certain tasks, for example typing. In such cases, small backrests which support the lumbar region only are suggested by many authors.

Backrest angle: 103 to 112 degrees. Like an angled seat-pan, the angle of the backrest to the seat-pan serves two purposes. First, it prevents the occupant from slipping forwards, and secondly, it helps the body to lean against the backrest with the lower (lumbar) part of the back and sacrum supported. From an orthopaedic viewpoint, the appropriate angle would be about 115 degrees, which Keegan and Radke (1964), for example, demonstrated produced the nearest to a 'natural' lumbar shape. However, when sitting comfort responses have been elicited from seated laboratory subjects, a less obtuse angle has consistently been found to be more 'comfortable'.

Jones (1969) studied posture and feeling of comfort in a highly adjustable car seat in many different positions. Subjects were trained to recognise the sensations of 'no sensation', 'conscious of contact with the seat', 'numbness', 'ache' and 'pain' after varying intervals. From his data he suggested a backrest angle of 108 degrees.

Grandjean (1973) discusses work which he carried out with Burandt to determine the optimum backrest angle for easy chairs when used for different reasons. Their data suggests that an angle of 101 to 104 degrees is optimum when reading, whereas 105 to 108 degrees is an optimum relaxed angle.

Armrest height: easy chair 2 cm to 24 cm above the compressed seat. The main function of armrests is to rest the arm and lock the body in a stable position. In an easy chair this is often accomplished by the arm being used to support the head. Armrests may also be useful in helping to change the sitting position or as an aid to getting up from the chair. However, it should be remembered that armrests may prove to be restrictive to the free movement of the arms and shoulders if they are incorporated in a working chair.

Cushioning and Upholstery

The importance of cushioning was demonstrated by Branton and Grayson (1967) in their observational study of sitters in two kinds of train seat. Although the dimensions of the two seats were about the same, the type and strength of seat spring and padding were different. One gave a relatively 'soft' subjective feel whereas the other appeared subjectively 'firm'. After analysing the number of 'fidgets' observed in the sitters and the length of time for which stable postures were maintained, the authors were able to state that 'by almost all counts II [the firmer seat] is much better'. Not only were there more different postures in the second seat, they were more 'healthy'.

Cushioning performs two important functions. First, it helps to distribute pressures on the ischial tuberosities and buttocks caused by the sitter's weight; as was shown earlier, if not relieved this pressure will cause discomfort and fatigue. The second function is to allow the body to adopt a stable posture. To this end the body will be able to 'sink' into the cushioning which then supports it. However, in this respect Branton (1966) raises a warning against the cushioning being too soft:

> A state can easily be reached when cushioning, while relieving pressure, deprives the body structure of support altogether and greatly increases instability. The body then 'flounders about' in the soft mass of the easy chair and only the feet rest on firm ground. Too springy a seat would therefore not allow proper rest, but may indeed be tiring because increased internal work is needed to maintain posture.

Kroemer and Robinette (1968) agree with Branton's position and also caution that soft upholstery will allow the buttocks and thighs to sink deeply into the cushioning. If this occurs all areas of the body that come into contact with the seat will be fully compressed, offering little chance for the sitter to adjust position to gain relief from the pressure. In addition, the body often 'floats' on soft upholstery, again causing the posture to have to be stabilised by muscle contraction.

Regarding seat covering, the important aspects are its ability to dissipate the heat and moisture generated from the sitting body (which, in turn, will be related to the type of environment in which the sitter is sitting) and its ability to resist the natural forwards-slipping movement of the body over time. For both of these criteria adequate thermal and mechanical techniques exist to allow the designer to make appropriate measurements.

SUMMARY

Sitting is often considered to be a natural posture, relieving the sitter of the need to maintain an upright posture. However, as this chapter has demonstrated, a seated posture can sometimes cause more problems than it solves. A seat which requires the sitter to adopt certain postures can create at the least muscular fatigue due to the static loads placed on the spinal and other muscles. At worst, permanent orthopaedic damage can result from spinal pressure maldistributions. The second part of this chapter considered chair dimensions for alleviating some of these problems—particularly in relation to increased sitter comfort.

10

THE PHYSICAL ENVIRONMENT I: VIBRATION AND NOISE

Aspects of the system such as the controls and displays are 'visible' to the operator; they can be perceived and they affect working behaviour in so far as they influence actions, judgement and immediate perceptions. The next two chapters will consider the less tangible (the more 'invisible') environmental features that arise both from the surroundings and from mechanical aspects of the workplace: environmental vibration, noise, temperature and illumination. Of course, these are not the only aspects of the environment that could affect behaviour; atmospheric pressure, dangerous chemicals or radioactive materials, adverse climatic conditions, cigarette smoke, and so on are other kinds of environmental features that could be encountered at work. However, only vibration, noise, temperature and illumination will be considered here.

The order in which the four factors are discussed is not intended to imply their relative importance to the operator. This depends entirely on the situation and the individual. Take, for example, two people standing on a small ship in cold, rough weather. One, a 'poor' sailor, will be concerned more about the ship's motion than any other factor; the other, a 'good' sailor, will probably worry more about the cold. The same environment may thus influence people in different ways because of the importance each attaches to its effects.

The various environmental features can affect people in one or more of three ways: health, performance and comfort. However, they are not independent. For example, poor health can create poor performance, and poor performance can lead to reduced work satisfaction; as was shown when discussing seating, reduced comfort may be a precursor to health hazards and can lead to poor performance; and so on. Although these aspects will be considered independently, their effects are therefore likely to be combined.

Purely physiological (health) effects of environmental stressors occur mainly at extreme levels of the stressor's intensity. But even before such extremes are reached the stressor can begin to affect the operator detrimentally, although this may not be apparent either to an observer or even to the person being affected. Although humans are extremely adaptable animals, the ideal range of any environmental factor for comfort or for performance is very narrow. Indeed, as has been stressed throughout this book, having to adapt to conditions outside this range can make the operator use more effort, which can lead to reduced performance. The concept of a limited store of 'spare mental capacity', for example, was discussed in Chapter 1. In terms of the present discussion, performing a task under normal circumstances and within the narrow optimum range of environmental factors will take up a certain amount of this mental capacity. Having to adapt to more severe conditions (for example to hear in loud noise or to read under glaring conditions) will further reduce the amount available, until a point is reached when the 'spare mental capacity' is exhausted. When this happens, the argument suggests, performance begins to decrease.

VIBRATION

Vibration will be discussed first because it is the most fundamental environmental factor. It underlies the production and perception of noise and sounds in the environment and, depending on the theory to which one ascribes, the production and perception of light stimuli. Understanding the definitions and parameters of structure-borne vibration, therefore, will help the reader to understand the effects of many other environmental parameters.

Definitions

Vibration may be defined simply as any movement which a body makes about a fixed point. This movement can be regular, like the motion of a weight on the end of a spring, or it can be random. The vibration experienced from machinery is usually a very complex, but regular, motion. Using appropriate techniques any complex motion can be analysed in terms of a number of simple components. This kind of analysis—Fourier analysis—is outside the scope of this book but can be found in most texts dealing with vibration theory.

If vibration is defined in this simple way, it follows that a body can vibrate in a number of different directions, although the International Organization

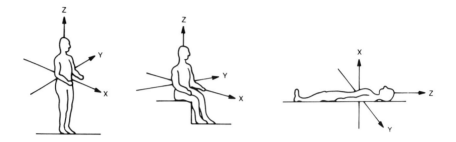

Figure 10.1 The three vibration coordinates for a standing, seated and lying person

for Standardization (1985) suggests that any movement should be defined and measured in terms of three orthogonal components: x, front to back; y, side to side; and z, foot to head (Figure 10.1). Using these coordinates a person jumping up and down, for example, would be vibrating in the z direction. If the same person was rotating about an axis from shoulder to shoulder (for example, tumbling face-forwards from a roof) then the body would be vibrating in the x and z axes at the same time. Finally, a weightless astronaut in space may rotate uncontrollably and might be vibrating in all three axes together. For most experimental purposes, however, the effects of vibration are normally considered in one axis only—and this has generally been in the vertical (z) direction.

Once the direction of the motion has been determined, the amount of vibration is defined in terms of two parameters: its 'speed' and 'intensity'.

The 'speed' of a vibrating body is expressed in terms of its frequency of movement—simply the number of times the body, the weight on the end of a spring, for example, completes one cycle of movement (i.e. from its fixed reference point to its highest point, to its lowest point and finally back to its reference point) within a specific time (usually 1 second). The normal unit of frequency is the Hertz (Hz), where 1 Hz = 1 cycle per second.

Vibration intensity is normally expressed in terms of the maximum amount of body movement from the fixed point—originally its distance or amplitude (in cm or in mm), but more recently acceleration units have been used to define vibration intensity. These are conventionally expressed in 'g' units (1 g being the amount of acceleration required to lift a body off the earth's surface); although the convention has been changed slightly in recent years to use the metric units of metres per second per second (1 g = 9.81 ms^{-2}).

Each of these parameters is related:

$$\text{Acceleration in 'g' units} = \frac{4\pi^2 f^2 a}{981}$$

where f is the frequency of the vibrating body and a its amplitude.

THE BASES OF VIBRATION EFFECTS

Any simple structure: this book, a table, a door, a building, can be excited at a particular frequency which is known as its natural or resonant frequency. If vibration is applied to the structure at or near this frequency then it will vibrate at a higher intensity than that applied to it. This amplification is known as resonance. (Indeed this effect can also occur if the original vibration input is situated close to, but not actually touching, the structure—this is how sopranos can sometimes shatter glass.) At other frequencies the opposite of resonance can occur, in that the body structure absorbs and so reduces the input intensity. This process is known as damping or attenuation (see Figure 10.2).

The human body is a very complex structure composed of different organs, bones, joints and muscles. Each of these parts, both individually and together, can be affected in the ways described above. At some frequencies they might vibrate at higher intensities than the vibrations applied to them, while at others they could absorb and attenuate the inputs. Because of resonance, therefore, body movements can sometimes become difficult for the operator to control, whereas at other frequencies, the vibration energy absorbed by the body during attenuation may be enough to cause structural damage.

The resonance effects of a particular system, for example the hand–arm complex, the head–neck complex, or the whole body itself, can be measured by comparing the vibration intensity of the system both at the point of stimulation and at the point of 'exit' for different frequencies. For example, to consider the resonance characteristics of the whole body, vibration-measuring devices (accelerometers) could be placed at the feet (entry) and the top of the head (exit) of a standing person. The resonant frequencies are those at which the 'exit' intensities exceed the 'input' intensities, i.e. when the exit : input intensity ratio is greater than 1. If the 'transmissibility' ratio is less than unity the system is absorbing (damping) the vibration.

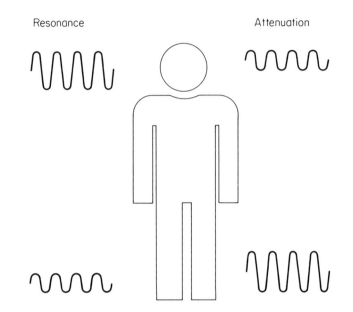

Figure 10.2   Vibration resonance and attenuation

A number of investigators have considered the biodynamic response of the whole body and there is general agreement that, for vertical vibration, the body has a whole-body resonance of around 5 Hz (for example Paddan, 1987). A seated operator, however, may be exposed to different vibration stimuli, particularly if the seat has a backrest which can help to transmit vibration to the operator. This was demonstrated well by Rowlands (1977), who also investigated seat–shoulder transmissibility. In this case, two resonant peaks occurred—one at around 5 Hz and another at about 10–12 Hz. These results were confirmed by Paddan and Griffin (1988).

Another important body system is the hand–arm complex: first, most control tasks use this system, and secondly, there is a growing awareness of the possibility of damage to the hand from using high-speed vibrating tools. Until relatively recently, however, little work had been carried out to investigate the dynamic response of this system.

Abrahams and Suggs (1969) analysed the vibration characteristics of a cadaver hand and arm by mounting accelerometers onto the bones. Their results showed that as the vibration frequency applied to the hand increased, less vibration was transmitted up the arm. Similar conclusions

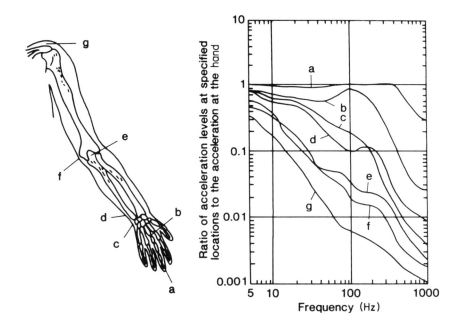

Figure 10.3 Hand–arm transmissibility obtained by Reynolds and Angevine (1977) at different test sites along the arm (reproduced with permission. Copyright: Academic Press Inc. (London) Ltd)

were reached by Reynolds and Soedel (1972) and by Reynolds and Angevine (1977). Reynolds and Angevine (1977) placed accelerometers at seven points between the fingers and shoulders of five subjects who were asked to grip a vibrating handle. Their results are shown in Figure 10.3 (the graph coordinates are arranged logarithmically to cover the ranges measured); it is clear that less vibration is transmitted the further up the arm the test site is situated. Indeed, vibration frequencies above about 100 to 150 Hz are almost totally absorbed in the hand itself. Reynolds and Soedel (1972) also demonstrated that changes in the position and stiffness of the arm had no significant effect on the vibration response of the hand–arm system. Not unexpectedly, however, grip tightness had a significant influence.

Just as the dynamics of the hand–arm–shoulder system have implications for understanding manual control difficulties under vibration, the behaviour of the eyes in their sockets can affect the operator's visual ability. In this case two aspects have to be considered: first, the movement of the head and eyes together, and second, the resonant characteristics of the eyes themselves.

The eyes are clearly not fixed inside the skull but are able to move by the action of muscles attaching them to the orbit in the skull. This means that the ways in which the eyes move during whole-body vibration are not necessarily the same as the head movements. Indeed, both Lee and King (1971) and Wells and Storey (1980) have demonstrated considerable damping effects in hand–eye transmissibility. Although the authors appear to differ slightly in their assessment of the extent to which this damping occurs, both agree that the most damping occurs above 20 Hz.

At higher frequencies the eyeballs themselves are in danger of resonating—irrespective of the head movement. Stott (1980) was able to map the course of these resonance effects for five subjects by measuring the movement of a spot of light shone onto the cornea of the eye. His results demonstrate the start of eyeball resonance after about 30 Hz, with a maximum (vibrating approximately four times as much as the head alone) at 70 Hz.

HEALTH EFFECTS OF VIBRATION

The health effects of vibration lie basically in two areas. First is damage caused to body organs as a result of their being buffeted by high vibration levels at relatively low frequencies. These effects are basically intensity dependent. Second comes the breakdown of body tissues owing either to continued resonance or to their absorption of high-energy vibration. These effects depend primarily on the frequency of stimulation.

Intensity-dependent Effects

For most working environments the potential damage to large body organs or to the musculoskeletal system by high-intensity buffeting is unlikely to be a problem. In vehicles that ride over rough terrain or can be buffeted about in other ways, however, the levels of vibration experienced for very short periods may, over time, cause structural damage.

Griffin (1990) presents an overview of well over 100 studies since 1947 that have considered health effects resulting from vibration—from tractor drivers to flamenco dancers. One of the most frequently cited complaints concerned back problems resulting from spinal buffeting, followed by digestive and reproductive system disorders. As Griffin points out, the symptoms of low back pain may appear before degenerative changes are radiologically detectable. Therefore, in environments where 'extreme' vibration levels may occur, it is important that subjective complaints are considered carefully.

Frequency-dependent Effects

Injuries that are caused by the frequency aspects of vibration normally occur after prolonged exposure to the vibrating stimulus, and mainly in the higher frequency ranges. In contemporary working environments the problem arises particularly from the use of powered hand-held machinery such as road drills, stone breakers and chain saws.

After reviewing much of the work, however, Seidel and Heide (1986) also suggest some frequency dependency for many of the severe injuries that arise from high-intensity vibrations. For example, although intense vibrations at around 20 Hz generally result in higher incidences of spinal problems, vibrations below 20 Hz often lead to digestive complaints while those above 20 Hz led to nervous system disorders.

Intense vibration from hand tools can be transmitted to the operator's fingers, hands and arms from the machines themselves and from hand-held objects. When this happens structural damage to the peripheral blood and nervous systems in the fingers can occur which, over time, produces 'intermittent numbness and clumsiness of the fingers, intermittent blanching of either all or part of the extremities, and a temporary loss of muscular control of the exposed parts of the body' (Agate, 1949). Because of the appearance of the affected limbs the condition is often referred to as 'white finger', although, since the symptoms are similar to a disease first described by Raynaud in 1862, it is sometimes referred to as 'Raynaud's disease of occupational origin' (Taylor, 1974).

In 1970 the Industrial Injuries Advisory Council rejected the various names in favour of the descriptive term 'Vibration Induced White Finger' (VWF) and described the complex of symptoms associated with vibrating tools as 'The Vibrating Syndrome'. These additional effects may include any or all of neuritis, damage to bones, joints or muscles (Taylor, 1974). Relief from all or some of these symptoms usually occurs after prolonged rest from exposure to the vibration stimulus, although they are likely to reappear promptly with renewed exposure. Table 10.1 describes the developmental stages of this complaint.

PERFORMANCE EFFECTS OF VIBRATION

Because body parts tend to vibrate in sympathy with vibrating machinery, either nearby to or on which they may rest, the effects of vibration on performance occur mainly in terms of reduced motor control. This might be the control of a limb (causing, for example, reduced hand steadiness) or of

Table 10.1 Stages of the symptoms of Raynaud's disease (adapted from Taylor, 1974; by permission of Academic Press)

Stage	Condition	Work and social interference
0	No blanching of digits	No complaints
0_T	Intermittent tingling	No interference with activities
0_N	Intermittent numbness	No interference with activities
1	Blanching of one or more fingertips with or without tingling and numbness	No interference with activities
2	Blanching of one or more complete fingers with numbness. Usually confined to winter	Slight interference with home and social activities. No interference at work
3	Extensive blanching, usually all fingers. Bilateral. Frequent episodes, summer as well as winter	Definite interference at work, at home and with social activities. Restriction of hobbies
4	Extensive blanching of all fingers. Frequent episodes, summer and winter	Occupation changed to avoid further vibration exposure because of severity of signs and symptoms

International Standard 5349 (International Organization for Standardization, 1986) provides general guidelines for the measurement of hand-transmitted vibration.

the eyeballs (causing fixation difficulties and blurring). Little evidence exists to suggest that vibration can affect central, intellectual processes.

Visual Performance Effects of Vibration

An object will only be perceived clearly if a stable image falls on the retina; a moving figure will stimulate different sets of receptors in the retina, producing a signal which has overlapping and confused images. This is clearly likely to cause difficulties in detecting much of the object's detail, particularly if the retinal image oscillates with a relatively large amplitude.

Although a fair amount of work has been carried out to investigate visual vibration effects, it is difficult to draw many conclusions about the types and levels of vibration which affect visual performance. This is because different investigators have used different tasks to measure visual performance; since different tasks require subjects to perform different activities it would be difficult to relate them to each other or to any standard performance criteria.

There are three combinations of observer and object vibration that can result in a moving image being perceived: first, if the object alone is vibrated; second, when only the observer is vibrated; and third, when both the observer and the object are vibrated. In the third case the degree of blurring will depend not only on the nature of the vibration experienced but on the phase relationship between the two moving bodies. The effect of these three aspects will be considered separately.

Vibrating the object alone

The effects on vision of vibrating the object alone appear to be mainly because of the vibration frequency and, to some extent, its intensity.

If the object is vibrating slowly enough (below about 1 Hz) the optical system can track it and so maintain a stable image on the retina. In doing so, however, the optic muscles have to work harder and muscular fatigue may occur quite quickly. This kind of tracking task is known as pursuit eye movements. At frequencies above 1 Hz, however, the system effectiveness decreases considerably until by about 2–4 Hz and above the tracking ability is almost non-existent. Interestingly, studies have also demonstrated that at very low frequencies the tracking performance for unpredictable motions is almost as good as for predictable stimuli. With increasing frequency this ability soon disappears, but at around 2–4 Hz and above (when pursuit eye movements are no longer effective) the system's inability to track unpredictable stimuli appears to be no worse than its inability to track predictable stimuli.

At higher object frequencies, when pursuit eye movements cannot usefully track a vibrating object, any performance reduction will be related directly to the degree of blurring on the retina. The quality of the image is thus inversely proportional to the number of extra retinal cells stimulated (i.e. the vibration amplitude), although at the same time it will be proportional to the length of time for which any one cell is stimulated. Since the time taken for an object to move through one cycle is inversely proportional to the frequency, it follows that the performance efficiency will be related to both the frequency and the amplitude of the vibrating image. Indeed O'Hanlon and Griffin (1971) have suggested that at frequencies above about 5 Hz an observer's error rate in perceiving fine detail in a moving object is proportional to the product of the frequency and the square root of the amplitude of the vibrating image (that is, $E \propto f\sqrt{a}$). This relationship appears to fit data produced by O'Hanlon and Griffin, and Meddick and Griffin (1976) state that the model has been confirmed by Alexander (1972).

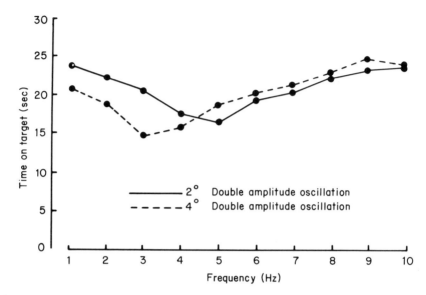

Figure 10.4 Tracking performance under vibration, showing how the main frequency effect is modified by an amplitude effect (from Huddleston, 1970. Copyright 1970 by the American Psychological Association. Reprinted with permission)

In an attempt to map the relationships between vibration frequency and visual performance, Huddleston (1970) measured the proportion of time during which subjects could maintain a stable image of an object vibrating at one or two different amplitudes. His results, shown in Figure 10.4, illustrate well the observer's problems when coping with vibrating material. Thus, for the smaller amplitude, the eye can track the moving object quite well at low frequencies. As the frequency is increased this ability is reduced in the way described earlier. The attempt to track the object continues, although with decreasing efficiency, until at about 5 Hz the subject gives up and stabilises on the object. At this point the decrement is related more to the degree of image blurring. For the higher amplitude vibration, however, the relinquishing of pursuit tracking occurs at a lower frequency, with the result that the upturn in performance occurs earlier.

Regarding the effect of the amplitude of the moving object, studies by Drazin (1962) and Huddleston (1970) demonstrate that at frequencies below about 4 Hz (at which pursuit eye movements are possible), visual performance is reduced with increasing vibration amplitude. At higher frequencies, however, these deficiencies are not sustained. Indeed, Huddleston's data shown in Figure 10.4 suggest that at 5 Hz the higher amplitude was beneficial, and Drazin's results suggest that at 6 and 8 Hz the larger amplitudes produced lower error scores than the smaller amplitudes. Conclusions from these results, however, should not be taken to extremes; it is not necessarily the case that reading becomes easier with increased displacement. Griffin and Lewis (1978), for example, suggest that the larger amplitudes were large enough to reduce the amount of confusion in the blurred image. More confusion is likely to result from smaller amplitudes and, when this occurs, the O'Hanlon and Griffin model of $E \propto f\sqrt{a}$ still holds true. It must be remembered, however, that their model was proposed for performance reductions in a visual acuity task (perceiving the gap in a Landolt C). Griffin himself questions (1976a) whether it also holds true for other types of perceptual tasks. Indeed, data from Meddick and Griffin (1976), who used digits of the form recommended in British Standards 3693A, suggest that the error rate for this kind of material is *not* proportional to $f \sqrt{a}$.

Vibrating the observer alone

The same problems appear when the observer is vibrated as when the object is vibrated—namely those concerning the optical system's tracking ability and the degree of blur experienced. These problems, however, are confounded by the dynamic characteristics of the body in which the eyes reside. These may be such as to produce head and eye motions that have different intensities to the input motion and, because the body is a flexible structure, the resultant eye motions may not even occur in the same axis as the input motion. (Indeed, Griffin (1976b) has demonstrated that in seated subjects vertical vibration is likely to cause some angular motions of the eyes.)

Because of these confounding problems, and because so much variability exists between individuals in their whole-body transmissibility, the only reasonable procedure for determining the effects of whole-body vibration on vision is to measure the level of vibration experienced at the head. During their study of seat to shoulder and head transmissibility, Guignard and Irving (1960) also asked subjects to scan blocks of the letter 'c' and to count randomly placed letter 'o's. Using the average time taken to complete the task as their measure of reading performance, Guignard and Irving demonstrated very close similarity between the shape of the performance curve as a function of frequency and that of the velocity of the head motion. Unfortunately, only four subjects were tested which, given the levels of individual variability known to exist for these types of reading task (for example, Griffin, 1976b), is likely to limit the value of the results.

Considering the frequency of the vibration alone, the problems that occur when a vibrating observer views a stationary display are similar to those arising when only the display is vibrated; that is, they operate in two frequency bands, first, low frequencies in which the moving observer's problem is to stabilise the eyes to maintain a stationary image, and second, at higher frequencies in which eyeball resonance is involved.

Because the low-frequency task essentially involves stabilising the eyes on a stationary display (rather than moving the eyes to keep up with a moving display) it is often referred to as compensatory (rather than pursuit) tracking. The difference between the two terms is more than simply semantic. For example, Guignard and Irving (1960) suggest that the upper frequency limit for compensatory eye movements is higher than that for pursuit movements. At frequencies higher than those which allow compensatory tracking, the problem of eyeball resonance must clearly be taken into account. As discussed earlier, Stott (1980) demonstrated the beginnings of resonance in the eye-orbit complex at about 30 Hz, with a maximum at 70 Hz.

Regarding the intensity aspects of the vibrating observer, the obvious problems relate to visual blur. In an experiment to map the frequency course of blurring when the observer alone is vibrated, Griffin (1975) vibrated subjects at frequencies between 7 and 75 Hz. At each frequency the subjects were required to adopt postures that resulted in the 'maximum sensation' at the head. They were then asked to adjust the vibration level to the minimum at which they observed any definite blurring of points of light. (Because subjects always adjusted down the intensity range, it is likely that this technique will produce 'conservative' estimates of the blur level.) The blur thresholds obtained from the subjects are illustrated in Figure 10.5, along with predicted blur levels from vibrating the object alone (assuming that a vibrating object produces blur when there is an image displacement of about 1 minute of arc at the eye; Griffin, 1975). The divergence of these two curves at higher frequencies illustrates, once again, the effect of eye movement relative to head movement. From these curves, however, it is not possible to determine by how much the eyeball resonance affects visual performance. Furthermore, any interpretation of them must take account of Griffin's own cautions regarding the high levels of inter- and intra-subject variability which were obtained.

In an attempt to relate vibration levels to performance reductions, Lewis and Griffin (1980a, b) considered the effects of vibration frequency (28 to 63 Hz) on a number-reading task. In addition, employing a model which assumed a linear relationship between error rate and vibration intensity experienced at the head at each frequency, the authors predicted performance contours outside the range of intensities which they investigated. Their results are shown in Figure 10.6.

Regarding the effect of the task on visual performance, the most obvious factor to consider is object size. Clearly larger objects are easier to see, and

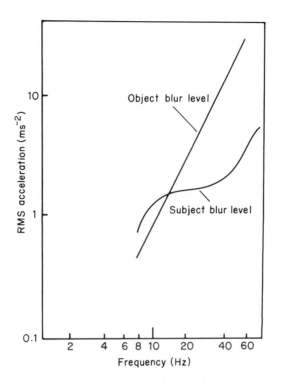

Figure 10.5 The average levels of vertical vibration needed to produce blur, compared with object blur levels (reproduced with permission from Griffin, 1975. Copyright Academic Press Inc. (London) Ltd)

this is also likely to be true under vibrating conditions. This was illustrated by Lewis and Griffin (1979b) who used four character heights (1–2 mm) while seated subjects were exposed to different vibration stimuli. Their results demonstrate significant increases in percentage reading errors with both increased vibration intensity and reduced character size.

Vibrating the object and the observer together

Although the previous two conditions have illustrated the many problems of viewing an object in a dynamic environment, they are quite simple compared with that in which both the observer and the object are vibrating. Unfortunately this is a common situation in real life environments whenever the observer and objects are both attached to or are inside a piece of vibrating machinery, such as a vehicle passenger or driver.

A number of conditions may occur when both the observer and the object are being vibrated, each of which is likely to affect the resultant visual

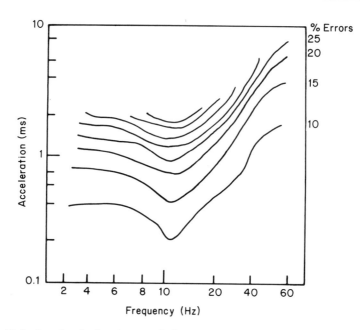

Figure 10.6 Levels of vibration needed to produce equal error rates for a reading task (reproduced with permission from Lewis and Griffin, 1980a. Copyright Academic Press Inc. (London) Ltd)

performance in an individual manner. For example, the two may be vibrating at different frequencies or intensities, they may be moving in phase or out of phase, and they could even be moving in different axes. Because of these problems, very few well-controlled studies have been carried out to investigate combined object and subject vibration effects.

A specific situation which has been investigated, however, is when the display is in some way attached to an observer's head—usually in a helmet. The helmet-mounted display allows information to be presented continuously to an operator such as a pilot—regardless of the head position.

Barnes, Benson and Prior (1978) investigated this form of the observer–object relationship for angular motion of the head (using both the 'yaw' and 'pitch' motions). Their results demonstrated a marked reduction in the ability to read the displayed digits at frequencies higher than about 1 Hz, with faster reductions for the smaller digit size. Some performance differences were apparent between axes, however: the overall number of digits read correctly was lower, and the reduction in reading efficiency higher, in pitch than in yaw.

A similar kind of experiment was reported by Furness and Lewis (1978), although their subjects were vibrated in the vertical axis only (1.4 to 45 Hz). As with the Lewis and Griffin (1980a, b) studies, from the performance measures Furness and Lewis produced equal performance decrement contours over the frequency range studied.

In summary, the effects of vibration on visual performance are extremely complex. They depend on whether the observer or the object is vibrating, on the vibration frequency and intensity, and on the object size (and thus the distance from the observer). In general it would appear that the extent of performance reductions is determined largely by the vibration frequency. At low frequencies it is a function of the optical system's ability to track an object to maintain a stable retinal image. At higher frequencies it is a function simply of the degree of blur. The cut-off frequency of these two bands, however, is determined by whether it is the observer or the object which is being vibrated.

Motor Performance Effects of Vibration

Two kinds of tracking task are normally used by experimenters to investigate the effects of vibration on motor performance: pursuit and compensatory tracking.

In pursuit tracking the operator's task is to move the controls so that the object (perhaps a spot on a display) follows a predetermined course (possibly following another moving spot). A 'real life' example of this situation might be a car driver's task of turning a steering wheel to keep the car on a winding road. The operator corrects errors by comparing the movement of the 'spot' (the car) with that of a standard (the road).

In the compensatory tracking task the operator 'sees' only errors. The task is to maintain an otherwise moving 'spot' in a particular position—to use the controls to compensate for the machine's movement. The spot only moves when the task is not performed correctly. The car driver's attempt to maintain a steady speed (i.e. to keep the speedometer needle at a particular place) is an example of such a task. Variations in the vehicle dynamics, the road incline, the weather or other environmental conditions may all act to influence the car speed and so cause the driver to have to compensate by using the accelerator and other pedals.

Compensatory tracking is more difficult than pursuit tracking. When tracking in a compensatory manner operators cannot see what is being done nor predict what is meant to be done; they can only compensate when an error has occurred. If tracking in a pursuit manner, however, we can see both the movements produced by the track program and the results of control movements.

Although the two forms of tracking task differ in their difficulty, it would appear that they are not differentially affected by vibration. Thus Lewis (1980) asked subjects to perform, separately, both kinds of tracking task while being subjected to different vibration stimuli. His results suggest that irrespective of the measures used to record the subject's performance, and although different frequency stimuli affected the performance to different degrees, the performance curves for the two types of task were very similar.

Whatever measure of motor performance is used, there appears to be general agreement that at low frequencies (below about 15 Hz) performance reductions are related to the amount of vibration experienced at the controlling limb. In this case, therefore, the important variable again concerns the individual's seat or foot to arm (shoulder) transmissibility. Thus Levison (1976) demonstrated that performance reductions in a vertical tracking task were linearly correlated with shoulder acceleration in the range 2–10 Hz. Furthermore, Buckhout (1964) showed tracking error to follow very closely a linear relationship with the intensity of vertical vibration measured at the sternum (at 6, 8 and 10 Hz).

Regarding the intensity domain, the results from a number of studies are extremely consistent and suggest that tracking performance decreases as the vibration intensity transmitted to the limb increases (for example, Catterson, Hoover and Asche, 1962; Lewis and Griffin, 1979b).

The lowest level of vibration before performance is affected appears to be very variable. Reviewing the field, for example, Lewis and Griffin (1978) point out that the levels of vibration at which some experimenters had failed to obtain an effect were higher than those at which other experimenters had obtained significant reductions in performance. They conclude, therefore, that:

> It seems reasonable to draw the general conclusion that increases in vibration level, above some threshold effect, will result in progressive degradation of performance. However, because of the great number of task variables which may affect the performance of specific systems blurring vibration ... it is not reasonable to expect to be able to discover an absolute threshold of effect, above which performance is affected by vibration and below which it is not.

Finally, Fraser, Hoover and Asche (1961) investigated the combined effects of vibration frequency and intensity on a tracking task. On the basis of their results they argued that the subjects' average tracking error (the number of subjects used was not reported) was proportional to the product of the vibration amplitude and the square root of the frequency (over the frequency range 2–12 Hz) (i.e. $E \propto a\sqrt{f}$).This is interesting, particularly when the expression is compared with that reported earlier by O'Hanlon and Griffin (1971) in terms of visual acuity errors ($E \propto f\sqrt{a}$). The two expressions clearly imply that visual performance degradation is mainly a function of the vibration frequency, whereas manual performance degradation is primarily intensity dependent.

In respect to the direction of the motion being applied to the operator, all of the studies conducted so far agree that the primary detrimental effect occurs in the axis in which the operator is being vibrated. For example, Fraser, Hoover and Asche (1961) demonstrated that horizontal tracking performance (2–12 Hz) was affected more by y-axis vibration than by z-axis vibration of the same intensity. Vertical tracking was affected more by z-axis vibration than by y-axis vibration. Front–back (x-axis) vibration had no effect on either horizontal or vertical tracking. Similar conclusions were reached by Shoenberger (1970) who argues, not unreasonably, that the results suggest that the primary mechanism responsible for decrements on tasks of this nature is the interference with perceptual processes and hand control caused by the short-duration whole-body vibration.

The studies by Fraser, Hoover and Asche and by Shoenberger were carried out using separate axes in different trials. Lovesey (1974), however, describes an experiment to investigate the effects of combined y- and z-axis vibration on a compensatory tracking task. He presented subjects with 2, 5 and 7 Hz vibration stimuli at 0.2 g in the z-axis and 0.1 g in the y-axis. These frequencies and levels were also combined at $2z+5y$, $2z+7y$, $5z+7y$, $7z+2y$ and $7z+5y$. His results are interesting since, in addition to illustrating decrements in tracking performance with all single-axis vibrations, when the axes were combined tracking performance tended to be degraded by an amount equal to the product of the tracking decrements produced by each single axis alone, i.e.

$$\text{combined error} = z\text{ error} \times y\text{ error}$$

Lovesey does add that this equation only holds true for cases when the task was difficult enough to be affected adversely by the single-axis vibrations. It does not hold if either the z or the y error was zero or if the vibration actually helped to improve performance. (More will be said later regarding the possibility of performance increases under vibrating conditions.)

As well as the vibration itself being a variable that could affect performance, the task to be performed by the operator must also be considered. In this respect its duration and the physical equipment provided could play important roles.

The variable of exposure duration (or 'time dependency') is one which has received considerable debate since it forms an important part in the levels set by the International Standards Organization for exposure to whole-body vibration. Unfortunately, as will be discussed later, there is little evidence to support the contention that performance decreases the longer that the individual is exposed to the vibration stimulus (for example, Lewis and Griffin, 1979a, b; Guignard, Landrum and Reardon, 1976; Maslen, 1972; Hornick and Lefritz, 1966). A recent study by McLeod and Griffin (1993), for example, demonstrated that, although motor performance decreased over time (3 hrs), the duration effects of subjects who were exposed to vibration were not significantly different from those who received no vibration.

McLeod and Griffin (1989) review a number of studies in this area and found some that had reported finding time-dependency effects in relation to vibration exposure. Of more importance is that some of the studies which demonstrated differential changes in performance over time implied a slight *improvement* rather than reduction in performance (for example, Khalil and Ayoub, 1970; Dudek, Ayoub and El-Nawawi, 1973; Wilkinson and Gray, 1974). Such results imply that the vibration stimulus may act as an alerting mechanism for subjects undertaking what is otherwise often a boring task.

Summarising the field, McLeod and Griffin (1989) conclude:

> There appears to be no simple factor which determines whether a task will be sensitive to time-dependency effects of vibration ... The only factor common to the tasks affected by vibration duration appears to be their dependence upon attention and cognitive processes. It is possible that the vibration effect occurred at a level upon which more complex and specific mental processes depend: the mechanism may depend upon 'fatigue' and 'arousal'.

Regarding the quality of the equipment provided for the operator, obvious variables to consider are the type and degree of body restraint afforded during the task. Without such support the vibration will be likely to destabilise the body and make the manual control task more difficult. In this respect two restraint systems can be considered—harnesses and armrests.

Although at first it would appear sensible to argue that a restraining harness is likely to increase stability and thus improve performance, the effects of the harness on the amount of vibration transmitted through the body must be considered. Thus, as was noted earlier, Rowlands (1977) demonstrated significant increases in vibration transmitted to the shoulder when the back was pressed against the backrest. Given the very strong relationship between the amount of vibration reaching the shoulder and performance decrement, it could well be hypothesised that a restraining harness would have a detrimental effect on motor control. This was illustrated by Lovesey (1971) for tracking in both the y- and z-axes.

As far as armrests are concerned, Torle (1965) tested three subjects on a tracking task using a 'small' armrest, a 'large' armrest or no armrest (unfortunately dimensions were not provided). His results demonstrated some improvement in tracking ability using the armrest although he observed no difference between the two armrests used. The armrest improvement increased with increasing vibration intensity. Whether the improvement was owing to increased overall body stability created by the armrests, or simply to forearm or elbow stability, is not, unfortunately, able to be deduced from the experimental report.

In summary, therefore, whole-body vibration clearly degrades motor control, particularly when the task demands movement in the same plane as the vibration. Furthermore, the degree of degradation is primarily intensity dependent and is thus a strong function of how the vibration is transmitted through the body.

THE EFFECTS OF VIBRATION ON REACTION TIME AND INFORMATION PROCESSING

For a number of years, particularly in the late 1950s and 1960s during the 'space race' era, a number of studies were carried out to investigate whether vibration affects operator response (reaction) times.

Much of the research in this area has demonstrated that reaction time is relatively unaffected by vibration (such as Weisz, Goddard and Allen, 1965; Holland, 1965). For example, Hornick (1962) asked subjects to press a foot-pedal each time a particular sequence of coloured lights appeared under various vibration conditions. Under no condition was reaction time increased, although, interestingly, he reported an increase during a post-vibration test in the y- and z-axes. In the light of information on similar responses after the cessation of other stressors (for example, Wohlwill et al., 1976), it could be argued that the vibration is acting in this case as a general stressor which causes the operator to have to work harder to maintain the same level of performance. When the stressor ends a 'let down' effect occurs which shows itself as reduced performance.

Despite experiments which show no effect of vibration, Shoenberger (1970) did demonstrate significant performance reductions using vibration, separately, in the x-, y- and z-axes. The main effect was in the y-axis (side–side), with highly significant decrements occurring at 1 Hz and 3 Hz. Very little reduction in reaction time occurred at either 11 Hz in the y-axis or in the other two axes at any frequency. It may be suggested, however, that Shoenberger's results simply reflect his apparatus arrangements: the stimulus lights and response buttons were arranged horizontally (i.e. along the y-axis) and so interference in the motor component of the reaction time task could have caused the increased reaction time.

An interesting validation of the hypothesis of peripheral, rather than central, interference was produced by Shoenberger (1974). He used a memory reaction time task in which subjects were required first to memorise letters and then to react (verbally) to their presence or absence within a matrix on a screen. The motor component of the reaction time task, therefore, was reduced to one simply of controlling the diaphragm for speech. Using an analysis technique developed by Sternberg (1966), Shoenberger demonstrated that although the peripheral components of this task (perceiving the test letter and verbalising the response) were susceptible to vibration, the central processing aspects (deciding to react) were relatively immune.

In terms of intellectual (cognitive) tasks, Shoenberger's conclusion of no vibration effects has been supported by some experimenters but not by others. For example, Schohan, Rawson and Soliday (1965) showed no appreciable effects of vibration on a navigation task, while Simons and Schmitz (1958) found no effects on mental arithmetic using 2.5 Hz and 3.5 Hz vibrations at up to 0.31 g. On the other hand Huddleston (1964), using a 'rolling arithmetic' task (which combined mental addition and recent memory), demonstrated that performance was significantly slower at 4.8, 6.7, 9.5 and 16 Hz at 0.5 g than during the static control condition. The wide frequency range over which an effect was obtained demonstrates that the performance reductions were not frequency dependent, as are both visual and motor control decrements. In a subsequent experiment Huddleston (1965) used the same intensity at 4.8 and 6.7 Hz and confirmed these results.

The results of the effects of vibration on cognitive tasks, therefore, appear to be inconclusive. However, it must be remembered that with such tasks a number of possible variables can interfere to cause unpredictable results unless they are controlled. As will be discussed in more detail later in this chapter, an individual's level of arousal, among other factors, is known to have effects (both facilitative and detrimental) on subsequent performance. In this vein Poulton (1978) argues that vibration at 5 Hz can act as an alerting mechanism to increase performance. Furthermore, the arousal level is known to be related to the time of day as a result of the human body's cyclical (circadian) activities. Thus Sommer and Harris (1970) have demonstrated time-of-day effects on the relationship between a combined vibration and noise stressor and mental performance. Subjects were tested on a mental subtraction task at either 6 a.m. or 3 p.m. while exposed to either a 5 Hz, 0.25 g vibration and 110 dB noise stressor or to no stress. Whereas the stress condition produced poorer performance at 3 p.m., no difference in performance was observed at 6 a.m. Thus the otherwise significant reduction in performance at 6 a.m. under the 'no stress' condition further supports the hypothesis that the degree of 'arousal' or 'alertness' plays a significant role in whether or not the stressor will affect performance.

THE EFFECTS OF VIBRATION ON COMFORT

The concept of comfort has already been discussed but two points should be re-emphasised: first, comfort is extremely difficult to define, and second, discomfort may both affect and be affected by performance decrements.

Qualitative Effects of Vibration on Comfort

Oborne (1975) reports a series of questionnaire surveys carried out on fare-paying passengers using a number of different vehicles (trains, hovercraft, helicopters). His results suggest that vibration can affect comfort in one or more of three main ways. First, in the manner discussed earlier, it affects our abilities to perform motor tasks. Large numbers of passengers complained that they were unable to read, write or eat under the conditions in which they were travelling. Since most people are not merely passive beings while being transported from one place to another, and since many passengers use different activities to pass the journey time away, he argues that the reported degradation in performance due to vibration and motion clearly has important implications.

The second effect of vibration on comfort is a positive one and relates to the information which the stimulus carries to the passenger. For example, one passenger travelling by helicopter reported that he found the vibration reassuring—it would certainly have affected his comfort had the machine suddenly stopped vibrating while in mid-air! Car drivers use the information from the noise and vibration of the car engine to know when to change gear or whether something is wrong. In such cases, therefore, it is the implications of the stimulus which are the important feature.

Thirdly, and under conditions of extreme vibration, physiological effects were described. In such circumstances reports of motion sickness and headaches predominated, although it is debatable whether the headaches arose from the buffeting action of the vibration or the noise caused by the vibrating structures. More will be mentioned about the problems of motion sickness later.

Quantitative Effects of Vibration on Comfort

Because of the many variables that impinge on passengers travelling in a vehicle, 'field' investigations of the quantitative relationship between vibration level and comfort are extremely difficult to undertake. For this reason most of the work in this area has been performed under more controlled, laboratory conditions, often using paid subjects. Much of this work has been criticised by Oborne (1976) on experimental grounds although, as will be seen later, many of their conclusions have appeared in the International Standard (International Organization for Standardization, ISO 2631, 1978, amended in 1985) which is presently accepted for this area. Only one study (Oborne, 1977) has used actual fare-paying passengers and this was carried out on a hovercraft service between England and France; each journey took approximately 35 minutes. By comparing measured vibration levels with passengers' comfort ratings the function illustrated in Figure 10.7 was able to be derived (the figure illustrates vibration levels in two frequency bands shown to predominate in the vehicle).

The curves shown in Figure 10.7 illustrate how rated vehicle comfort varies with either the intensity of the vehicle vibration (8–16 Hz band, from the engines) or the motion (0–4Hz band, from the vehicle motion over the water). Although the two curves have similar shapes they show that, at lower intensity levels, the higher-frequency vibration is more important to comfort than is the lower-frequency motion. As intensity levels increase, however, the importance of the motion increases until, after about $1.4m^{-2}$, it becomes more important to comfort than the vibration is. This was presumably because at the higher motion levels the motion was more likely to cause motion sickness and to affect the passengers' abilities to read, write or drink. Figure 10.7 also shows, of course, that this crossover point is also related to the change from 'comfortable' to 'uncomfortable' experiences.

Motion Sickness

Motion sickness is one aspect of vibration which certainly causes discomfort and performance loss. This distressing effect is experienced by a large proportion of travellers and is caused by the low frequency (about 0.3–0.5 Hz), high-amplitude motion conditions prevailing in rough seas or

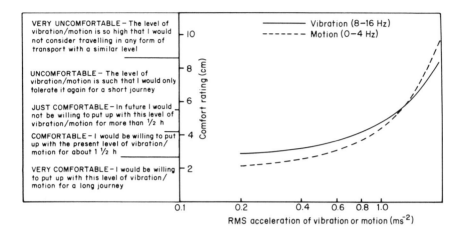

Figure 10.7 Levels of vehicle vibration and motion needed to produce varying levels of passenger comfort (from Oborne, 1977; reproduced from *Applied Ergonomics*, **8**, 97–101, by permission of the publishers, Butterworth-Heinemann Ltd. Copyright)

air turbulence. The most commonly reported symptom is nausea, often leading to vomiting. For many, the act of vomiting leads to a rapid recovery of well-being, but in some people the nausea exists even after vomiting— resulting in further bouts of vomiting and retching, and a continued decline in well-being. Nevertheless it is possible to become adapted to the stimulus. Prolonged exposure to the sickness-inducing motion is likely to lead to a diminution and eventual disappearance of the signs and symptoms in most people. This 'protective adaptation' can be influenced by the type of activity in which the person engages, the abruptness with which the stimulus is presented (gradual presentation leads to better adaptation), the victim's level of arousal, and the extent of the person's visual activity (Reason and Brand, 1975).

The part of the body which triggers the sensation of motion sickness very clearly lies in the vestibular system in the ear, since an intact aural system is necessary before the symptoms can occur. However, Reason has suggested that its cause also lies in the fact that, in a moving environment, discrepant information is received by the brain from either the eyes and the vestibular apparatus (visual–inertial conflict) on the one hand, or from the semicircular canals sensing rotational motion and the otoliths sensing vertical motion (canal–otolith conflict) on the other. Reason's suggestion is therefore one of sensory conflict; that the sensations received from the body's position sensors are at variance not only with one another but also— and this is the crucial factor—with what is expected on the basis of previous dealings with the environment (past experience). Continued experience of the conflict, therefore, will help the individual to adapt his or her 'experiential template' and reduce the sensory conflict.

Reason (1978) makes various practical suggestions for alleviating such conflicts, all of which attempt to reduce the discrepancies of the incoming information. These include adopting a supine position, fixating on an otherwise stable object such as the horizon, closing the eyes, and wearing spectacles with thick, heavy frames.

Riccio and Stoffregen (1991), however, have criticised the sensory-conflict theory on the grounds that our perceptual systems are not sensitive enough to detect and interpret the variations in sensory inputs between what is being experienced and what is expected or learned on the basis of past experience. They suggest that the mechanism lies more in terms of the extent to which we can control the effects of the motion on our bodies; that is, the extent to which we can maintain postural stability. They argue, therefore, that we become sick in situations in which we do not have (or have not yet learned) effective strategies for postural stability.

Whatever the behavioural cause of motion sickness, the fact that it is physiologically based means that it might be able to alleviated using appropriate drugs. However, before such a drug can be prescribed the true site of the cause of motion sickness has to be determined. In this respect, controversy has raged for a number of years over whether the site of the important vestibular symptoms lies in the otoliths (the vertical motion receptors) or in the semicircular canals (which sense angular acceleration). Much of this controversy has been caused by the difficulty of delivering a stimulus to one part of the vestibular system (for example, the semicircular canals by rotation) without also stimulating the other part (for example, the otoliths by centrifugal force). Evidence using high-amplitude lifts, however, tends to suggest that the otoliths represent the prime motion sickness centres. With information of this nature Reason (1978) suggests a number of drugs that can be used to combat the sickness symptoms, each having different qualities.

A VIBRATION STANDARD

Since the early 1960s attempts have been made to combine all the information relating vibration to health, performance and comfort into an accepted standard for human exposure to whole-body vibration. Such a standard was finally produced as a discussion document in 1974 and as a standard in 1978—ISO 2631, *Guide for the Evaluation of Human Exposure to*

Whole Body Vibration. The committee which steered the standard through its various stages (Working Group No. 7 of the ISO Technical Committee 108, i.e. ISO/TC 108/WG7) was initially composed of representatives from the USA, Germany, the Netherlands and Sweden, although representatives from other countries including Czechoslovakia, Japan and the UK joined later (Cowley, 1976). Slight ammendments were made in 1982 to 'simplify' the section dealing with time dependency.

The guide deals with vibration in all three axes, but treats the two lateral axes (x, y) as being the same. It only considers vibrations in the strict range 1–80 Hz, thereby purposefully not including the problems of motion sickness (ISO 2631 Part 3 (1985) deals with vibration in the frequency range 0.1 to 0.63 Hz).

As far as vibration in the range 1–80 Hz is concerned, the standards lay down limits of exposure to both vertical and lateral vibration under three criteria: the preservation of health (exposure limit, EL), working efficiency (fatigue–decreased proficiency boundary, FDP) and comfort (reduced comfort boundary, RCB). As an innovation the levels for each criterion are defined in terms of the maximum time for which an operator should be exposed to the vibration (time dependency). These levels range from one minute to eight hours (i.e. a 'working day'). For any exposure time, EL = 2 × FDP and RCB = FDP/3.15. Figure 10.8 illustrates the levels ((FDP) produced for exposure to vertical and lateral vibration for 1–4 minutes and for one and eight hours. It should be noted that the shape of the response curve for either vertical or lateral vibration is assumed to be the same whatever intensity (i.e. time dependency) level is being considered.

Despite its acceptance by so many countries, and despite its incorporation into electronic machines which are used to measure 'human response to vibration', there is little detailed experimental evidence on which the committee based the guide. Thus Oborne (1976) has criticised many of the studies which are referred to in the guide's reference list, primarily from the viewpoint of a lack of experimental design and/or reporting. Furthermore, Oborne (1983) has critically evaluated the guide's empirical bases. He has demonstrated that many of the guide's recommendations, including the shape of the weighting curves shown in Figure 10.8, the suggestion that response to vibration shape remains stable over the intensity range, the concept of time dependency and the response criteria, are not supported by empirical data.

The main innovation of the standard is to relate vibration to exposure time. Thus an operator who is likely to be working in an environment for eight hours in which, for example, 20 Hz vibration predominates, should only receive an average of 0.8 ms^{-2} vibration before performance deteriorates.

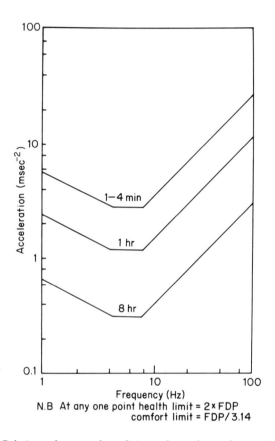

Figure 10.8 ISO fatigue decreased proficiency boundaries for vertical vibration

The same person experiencing the same frequency vibration, but for a short, 1-minute period, would be able to accept about 6.5 ms^{-2}.

Unfortunately, like the rest of the standard, the experimental evidence for this time dependency is sadly lacking. Indeed, as has been shown already, there is little evidence to suggest that any performance reductions which do occur over time arise from anything other than the 'natural' fatiguing effects of performing relatively boring tasks for long periods.

How much trust can be put in many aspects of the guide, therefore, is open to debate. Nevertheless, the ISO document does provide useful starting points from which designers may begin to decide appropriate vibration levels—but these decisions will be more valid if its restrictions are understood. Thus the document refers, primarily, to whole-body vibration applied to seated or standing human beings. It provisionally applies to recumbent or reclining human beings but not to local (for example, hand–arm) vibration. Further, it covers only people in 'normal health', and most of the evidence for the limits appears to be based on averaged laboratory data obtained from fit young men. (Jones and Saunders (1972), for example, have demonstrated some significant differences between men's and women's reactions to higher-frequency (greater than 30 Hz) vibration stimuli.) Finally, and this restriction applies to all composite curves, different individuals react differently to vibration, and curves such as the ISO standards which depict average reactions may mask these differences (see, for example, Oborne and Humphreys, 1976).

Despite such negative conclusions, however, Oborne (1983) does suggest that the committee can claim a significant success in having stimulated discussion and research in an area that has been poorly investigated before their work. Indeed, it might be postulated that the encouraging increase in controlled experimentation in this area, alluded to at the beginning of this chapter, arose largely because of the stimulation provided by ISO/TC 108/WG7. Furthermore, Oborne points out that some revision of the standard is currently taking place, although given the slowness of committee decisions—particularly committees involving a number of different countries—it is likely that it will be a few years before the revised standards will emerge. In the meantime, however, the present standard is in operation and is being used to assess how the complex physical and behavioural structures known as humans are likely to respond to mechanical vibration.

NOISE

Noise is an aspect of the working environment which has received much attention for many decades. Indeed, audiometric surveys were being carried out before the effects of vibration on people even began to be considered. This is probably because the sites of the body which receive the noise stimuli (the ears) are obvious and are able to be stimulated directly, and the equipment used to produce acoustic stimuli is fairly easy to obtain.

Definitions

Noise is conveniently and frequently defined as 'unwanted sound', a definition which in its looseness enables a sound source to be considered as 'noise' or 'not noise' solely on the basis of the listener's reaction to it. Unlike the concept of noise in electronics, for example, no specific characteristic of the noise source (frequency, groups of frequencies, or intensity) is involved.

Acoustic noise is simply sound that is unwanted by the listener—presumably because it is unpleasant or bothersome, it interferes with the perception of wanted sound, or it is physiologically harmful. Furthermore, this definition implies that sounds which are labelled as being 'noise' by an individual on one occasion may not be so labelled at other times or in a different environment.

Because sound is vibration which is normally experienced through the air, the parameters of a single tone are the same as those of a single vibration stimulus—frequency and intensity.

In terms of the frequency, for the human listener sound is defined as acoustic energy between 2 and 20 000 Hz (20 KHz). These are the typical frequency limits of the ear. The ear can still separate the wave changes of the air below about 16 Hz but the sensations are perceived as 'beats'. Above about 16 Hz the beats begin to fuse and produce a tone-like quality.

Noise below about 16 Hz is normally described as infra-sound. This is a stimulus which is receiving more attention and can be produced by any pulsating or throbbing piece of equipment. Leventhall and Kyriakides (1976), for example, have measured significant levels of infra-sound in transport, close to blast-furnaces and diesel engines in industry, and from ventilation systems in offices.

The effects of the levels of infra-sound encountered in normal working conditions are not clear. At high intensities, such as those produced near rockets and extremely large jet engines, detrimental performance effects have certainly been described. However, the infra-sound levels measured in industry and transport, for example, do not reach these high intensities and the evidence of reduced performance caused by levels of infra-sound less than about 120 dB is very weak. This has led authors such as Harris, Sommer and Johnson (1976) to conclude:

> Regardless of whether performance, nystagmus (loss of balance), or subjective measures are considered, it seems certain that the adverse effects of infrasound reported at low-intensity levels either do not exist or have been exaggerated.

Whereas the basic intensity measure of a vibration stimulus is its acceleration, the intensity of a pure tone is defined in terms of pressure changes associated with the compression and refraction in the air caused by the sound source. Sound intensity, therefore, is defined in terms of sound pressure level (SPL) and is measured in the logarithmic units of decibels (dB).

Because the decibel scale is logarithmic in nature a simple, linear relationship with sound intensity does not exist. Thus 100 dB is not twice as intense as 50 dB. Being logarithmic a tenfold increase in power (intensity)

Table 10.2   Some commonly encountered noise levels

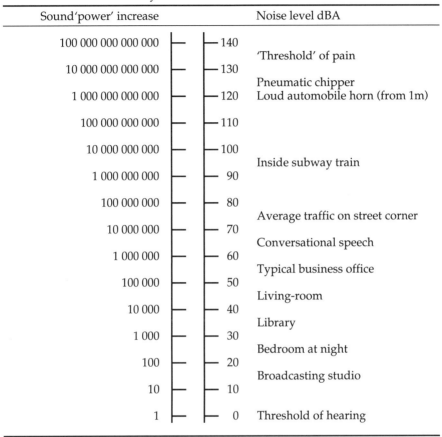

Sound 'power' increase	Noise level dBA	
100 000 000 000 000	140	
		'Threshold' of pain
10 000 000 000 000	130	
		Pneumatic chipper
1 000 000 000 000	120	Loud automobile horn (from 1m)
100 000 000 000	110	
10 000 000 000	100	
		Inside subway train
1 000 000 000	90	
100 000 000	80	
		Average traffic on street corner
10 000 000	70	
		Conversational speech
1 000 000	60	
		Typical business office
100 000	50	
		Living-room
10 000	40	
		Library
1 000	30	
		Bedroom at night
100	20	
		Broadcasting studio
10	10	
1	0	Threshold of hearing

occurs with each 10 dB increase. So 50 dB represents a 100 000 times intensity increase (10^5) and 100 dB represents a 10 000 000 000 times increase (10^{10}) (so 100 dB is 100 000 times as intense as 50 dB). The starting point of the logarithmic scale (0 dB) is arbitrarily set to be at a sound pressure level of 0.0002 dynes/sq cm—the 'average hearing threshold' of the population at 1000 Hz. For this reason a negative decibel value indicates an extremely quiet sound with an SPL of less than 0.0002 dynes/sq cm. Examples of different sound sources on a decibel scale are shown in Table 10.2.

Just as the ear converts acoustic energy into nerve impulses to be decoded and 'measured' by the auditory cortex, electrical sound-measuring machines (sound-level meters) also convert the sound received from the microphone into electrical energy which is then measured. The ear, however, is more sensitive to some frequencies than to others, whereas,

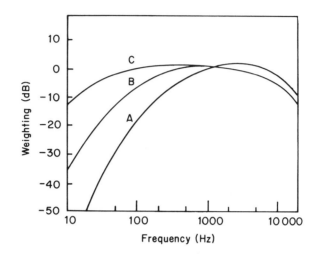

Figure 10.9   The A, B and C noise weightings

unless modified, the microphone and amplifier would treat all frequencies in the same way. For this reason weighting networks are often included in sound-level meters to make them operate in the same way as human ears. The three internationally recognised scales are the A, B and C scales.

As can be seen from Figure 10.9, the A scale tends to attenuate the lower frequencies more than do the B and C scales respectively. These weightings have been produced after measuring the response of the human ear under (A) normal (40 dB), (B) moderate (70 dB) and (C) intense noise conditions and thus would be used in these types of conditions. Because it affects any readings which are made, the scale used should always be quoted in any noise level report, the normal convention being to describe the sound pressure level in either dB(A), dB(B), or dB(C) terms.

HEALTH EFFECTS OF NOISE

Noise can affect health in one or both of two ways: perhaps the most obvious being deafness from long-term exposure, but some types of noise have also been shown to affect personal and mental health.

Noise-induced Hearing Loss

A reduced ability to hear can have two causes. The first, conduction deafness, occurs because the airborne vibration cannot make the eardrum vibrate adequately. It might be caused by such factors as wax in the ear canal, infection or a scarred eardrum. Although conduction deafness does not occur because of a noisy environment, it still has consequences for the individual's social life and safety.

The second kind of deafness, nerve deafness, is caused by reduced sensitivity of the nerve cells in the inner ear. This is likely to result in the operator's hearing loss occurring at or near the frequency range of the environmental noise experienced. Dixon-Ward (1984) points out that temporary changes in the chochlear structure and in the chemical composition of the fluids in the inner ear are produced by even very moderate noises. As the severity of exposure increases such changes also increase, eventually being irreversible. Lim and Dunn (1979) have reviewed many of these physiological effects.

Noise-induced deafness is a significant health problem in most modern countries. It is an insidious complaint since an operator whose hearing is being damaged is unlikely to demonstrate reduced performance owing to the deafness. Without continuous, objective audiometric testing the gradual hearing loss which may be caused by noise will not become apparent.

As will be discussed in more detail later, it is difficult to establish firm links between hearing loss and exposure to specific noises. This is because other environmental and natural sources can also lead to reduced hearing ability. For example, hearing loss can result from the combined effects of the normal noises and sounds that we encounter every day—loud vehicles, music, applause, etc. Hearing loss which occurs from these types of source is generally termed sociacusis. Such exposures, of course, vary from individual to individual. Secondly, infections, and drugs used to control them, can lead to hearing impairment, as can injuries such as a blow to the head. The net effect of these non-acoustic environmental factors on auditory sensitivity is called nosoacusis.

Finally, hearing loss can also occur as a result of the normal process of ageing because of changes that occur in the structure of the auditory apparatus (deposition of substances such as cholesterol, changes in the elasticity of parts of the inner ear, etc.). These have the effect of causing the normal threshold of noise detectability to decline more rapidly at higher frequencies. This ageing factor is termed presbyacusis and, because it does not occur consistently in all individuals, it also complicates the task of determining the extent to which long-term noise exposure contributes to deafness overall.

Noise-induced deafness can be temporary (up to 16 hours) or permanent, and these effects are commonly described as temporary threshold shift (TTS) or permanent threshold shift (PTS) respectively. Although TTS is not

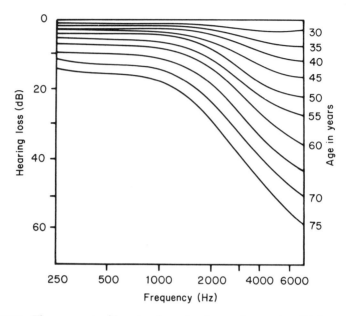

Figure 10.10 The amount of hearing loss due to presbyacusis with increasing age (male subjects) (from Spoor, 1967, reproduced by permission of the International Society of Audiology)

damaging to health, Kryter (1970) considers that the two types of deafness have so many factors in common that it is likely that the continued experience of TTS will lead eventually to PTS. Perhaps the most important of these similarities is that the same areas of the ear are affected in workers suffering from both TTS and PTS.

Variables which Affect Susceptibility to Hearing Loss

Exposure duration

Since becoming progressively deaf is a relatively long-term process, an operator who is continually exposed to a noise stimulus will also become older, and this brings all of age's attendant problems of presbyacusis. Any assessment of the affects of long-term noise exposure, therefore, will be complicated by a need to account for the normal ageing effects.

As was discussed earlier, presbyacusis is symptomatised by a more rapid decline in the hearing threshold at high frequencies than at low. In addition it appears to occur more severely for men than for women. The variations in hearing threshold at different ages are illustrated in Figure 10.10.

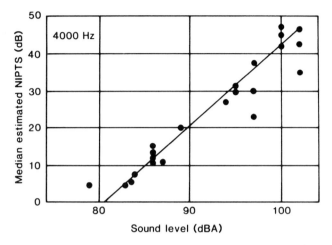

Figure 10.11 Estimated industrial noise-induced permanent threshold shift at 4 kHz produced by ten years or more of exposure to noise (after Dixon-Ward, 1984)

Nixon and Glorig (1961) have considered in detail the relationship between presbyacusis and hearing loss. They demonstrated that a significant increase in hearing loss with exposure was produced only in an industry in which the noise level exceeded 94 dB(A). Furthermore, only workers with more than six years' exposure to the noise in this industry had significant hearing losses at 2 KHz. Other authors have also demonstrated similar effects in other industries (for example Baughn, 1966).

Exposure intensity

In addition to duration, the intensity of noise is an obvious variable which affects the extent to which an operator may become deaf (PTS). As Nixon and Glorig's results show, for example, workers in the industry which had an average noise level greater than 94 dB(A) were liable to PTS, whereas the incidence of hearing loss was lower in the other industries with lower noise levels.

Figure 10.11 illustrates a relationship between sound level and hearing loss described by Dixon-Ward (1984) for different test tones (using a criterion of 8 hours/day, 200 days/year). This figure suggests that damage is likely to occur in exposure above 80 dB(A), although losses for lower-frequency tones occur only at higher intensities.

Because high noise levels can damage hearing permanently, and lower levels can temporarily interfere with hearing, most modern industrialised countries have produced legally enforceable maximum noise levels for

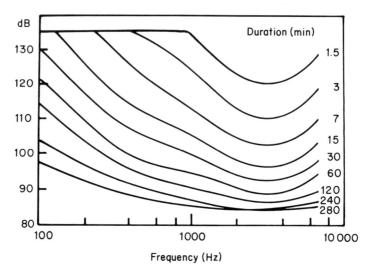

Figure 10.12   Damage risk contours for continuous noise (from Kryter *et al.*, 1966, reproduced by permission of the *Journal of the Acoustical Society of America*)

workers. Such levels are often derived from 'damage risk contours' and Figure 10.12 illustrates one such set of contours produced by Kryter *et al.* (1966). Like the ISO standard for exposure to whole-body vibration, the damage risk contours also relate exposure risk to exposure duration.

Type of noise

In addition to being defined in terms of the total length of time for which the operator is exposed to the noise, the duration of exposure can also be considered in terms of the intermittency of the stimulation; that is, whether the noise is continuous or the continuity is broken either by bursts of louder noise or periods of quiet.

Although most of the studies of hearing loss have been carried out using continuous noise, the effects of intermittent noise on hearing are gradually being documented. The few results available suggest that the important stimulus characteristic, at least for recovery from TTS, is the average energy level of the noise to which the operator is exposed. Johnson, Nixon and Stephenson (1976), for example, exposed subjects to pink noise for different on–off periods (pink noise is a special type of random noise which is composed of frequencies within a specified bandwidth and with constant energy levels). It is important to note that the levels of intermittent noise were set to produce equivalent energies to 85 dB(A) continuous noise. The authors measured their subjects' hearing levels

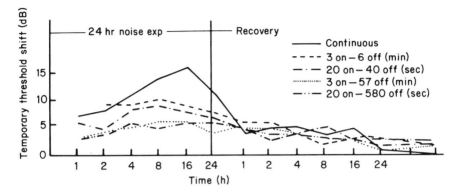

Figure 10.13 Growth and recovery from TTS using different types of noise (from Johnson, Nixon and Stephenson, 1976, reproduced by permission of the Aerospace Medical Association)

at different times during the 24-hour exposure period and for 24 hours after (recovery). Their results are shown in Figure 10.13, from which it is clear that although the continuous noise produced slightly more TTS than the intermittent noise, the recovery trends for each type of noise were very similar.

Kryter *et al.* (1966) discuss in more detail the damaging effects of interrupted noise, and have produced a series of damage risk contours for such noises (see Figure 10.14).

Another kind of intermittent noise occurs as a sudden large 'bang' or impulses arising from any percussion type of machine such as a gun, steam hammer or road hammer. Impulsive sound is characterised by an initial high-energy surge which reaches its peak extremely quickly (a near-instantaneous rise time), but which decays gradually over about 1 msec. The damaging effects of the stimulus are the intensity of the initial surge and the decay duration. Coles *et al.* (1968) reviewed many of the studies concerning the TTS and PTS resulting from such noise. On the basis of these studies they produced a damage risk contour for impulsive sounds (shown in Figure 10.15) which relates the maximum sound pressure level acceptable to the ear (i.e. the noise from both the machine itself and reflected from the surroundings) to the impulse duration. They point out that such criteria will protect 75 per cent of the population at risk; to protect 90 per cent the contour should be reduced by 5 dB at each duration. They also emphasise that the criterion is based on repetition rates in the order of 6–30 impulses per minute, 'with the total number of impulses limited to around 100 per exposure'.

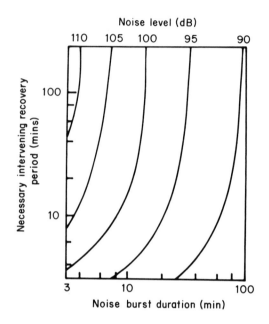

Figure 10.14 Damage risk contours for intermittent noise containing frequencies 1200–2400 Hz (from Kryter *et al.*, 1966, reproduced by permission of the *Journal of the Acoustical Society of America*)

PERFORMANCE EFFECTS OF NOISE

Communication

Effective verbal communication depends on both the speaker's ability to produce the correct speech sounds and the listener's ability to receive and decode these sounds. A noisy environment is likely to interfere with this last stage in speech transmission because of an effect which is described as 'masking'.

The American Standards Association (1960) defines auditory masking as 'the process by which the threshold of audibility for one sound is raised by the presence of another sound'. Deatherage and Evans (1969), however, have redefined the concept as 'the process by which the detectability of one sound, the signal, is impaired by the presence of another sound, the masker'. This reformulation recognises that masking occurs at higher signal intensities than threshold (minimum audible) levels.

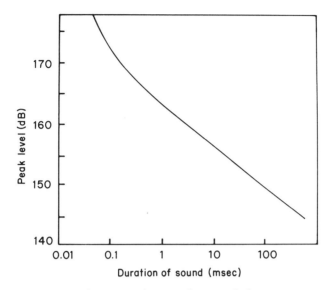

Figure 10.15 Damage risk contour for impulse sounds having near instantaneous rise times (from Coles *et al.*, 1968, reproduced by permission of the *Journal of the Acoustical Society of America*)

Since masking impairs the perception of a signal (in the present context the 'signal' is either speech or the output of an auditory display) it is important to realise the conditions under which masking occurs so that its effects can be reduced. However, masking depends on almost any aspect of the signal and of the masker (noise) that could be considered: their respective intensities, frequencies, phases, durations, etc.

As far as intensity relationships are concerned, the results of many studies over the years have proved to be fairly consistent: more masking occurs as the masker (noise) intensity increases when the signal intensity remains constant; less masking occurs as the signal intensity increases if the masker intensity remains constant.

The frequency relationships, however, are slightly more complex. Although the amount of masking increases as the masker frequency approaches that of the signal, Fletcher (1940) demonstrated that this effect occurs within a 'critical band' of frequencies. He demonstrated that a pure tone is really masked only by a certain narrow band of noises which are centred at the frequency of the tone. Frequency components outside this critical band are relatively ineffective in their masking ability. He also showed that the breadth of the critical band increases as the central frequency of the masker (noise) increases above 1000 Hz.

Although the notion of a critical band is adequate for most circumstances, if the noise intensity is 'sufficiently' high it can mask tones which lie outside its critical band. Bilger and Hirsh (1956) describe these effects as 'remote masking' and suggest that they occur as a result of the high noise intensity 'scattering' acoustic energy in the cochlea causing distortion, the products of which may act as masking stimuli.

Finally, phase relationships: a pure tone is produced by the action of an earphone diaphragm (A) vibrating sinusoidally. If a second diaphragm (B) is made to vibrate with the same frequency but A is at its peak position when B is at its lowest, then the two diaphragms are said to be out of phase. They are in phase when both move in the same direction at the same time. Different phase relationships occur between these two extremes of 0 degrees (in phase) to 180 degrees (out of phase).

During the Second World War workers at the Harvard psycho-acoustic laboratory showed that when the noise and the signal (speech) are presented to both ears a substantial improvement in hearing could occur if either was reversed in phase at one ear relative to the other ear. Using speech as his signal, Licklider (1948) showed that intelligibility was highest with the antiphasic relations and lowest with the homophasic arrangements—with the heterophasic conditions allowing intermediate intelligibility.

The reason for such differential phase effects probably lies in the fact that as tones vary in phase between the two ears the position of the resultant tone appears to 'rotate' around the head. If both the signal and masker are in phase, therefore, the two appear to be in the same position in space. As one moves out of phase between the ears, however, it appears to 'separate' from the other and thus becomes more discriminatable. This is simply a further example of the general observation that masking decreases as the signal and masker become less 'similar'.

Such phenomena also enable 'three-dimensional' auditory stimuli to be produced which will provide the basis for special alerting stimuli to be presented, as well as the potential development of effective 'virtual reality' in the acoustic domain (for example, Begault and Wenzel, 1993).

Implications for Communication

The evidence from masking studies has implications for speech communication in noise. For example, if the environmental noise has a similar bandwidth to that of normal speech, or if it is louder, then masking will occur.

Kryter (1970) indicates that speech (for both males and females) tends to predominate at around 400–500 Hz, but includes frequencies up to 5000 Hz. Clearly, therefore, significant environmental noise having these frequencies should be avoided. However, Licklider's (1948) data suggest that if the speech can be presented to the observer through earphones, adjusted so that one diaphragm is out of phase with the other, then masking may be reduced.

The normal behavioural response to increased ambient noise levels will be for the speaker's voice to be raised. Increases of 10 dB in the noise level, for example, have been shown to cause normal-hearing talkers to raise their voice levels by amounts varying between 3 dB (Van Heusden, Plump and Pols, 1979) and 6–10 dB (Pearsons, Bennett and Fidell, 1977). However, such increases in effort are generally insufficient to overcome the increases in noise level completely.

If the signal is masked by noise which is interrupted by periods of quiet, then the degree of masking changes in quite a complex manner which is determined by the rate of interruption. Miller and Licklider (1950), for example, explain the relationship as follows:

> At interruptions of less than 2/sec, whole words or syllables within a word tend to be masked; at interruption rates of between 2 and 30/sec, noise duration is so brief that the listener is able to hear a portion of each syllable or phoneme of the speech signal, thereby tending to reduce the amount of masking; when the interruption rate is more frequent than 30/sec the spread of masking in time around the moment of occurrence of a burst of noise results in increased masking until by 100 interruptions per sec there is, effectively, continuous masking.
>
> (Reprinted from the *Journal of the Acoustical Society of America* by permission of the publisher.)

In conclusion it should be pointed out that most studies of this nature have been conducted using young (usually male), articulate subjects with normal hearing in situations where no face-to-face contact is permitted (which is analogous to using the telephone). Little attention has been paid to the social and non-verbal cues which also occur between people who are speaking. For example, Waltzman and Levitt (1978) reported that face-to-face encounters using visual cues improve the intelligibility of noisy messages quite considerably. Furthermore, Webster (1973) has shown that the speech-intelligibility criteria used, which are based on speech without visual cues, overestimate the effect of noise for face-to-face communication by as much as 20 dB. Finally, virtually nothing is known of the skills that we use to perceive speech in noisy conditions. This is despite the fact that there is ample anecdotal evidence to suggest that individuals who are practised at conversing in noisy settings are able to pick out speech more accurately than those who are not practised.

Cognitive Performance

There is currently a great deal of controversy over the question of whether environmental noise affects anything other than auditory-based performance. Stevens (1972), for example, insisted that noise has no direct detrimental effects on humans, apart from producing deafness and annoyance. After including masking as an effect, this suggestion has also been supported by Kryter (1970), Poulton (1977), and Koelega and Brinkman (1986).

Other authors, however, claim that continuous broad-band noise at higher levels than 100 dB(A) has a detrimental effect on work. This is distinct from the effects of the noise masking any auditory feedback cues which the operator can derive from the task.

The available evidence, however, remains very difficult to interpret and does not lead to any firm conclusions about whether or not noise affects cognitive performance. Jones (1983), for example, argues that, given the disparate nature of the results from many dozens of studies, it would be foolish to search for generalisations. Koelega and Brinkman (1986) summarise a variety of task and stimuli characteristics that have been thought to influence the effects of noise on cognitive performance, including the kind of experimental design, noise intensity and frequency, the meaningfulness of the noise, its time course and scheduling; but also conclude that the effects are too nebulous to be meaningful.

Any effects which do occur have been proposed by Poulton (1976, 1977) to be the result of some kind of masking. He suggests that in such studies 'inner speech' is also masked by the noise: 'you can't hear yourself think in noise'. Thus many of the tasks which have demonstrated a detrimental effect of noise had a large short-term memory component: subtracting a four-digit number from a memorised six-digit number; counting and holding in separate cumulative totals the number of flashes from each of three sources; searching for a series of two-digit numbers, etc. In such tasks Poulton argues that the noise masks the individual's internal verbal rehearsal loop, causing the person to work more slowly and to make more errors.

A separate hypothesis to account for some of the possibly observed detrimental effects of noise has been advanced by Jerison (1959). He suggests that the noise affects the operator's judgements of time. He asked his subjects to press a key at what they considered to be 10-minute intervals. Throughout the experimental period his subjects progressively contracted their internal timescale when in the noisy condition but not in 'quiet'. Whereas in the first 15 minutes of noise the key was pressed after an average period of 8¾ minutes (to signal the end of a 10-minute period), after 2¾ hours '10 minutes' was contracted to about seven minutes. It is not entirely clear, however, how such distortions in time judgement can influence all kinds of cognitive or motor work performance.

Environmental noise can also affect memory, although it is not clear whether this occurs only at the input (memorising) stage, at the output (retrieval) stage, or both. Furthermore, the direction of the effect (an improvement or reduction in memory) is equivocal. Some studies have suggested that noise improves immediate retention while others have shown an impairment. Indeed, still others have suggested that noise has no effect on immediate retention.

The levels of noise used in experiments of this nature, however, have generally been very high (greater than about 80 dB(A)). Slightly lower noise intensities (65 dB(A)) generally improve immediate recall (for example, Berlyne et al., 1965; Wesner, 1972). This is probably because of the inverted-U, arousal–performance relationship discussed in Chapter 1. Thus moderate noise levels increase body arousal so that performance also increases. Too much noise, however, causes arousal to become too high with resultant reductions in performance. This suggests, therefore, that noise acts on cognitive behaviour as a general stressor, and that any performance increases or decreases in noisy conditions can be explained in these terms. This possibility will be considered later.

Finally, authors such as Broadbent and Gregory (1965) and Hockey (1970) suggest that noise may not affect so much the observer's ability to monitor a signal but both the criteria used to decide whether a signal is present and the search pattern employed. Thus Broadbent and Gregory demonstrated that in 100 dB noise observers were more likely to report being 'sure yes' or 'sure no' of perceiving a signal than in quieter conditions. Hockey showed that in noise the subject's search pattern changed to give more weight to areas of the panel which contained the highest proportion of signals. Results such as these, therefore, imply that observers' cognitive strategies change in noise to become more efficient and less wide ranging.

From laboratory-based studies at least, therefore, a detrimental effect of noise on cognitive performance alone has not been shown to occur for all types of task. Noise clearly has an effect on overall performance, but this could be as much owing to masking acoustic cues as to any deficiency in central cognitive processing.

In general, the conclusion must be that the relationship between noise and cognitive performance is similar to that between any environmental stressor and cognitive performance, as discussed at the beginning of this chapter. That is, the stressor is unlikely to affect cognitive performance as long as it does not demand more mental capacity than the task leaves spare.

With stress, however, there is general agreement that it not only brings about quantitative changes in performance but also qualitative changes. Easterbrook (1959), for example, proposed that in overaroused subjects attention tends to be concentrated on the dominant and obvious aspects of the situation. This suggests that some aspects of task performance might be relatively unaffected by stress but that performance on other, more difficult or less important, aspects may be impaired. For example, Boggs and Simon (1968) examined noise effects in relation to task complexity. They found a reliable noise–complexity interaction in which noise produced more errors in complex rather than simple tasks.

Views such as this have been extended to emphasise that stress also reduces the stability of attention and interferes with the capacity to discriminate relevant from irrelevant aspects of a task. Since stress is also likely to narrow the span of attention in the way described above, Jones (1979) suggests that the qualitative results of stress are that it seems to produce strategic changes in behaviour rather than simply depressing performance.

The idea that coping with noise involves some cognitive intervention has also evolved in other areas of enquiry. Over the past decade or so there has been an increasing amount of interest in the notion of 'perceived control' as a means of alleviating the deleterious after-effects of noise. For example, Wohlwill *et al.* (1976) suggest that individuals can cope with noise through increased concentration and effort. They make the observation that subjects in such experiments sometimes experience considerable 'release of tension' after the experience—even to the extent of breaking down and crying. In a series of studies (Glass and Singer, 1972) subjects exposed to loud intermittent noise over which they had no control showed no detrimental effects in their performance during the noise (indeed, physiological indices indicated that the subjects had adapted to the noise), but they performed badly when the noise had ceased and they moved to another room. These results contrasted with those from similar groups of subjects who were told that they could terminate the noise although they were encouraged not to do so. These subjects showed no detrimental effects after the noise.

BACKGROUND MUSIC AND PRODUCTIVITY

In many respects the topic of background music should not be considered in a section that discusses the effects of noise on performance. By definition noise is unwanted sound, whereas background music is often wanted and enjoyed by many workers. In cases where it is not wanted (and thus becomes 'noise') the sound pressure levels produced are not high enough to cause the direct performance reductions discussed above, so the effect is more likely to become one of annoyance, as will be discussed later. Nevertheless, the effects of background music on performance will be considered here since music is an acoustic stimulus which, it has been argued, may affect performance. As with the effects of noise on cognitive performance, the evidence regarding music and productivity is controversial.

Fox (1983) distinguishes between two kinds of music at work—background music and industrial music. Although each might be used to increase commercial profitability, they are quite different in their mode of operation. Background music is the type of music often heard in shops and supermarkets; as 'acoustic wallpaper' it is an endless stream of light, quiet music designed to put shoppers at ease. Industrial music, on the other hand, generally varies in kind; it does not occur all of the time but only at selected periods during the day. Indeed, if the music were to be played all of the time it would defeat the reason for its presence.

The theoretical basis for suggesting that music might aid performance lies in alleviating the boredom and fatigue which often accompany repetitive work. Again the inverted-U, performance–arousal relationship is invoked (Fox, 1971). Thus the normal stimulation which an operator receives from the task not only gives information about the job but provides stimulation for the reticular activating system (RAS) in the brain which determines how much attention, alertness or vigilance the operator brings to the job. Repetitive work with little stimulation can lead to underarousal and reduced efficiency; so the basis of any effects of industrial music is that the varying, secondary stimulation provided by the music might create the stimulus required to 're-activate' the RAS.

It is difficult to measure the effects of background music in actual organisational studies because other performance influencers are often also present. Thus music may influence not only attention and vigilance but feelings of well-being and job satisfaction, and these effects could be reflected in reductions in absenteeism, bad time-keeping and labour turnover which are likely to increase overall productivity.

Studies investigating the effects of industrial music on productivity have been reviewed by Fox (1971, 1983). Although many were poorly controlled he concluded, from studies based in both laboratory and industrial settings, that under the right conditions music can be beneficial. Thus subjects increased their performance in the laboratory; and the industry-based studies showed reduced errors, staff turnover and accidents, better time-keeping, and increased output and production quality.

When considering the music to be used for such purposes, two important questions are when the music should be played and what kind of music should be used. Answers to these two questions can be found in the theoretical rationale for using industrial music—to increase arousal. Regarding the times for music, the inverted-U arousal–performance hypothesis suggests that it should be played at times during the day when arousal would otherwise be low. Daily variations in human performance and efficiency have long been recognised and are generally termed 'circadian rhythms'. For example, Blake (1971) demonstrated increases in performance between 0800 and 1030 hours, with a 'post-lunch' dip at about 1400 hours. Unfortunately, precise times during the day for these peaks and troughs are not available (see Folkard and Monk, 1979) and so the appropriate times need to be determined empirically within different working environments.

Finally, with regard to the content of the music, a series of studies carried out by Fox and Embrey (1972) suggests that the workers themselves should be able to choose their music. In a laboratory experiment the authors tested six subjects on a detection task using four conditions:

(1) No music.

(2) Music played during the 15th to 20th minute of the test session using a programme of randomly selected music.

(3) As in (2) but using a commercially prepared, lively programme.

(4) As in (2) but allowing the subjects to select a programme from the tapes used in (3).

Their results demonstrated that average detection efficiency increased significantly from the 'no music' to the 'commercial music' conditions, with the detection rate being higher when the subjects were able to choose their music—(4) rather than (3).

NOISE ANNOYANCE

Annoyance is a common subjective response which we all exhibit when exposed to something we do not want. Since, by definition, noise is unwanted sound, in whatever form it presents itself (speech, music or random acoustic energy) it can cause annoyance. The extent to which particular sounds are likely to cause annoyance will be determined not simply by their physical characteristics but by the extent to which they are unwanted by the listener. So what is annoying to one person may not be so to another, and even what is annoying to someone on one occasion may not be so at another time. It is not possible, therefore, to define strictly the acoustic conditions likely to cause annoyance (as, for example, the conditions likely to lead to deafness or to reduced speech intelligibility can be defined). Nevertheless, there are some physical aspects of noise which are more likely to be annoying than others.

Physical Aspects of Noise Annoyance

Contrary to popular opinion the mere physical intensity of a noise is not the only feature likely to cause annoyance. Two noises can have the same intensity but cause different degrees of annoyance, perhaps because of the frequencies which they contain, their respective durations, or even their meaning to the listener.

Kryter (1970) suggests that five physical aspects of a noise stimulus can be identified as affecting its annoyance level:

(1) The spectrum content and level.

(2) The spectrum complexity.

(3) The sound duration.

(4) The sound rise time (i.e. the length of time it takes to reach its maximum level).

(5) The maximum level reached (for impulsive sounds such as a door bang).

The relationships between most of these parameters and annoyance are likely to be fairly obvious. For example, annoyance increases the louder the sound, the longer it continues, etc. (although Poulsen, 1991, demonstrated that rated annoyance does not increase significantly after about five minutes of exposure). With regard to the spectrum content, however, the relationship is not as straightforward. By asking subjects to adjust tones of different frequencies to make them equally 'noisy', Kryter and Pearsons (1966) produced bands of equal 'noisiness' over a frequency range of 40 to 10 000 Hz (a distinction was made between 'noisiness' and 'loudness'). These bands indicated that the higher frequencies (above about 2000 Hz) tend to contribute more to the sound noisiness (and thus are likely to be more annoying) than the lower frequencies—even though they were equally loud. This relationship can be seen in Figure 10.16: as the noise frequency increases above about 1000 Hz it appears to become more 'noisy' (or, interpreting the graph literally, with increasing frequency a lower

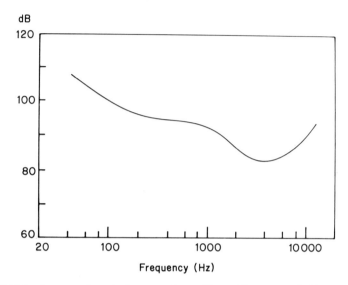

Figure 10.16 An equal noiseless contour (from Kryter and Pearsons, 1966, reproduced by permission of the *Journal of the Acoustical Society of America*)

intensity is needed to maintain the same noisiness level). Although the same relationship is apparent when the sounds are made to be equally 'loud', the increase in sensitivity for higher frequencies is not so marked.

Details of the procedures used to record and measure noise levels at a workplace are provided by Michael and Bienvenue (1983).

Subjective Aspects of Noise Annoyance

In many respects what is conveyed by the term 'annoyance' is not just 'noisiness'; annoyance implies something more. It commonly signifies one's reaction to sound that is based not only on physical characteristics of the stimulus but also on what it means; the emotional content and the novelty that the sound can have for the listener. For example, Raw and Griffiths (1990) point to studies which have shown that people's negative responses to reductions in road traffic noise generally decrease more than a 'simple' noise-reduction model would suggest. This implies, therefore, that dissatisfaction and annoyance with noise include components additional to the content of the noise itself. As Wilson (1963) suggests:

> The annoyance may be ascribed to the 'information' which sounds may carry from the source to the recipient. The physical energy in the noise of a creaking door, a crying baby, or a distant party may be very small, and if distributed in the form of random noise probably would be quite unnoticed. But it may

convey manifold suggestions of alarm, neglect, sadness, loneliness, and so in some people it has an emotional effect out of all proportion to its physical intensity.

Reviewing the many studies and surveys that have been carried out to investigate the types and levels of noise which cause disturbance, it is clear that annoyance generally occurs either when the noise interferes with people's ability to carry out some activity that they wish to do, or when the individual feels unable to be in control of the situation. For example, Levy-Leboyer and Naturel (1991) surveyed reactions of residents in a neighbourhood to noise experiences. They demonstrated that the most annoying noises were those that were judged to be not normal and possible to avoid. The residents' reactions did not seem to be linked to the level of annoyance experienced, but rather to the degree of control they felt they had over the situation and to the motives they attributed to the person making the noise.

Speech is a kind of noise which carries with it a great deal of information; it is also a significant source of noise in rooms such as offices. Thus Nemecek and Grandjean (1973) surveyed the noise requirements of employees working in landscaped offices. Of the employees who considered that they were disturbed by noise, 46 per cent felt that the noise produced by conversations was most annoying; 25 per cent disliked office machinery noise and 19 per cent the telephones. Interestingly, further questioning revealed that the majority who indicated that conversation noise disturbed them most felt that it was the content of the conversation rather than its loudness which was most disturbing.

The problem of overhearing conversations was also advanced as a cause of annoyance by Cavanaugh et al. (1962) and Waller (1969). Proposing the concept of 'speech privacy' these authors have argued that the disturbance might be caused by the worry that if one can hear other people talking then one can also be heard by other people. They also suggest that it is the degree to which the intruding speech can be understood, rather than its loudness, which destroys the feeling of office privacy.

Some studies have attempted to relate the noise sensitivity of individuals to individual traits. For example, Stephens (1970) examined the relationship between the judgement of loudness and annoyance in conjunction with various personality measures. He found that among tests measuring introversion, need achievement, test anxiety, social desirability and general annoyance, only the test anxiety scores correlated significantly with noise sensitivity. He ascribed this result to the tendency for anxious subjects to give extreme responses to very different stimulus levels. Interestingly, noise annoyance did not correlate at all well with noise sensitivity.

Evidence is also available to suggest that continued noise does detrimentally affect social behaviour. For example, Mathews and Cannon (1975) investigated the influence of noise on the willingness to help an experimenter's confederate pick up materials which had been 'accidentally' dropped. Subjects who were exposed to 85 dB(A) noise were less likely to help than those exposed to a maximum of 65 dB(A). Similar results were obtained in a more naturalistic setting. In addition, a study by Crook and Langdon (1974) of classroom activity in schools around a London airport demonstrated the distracting effects of noise and the results that this can have on social interaction. As well as the aircraft noise interfering with lessons, the authors also reported changes in the style of teaching on the noisier days (lessons abandoned and more pauses in the flow of the teacher), increased pupil fidgeting, and reduced teacher satisfaction with the class as a whole. Thus teachers often felt that the noise caused the whole atmosphere of the proceedings to deteriorate, that they and their pupils became irritable and tired, that they developed headaches and that the pupils became noisier and less inclined to work. Hetu, Truchon-Gagnon and Bilodeau (1990) have recently reviewed studies which have investigated the effects of all kinds of noise within classroom settings, and point to reported disturbance effects on attention and learning, speech intelligibility, and the children's health and well-being.

As well as directly interfering with tasks, the indirect consequences of noise can also be annoying. For example, Griffiths and Langdon (1968) investigated community responses to road traffic noise. In addition to causing problems such as headaches, noise was annoying because it made the respondents keep their windows shut during the summer months. In addition there were also complaints that living next to a noisy road resulted in house values being reduced. Similar points were also raised by Stockbridge and Lee (1973), while Öhrstrom (1989) and Öhrstrom and Rylander (1990) have shown clear effects of noise on sleep disturbance. Annoyance, therefore, appears to be a subjective reaction to interference in the ability to carry out a preferred task (for example, talking or sleeping). It can also arise as a result of changes in the listener's physiological state, perhaps causing headaches and high blood pressure. In these cases, however, the effects of noise are owing not to the specific attributes of the noise but to the stress or distress which it causes.

Finally, one extreme response to noise as a stressor that has been documented slightly is reduced mental health. In this case, several lines of indirect evidence point to some increase in incidence of minor psychiatric disturbance as a result of exposure to noise. For example, Cohen, Glass and Singer (1973) have suggested that:

Existing evidence suggests that noise may indeed have some res[...]
the personal disorganisation of those living or working
environments. Industrial surveys, for example, report that noise [...]
results in increased anxiety and stress responses. Workers habitually ex[...]
to high intensity noise show increased incidence of nervous complai[...]
nausea, headaches, instability, argumentativeness, sexual impotency, change
in general mood and anxiety ... Jansen (1961) reports that workers in the
noisiest places in a steel factory have a greater frequency of social conflicts
both at home and in the plant.

Cohen, Glass and Singer do point out, however, that it is difficult to ascribe
these effects solely to noise. There is a variety of other stresses associated
with noisy workplaces and a number of variables which are related to the
types of people who are likely to work in them. At the very least, however,
the evidence is suggestive of some distinctive social effects.

SUMMARY

This chapter has considered in detail the effects which two environmental
parameters, vibration and noise, have on human beings. In both cases the
effects can be threefold. At extreme intensities they can be dangerous,
causing either a breakdown of body parts (in the case of vibration) or
deafness (from noise). At lower intensities, however, they are more likely to
affect performance, although more diversely. Thus vibration interferes
primarily with the ability to control the affected body part (either a limb or
the eyes); the performance effects of noise are likely to occur in interference
with hearing. Some evidence exists to suggest that both environmental
parameters affect cognitive performance, although it is likely that they act
in the manner of general stressors rather than affecting the brain directly.
The final reaction to both vibration and noise is one of reduced comfort and
increased annoyance. In both cases, however, although it is possible to
relate the degree of annoyance or comfort reduction to physical aspects of
the stimuli, the reaction is likely to be determined by the meaning of the
stimulus to the individual and its effects on the ability to carry out a
preferred task.

11

PHYSICAL
...RONMENT II:
...RATURE AND
ILLUMINATION

Chapter 10 considered two aspects of the environment (vibration and noise) which affect health, performance and comfort. Each has a fairly clear relationship between its intensity and its importance to the human operator, in so far as the intensity effects fall along a single dimension that extends between no (or relatively little) effect to maximum interference. For example, if all machine-borne vibration could be eliminated from the environment there would be no interference with motor performance; when levels are high it interferes considerably.

The position is slightly different, however, for both temperature and illumination, since for both stimuli there is a narrow range of intensities under which a person can, and should, operate. Departure from this optimum, either by increasing or by reducing the intensity, is likely to affect performance, comfort and, in extreme cases, health. For example our ability to see fine detail is impaired in both dark and very bright conditions; our ability to perform complex mental operations is affected by both hot and cold conditions.

Just as vibration and noise were treated separately in Chapter 10, so temperature and illumination will be in this chapter. Again, however, this is not to imply that their effects are independent or that one is more important than the other. As was stressed in Chapter 10, the importance of any environmental factor can vary in different circumstances and their interactive effects can be unpredictable.

TEMPERATURE

A human's response to the thermal environment depends largely on a very complex balance between the levels of heat produced and heat lost. The

Existing evidence suggests that noise may indeed have some responsibility for the personal disorganisation of those living or working in noisy environments. Industrial surveys, for example, report that noise exposure results in increased anxiety and stress responses. Workers habitually exposed to high intensity noise show increased incidence of nervous complaints, nausea, headaches, instability, argumentativeness, sexual impotency, change in general mood and anxiety ... Jansen (1961) reports that workers in the noisiest places in a steel factory have a greater frequency of social conflicts both at home and in the plant.

Cohen, Glass and Singer do point out, however, that it is difficult to ascribe these effects solely to noise. There is a variety of other stresses associated with noisy workplaces and a number of variables which are related to the types of people who are likely to work in them. At the very least, however, the evidence is suggestive of some distinctive social effects.

SUMMARY

This chapter has considered in detail the effects which two environmental parameters, vibration and noise, have on human beings. In both cases the effects can be threefold. At extreme intensities they can be dangerous, causing either a breakdown of body parts (in the case of vibration) or deafness (from noise). At lower intensities, however, they are more likely to affect performance, although more diversely. Thus vibration interferes primarily with the ability to control the affected body part (either a limb or the eyes); the performance effects of noise are likely to occur in interference with hearing. Some evidence exists to suggest that both environmental parameters affect cognitive performance, although it is likely that they act in the manner of general stressors rather than affecting the brain directly. The final reaction to both vibration and noise is one of reduced comfort and increased annoyance. In both cases, however, although it is possible to relate the degree of annoyance or comfort reduction to physical aspects of the stimuli, the reaction is likely to be determined by the meaning of the stimulus to the individual and its effects on the ability to carry out a preferred task.

11

THE PHYSICAL ENVIRONMENT II: TEMPERATURE AND ILLUMINATION

Chapter 10 considered two aspects of the environment (vibration and noise) which affect health, performance and comfort. Each has a fairly clear relationship between its intensity and its importance to the human operator, in so far as the intensity effects fall along a single dimension that extends between no (or relatively little) effect to maximum interference. For example, if all machine-borne vibration could be eliminated from the environment there would be no interference with motor performance; when levels are high it interferes considerably.

The position is slightly different, however, for both temperature and illumination, since for both stimuli there is a narrow range of intensities under which a person can, and should, operate. Departure from this optimum, either by increasing or by reducing the intensity, is likely to affect performance, comfort and, in extreme cases, health. For example our ability to see fine detail is impaired in both dark and very bright conditions; our ability to perform complex mental operations is affected by both hot and cold conditions.

Just as vibration and noise were treated separately in Chapter 10, so temperature and illumination will be in this chapter. Again, however, this is not to imply that their effects are independent or that one is more important than the other. As was stressed in Chapter 10, the importance of any environmental factor can vary in different circumstances and their interactive effects can be unpredictable.

TEMPERATURE

A human's response to the thermal environment depends largely on a very complex balance between the levels of heat produced and heat lost. The

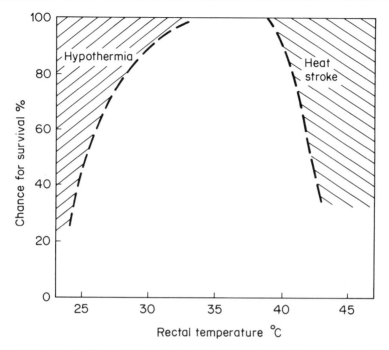

Figure 11.1 The likelihood of survival with different rectal temperatures (adapted from Luczak, 1991; reproduced from *Ergonomics*, **34**, 687–720, by permission of Taylor & Francis)

heat resulting from the normal body metabolism, during work for example, maintains the body at a temperature well above that of the usual surrounding environment. At the same time heat is constantly being lost from the body by radiation, convection and evaporation, so that under ordinary resting conditions the deep body temperature is maintained within its normal narrow range of between 36.1 and 37.2 °C (97–99 °F). Although the skin temperatures may fluctuate over quite a wide range without serious damage to performance or health, the deep body temperature must stay within this narrow range. Figure 11.1 illustrates the narrowness of this range of deep body temperatures.

The body's thermal balance is maintained by a very complex self-regulating system situated in the hypothalamus in the brain (see Mekjavic and Bligh, 1987, for a comprehensive treatment of the body's thermoregulation system). Put in its simplest form, the system depends on blood temperature being sensed by sensors, some of which have been found in the epidermis, the lining of the veins, and the gut. Whenever the body needs to lose heat hypothalamic activity causes the blood vessels to dilate, the sweat glands to produce cooling sweat, the respiration rate to increase, and the body's metabolic rate to be lowered. Under cold conditions, when the body needs to conserve and even generate heat, the hypothalamus causes the blood vessels to constrict and to route the blood away from the extremities (causing the characteristic 'blue' appearance), and increases the metabolic rate by inducing the often uncontrollable muscle activity described as shivering. By these processes the optimum body temperature is maintained through quite adverse external environmental conditions.

In some cases, however, this self-regulating system proves to be inadequate and the body either gains or loses too much heat. Depending on the amount of heat gained or lost the process can lead, progressively, to reduced performance, damaged health and, eventually, to death. Any discussion of the effects of the thermal environments, therefore, is complicated by the need to consider the effects of heat and cold separately. Thus, the first part of this section will deal with health and performance effects of hot conditions. In the second part these aspects will be discussed in relation to cold conditions. The final part will deal with less extreme departures from optimal balance and their effects on comfort.

HOT ENVIRONMENTAL CONDITIONS

Health Effects (Hyperthermia)

The health of a worker exposed to high levels of radiant or convected heat may be damaged in one or both of two ways. First, elevated temperatures on the skin can result in tissue damage from burning, particularly at skin temperatures of over 45 °C (113 °F). These effects, however, are immediately observable and under normal circumstances pain will cause the operator to remove the exposed body part from danger.

The more insidious effects of an elevated body temperature occur if the deep body temperature increases to a level of about 42 °C (108 °F) (i.e. a core temperature increase of about 5 °C (10 °F)). When this occurs the onset of heat stroke (hyperthermia) can be very sudden with the collapse and (unless treated promptly) the imminent death of the individual. In some cases the loss of consciousness is preceded by a short period of general weakness or confusion and irrational behaviour (under hyperthermic conditions, as well as transporting oxygen the blood has to transport heat from the interior of the body to the skin, so limiting the amount of oxygen that can be transported; see Rodahl and Guthe, 1988).

There are three related reasons why the body may be unable to rid itself of the excess heat generated. First, when the individual is exposed to environmental conditions which are so humid that the body cannot reduce heat by evaporating sweat. For example, small microclimates can be produced around a body that is inside protective clothing which become supersaturated with water, thus impairing adequate evaporation. Secondly, heat stress can also be caused by the insulating effects of some protective clothing. In this case the stress arises because of impaired evaporation owing, perhaps, to the impermeability of the clothing and to its heat-retaining properties. Finally hyperthermia can occur when the environmental conditions are too hot (although not dangerously so) but may still interfere both with the body's ability to produce sweat and sweat's ability to cool the body. In such conditions, of course, more and more sweat may be produced and dehydration (hypohydration) from excessive sweating can, itself, lead to dangerous conditions.

Since heat stress is a function of the body's core temperature rather than the external conditions, it may still occur even if the surrounding temperature is less than the critical 42 °C. Thus strenuous physical exercise can cause heat stroke if the metabolic heat released by the effort is greater than the body's ability to rid itself of the excess. Indeed, after reviewing many studies of the affliction, Shibolet, Lancaster and Danon (1976) argue that heat stroke is most likely to strike highly motivated young individuals who are engaged in hard work, military training and sport. Under other circumstances these individuals would rest when tired, take liquid when dry, or remain at home when ill. The authors suggest, therefore, that heat stroke prevention requires adequate rest and liquid consumption (to compensate for the increased liquid loss during sweating) before physical exertion, as well as periods of rest during work when the individual can cool off and drink adequately. When such seemingly obvious precautions were implemented in the South African mining industry, Wyndham (1966) demonstrated a significant reduction in the incidence of heat stroke mortality among South African miners.

Another significant factor in the likelihood of collapse from heat stroke is the duration for which the worker is exposed to the heat source. In this respect Bell, Crowder and Walters (1971) carried out an experiment using fit, unacclimatised young men who were asked to perform a stool-stepping task under different thermal conditions. Each subject was encouraged to push himself to his individual limit of exhaustion, knowing that he would be protected from hazard by the presence of two competent and experienced observers in the hot chamber. From their data Bell, Crowder and Walters produced a series of graphs of predicted safe exposure times for different combinations of dry and wet bulb temperature conditions. Two of these curves are shown in Figure 11.2. As can be seen, the figures match very closely similar limits produced by the American Society of Heating and Refrigeration Engineers (ASHRAE) (1965) based on

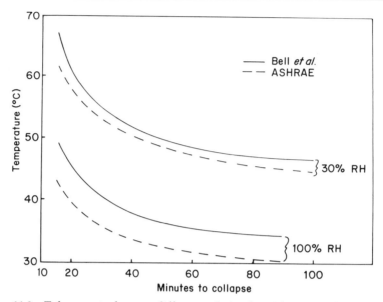

Figure 11.2 Tolerance to heat at different relative humidities, produced by Bell, Crowder and Walters (1971) and the American Society of Heating and Refrigeration Engineers (ASHRAE) (1965)

physiological data (the average time taken to raise the pulse rate from 75 to 125 beats per minute, and the deep body temperature from 37 to 38.3 °C (98–101 °F)), although the ASHRAE guidelines are more conservative in their levels.

Bell, Crowder and Walters do caution against the overuse of these figures, however. Thus they point out that the data were obtained from fit young men and it would be dangerous to extrapolate the findings to other populations of workers with different work rates, ages and physical fitnesses. Secondly, the safe exposure times relate to subjects who were required to work continuously, whereas workers who normally carry out lighter or more intermittent work could be expected to endure longer exposure.

The third point to be made about these data is that they apply to workers with very little heat acclimatisation, whereas it has been shown that acclimatised men may be able to endure the heat for longer. For example, for periods of 400 minutes or longer Wyndham et al. (1970) have shown that resting acclimatised men can tolerate body temperatures nearly 2 °C higher than unacclimatised men. This is related to increased sweat production, a lower skin temperature and a reduced heart rate (Åstrand and Rodahl, 1986).

In a naturalistic study Clark and Edholm (1985) describe work carried out using acclimatised and unacclimatised soldiers in Eden. The platoon which had been acclimatised naturally by a prior period in Bahrain demonstrated higher sweat rates and lower deep body temperatures and heat rates than did their unacclimatised comrades. Although the differences between the two groups diminished over the 12-day test period, significant differences still existed on the last day. Clark and Edholm note that the most dramatic differences between the two groups appeared in terms of heat collapse: three cases in the acclimatised group versus over 30 cases in the unacclimatised soldiers.

Performance Effects of Heat

Over the years many studies have been carried out to investigate the effects of thermal conditions on performance—usually employing some type of cognitive task such as memory or vigilance. Unfortunately, however, because of experimental limitations and wide differences between tasks, techniques and conditions, no firm conclusions can be drawn from the combined results. As Kobrick and Fine (1983) point out following a comprehensive survey of the relevant literature, although numerous studies have demonstrated some performance impairment in heat, others have shown no differences, and some even improvements. Despite such negative conclusions, however, studies which do suggest some performance impairment generally imply that losses occur at around 29–30 °C (approximately 85 °F), although there appears to be a wide band above and below this level (for example, Wyon, Andersen and Lundqvist, 1979).

Figure 11.3 illustrates the extent to which varying the thermal conditions affects various types of cognitive performance.

COLD ENVIRONMENTAL CONDITIONS

Health Effects (Hypothermia)

Just as slight rises in deep body temperature can rapidly lead to hyperthermia, fairly small amounts of deep body cooling are likely to produce a severe risk to health. In this case the condition is known as hypothermia. Accidental hypothermia can result from exposure in bad weather; short-term immersion in very cold water or long-term exposure in slightly cold water; or, particularly in the elderly, it may be a consequence

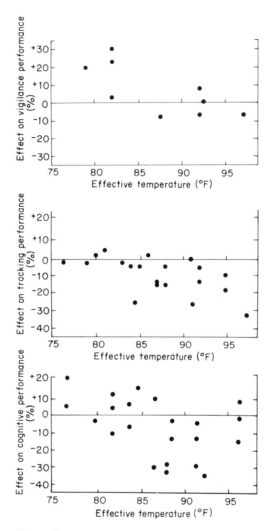

Figure 11.3 The effects of temperature on different forms of cognitive performance (after Grether, 1973)

of illness or accident. Harnett, Pruitt and Sias (1983a, b) present a comprehensive review of problems and techniques relating to resuscitation from hypothermia.

Clinically, a state of hypothermia is said to exist when the body's core temperature falls to about 35 °C (95 °F). Below this the risk of fatality increases, until at temperatures below 30 °C (86 °F) imminent death from cardiac arrest is likely. Again, therefore, it requires the deep body temperature to depart only slightly from its optimum (in this case 2–4 °C) for fatalities to occur.

Following exposure to cold, the body's regulation system attempts to produce heat rapidly by increased muscular activity, manifested by an increase in muscle tone and shivering. Violent shivering appears not to begin until the deep body temperature begins to fall but, once started, its effect can be marked causing the falling trend to be reversed and the core temperature to rise. Shivering reaches a maximum at body temperatures around 34–35 °C (93–95 °F). During the shivering stage the cardiovascular system responds to the cold by constricting the peripheral blood vessels and this increases the blood pressure. If the temperature falls further, however, the heart rate also falls owing to a direct effect on the heart pacemaker. When the heat loss cannot be compensated for further, the deep body temperature falls until at temperatures around 30–33 °C (86–91 °F) shivering gradually ceases and is replaced by muscular rigidity.

Tolerance to cold exposure, and thus susceptibility to hypothermia, varies considerably between individuals. For example, Timbal, Loncle and Boutelier (1976) immersed subjects in cold water at 30 °C for 15 minutes. After this time some subjects' temperatures had dropped by 2 °C, whereas others had dropped by only 10 per cent of this amount. These differences in susceptibility are owing, primarily, to morphological factors of which the amount of subcutaneous fat around the body is probably the most important. This acts as good insulating material, particularly when the blood vessels constrict in response to the cold and blood is routed away from the body surface.

Hayward and Keatinge (1981), however, found that the ability of people to stabilise body temperature in cold was related as much to their metabolic rate as to their subcutaneous fat thickness. They felt that high muscle mass in relation to surface area and a high state of training is important in promoting high rates of shivering heat production. In addition, the individual's size and weight are important factors in cold susceptibility. This is because the degree of heat loss is proportional to the body's surface area, and the amount of heat which can be generated (perhaps by shivering) depends on the mass of active muscular tissue in the body.

Performance Effects of Cold

After reviewing much of the work of the effects of environmental cold on human performance, Fox (1967) concluded that cold can affect performance in five areas: tactile sensitivity, manual performance, tracking, reaction time, and 'complex behaviours'. These five behaviours can be grouped into two main categories: motor performance and cognitive performance. As far as motor performance is concerned, two factors have consistently been shown to be important: first the temperature of the limb which is being used, and secondly the rate of cooling.

Motor performance

The limb temperature, rather than the overall body temperature, affects motor ability because of the effects which cold has on muscular control. It causes a loss of cutaneous sensitivity, changes in the characteristics of synovial fluid in the joints, and a loss of muscular strength. With respect to finger performance Morton and Provins (1960) demonstrated a significant reduction in dexterity for skin temperatures below 20–25 °C (68–97 °F), although there was large individual variability. They suggest that the true relationship for any one person may be such that most of the change in performance is spread over only a few degrees. Thus skin sensitivity remains fairly normal for small reductions in skin temperature, but deteriorates considerably after the individual's critical hand skin temperature has been reached. Data from Clark (1961) tend to support this contention of a critical temperature. He showed that the longer his subjects were exposed to the cold the more their performance decreased as the skin temperature was lowered from 15 to 10.5 °C (51–59 °F). At a higher overall temperature (13–18 °C, 56–64 °F), however, this performance/exposure duration relationship was not apparent.

Effects of the rate of cooling were investigated by Clark and Cohen (1960) on a knot-tying task. They found that slow cooling to a finger temperature of 7.2 °C (45 °F) resulted in more knot-tying errors than did fast cooling to the same temperature. The authors suggested that this was because the slow cooling procedure allowed relatively lower subsurface temperatures to occur. Although the rate of cooling results have been unable to be replicated, their data do indicate significant performance reductions on a number of dexterity tasks when the temperature fell from 18 °C to 9 °C (65 to 48 °F).

To investigate the effects of long-term exposure to cold conditions on manual performance, Teichener and Kobrick (1955) asked subjects to perform a tracking task for approximately five minutes each day over a 41-day period, during which time they lived in a constant temperature chamber. For the first 16 days the room temperature was maintained at 24 °C (65 °F); during the next, cold, period lasting 12 days the temperature was held at 13 °C (55 °F); and finally, during the 13-day recovery period, the temperature was again set to 24 °C.

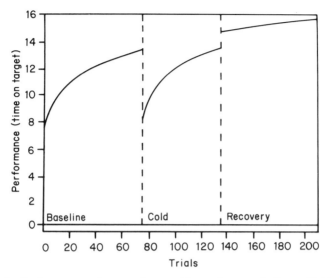

Figure 11.4 Performance changes in a cold environment (from Teichener and Kobrick, 1955)

Teichener and Kobrick's results are shown in Figure 11.4, and a clear performance reduction in the cold conditions can be seen. Interestingly, the results also suggest that the subjects because adapted to the cold conditions fairly quickly. Whereas even at the end of the cold period the subject's performance was not as good as their performance the next day in the warm, within the cold period their performance increased by approximately 50 per cent.

Because the main factor affecting manual performance in the cold is related to the skin temperature of the affected limb, when gloves cannot be worn it would appear sensible to attempt some local warming of the skin. Lockhart and Keiss (1971), for example, showed that for most tasks the impaired manual performance experienced during the cold conditions (when the average skin temperature of the little finger was 12 °C (54 °F)) was alleviated considerably by applying radiant heat to the hands only (raising the temperature of the little finger to 19.5 °C (67 °F)). Indeed, performance using the radiated heat in very cold conditions (–18 °C; 0 °F) was no worse than working in 15.5 °C (60 °F) conditions (when the average temperature of the little finger was 30 °C (80 °F)).

Artificially raising the temperature of the affected limb, however, cannot fully overcome the effects of the cold if the rest of the body is not similarly heated. For example, Lockhart (1968) maintained the temperature of his subject's hands at 'normal' temperature while cooling the body from 25.5 to

19 °C (78–66 °F). His results suggest that cooling the whole body affects the operator's ability to carry out some manual tasks even though the hands were kept 'warm'. The tasks affected involved fine dexterity and Lockhart suggests that part of the reason for the performance reduction could have been shivering. Support for this contention has been provided by Peacock (1956) who examined the effects of cold exposure on rifle-aiming steadiness after vigorous exercise. Although steadiness was reduced, Peacock's results showed that if shivering is excluded as a cause of unsteadiness, rifle steadiness was not seriously affected in the standing position when compared with results taken during normal temperatures.

The effects of cold on manual performance appear therefore to be twofold. First, if the cold is applied locally to the operating limb it can directly affect that limb's muscular control, reducing such abilities as dexterity and strength. This may be overcome somewhat by locally warming the limb. Cold applied to the whole body, however, can reduce performance because of shivering. If the body can be stabilised during this shivering, generalised cold would appear not to affect manual performance to any great extent.

Cognitive performance

As far as cognitive performance in the cold is concerned, the available experimental work does not lead to any firm conclusions—an argument supported by Kobrick and Fine (1983) after a detailed review of the available literature. Many of the problems that arise when interpreting the various results can be placed at the feet of notable differences in experimental techniques, tasks and environmental conditions.

Coleshaw et al. (1983) demonstrated impaired memory performance and calculation speeds when core temperatures fell to between 34 and 35 °C. In a test involving serial choice reaction times, Ellis (1982) reported that consistently large increases in error accompanied reductions in mean skin temperature rather than a fall in rectal temperature. This is probably because of the local cooling effects of the cold on the peripheral tissues, as discussed earlier. Reaction times themselves, however, were unaffected. Giesbrecht et al. (1993) demonstrated important task-dependent effects in relation to the impact of cold environments. Thus 55–80 minutes of immersion in cold water (2–4 °C) had no effect on simple tasks but adversely affected more complex tasks.

Vaughan (1975) studied a number of performance tasks during 6-hour tests when diving in water at 2 °C. His results also suggest a complex task-dependent effect of cold stress, but he also concluded that rectal temperature change was probably a poor index of cold stress when being used to test cognitive performance.

Some evidence is also available to suggest that cold interferes with an individual's ability to estimate time accurately. Baddeley (1966) asked 20 amateur scuba divers to count up to 60 at what they considered to be a one-second rate. His data indicate that after the divers had entered the 4 °C (39 °F) water their estimation of time increased, i.e. one second was judged to be a longer period than in fact it is. It may be remembered that a similar effect was obtained by Jerison (1959) from subjects working under noisy conditions (Chapter 10). The similarity of these results with those of noise suggests that the cold is acting in the way of a general stressor when dealing with cognitive efficiency, rather than on particular physiological functions such as muscle control or skin sensitivity.

THE EFFECTS OF TEMPERATURE ON COMFORT

From the foregoing discussion it is quite clear that the body's core temperature must be kept to within quite narrow limits. A temperature increase of about 5 °C (9 °F) is likely to lead to death, as is a reduction by only 3–4 °C (5.5–7 °F). Furthermore, small departures from this critical band can lead to reductions in both motor and cognitive performance, as can large changes in general environmental conditions.

In addition to these effects, changes in the thermal environment can affect an individual's comfort. As with any interaction with the environment the resultant sensations of comfort experienced by an individual depend both on the environmental conditions and on the individual factors which the person brings to the situation. For most purposes the physical environmental factors can be distilled to a consideration of the air temperature, the air humidity and the amount of air movement. Each is likely to become stressful when it interferes with the body's ability to maintain an adequate thermal balance.

The effect of the air temperature, measured with any type of dry bulb thermometer, will be to raise or lower the overall body temperature. This requires balancing mechanisms to produce sweat in hot conditions or to constrict peripheral blood vessels when cold. However, in very hot conditions, for example near a furnace, the amount of heat radiated from the hot source (the furnace) is also important in affecting the operator's feelings of 'comfort'. Radiation is emitted by the heat source as electromagnetic waves which are absorbed and converted back into heat when they fall on to solid objects. If the radiation is severe enough, the skin tissue can burn—as most people who have spent too long in the hot sun will know.

Radiant temperature is usually measured using a globe thermometer. This is a hollow, 6 in diameter, metal globe that is painted matt black (the original equipment used by Bedford and Warner in the early 1930s was a cistern ballcock) with a normal mercury thermometer placed in an opening in the bulb. In this apparatus, the thermometer receives radiant heat from all directions and an indication of the 'mean radiant temperature' can be obtained after noting also the air temperature and the air speed.

The humidity is an index of the amount of water vapour in the air and is normally measured using two mercury thermometers. On one, the 'wet bulb' thermometer, the bulb is kept damp and is thus cooled by the evaporating water. The other, the 'dry bulb' thermometer, indicates the 'normal temperature'. Since the amount of water that can evaporate from the wet bulb depends on the air humidity, and since the degree of evaporation is reflected by a lower wet bulb temperature, taken together the two temperatures (wet and dry bulb) indicate the amount of water vapour present in the air.

Excessive water vapour in the air, indicated by a high relative humidity, is likely to interfere with the efficiency by which sweat will evaporate from the skin for cooling purposes. At the other end of the scale, very low humidities are likely to cause discomfort by drying the normally moist membranes in the nose and throat, particularly if the air temperature is rather high.

Air that moves over the body has a cooling effect because it helps both to evaporate the sweat and to dissipate heat from the body surface. Although this is likely to result in increased comfort, air movement that is too fast can lead to complaints of draughts. It should be remembered, however, that velocity is a relative term; in this case it applies to the relative motions of the air and the observer. If the observer is stationary the relative velocity is equal to the air speed. For a moving observer, however, the air velocity is a function of both the observer's speed and direction of movement with respect to that of the air.

The two important variables that the observer is likely to bring to the situation are activity (type and level) and clothing. Other variables such as age and physical condition are also likely to affect whether a particular thermal environment is perceived as being 'comfortable' or 'uncomfortable', but these act solely on the body's ability to maintain a thermal balance through sweating or vasoconstriction. Activity and clothing, on the other hand, act independently of the observer's physical capacities—unless there is evidence of any physiological deficiency.

The effects of activity level on body temperature have already been considered when discussing heat stress. Thus when the muscles do work, heat is produced as a by-product of the oxidation process which must be dissipated. The transfer of dry heat between the skin and the outer surface of the clothed body is quite a complicated process and involves internal convection and radiation processes in the intervening air spaces, and conduction through the cloth itself. The relationship between these variables is accounted for by the now internationally accepted dimensionless unit of thermal resistance from the skin to the outer surface of the body—the 'clo' (Gagge, Stolwijk and Nishi, 1971). The range of clothes investigated extends from nude (clo = 0) to heavy wool suits for polar environments (clo = 3–4); within these extremes Fanger (1970) lists the clo values of twelve other clothing ensembles. In addition to the nude state, Goldman (1988) lists measured clo values for 16 clothing sets.

As well as the conductive resistance of the textile itself, the air between textile layers also acts as an important insulator and so the quality of tailoring and fit will influence the clo value. With very loose and hanging clothing, like that worn by inhabitants of very hot countries, the heat which rises from the bottom of the airspace can help to create 'chimney' effects, which force ventilation over the skin.

A Combined Temperature Scale

Since each of the thermal variables, air temperature, air velocity, radiation and humidity, can, separately and together, affect thermal comfort, it is useful to attempt to combine them to produce a single temperature scale. The most used such scale is the Effective Temperature Scale first proposed by Houghton and Yaglou in 1923. Unfortunately, since the scale only took account of air temperature, humidity and velocity, it was inapplicable for environments with high levels of thermal radiation.

Vernon and Warner (1932) applied a radiation correction factor to the ET scale by using the globe thermometer to measure thermal radiation rather than a simple mercury thermometer to measure dry bulb temperature. Their resultant scale, the Corrected Effective Temperature Scale (CET), has been used extensively in many conditions and is shown in Figure 11.5. Under 'normal' conditions, however, the ET and the CET scales can be taken as being the same.

More recently, attempts have been made to reassess the CET scale to bring it more up to date. For example, Nevins and Gagge (1972) suggest that there is substantial evidence that the temperature criteria for thermal comfort have risen steadily from a range of 18–21 °C (65–70 °F) in 1900 to 24–26 °C (75–80 °F) in 1960. Although they do not support their contention with any written evidence, they suggest that this shift has probably resulted from changes in clothing types and building construction.

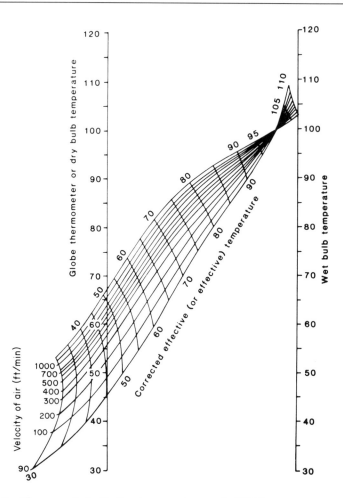

Figure 11.5   The corrected effective temperature scale (CET)

A second reason for reassessing the scale has been the fear that both scales overemphasise the effects of humidity in cool conditions and underemphasise it in warm environments. Indeed, 25 years after the introduction of his original scale Yaglou (1947) himself recognised that the scale may perhaps have overemphasised the effects of humidity towards the lower temperatures. It was also felt that the old scales did not account sufficiently for the physiological processes which regulate the body's thermal response, including the 'insensible' heat lost from surfaces such as the lungs during breathing and vaporised water diffusing through the skin.

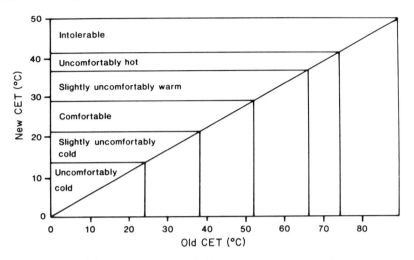

Figure 11.6 The old and new corrected effective temperature scales

The American Society of Heating and Refrigeration Engineers therefore commissioned studies to produce a new comfort scale—the ASHRAE comfort scale (see Gagge, Stolwijk and Nishi, 1971). The New (Corrected) Effective Temperature Scale which was produced (designated the ET* scale to distinguish it from the old ET scale) is shown in Figure 11.6 and is compared with the old ET scale.

Variables Which Affect Thermal Sensation

A number of variables contribute to the assessment of thermal comfort. Besides the obvious physical aspects of the environment discussed above, Rohles (1967) has listed such aspects as the room colour and size, the season of the year, the subject's age, activity, clothing and duration of exposure. To these Fanger (1970) adds national and geographical location, body build, the condition of a woman during her menstrual cycle, circadian rhythms, and ethnic differences. Some of these will be discussed below.

Age

It would be reasonable to expect the elderly to prefer higher temperatures than younger people, since it is well known that metabolic rate falls slightly with age. Furthermore, the elderly are less likely to lead the active life required to help maintain a higher metabolic rate. Reduced body heat should therefore be compensated for by an increased need for warmth.

The research in this area, however, suggests that as long as their physiological regulatory mechanisms remain effective, the thermal preference of the elderly is no higher than that for younger subjects. For example, Rohles (1969) asked elderly subjects (mean age 75 years) to indicate whether they thought that each of 41 temperatures ranging from 32 to 110 °F (0–43 °C) would be 'too warm', 'too cold', or 'comfortable'. His results demonstrated that the distribution of responses for each category compared well with the distributions of more empirically derived responses from younger groups in other experiments.

Fanger (1970) conducted a more controlled series of experiments to investigate the same problem and found similar results. He ascribes the failure to show differences in preference to the body's bioregulation system. His measurements indicated that 'insensible' sweating (i.e. the evaporation of imperceptible amounts of sweat from the body which help to maintain thermal balance) in the elderly decreased in proportion to their reduced metabolic rate. Thus, although less heat is produced by the body, less is lost.

Sex

In an experiment which measured the metabolic rate of subjects carrying out different levels of activity, McNall et al. (1968) demonstrated that males have higher metabolic rates than females. Again, therefore, the argument could be advanced that females might prefer warmer environments and, unlike for age, there is some slight evidence to suggest that this is the case. Thus, Beshir and Ramsey (1981) exposed subjects to different temperatures and asked them to rate their thermal sensation on a nine-point scale ranging from 'cold' to 'extremely hot'. Female subjects consistently rated lower (i.e. cooler) than males, although no statistical data are provided to assess the significance of the difference. Similar work (using a five-point scale) by Fanger (1970) resulted in similar conclusions although, in this case, the male–female difference was slight and non-significant for Danish subjects but just significant for American subjects. Even the American difference, however, was only very small: the females preferred, on average, temperatures 0.3 °C higher than the males.

A reason for the lack of any significant difference between the thermal preferences of the two sexes could again lie in the respective levels of insensible sweating. Thus, Fanger's data suggest that males sweated slightly more than females. This contention is borne out by data from Cunningham, Berglund and Fobelets (1985) who showed that men produced higher levels of sweating ('skin wettedness') than women.

Colour

A considerable body of anecdotal evidence has built up which suggests that the colour of the surroundings can influence our thermal preferences. For example, red colours are considered to produce more feelings of warmth than blue colours.

Perhaps the first experimental study which bears on this question was conducted by Morgensen and English in 1926, who asked subjects to judge the temperature of heating coils wrapped in different colours. Apparently, the green ones were judged to be the hottest.

Unfortunately, however, empirical work relating to thermal preference shows no such conclusive results. For example, Berry (1961) exposed each of 25 subjects to a temperature chamber illuminated by one of five colours: blue, green, white, yellow or amber. His subjects showed no change in the upper comfort limit in different coloured surroundings. Similar conclusions were reached by Fanger, Breum and Jerking (1977) who concluded that 'the effect of colour on man's comfort is so small that it hardly has any practical significance'. Indeed, Fanger (1970) rightly points out that any influence which colour has on the thermal sensation must be of a 'psychological nature'. The possibility cannot be denied, therefore, that an individual who is away from the oppressive, controlled laboratory environment may feel more at ease, more comfortable and, perhaps, experience more 'warmth' with different lighting conditions.

ILLUMINATION

Definitions

When discussing vibration and noise, the two defining characteristics of the stimulus were the signal's intensity and frequency. The defining parameters of a light stimulus are very similar: intensity and wavelength. The concept of wavelength is similar to that of frequency, except that it is related more to the distance between two peaks of a sinusoidal stimulus (like the distance between two waves on the sea) rather than the frequency with which the peaks occur. Wavelength, therefore, is measured in terms of distance but, because the distances between two energy 'peaks' are so small, the wavelength of light is normally described in terms of nanometers (1 nm $= 10^{-9}$ m, or one-billionth, of a metre). Visible light is simply a form of radiation with wavelengths between 380 and 780 nm, and the eye discriminates between different wavelengths in this range in terms of the sensation of colour. The violets are around 400 nm, blending into the blues (around 450 nm), the greens (around 500 nm), the yellow-oranges (around 600 nm), and the reds (around 700 nm and above).

Illumination and Luminance

The intensity of a light source is expressed in terms of the amount of luminous flux (energy) which it generates. Just as the power of a car is described in relation to the power produced by a 'standard' horse (horsepower), the luminous flux produced by a light source is measured by comparing it with the flux produced by burning a standard candle of a specified material and weight. This candle is said to produce one candle power (or 1 candela, 1 cd) of energy.

Although flux is used here as a synonym for energy, strictly speaking it refers to the rate at which the energy is produced and is measured in 'lumens'. Indeed, because a light source emits light in all directions, 1 candela is also defined as 1 lumen per steradian (i.e. the rate of flux produced per solid angle of the body).

As energy radiates from a source and travels through a dense medium such as air, water or glass, it spreads out and loses its intensity. The amount of energy lost is inversely related to the square of the distance travelled (this is known as the inverse square law). Thus the level of illumination that falls on a surface will be lower than that which originated from the light source and, because of the diffusive nature of the medium through which it is travelling, will spread over the surface. Illumination, therefore, is defined in terms of the rate of flux (lumens) produced and the surface area over which it spreads (that is, lumens per square foot or lumens per square metre).

Unfortunately, the amount of flux emitted from a source is not the only measure of the illumination of a surface. As well as the inverse square law, there exists another law of illumination—the cosine law—which states that the surface illumination varies with the cosine of the angle between the surface and the light's direction. This is important for two reasons. First, the efficiency of a light source can be varied by altering its angle of incidence to the surface; for example, by raising or lowering it. Secondly, the light that falls on a surface only rarely, and under specific conditions, emanates from a single source. Generally, it arises both as direct illumination and as reflections from other surfaces—walls, ceilings, other objects, etc. These can be considered to be individual light sources and the efficiency of each depends on the angle at which they reflect light onto the surface.

In any environment, therefore, the amount of light falling on a surface depends on a number of factors. These are the luminous intensity of the light sources, the distances of the sources from the surface, the angles of the sources to the surface, and the number of original and reflecting sources in the immediate environment.

Luminance

Although a particular light level may fall on a body, this is not to say that the observer 'sees' that level. Depending on their surface characteristics different bodies absorb and reflect different amounts and qualities of light. In this case the term used to define the amount of light reflected from the body's surface is its luminance, which refers, in simple terms, to the amount of light falling on the body multiplied by the proportion of light which the body reflects (its reflectance). Unfortunately for the novice illumination engineer, however, there are a multitude of terms to define luminance. It can be expressed either in terms of the luminous intensity per unit area (candelas per square metre), or in terms of the 'equivalent illumination' (equivalent lux), or apostilbs (asb), or in foot Lamberts (ft-L). The modern standard is to express it in terms of the candela per square metre, but a number of conversion tables exist to relate the various measures (see, for example, Megaw and Bellamy, 1983).

Brightness and Retinal Illuminance

The luminance qualities of an object will only be perceived by an observer after the light has stimulated the retinal cells and the information has passed to the optic cortex in the brain. At this point the concept of the body's brightness is invoked, which is the subjective aspect of its luminance. When considering the response of the visual system to light, however, it is sometimes necessary to talk about the retinal illuminance. This is because the brightness of any image depends on the diameter of the limiting aperture of the image-forming device. In the eye this is set by the diameter of the pupil and retinal illuminance is measured in trolands (td). One troland is equal to the retinal illuminance obtained by looking through an artificial pupil having an area of 1 square millimetre at a matt surface whose luminance is l cd per square metre.

The relationship between these definitions can perhaps be explained by reference to Figure 11.7. Thus a source (for example, a light bulb) illuminates a body. The level of illumination or illuminance is likely to be measured in units such as lux or lumens per square metre ($lm\ m^{-2}$ (1 lux = 1 $lm\ m^{-2}$)). This is unlikely to be the only source of light falling on the surface, however, and the total surface illuminance will depend also on the distance of the light sources and their angles to the surface. The surface of this body reflects light to the eye of the observer, the intensity being determined by the surface reflectance and being measured in many units such as candelas per square metre ($cd\ m^{-2}$). The observer then reports the body's brightness, the intensity of the report being determined by the amount of retinal

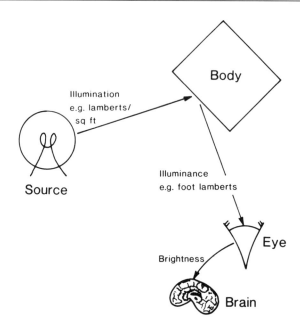

Figure 11.7   The relationship between illumination, luminance and brightness

illuminance allowed by the pupil and the experiences of the observer. These experiences, being subjective, are likely to depend on many factors including past experience and the brightness of other bodies in the visual field.

LIGHTING AND BEHAVIOUR

Most of the important information regarding the relationship between illumination quality and performance has been discussed already when considering how the visual system operates. However, it is appropriate to recall some of the material here. Thus performance is a function, primarily, of the overall illumination levels, the size of the object being viewed and the contrast between the object and its surround. This latter aspect of the relationship between the object and its surround—comprising aspects such as contrast and location—is very important since it introduces the topic of glare and the effects that this can have both on comfort and performance.

Illumination Level and Object Size

With regard to the relationship between overall illumination levels and performance, Gilbert and Hopkinson (1949) demonstrated that the potential for a particular type of performance (visual acuity) reduces after about 10 lumens/sq ft (107 lux). Subjects with visual impairment, however, required much higher illumination levels. A similar finding, that increased lighting will be of value only until a certain level has been reached, was demonstrated by Smith and Rea (1979). They asked subjects to check a list of numbers for agreement with a comparison list, under different conditions of task luminance (i.e. the light reflected from the page). Performance increased with luminance levels up to 10 cd m^{-2}, but not above this level.

The relationship between overall illumination and more subjective factors such as comfort gives rise to similar conclusions. For example, Saunders (1969) allowed subjects to adapt to windowless rooms lit only by ceiling lamps and then asked them to read from a book. Subsequent ratings of the illumination quality to which they had been exposed show that with increasing illuminance levels, subjects judged the lighting to increase in quality until at about 800 lux there was no further value in increasing the levels (see Figure 11.8).

As far as the size of the object (i.e. the task) is concerned, Gilbert and Hopkinson's (1949) results demonstrated that as the objects (letters on the Snellen chart) became smaller, more light was required for them to be read accurately. In its code for interior lighting (1977), the Illuminating Engineering Society (IES) suggests illumination levels for many different types of work interiors which are related to the type of work carried out. Overall, seven levels are suggested, as shown in Table 11.1. The code

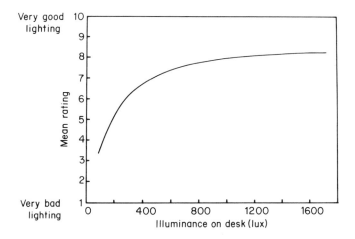

Figure 11.8 Quality of the lighting in a windowless office at different illuminations (Saunders, 1969; reproduced by permission of the Chartered Institution of Building Services)

Table 11.1 A flowchart for modifying standard service illuminances for unusual conditions (after IES Code, 1977)

Task group and typical task or interior	Standard service illuminance (lx)	Are reflectances or contrasts unusually low?	Will errors have serious consequences?	Is task of short duration?	Is area windowless?	Final service illuminance (lx)
Storage areas and plant rooms with no continuous work	150					→ 150
Casual work	200				no → 200 yes	→ 200
Rough work Rough machining and assembly	300	no → 300 yes	no → 300 yes	300 ← yes	no → 300 yes	→ 300
Routine work Offices, control rooms, medium machining and assembly	500	no — 500 yes	no — 500 yes	no — 500 yes	no → 500 yes	→ 500

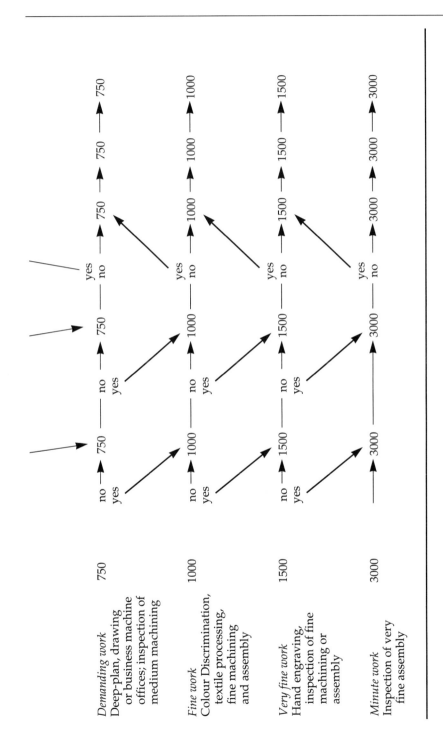

suggests, however, that before deciding on an appropriate illumination level for the task in hand, four important questions should be asked:

(1)   Are the reflectances or contrasts unusually low (for example, having to pick out dark objects from a dark, matt background)?

(2)   Will errors have serious consequences?

(3)   Is the task of short duration?

(4)   Is the area windowless?

On the basis of the answers to these questions an appropriate illuminance level can be chosen, as indicated in Table 11.1.

Contrast

An object's contrast refers simply to the relationship of its luminance to its surround; it is a measure of how well the object 'stands out'. Without contrast an object cannot be seen and this principle applies equally to such stimuli as words on the printed page or on a visual display, to a large machine in a dimly lit room, to a well-camouflaged soldier, or to insects.

Contrast is normally expressed in terms of a ratio between the luminance difference of the object and its surround to the surround luminance. So an object that is illuminated by 100 units of light placed on a background of 10 units will have a contrast ratio of $((100-10)/10) = 9$, as will a 10-unit object placed on a 1-unit background.

Unfortunately, however, as Hopkinson and Collins (1970) point out, the observer's visual behaviour also has to be taken into account when determining contrast relationships. For example, whereas two light meters may register 100 and 10 units in one case and 10 and 1 units in another, and so 'deduce' that the contrast ratios in the two cases are the same, an observer's perceptual system will probably treat the two sets of stimuli differently because of a phenomenon known as brightness constancy.

To explain this phenomenon, suppose an observer is looking at two different flat surfaces—one grey and one white—which are illuminated so as to ensure that the luminances arising from them are equal. Since the stimulus received by the retinal cells is related to the surface luminance, and since the two luminances are the same, it might be assumed that they would look the same. Unfortunately, they will not; the grey will still look greyer than the white unless they are viewed separately (say each is viewed through a tube in such a way that each surface covers the whole of the observer's field of view). Only under these very specific circumstances will the two appear to have similar luminances. Because an object exists within a frame of reference which contains other objects and surfaces, well-defined textures, contours, contrasts and colours, the optic cortex interprets the stimuli in terms of past experiences and expectations to ensure that the visual world remains 'constant'.

Because of this phenomenon Hopkinson and Collins (1970) suggest that contrast should be expressed not in terms of the actual luminance levels but of the difference between the 'apparent brightnesses' of the object and its surround. This rests on the assumption that everything we see is evaluated, as far as brightness is concerned, in terms of some reference level which is associated with the state of adaptation of the eye at the time. Light entering a large window, therefore, is likely to alter the eye's adaptive state and so affect vision by altering the apparent brightness of, say, characters on the page. Hopkinson, Waldram and Stevens (1941) have produced a set of curves from which one can read the apparent brightness of the object or surround given their respective brightnesses.

Although a high contrast is clearly important in ensuring that the object is perceived accurately, it is also important that the direction of the contrast effect is considered, for two reasons.

First, as has been discussed already in Chapter 5, some evidence exists to suggest that dark characters on a brighter background (negative contrast; positive polarity) lead to slightly higher performance and preference ratings than the reverse. This is possibly because the printed page is normally also in negative contrast so that adaptation is maintained when the gaze has to move from the screen to paper and back again.

The second reason for concern about the contrast direction arises if the surround is considerably brighter than the object, perhaps because of reflected light falling on the screen. If this occurs then both the object's visibility and the observer's visual comfort are likely to be reduced by glare. This will be discussed in more detail below.

As an example of the importance of contrast to efficient visual performance, in their illumination study Gilbert and Hopkinson (1949) asked their subjects to read the letters on a Snellen chart under different illumination levels, using different contrast ratios between the letters and the background. Their results indicated strongly that as the contrast was increased the subject's ability to read the letters accurately also increased. This effect was particularly marked at the lower levels of overall illumination, whereas the performance increase was not so marked when the overall illumination level was reasonably high.

Glare

Glare occurs whenever one part of the visual field is brighter than the level to which the eye has become adapted. Excessive luminance levels can arise in one or both of two ways. First, direct glare occurs when the light appears directly from the source itself, such as a car headlight at night, the sun during the day, or perhaps a badly positioned light bulb. Second, and perhaps more insidious, reflected or specular glare is caused by very bright reflections from polished or glossy surfaces. VDUs, for example, often act as very good sources of specular light, as do glossy paper and even the keys on a keyboard. White walls and ceilings can also be a source of specular glare. The effects of these glare sources can often be unpredictable since they may occur under various circumstances, for example when the object is placed at a certain angle to the light, when more than one light is brought together, or at certain times of the day when the sun is reflected off other surfaces.

Glare is commonly described as being of two types. If there is direct interference with visual performance the condition is referred to as *disability glare*. However, if performance is not directly affected but the bright stimulus still causes discomfort, annoyance, irritation or distraction, the condition is called *discomfort glare*. The distinction between these two terms is often blurred—the same lighting conditions can produce disability and discomfort simultaneously and, to confuse matters further, different lighting conditions can cause disability and create discomfort independently.

The effects of both types of glare, however, may eventually be to cause reduced performance, through distraction, increased arousal or, because having to avoid the glare can constitute another task that the operator has to perform, through reduction in the available spare mental capacity. Furthermore, because the eye always tends to move to the brightest part of the visual field (the so-called phototropic effect), a consequence of glare can often be to draw the eyes away from the task in hand.

Disability glare

The reduced ability to see accurately because of interference from a bright light source has probably been experienced by everyone at some time or another, so the potential disabling effects of glare are well known.

At a descriptive level two of the earliest workers in the field, Lukiesh and Holladay (1925), considered disability glare to be of three types. Veiling glare, they felt, was owing to light from the glare source being scattered in the fluids of the eye, so reducing contrast and hence visibility. An effect is caused, therefore, which is similar to illuminated fog or mist. This was illustrated by Stiles and his colleagues (Stiles, 1929; Crawford and Stiles, 1937) who performed an experiment in which the glaring light source was presented to the blind spot of the retina. Although the light source itself was invisible, its veiling effect was still present.

The second kind of disability glare, which Lukiesh and Holladay describe as 'dazzle glare', occurs as a short-term effect for the duration of the glare source. Finally, 'blinding glare' lasts beyond the period of the glare stimulus due to the formation of 'blinding after-images'.

In a comprehensive series of experiments Holladay (1926) investigated many aspects of disability glare and he is perhaps best remembered for producing a glare formula which is still in use. His experiments indicated that the amount of glare (defined in terms of contrast reduction), is determined by both the position of the glaring source with respect to the observer and the amount of light entering the observer's eye. Thus:

$$\text{Contrast reduction} = \frac{k \times \text{illumination produced by the glaring source at the eye}}{\text{angle at the eye between the source and the object being viewed}^{2.4}}$$

The value of k in this formula appears to depend on the age of the observer since age causes changes in the consistency of fluids in the eyeball.

There are two important implication of Holladay's formula. First is its suggestion that the extent of the glare will decrease as the angle of the glare source to the observer increases. The other important factor concerns the amount of illumination produced by the glare source. As Hopkinson and Collins (1970) point out, the effect will be the same whether the glaring source is a small source of high illuminance or a large source of flow illuminance—provided the illumination at the eye is the same. This means that, for example, a dark sky seen through a large window can cause as much disability glare as a small, more intense light bulb—even though its brightness may not be sufficiently high to cause any discomfort.

Discomfort glare

Paradoxically, discomfort glare appears to have been studied more extensively than disability glare, and a number of formulae have been derived which relate various physical parameters of the glare source to levels of 'discomfort' (see, for example, Murrell (1971) or Boyce (1981) for details of many of these formulae).

The discomfort produced by a glare source appears to have a different physiological origin to disability glare. Thus Hopkinson (1956) has demonstrated a link between the level of discomfort and the activity of the eye musculature which controls the iris. This relationship is not perfect, however, and Hopkinson concludes that discomfort sensations came only in part from the conflict which arises between the requirements for pupil control between the areas of the retina stimulated by the glaring source, and those receiving lower levels of illumination.

The most modern glare formula, which has become generally accepted, has been produced by the Illuminating Engineering Society based on empirical work developed by the Building Research Station in Great Britain. This work was carried out over a number of years by Hopkinson and his colleagues (see, for example, Hopkinson, 1940, 1972; Petherbridge and Hopkinson, 1950). The results of the various investigations produced the following glare formula:

$$\text{Glare constant } (G) = \frac{B_s^{1.6} \times \omega^{0.8}}{B_b \times \phi^2}$$

where B_s is the luminance of the source, ω is the solid angle subtended by the source at the eye (i.e. this is related to its apparent size), B_b is the general background luminance and ϕ is the angle between the direction of viewing and the direction of the glare source.

The Glare Index, therefore, is computed by summing the glare constants from each source in the visual field, obtaining the logarithm of this sum, and multiplying this figure by a factor of 10. Thus:

$$\text{Glare Index} = 10 \log_{10}(\text{sum } G)$$

Using formulae of this nature, the glare constant obtained can be related to some criterion of discomfort. Thus a glare constant of 600 indicates the boundary of 'just intolerable'; 150 the boundary of 'just uncomfortable'; 35 the boundary of 'just acceptable'; and 8 would be 'just perceptible'. A more useful criterion, however, might be to express the glare ratings in terms of the probability of producing 'visual comfort'. This the IES has done, adapted by McCormick (1976) to form a single graph as shown in Figure 11.9.

If more than one glaring source is present in the environment, Hopkinson (1940) showed that the simple arithmetical addition of the glare constants obtained from each source gave a glare value which corresponded closely to the sensation from the complete array of the sources. Later however (1956), he modified his position slightly when he showed that the additive

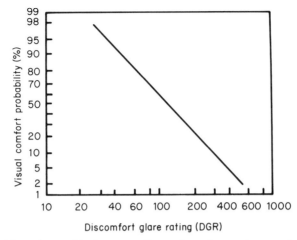

Figure 11.9 The relationship between discomfort glare ratings and the probability of retaining visual comfort (from McCormick, 1976, reproduced by permission of the McGraw-Hill Book Co.)

nature was a highly complex phenomenon, the exact function depending, among other things, on the luminance of the sources and their position in the field of view.

Finally, although the values of the exponents in the glare formula depend to some extent on the experimental conditions, it is possible to see that decreasing the size and luminance of the source (B_s) would increase glare, as would increasing the background luminance (B_b). In practice, however, increasing the source luminance is also likely to increase background luminance. Furthermore, as with disability glare, increasing the angle between the glare source and the observer also decreases glare. As a rough guide Hopkinson and Collins (1970) state that a Glare Index of less than 10 is rated as 'barely perceptible' glare, while a value of over 28 is rated as 'intolerable'. Unfortunately, however, as Boyce (1981) has shown, there is wide individual variability in the extent to which glare (as measured by the Glare Index) causes discomfort.

Veiling reflections

As well as these two kinds of glare, a special case of glaring sources can occur when high levels of background illumination appear in the visual field and cover the objects of interest. For obvious reasons, these are called veiling reflections and their effect is to increase the overall levels of both the object and the background luminances. To measure the contrast between the object and surround, therefore, the basic formula discussed earlier has to be modified slightly to include the luminance of the veiling source (B_v).

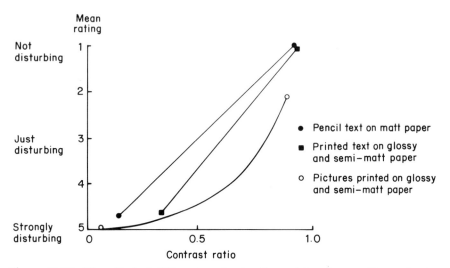

Figure 11.10 The effect of different contrast ratios, arising from veiling reflections from various surfaces, on perceived disturbance (De Boer, 1977; reproduced by permission of the Chartered Institution of Building Services)

Thus the new task contrast (C) will be:

$$C = \frac{(B_o + B_v) - (B_b + B_v)}{B_b + B_v}$$

To discover how veiling reflections affect viewer satisfaction, De Boer (1977) asked subjects to read two journals; one printed on a moderately glossy paper, the other on semi-matt paper, and also a piece of text written in pencil on matt paper. Figure 11.10 shows that there is a clear relationship between comfort and veiling reflections, with the 'just disturbing' category having a contrast ratio of about 0.6.

Veiling reflections mainly present themselves at work as reflections from the working surface, and in modern office environments this is often at computer screens. However, they can also occur over shiny keyboard keys and on glossy source document paper. As far as the screen is concerned, Cakir, Hart and Stewart (1980) point out that the smooth glass surface of a screen face typically reflects about 4 per cent of the light that falls on it, which is sufficient to produce clearly visible and sharply defined reflections. When the phosphor is bonded directly onto the inner surface of the screen glass, without any intervening filter, this reflectance can rise to 22–27 per cent.

Cakir, Hart and Stewart also point out that veiling reflections can affect the eye's accommodation. Reflections on the face of a VDU screen, for example, represent an additional image which is interposed between the operator's eye and the plane on which the character images are displayed. Thus a 'double image' occurs which the optic cortex attempts to resolve (often unsuccessfully) by using the ciliary muscles to alter the lens curvature. In the long term this is likely to lead to visual fatigue.

Reducing Glare

It is clear, therefore, that glare arises mainly from two sources: specular glare reflected off material that is being used, and glare from large light sources such as windows or badly positioned lights.

Glare from screens

Perhaps the most obvious way to control reflected glare from VDU screens is to control the glaring source; to pull blinds, position the screen so that the window does not shine on it, arrange lights so that they are not reflected, and so on. Often, however, this is not possible or convenient. For example, sun shining through a window at such an angle or intensity that it is reflected on the screen may only occur for a relatively short time. Rearranging the workstation to take account of such possibilities may not be a feasible proposition. For these kinds of situation, screen filters are often used by manufacturers and individual operators to combat the problem of screen reflections.

Unfortunately, little work appears to have been reported which has investigated the efficiency of different types of screen filter. Nevertheless, Cakir, Hart and Stewart (1980) present a useful discussion of the different types of filter currently available and the advantages and disadvantages of each. As they point out, however, screen filters can have only limited value. It is not possible to place a filter between the eye and visual display and thereby improve all the characteristics which contribute to the 'quality' of the display. While using an appropriate filter can be effective in reducing screen reflections, it is invariably accomplished at the expense of reduced character brightness and resolution.

Glare from windows

Consideration of the glare formula discussed earlier suggests two features of the illumination environment which can contribute to increased glare from large areas such as windows. Glare is increased as the luminance of the glaring source (B_s) is increased and as its angle to the observer is decreased. This suggests that simply reducing the amount of light entering the room will go some way to reducing glare—but not the whole way.

Hopkinson (1972) therefore suggests that if the simple expedient of window blinds is not appropriate, architectural techniques can be used such as fitting tinted glass, limiting the area of sky visible from any position in the room by using large, vertical fins on the window or by fitting translucent blinds, building an overhang above the window, or, to increase the angle of the glaring source, having windows higher up the wall. Furthermore, remembering that glare is a contrast effect, he suggests that it might be reduced if this contrast is also reduced, for example by painting the window surrounds a very light colour (possibly even white). Care should be taken in this case, however, to ensure that the white surrounds do not themselves become glaring objects.

Windowless rooms

If glare from windows is a serious problem one obvious design possibility is to remove the windows and install lights, the intensity and angle of which are under the control of the operator. Research data suggests, however, that to do so can often create problems of a different form, possibly of reduced satisfaction with the workplace. Boyce (1981) presents a valuable review of such studies which have demonstrated mixed reactions to windowless rooms, often depending on the room function and the number of other occupants it contains. For example, Ruys (1970) surveyed occupants in five different buildings in America, each containing a number of windowless offices. Whereas there appeared to be few complaints about the level of artificial lighting provided, nearly 90 per cent of the occupants expressed dissatisfaction with the lack of windows. Office workers who often had to work alone complained that a lack of windows meant a lack of daylight, poor ventilation and an inability to know about the weather or to have a view. It also gave an impression of being cooped up and led to feelings of depression and tension.

On the other hand, studies performed in factories, which are often windowless but in which space is usually large and contains a number of other people, suggests few complaints (Pritchard, 1964). Boyce also reports similar findings from studies investigating the effects of windowless classrooms on schoolchildren. Indeed, in some cases the children performed better in rooms without windows.

Contradictory data such as these led Boyce to suggest that it is not the lack of windows *per se* which is a cause for discontent but the social setting of the environment and the size of the windowless space. In environments in which there was adequate scope for social interaction (factories and schools), with larger rooms, the complaints were rare. In smaller, office-type environments, however, with reduced chances for social interaction, complaints were heard. Furthermore, Boyce argues that equality of circumstances is important in such cases. For example, Sommer (1974) found that the dislike of a windowless environment in the underground offices he studied was amplified by the fact that the executives had offices above ground with windows overlooking fine views.

SUMMARY

As this chapter has demonstrated, small departures from the ideal levels of both illumination and temperature can lead to fairly large reductions in performance and, in the case of temperature, even to death. Both of these environmental parameters, however, are extremely complex in their composition and their effects on the operator, some of which this chapter has explained.

12

ERGONOMICS AND SAFETY

At first it might appear strange that safety is considered as a separate chapter in an ergonomics text which stresses throughout the variety of ways in which different kinds of interactions with the environment can lead to unsafe acts. Safety, after all, was considered when discussing features such as the maximum loads the operator should lift (Chapter 3), display design for accurate perception and performance (Chapter 5), designing and arranging controls for safe use (Chapters 6 and 7), and so on. What further information can a chapter on safety add?

Whereas it is true that safety and accidents have been examined in detail throughout this book, they were approached primarily from the viewpoint of the system and of the operator's interaction with it (for example, loads that can be carried; the design considerations of displays, controls, machines; the effects of noise, temperature). This chapter will examine some of the factors the operator brings to an otherwise 'safe' situation which may make it 'unsafe'. Even if the system has been designed to take account of all ergonomic principles so far discussed, therefore, experience tells us that accidents can still occur when a human operator is present. This chapter will consider some of the reasons.

Although the main emphasis will be on characteristics of the operator's behaviour that lead to accidents, the man–machine systems concept is still valid and should not be forgotten. It is still argued that an accident occurs because the environment (including machines) demands more of the operator than can be given; that the environment demands more 'spare mental capacity' from the operator than there is available.

At this point it is useful to ask the basic question, 'What is an accident?' When does an accident become deliberate and hence blameable? A number of definitions exist but all contain concepts which can be distilled to three main points, the more of which are present, the more likely the event will be to be called an 'accident'. An accident has a low degree of:

(1)   expectedness

(2)   avoidability

(3)   intention to cause the accident

Thus accidents are unfortunate, unpredictable, unavoidable and unintentional interactions with the environment. Their very unpredictability and rarity make them extremely difficult to investigate directly, and so most accident research has been carried out either on accident reports, or using the painstaking method of direct observation of minor 'incidents' or 'near misses' which do not result in reported accidents. Both of these techniques, however, have their drawbacks and can result in biases in interpretation, as will be discussed in Chapter 14.

Green (1988) presents an 'anatomy' of an accident that provides some basis against which the actions of different parts of the system can be judged. He argues that:

> the typical accident in an installation of balanced design is not caused by only one simple equipment fault or human error; on the contrary, major events will depend on a complex chain of events including equipment faults, latent risky conditions from repair and modifications as well as human mistakes and decision errors.

Green's model has three different phases which can lead to the development of an accident within process control situations. Thus transition from a 'normal' state to an 'abnormal' one can be caused by equipment failure or human error (or a combination of both) and involves passing from the normal process system to a system in which the safety mechanisms would normally apply. Failure of this second stage leads to the potential 'loss of control' in which 'energy is released'. Human error and/or equipment failure at this stage can increase the chance of an accident occurring.

THE COST EFFECTIVENESS OF ACCIDENT PREVENTION

In many respects it could be argued that to consider the cost-effectiveness of accident prevention is both morally wrong and inherently difficult. How much value does one put on human life, grief, pain and so on? However, the question is an important one if people are to be persuaded to develop safe and effective working systems. Thus the benefits of reduced costs can often be as powerful a motivator as the pressure of legislation.

As an example of the costs associated with accidents, Powell et al. (1971) considered the costs of over 2000 accidents which occurred during a study of four different types of shop-floor. They calculated that the number of

man-hours lost through accidents was roughly equivalent to the permanent absence of four people. At that time the total wages cost was in the region of £3500 per annum and, assuming the labour content of a factory product to be 20 per cent of the equivalent produced, the sales loss was calculated to be £16 500 per annum. Although these figures seem high, the study emphasises the problems facing an ergonomic drive towards safer workplaces. As the authors point out, 'to a large factory this is peanuts and is no doubt one of the reasons why accidents are not regarded as a serious problem'.

The straightforward loss of productivity from injuries, however, cannot represent all of the costs in any cost–benefit analysis. As Powell *et al.* also argue, the burden of an accident is not just a burden on the factory; it is also a burden on the community:

> A factory may have a first-aid service included in its on-costs but the community has a hospital service, a national insurance scheme, and a legal service to pay for, thus relieving the factory of further responsibility for the people it maintains. The factory produces goods and injuries; the community at large pays for both.

Bearham (1976) takes this point a little further and divides accidents into three types:

(1) *Lost-time accident*: because of, for example, hospitalisation, this causes a loss of time beyond the shift during which the accident occurred.

(2) *Non-lost-time accident*: causes no loss of time beyond the shift during which the accident occurred.

(3) *Damage accident*: no injury is caused to people, but facilities, equipment or materials may be damaged.

He further suggests that these three types of accidents occur in the ratio of approximately 1 : 60 : 400, so that for every lost-time accident occurring in industry there will be approximately 400 property-damage/no-injury accidents. The costs of all three types of accident, Bearham suggests, can be divided into direct and indirect costs (sometimes referred to as 'known' and 'hidden' costs). Direct costs are incurred through such aspects as settling claims for damage to equipment; compensation for loss of earnings, pain and suffering as a result of injury; legal liability under health and safety laws; and insurance premiums. This type of information is readily available since it is directly paid out. Because indirect costs tend to be hidden, they are more difficult to evaluate. However, Bearham's list includes the following items:

- *Safety administration costs*: the time of the safety officer and committee dealing with the accident investigation and a proportion of time for any secretarial support.

- *Medical centre costs*: doctors' and nurses' time and the medical supplies used in the treatment of injuries. (Bearham does point out that these types of cost would still exist even if accidents were greatly reduced, since they promote the well-being of employees. However, they are still costs which result from accidents.)

- *Welfare payments*: the proportion of the payment made by the company to the employee while off work

- *Ambulance service costs*: running and depreciation of the ambulance and the ambulance driver's time.

- *Cost of time of other employees*: including the time taken by other employees to help the injured person; the time taken by the foreman in aiding the injured person; the time taken by the witnesses in answering questions during the accident investigation, etc.

- *Replacement labour costs*: if the injured person is replaced.

- *Loss of production costs*: due to the unavailability of staff and machines.

- *Damage to plant and machinery costs*: incurred when repairs are required and replacements are ordered and fitted.

- *Other costs*: arising from the accident investigation—these include stationery and secretarial and clerical work performed in processing and recording the accident and corresponding with solicitors and insurance companies.

When all these costs are understood and are taken into account, the balance of the cost–benefit equation must clearly tip towards the importance of increasing safety practices. The remainder of this chapter will consider some of the reasons (models) for accidents occurring. Two kinds of models will be discussed in detail: behavioural and physiological.

BEHAVIOURAL MODELS OF ACCIDENT CAUSATION

Learning Theories

The skills developed at work arise as a result of a complex series of behaviour patterns learned over long periods. In developing these skills feedback, both from the sense organs and in terms of a knowledge of results, plays an extremely important role. One of the basic requirements for learning an action or a skill rests in reinforcing, by feedback, the consequences of the response to a particular stimulus. For example, when attempting to knock a nail into a piece of wood a novice carpenter might sometimes miss the nail and hit some fingers (producing negative reinforcement) which would cause subsequent behaviour patterns to be altered (maybe to move the fingers or alter the hammer swing). Eventually a correct response (hit) to the stimulus (nail) is made and the resulting (positive) feedback (of a nail properly embedded in the wood without painful fingers) will reinforce the correct behaviour.

This type of learning is very similar to that described by Pavlov whose dog learned to salivate to the sound of a bell, and is known as conditioning. (To distinguish it from the 'passive' behaviour observed in Pavlov's dog—often called 'classical' conditioning—the form of conditioning in which a motor response is made is known as 'instrumental' conditioning.) Two main principles apply in determining the strength of a conditioned response: first, positive reinforcement is more effective than negative reinforcement; and secondly, the more frequently the action is reinforced (either positively or negatively) the greater the learning effect will be.

Since skilled behaviour is composed of a collection of skilled responses it is possible to understand how inappropriate (dangerous) behaviour can soon become incorporated into the repertoire. First, in many respects safe behaviour is often negatively reinforcing. It generally takes more time, it may involve using safety clothing, and it sometimes attracts unwelcome comments from fellow workers. (Although this attitude is gradually being eroded, in many industries it is still considered 'unmanly' to take safety precautions.) Unsafe behaviour, on the other hand, is often quicker (one talks of 'cutting corners'), more comfortable, and is often more socially acceptable. As an example of these effects Winsemius (1965) describes the operation of a machine used to punch the index letters on the sides of pages in address books:

> In order to start the machine a pedal was pushed down. As long as it was down the machine ran; as soon as the foot was lifted from the pedal the machine stopped almost instantaneously.

> The machines were operated by female workers. During their learning period they stopped the machine at every page so that the operator fixed the speed of work. Experienced workers, however, started the machine after having inserted a booklet and did not stop it again until the whole booklet had been punched. Experienced workers thus moved their fingers at the same rhythm as the machine. As the booklet approached completion, the index finger came nearer and nearer to the edge of the punching die, and was indeed very close to it during the punching of the last two or three leaves.

The experienced operators had learned to use unsafe behaviour patterns to change pages without stopping the machine. This behaviour was easier and less time consuming than the safe operation and so it was positively reinforced. The safe behaviour (stopping the machine before changing the pages), however, led to fatigue, lost time, and no obvious rewards once the action had been undertaken. Only when the press descended on the operator's fingers was the negative reinforcement stronger than that resulting from the safe behaviour.

The second principle, concerning the frequency of reinforcement, is also important when applying learning theory to safety. Accidents are extremely rare occurrences, even when the behaviour is unsafe. For example, Winsemius calculated that accidents using the alphabet punch occurred less than once in 6 million operations. The stronger negative reinforcement of a punched finger, therefore, is unlikely to be experienced.

Taken together, these two aspects (unsafe behaviour is positively reinforcing and its negative effects are extremely infrequent) suggest that training alone is unlikely to reduce unsafe behaviour. Unless the negatively reinforcing aspects have been sufficiently incorporated into the training repertoire, almost by a change in attitudes, the unsafe behaviour is likely to become positively reinforced as soon as the training period ends.

Memory Lapses

Many of the tasks commonly carried out at work involve large memory components. Operators have to remember sequences of operations, the meaning of different stimuli and responses to make, and so on. However, just as our capacity to process information is limited, so is our ability to retain it. The more which has to be remembered but which is not in the normal repertoire of behaviour, the more likely particular aspects are to be forgotten. Forgetting (the loss, permanent or temporary, of the ability to recall or to recognise something learned earlier) is therefore a clear candidate for causing accidents.

The reasons why we forget are complex and are still not fully understood. In some cases it may be due to repression of the action—blocking recall of the operation. Repression, a Freudian concept, is extremely difficult to investigate scientifically. More likely answers lie in the decay of the memory trace over time, interactions of the memory trace with other traces, or errors in storing and/or selecting the material to be remembered.

It is common experience that our ability to retain information decays from the time the information was sorted in memory. Originally this was thought to be because of a physiological decay in the brain which loses the information (much like a leak in a cylinder). However, more modern thinking suggests that laying down the memory trace may be impaired by the presence of previously learned material (proactive interference) or that its retention is impaired by material which was learned subsequently (retroactive interference). For example, an operator's inability to remember a correct sequence of control actions could be either because other, different sequences had been learned which interfere with memory for the new ones, or because other tasks have to be learned subsequently and carried out, again interfering with the memory trace.

In most cases a complete memory breakdown is unlikely to lead to accidents since performance will stop. Accidents are more likely to occur when an incorrect memory trace is recalled; that is, when the wrong control sequence is carried out without the operator's awareness.

The causes of such 'absent-mindedness' have not been studied in as much depth as the causes of forgetting. Reason (1979) asked people to keep a diary of their 'non-planned actions' for two weeks. From his results he categorised absent-minded acts into one of four types: storage errors, in which the original memory trace was incorrectly stored; test errors, in which the operator incorrectly checks the progress and outcomes of a sequence of actions; discrimination errors, in which the initial stimulus to carry out a sequence of activities is wrongly identified; and selection errors, in which the incorrect response is selected. Reason argues that absent-minded errors are a hazard for the skilled rather than for the unskilled operator:

> They seem to be a feature of well-practised or habitual tasks which are carried out fairly automatically, with only intermittent conscious checking. As one's conscious mind is rarely still, it is likely to be engaged with something other than the present routine action most of the time.

Personality

Much of the work investigating the role of personality factors in accident causation has been carried out in the field of motor vehicle accidents. Two types of study can be seen: searching for evidence of the 'accident-prone' personality, and considering causal relationships between accidents and various measured personality variables such as intraversion and extraversion, curiosity, aggression, and so on.

Accident proneness

The idea that an individual might have some personality trait which predisposes him or her to accidents was first suggested by three statisticians, Greenwood, Woods and Yule, in 1919. Supported by the Industrial Fatigue Research Board, they published an account of accidents sustained by workers in a munitions factory during the First World War and showed that a small minority of workers had more accidents than they would have done if chance factors alone were operating.

The next significant study in the area was carried out by Newbold in 1926. She described a similar analysis on nearly 9000 workers in factories manufacturing products of all sorts from cars to optical instruments, chocolates to cardboard boxes, and her data substantiated many of the findings of Greenwood, Woods and Yule.

Both sets of authors, however, were careful to emphasise that the statistical analysis of accident records is a study only of what happened—not of why or how it happened. In addition they record only the occurrences of accidents—not those of near accidents. Merely because an 'accident' was not sufficiently serious for it to be reported does not mean that the individual or the situation is not prone to causing accidents. Furthermore, Newbold pointed out that in her particular sample there were definite indications that youth, inexperience and possibly even poor health were associated with accident occurrence, and that it was not possible to rule out increased risk of exposure to dangerous situations as an important factor in the individual differences in proneness to accidents.

The concept of accident proneness as a personal idiosyncrasy predisposing the individual to a relatively high accident rate was first suggested by Farmer and Chambers in 1939. They examined the accident records of a large group of drivers and found, again, that a few had a disproportionately large number of accidents. However, in their description of accident proneness they went a stage further than their statistical data should have allowed. They argued that we can talk about an individual's personal proneness (regardless of the environmental circumstances) rather than the individual's and the environment's combined tendency to create a situation in which an accident is likely to occur.

If, as Farmer and Chambers suggest, accident proneness as a trait is 'no longer a theory but an established fact', using appropriate personality tests it should be possible to differentiate between the personalities of 'accident-free' people and 'accident repeaters'. A number of investigators have tried to do just this but without much success. Many traits have been established—aggressiveness, inconsiderateness, hostility, temerity—but no single personality dimension has been found.

Such difficulties have led to a reformulation of the concept of an accident-prone personality. Current thinking now suggests that if the trait of accident proneness does exist it is one which is not a permanent, unchangeable state of the individual. Rather it is an attribute influenced by both personal and environmental factors which vary from one period to another.

Thus age, experience, hazard exposure and a multitude of other factors may contribute to cause an individual at some times to be more liable to have an accident than at others. On the basis of a developed 'Accident Proneness Questionnaire', for example, Porter (1988) suggests that if there is any stability in the concept it is permanent for periods of at least 18 months, although she also accepts the likelihood of temporary 'accident-prone' states. Her research suggests that accident proneness relates more to abilities at other important aspects of working situations, such as attention. Thus work such as this suggests that accident proneness is not a single (or even a complex) personality trait—it occurs as a result of a complex interaction with the environment when individual features of the person do not match the requirements of the system. Rather than being relatively isolated events, such mismatches occur over a period, when the individual will appear to be accident prone.

The accident-proneness trait, therefore, can be represented by a continuum with the non-accident prones at one end and accident prones at the other (Porter and Corlett, 1989). Given that it is the result of potential mismatches, it is also as much a 'fault' of the current man–machine system with all its complexities as of the person.

Other personality traits

Even though it is unlikely that a single dimension of 'accident proneness' exists, it is not necessarily the case that personality traits or dimensions do not predispose an individual towards interacting with the environment in a dangerous manner. A number of studies have been carried out to consider the relationship between particular personality dimensions and the likelihood of accidents.

One of the earliest such studies was carried out by Shaw and Sichel (1971) who used the Eysenck Personality Inventory to compare the personality profiles of a group of South African bus drivers with their accident records (categorised as 'good', 'fair', 'poor' and 'bad'). All but one of the 'good' drivers had personalities measured as being towards the 'stable introvert' type (thoughtful, peaceful, controlled, calm, etc.), while the 'bad' and 'poor' drivers tended towards the 'unstable extravert' ends of the dimensions (outgoing, anxious, touchy, active, etc.). Similar results have been found by other workers. For example, Mackay et al. (1969) have demonstrated that a sample of accident drivers showed a mean extraversion score higher than the norms for the general population.

Intraversion–extraversion, however, is not the only personality trait to be considered. Hansen (1988), for example, demonstrated that extraversion, locus of control, impulsivity, aggression, social maladjustment and aspects of neuroses are all related to the occurrence of accidents. In addition, Sah (1989) showed that railway drivers who were involved in higher rates of accidents tended to display more uncontrolled impulsiveness, aggression and 'emotion of an explosive variety' than the accident-free individuals in his sample.

Table 12.1 provides details of some of the studies that have been undertaken to relate personality characteristics to accident behaviour (after Porter, 1988).

Age and Experience

Age is one of the most frequently considered factors in accident research, but its effects are confounded by experience, the task and, indeed, by the accidents themselves causing individuals to leave employment. For example, it is reasonable to assume that employees who have a high accident rate will tend to drop out of the system—because of injury, separation or leaving voluntarily. Any simple fall in accident rate with age, therefore, might reflect this trend.

Despite these confounding variables the overall trend indicates that during the teens and early twenties the accident rate is high; it then falls sharply, levelling out in the mid-twenties. When such factors as employee turnover are taken into account, some authors have then found a slight rise in accident rate towards ages in the mid-fifties.

The effects of experience and training cannot be excluded from these age effects—younger workers are likely to be less experienced and thus are more likely to make an error. A number of other reasons have been advanced for younger workers being more likely to have accidents, although few are based on any empirical evidence. Reviewing the literature, for example, Hale and Hale (1972) suggest that factors such as inattention, indiscipline, impulsiveness, recklessness, misjudgement, overestimation of capacity, pride, and lack of family responsibilities can be blamed. Although it is possible that all these suggestions are valid in particular circumstances, as the authors point out they are based on very slim evidence and mainly on the subjective impressions of individual investigators.

While younger workers labour under the handicap of the traits often ascribed to youth, such as impulsiveness, the problems of older workers lie in reduced and failing capacities which come with age. For example,

Table 12.1 The relationship between personality and accident proneness (after Porter, 1988; reproduced from *International Reviews of Ergonomics*, **2**, 177–206, by permission of Taylor & Francis)

Author	Tests administered	Results	Details
Dunbar, Wolfe and Rioch (1936) Dunbar *et al.* (1939)	Neuroses, spheres of conflict, attitude to injury/illness, etc.	80% of all cases involved a distinct psychic component; tendency to conflict, impulsiveness, fatalism, unstable education	Looking at psychomatic diabetes and heart disease. Fracture group intended as a control but found to suffer to the same degree with psychic problems
Adler (1941)	Personality, dreams and emotional reaction to accidents	60% of accident repeaters were bitter and revengeful towards parents, 40% needed attention. These attitudes cannot be seen in control group	104 industrial workers who had had repeated accidents in the previous six years. 20 control subjects
Tillman and Hobbs (1949)	Past life and adjustment to adult life	Significant differences between the two groups: parental divorce rate higher; juvenile violation rate higher; truancy from school higher; job changes more frequent; few close friends in high accident group	20 low and 20 high accident taxi drivers

Table 12.1 (cont.)

Author	Tests administered	Results	Details
Wong and Hobbs (1949)	Interviewed concerning broken home, juvenile court, truancy, irregular work, marital discord, job record. One point allocated for each	14/17 high accident group had at least 1 point, 7/14 had >3 points. 5/17 low accident group had at least 1 point, 1/14 had >3 points	17 high and 17 low accident workers in a job where minor cuts were common. Accident rate ascertained by observation
Smiley (1955)	Interviewed concerning work record, illness, etc.	72% of accident prones suffered from neuroses and nervous complaints as compared to 8% of controls	87 workers who had >11 accidents, 100 workers randomly chosen from the same workplace (they could presumably also have had >11 accidents)
Jenkins (1956)	131 primary personality factors and 52 indicators of occupational interests	Seven traits are predictive of accident proneness: ease of distraction, less restraint, lower independence, less sensitive, more tolerant of pain, more superior, more socially orientated	15-year study. Large group of accident repeaters matched with non-repeaters
Fine (1963)	Used MMPI to measure extraversion	Extraverts had significantly more traffic accidents than introverts	993 male students whose driving records were available

Study	Measure	Findings	Sample
Kunce (1967)	Accident proneness score derived from adventuresomeness and cautiousness scale in Strong Vocational Interest Blank	A higher than average accident rate was significantly related to high accident proneness scores	62 male industrial workers were given an accident proneness score based on the number of visits to the nurse to years on the job
Craske (1968)	Introversion/extraversion measured by EPI	Accidents significantly related to extraversion in the male group. No significant results for women	70 men, 30 women visiting an outpatient clinic. Interviewed concerning past accidents
Powell et al. (1971)	EPI	51 males with high extraversion scores had significantly more accidents than individuals with low extraversion scores	Large population of factory workers
Plummer and Das (1973)	Dichotomous thought processes, the extent to which individuals see life in 'black and white'	Dichotomous thinking used to a greater extent by the accident than by the non-accident group	30 high accident and 30 non-accident drivers, based on driving records over 3 years
Prather, Crisera and Fidell (1975)	Zimmerman Temperant Survey	No significant differences	High and low accident groups of roofing workers
Sanders and Hoffman (1975)	16PF, Mehrabian Achievement Scale, decision-making task	Accident-free subjects were more self-sufficient, imaginative and forthright	51 army pilots divided into accident-free and pilot error accident groups

Murrell (1962a) has suggested that tasks which have heavy perceptual demands, particularly when these are accompanied by speed, are not tolerated well by older people. This was supported by earlier studies which demonstrated that fewer older men were employed on jobs involving severe demands on attention to fine detail, or sustained care and attention.

Despite sensory and cognitive deficits that are the natural process of ageing, it is often pointed out that higher levels of skill and knowledge are associated with increasing age and these can often compensate for poorer faculties elsewhere. Holland and Rabbitt (1992), for example, have shown that, when deficiencies in their perceptual processing are pointed out to them, elderly drivers take active steps to avoid dangerous situations and so their accident rate does not increase.

Life Stress

Life stress is a concept which is becoming widely recognised as an influence on both health and behaviour. Significant stressful life experiences (such as a bereavement, divorce, or taking out a house mortgage) have been shown to play a role in precipitating episodes of serious illness, and even in the susceptibility to the common cold (Totman and Kiff, 1979).

The effects of life experiences on a worker's predisposition to accidents, however, have not been studied in any great detail. Verhaegen et al. (1976) quote a study which apparently demonstrated that subjects who had been responsible for an accident differed by their heavier 'psychological burden' from subjects who were the victims of an accident. 'Heavier psychological burden' was defined in terms of worries about children, housing, money, a marital partner, etc. However, when the authors attempted to replicate this study they obtained conflicting results. In one industrial plant they investigated, no differences were obtained between the stress experiences of accident causers and victims. In another plant, however, they obtained differences in the expected direction for worries about children's health and satisfaction with the home, but not for the subject's own or spouse's health, their children's educational progress, or the repayment of mortgages.

Despite these conflicting conclusions some other authors have found a significant relationship between accidents and life stresses. For example, Whitlock, Stoll and Rekhdahl (1977) compared the life experiences of 17–65-year-old orthopaedic patients who had sustained accidents, with a further group of control subjects drawn from routine surgery wards who were matched for age, sex and marital status. Their results demonstrated that the accidentally injured patients had experienced more changes in their lives over the previous six months. Unfortunately, however, a number of the accident victims had been taking various drugs for complaints such as hypertension, depression and diabetes. The possibility that the life stresses had helped to cause these complaints, and therefore that the drugs had contributed to the accidents, cannot be ruled out.

Levenson, Hirschfield and Hirschfield (1980) also considered patients, this time at a centre designed to evaluate, diagnose and treat problems of disability related to job accidents. When compared with control subjects the patient group were experiencing 25 per cent more life changes and 77 per cent more life stresses than the control group.

In summary, it is difficult to decide on the importance of life stressors in accident causation, particularly since most of the studies which have been carried out have been retrospective in nature. As has been demonstrated throughout it is certainly the case that distraction at an important point in carrying out a task can lead to an accident, and personal worries can be distracting. Whether life stresses *per se* (rather than specific worries) can make an individual liable to an accident cannot be decided until more evidence is available.

Accidents as Withdrawal Behaviour

In 1953 Hill and Trist advanced the theory that people may be motivated to have an accident so that they can take time off work. Their withdrawal hypothesis was supported by comparing the uncertified absence rates of 200 men who had remained free from accidents with those of 89 men who had sustained one or more accidents. Their results indicated that those sustaining accidents had had significantly more other absences than those who had remained free of accidents. Unfortunately, since the authors only reported the number of accidents, it is not possible to determine whether the people who had high accident rates had more accidents or merely reported more. Only the former would directly tend to support the theory.

Hill and Trist's survey can also be criticised on the grounds that they did not match the jobs of their high and low accident groups. As Hale and Hale (1972) point out, it is plausible to suggest that those with higher accident rates came from dangerous jobs, which also tend to be heavier jobs and make greater physical demands on people. The workers, therefore, might feel incapable of doing the job when slightly 'under the weather' and so take more days off work uncertified. This view is lent some support by the fact that Castle (1956) found no relation between accidents and uncertified absence in a photographic processing works where the work was much lighter. Powell *et al.* (1971), however, did show such a relationship in both men and women in a machine shop (heavier work), but not in an assembly shop.

It would appear, therefore, that there is very little evidence to support the hypothesis that workers either consciously or unconsciously cause an accident in order to escape from work.

PHYSIOLOGICAL MODELS OF ACCIDENT CAUSATION

Physiological models suggest that accidents are caused as a result of the worker's body being unable to cope with the task requirements. In this respect, disabilities such as deafness, blindness (or at least poor eyesight) or a lack of muscular strength might each be a cause of accidents. Such 'actors' have been discussed elsewhere. This section will discuss two aspects which might detrimentally influence the body's processing capacities: physiological rhythms and drugs (particularly alcohol).

Physiological Rhythms

Our bodies contain a number of systems which regulate functions in a rhythmical fashion. Perhaps the most obvious is the heart which beats consistently throughout life, normally at between 60 and 80 beats per minute. Less obvious are the rhythmical contractions of the intestinal muscles and the fairly high-frequency voltage changes (about 13 Hz depending on one's alertness) generated by the brain (as measured by electroencephalography, EEG). Over slightly longer periods, but still within 24 hours, we have rhythms of waking and sleeping and of temperature regulation. These daily variations are known as circadian rhythms (from the Latin *circa* (around) and *dies* (day)). Over even longer periods, up to a month, other bodily functions also cycle, for example the changes which occur in the lining of a women's uterus culminating each month in menstruation. In addition there are thought by some to be cycles of emotionality, and of intellectual and physical performance. These longer-term variations are commonly known as biological rhythms and biorhythms.

Circadian rhythms and accidents

Daily variations in human performance and efficiency have long been recognised. Indeed, Rutenfranz and Colquhoun (1979) have traced these observations back to Kraepelin in 1893:

With continued work the performance usually rises until noon. Soon after the meal it has decreased very significantly. Simultaneously a predominance of external associations and lower stability of imaginative combinations can be shown. These phenomena are no indication of work fatigue, since they disappear after 2–3 hours, even when work is continued. [After the noon meal] the performance again increases slowly. Sooner or later, however, without fail, fatigue gains the upper hand.

Rutenfranz and Colquhoun add the observation that much greater overall variation can be expected when the night hours are included. Rhythmical variations in performance on a number of tasks have been shown to occur under laboratory conditions. For example, Folkard and Monk (1979) demonstrated that the amount of information able to be remembered is influenced by the time of day of presentation, although no such influence occurred for the ability to retrieve information from memory.

Using a number of tasks (such as reaction time, calculations, card sorting, letter cancellation) Blake (1971) demonstrated performance increases between 0800 and 1030 hours with a 'post-lunch' dip at about 1400 hours. However, on one task (digit span, i.e. the number of digits which can be remembered) the post-lunch performance dip did not occur until late evening. Rutenfranz and Colquhoun (1979) interpret these findings to imply that just as physiological processes show different circadian rhythms, so do different psychological functions.

There are fewer industrial studies relating circadian rhythms to performance, a fact which Folkard and Monk (1979) ascribe to aspects of the working system such as union or management opposition and problems in finding appropriate measures. However, there appears to be agreement between the studies which have been carried out, primarily in relation to shift work. For example, Hildebrandt, Rohmert and Rutenfranz (1974) demonstrated a typical 24-hour circadian pattern of unintended brakings by train drivers (i.e. when the train came to a stop because the driver failed to respond to a signal in the cab). Other, similar conclusions from different situations have been reviewed by Folkard and Monk (1979, 1985).

The relationship between such rhythms and accidents, and the implications for shift work, have been discussed by Colquhoun (1975b). Investigating sailors on a four-hour watch-keeping schedule he demonstrated a circadian variation in alertness (detecting a very faint auditory or visual signal) and in reaction time, implying that the potential for accident causation also varies rhythmically. Similar results were obtained using eight-hour shifts without any 'weekend break'. Furthermore, Folkard, Monk and Chobban (1978) demonstrated a highly significant rhythmical variation over the day in the frequency of 'minor accidents' occurring to patients during their stay in hospital. The changes in the rhythm coincided well with the timing of the nurses' early day, late day and night shifts. Although the authors point out that the relationship between the two findings could be spurious (the tendency for accident peaks to occur in early morning or late night could be attributed to the patient's need to 'pass water' immediately before going to sleep or on awakening) they also suggest that a causal relationship might exist.

Biorhythms and biological rhythms

Whereas circadian rhythms have been demonstrated and occur over a 24-hour period, the evidence for biorhythms is not as secure. If they exist they occur over periods of up to one month. The biorhythm theory suggests that there are cycles of 23, 28 and 33 days in duration which govern physical, emotional and intellectual performance respectively. Each cycle is described by a sinusoidal curve having a positive and a negative phase, the cycle starting on a positive half-cycle at the moment of birth. (Why the theory should consider that the rhythm should begin at birth rather than at the time of conception is unclear.) The positive phase corresponds to periods when performance is best, the negative phase to periods of poorer performance, and the crossover points are termed 'critical'. The length of this critical period is usually considered to be 24 hours. According to the theory, accidents would be more likely to occur on critical days, that is on days when more than one cycle is in the critical phase and days when one cycle is in a critical phase and the other cycles are in a negative phase. In addition, days when all cycles are in a negative phase are said to be critical because of the change from 'positive' to 'negative' behaviour—'just as the most "dangerous" time for a light bulb to burn out is when power surges through it as it is switched on' (Gittelson, 1978).

Controversy continues in both the scientific and popular press concerning the existence of such cycles—whether they exist at all and, if so, whether they are fixed from birth. Certainly, it is not the purpose of this chapter to fuel the arguments. However, the theory does propose testable hypotheses with respect to accidents and a few investigators have attempted to correlate recorded accident data with that which would have been predicted according to the theory. After reviewing the studies, however, and after carrying out a study of their own on over 4000 pilot accidents, Wolcott et al. (1977a, b) concluded that there is no statistically significant correlation between the occurrence of an accident and biorhythmicity.

Support for these conclusions has also been provided by Khalil and Kurucz (1977). They investigated the relationship between the timing of 63 aircraft accidents in which 'pilot error' was said to be to blame, and the position of each pilot's biorhythm. Again, their analyses indicated that 'biorhythm' had no significant influence on accident likelihood.

Alcohol

A great deal of work has been conducted on the effects of alcohol on judgement and on the performance of skilled tasks. In general the experimental work has shown that alcohol has a deleterious effect on performance because of its effects on vision, perceptual motor functions, judgement, reasoning and memory.

Many of the studies in this area have concerned driving tasks. For example, Bjerver and Goldberg (1950) used a special truck designed to measure the driver's ability to operate a car within close limits. Such manoeuvres as parallel parking, driving out of a garage, and turning around in a narrow roadway were required. Their results showed that the time taken by skilled drivers to perform tests correctly was significantly lengthened when the subjects were at a blood-alcohol level of about 40 mg/100 ml of blood. Because of studies such as these which have consistently shown a positive relationship between alcohol level and performance decrement, most countries have fixed by law a blood-alcohol level beyond which it is an offence to drive. The levels vary from 50 mg/100 ml of blood to 150 mg/100 ml.

The role of alcohol in industrial accidents has been less extensively studied. Some studies have certainly indicated, as did the Bjerver and Goldberg study, that the accident rate rises with the proportion of drinkers in the workforce. However, these are cases of alcohol consumed while at work— the accident likelihood of the alcoholic worker who drinks heavily but not at work might well be considered. As Trice and Roman (1972) point out, it is logical to expect a deviant drinker to have more accidents than other workers, since steadiness would be impaired in addition to coordination, timing, motor responses and sense of danger. In addition, hangovers on the job could cause accidents. As some support of such contentions, Haberman (1987) reports that autopsy analyses of liver and pancreas disorders from fatal accident victims showed that non-traffic accident deaths were associated with alcoholism and alcohol use significantly more often than were traffic deaths.

Unfortunately the research data which have emerged over the years make generalisations about the relationships between alcohol and industrial accidents difficult. For example, 'Observer' and Maxwell (1959) ('Observer' was a pseudonym) concluded that problem drinkers do have more accidents than other workers. They recorded three times as many accidents caused by problem drinkers than by members of their control group. Furthermore, in another study Brenner (1967), who considered the fatal accidents in a sample of 1343 patients in four alcoholism rehabilitation clinics, concluded that the alcoholics were seven times as likely to become the victims of fatal accidents than the non-alcoholic controls. Of the 35 fatal accidents, however, only one was reported as occurring while at work.

A direct comparison of alcoholism and accident rate, however, has many pitfalls. The first concerns the problem of accident statistics as a source of data: they give no indication of the situation leading to the accident, nor usually of the accident severity. Secondly, the evidence appears to suggest that the risk of accidents from alcohol is related to the extent to which the alcoholic is able to cope with his or her 'disability'. When breaking down their accident data for different age groups, for example, Observer and Maxwell considered that while problem drinkers do account for more accidents than other workers of the same age during the early problem drinking years, by the time that the problem has developed fully problem drinkers are generally no more prone to on-the-job accidents than other employees.

These findings have been explained as owing to the improved coping behaviour of the committed alcoholics and their colleagues. Such factors include the routine nature of the job, extra caution, protection from accidents by fellow workers, absenteeism when incapacitated (e.g. from hangovers), and assignment by supervisors to less hazardous work. Apparently these factors—or at least some of them—do not play the same role during the early problem drinking period in protecting the individual from on-the-job accidents.

SUMMARY

Although one of the main themes of this book has been to illustrate ways in which the environment can be designed to promote safety, this chapter has dealt specifically with human accident behaviour. It has taken as its thesis the suggestion that accidents occur when the environmental demands surpass the operator's capabilities. Various behavioural and physiological models were proposed to account for why the operator's capacities may be reduced at the important time.

13

INSPECTION AND MAINTENANCE

Like the last chapter which dealt with accidents, in many respects a chapter dealing with inspection and maintenance could be considered to be out of place in a general ergonomics text. Ergonomics is an applied discipline; an ergonomist applies knowledge and experience about how people interact with the environment to ensure that the environment fits the individual's behaviours and abilities. This theme has been stressed throughout this book, and various routes to this grail have been illustrated. Both inspection and maintenance are areas of ergonomics application, in the same way that the ergonomics of space flight, of agriculture or of medicine are different areas of interest to different ergonomists. Why then should inspection and maintenance be singled out for special consideration?

Two answers can be given to this question. First, although it is true that inspection and maintenance are specific areas of interest, both exemplify the necessity to consider the total working system. They each provide ideal examples of how ergonomics can be implemented to help solve specific problems. Secondly, both are important in their own right when designing a system; they have to be considered just as much as the design of individual displays, controls or workplaces. It is a fact of life that components in a system occasionally break down, and if system maintainability has been considered in the original design the fault will be able to be discovered and rectified more quickly and more easily.

The distinction between inspection and maintenance, of course, is often a distinction without a difference. It is hard to draw a dividing line between the two processes since both involve detecting and eliminating faults. However, for the purposes of this chapter inspection will be taken to be the process by which a faulty item is detected. Maintenance involves rectifying the fault, usually within the system.

INSPECTION

With the increasing efficiency and output of machines, the task of an industrial inspector has become more complex over the years. Faster, more productive, more accurate machinery is likely to produce goods at a pace which causes greater difficulties in detecting product defects. In addition, the consequences of missing a defect have also grown in importance. At one level reduced vigilance or bad inspection could cause dissatisfaction among customers, evidenced by the return of faulty goods and perhaps a loss of custom. As Drury and Sinclair (1983) point out, these days customers are demanding defect-free products, often in the courts. At another level poor inspection may increase production costs by causing unnecessary machine stoppages, by interrupting the production flow, or by wasting material.

Engineers will tell us that it is possible to design machines to carry out some aspects of the inspector's job with almost 100 per cent efficiency. At present, however, this is feasible only if there is a limited number of specific faults that would occur within a product and if the decisions remain simple. For example, Drury and Sinclair (1983) compared human and machine inspectors and found that whereas the machines located more faults than the humans did, they were unable to classify them as acceptable or rejectable with the same consistency. This ought to be expected when one remembers the list of functions best carried out by man and by machine that was discussed in Chapter 1. Thus, man is normally more efficient in complex, variable situations, particularly when fine form, depth or texture has to be perceived. It would be difficult to find a machine that could match human powers of examining for numbers of different faults at once over a wide range of products; that could assess a surface 'finish' or colour uniformity; or could take note of a rare, perhaps unspecified, fault. Man is as yet unsurpassed where discrimination is required between a large number of faults, where classification and diagnosis are necessary, and where eliminating the fault involves liaison with other individuals or with other machines.

Regarding the types of task that would normally be carried out under the title of 'inspection', Czaja and Drury (1981) compared several taxonomies. From their review they distilled four task categories:

(1) *Monitoring:* observing a continuous process and reporting any deviations.

(2) *Examining:* searching items, or arrays of items, for defects. Judgements are made without numerical measurement.

(3) *Measuring:* using instruments and measuring tools to provide numerical measures on which decisions are based.

(4) *Patrolling:* checking and organising the work of other inspectors.

Clearly, the first two of these groups require some kind of subjective evaluation; the third group depends entirely on an inspector's ability to measure accurately (and on the ergonomic quality of the measuring instrument); while the fourth group may use any task covered in the first three groups. The following discussion will deal primarily with monitoring and examining.

A SIMPLE MODEL OF INDUSTRIAL INSPECTION

Based on reports from inspectors a fairly simple model can be developed to explain the extremely complex inspection process. Generally, inspectors suggest that their task is to keep the idea of what constitutes a 'good' item in mind and then to look for faults in the object being inspected. In other words, they appear to compare the object's 'external' appearance with an internal representation of the acceptable item. Any mismatch between the two perceptions would cause a decision to be made to reject the item. This model explains why an inspector who is asked to identify the fault will sometimes need to re-examine the item. Because the task is simply to identify a mismatch between the item and the internal model of it, time will not normally have been wasted in classifying the nature of the mismatch.

Toms and Patrick (1987, 1989) take this model slightly further by considering the nature of the process by which the inspector compares the 'given' state with the 'ideal'. They suggest that the task becomes one of generating a set of possibilities consistent with the symptoms of the problem. This set they call the 'consistent fault set' (CFS), after Duncan and Grey (1975). Following Rasmussen (1981, 1984) they suggest that inspectors may adopt two different kinds of strategies to derive this CFS:

(1) *Symptomatic strategies,* in which possible failures corresponding to the symptoms are accessed via some cognitive searching through a 'library' of possible abnormal 'patterns'. These obviously make use of past experience.

(2) *Topographic strategies,* in which possible failures are inferred on the basis of the structure of the system. These are clearly more 'rule based' strategies.

In addition to these features, Thomas (1968) points out that an inspector often requires the nature of the faults to be recognised—perhaps to send defective items for appropriate remedial treatment or to record the occurrence of various types of faults. To do this the inspector's model must contain sets of alternatives, similar to subroutines in a computer program, so that scanning can be continued beyond the stage of identifying a rejectable mismatch. The object's appearance will thus have to be matched with detailed characteristics of a specific 'fault subsection' in the model.

Finally, the simple model recognises one very important consequence of repetitive inspection—a possible drift in inspection standards. Since the task involves matching an external stimulus to an 'internal' representation, it is quite possible that the internal representation may undergo small, subtle changes, perhaps because of past experience, social pressures, or a host of other factors. These changes will cause a corresponding change in the inspector's decision criteria for accepting or rejecting an item.

The ergonomist's task, therefore, is twofold: first, to obtain the best possible stimulus of the object to be perceived; second, to assist in developing suitable internal models. Both aspects can be carried out by implementing many of the ergonomics principles discussed elsewhere in this book. As will become evident, however, this is an extremely complex task.

FACTORS AFFECTING INSPECTION ACCURACY

Megaw (1978) suggest four groups of factors which could influence inspection accuracy:

(1) Into the first category fall the variables which the inspector brings to the task: visual ability and performance; age and experience; personality and intelligence; and so on. There is little that the ergonomist can do to influence these variables alone, although, having recognised their effects, aspects of the work can be altered either to compensate for them or to accentuate them.

(2) Some of these features fall into Megaw's second category—physical and environmental factors in which the inspection task is carried out. Thus aspects such as the lighting, the workplace layout, background noise and the presence or absence of visual aids are important.

(3) Megaw's third category contains organisational factors and characteristics of the inspector's overall job. These include the number of inspectors available; the type of training and feedback received; rest pauses and shiftwork; social aspects of the job; and so on.

(4)   Finally, Megaw collects together factors which pertain specifically to the inspector's task—whether the objects to be viewed are moving or stationary; the probability that any one piece is defective; the complexity of the object; the density of the items; and so on.

INSPECTOR VARIABLES

Visual Acuity

Since in most cases inspection is a visually based task, it is reasonable to expect that inspection performance will degrade as the inspector's visual ability decreases. On the other hand, it is not unreasonable to expect the reverse—that inspection performance increases with increasing visual ability.

For some time visual acuity has generally been the accepted criterion of visual ability for an inspection task. As an indication of the relationship between acuity and performance, McCormick (1950) measured the visual acuity of over 5000 employees doing different jobs (the sample included sewing machinists and close assembly workers in addition to visual inspectors). The relationship between visual acuity and performance that he obtained is shown in Figure 13.1. It would appear from the graph, for example, that approximately 55 per cent of the employees who have fairly good near acuity (minimum visual angle of about 1 min of arc) were from

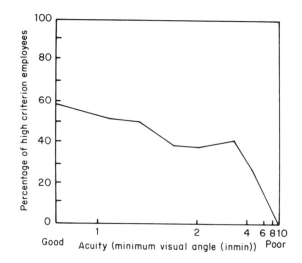

Figure 13.1   The relationship between visual acuity and good performance (from McCormick, 1950)

the high criterion group, whereas all of the employees having poor acuity (for example, 10 min of arc) were from the low criterion group.

Whereas McCormick's data suggest a trend of reduced performance with much reduced acuity, the converse is by no means the case—about 45 per cent of the employees with good acuity fell into the low criterion category. As Megaw concludes, 'the results demonstrate that the possession of good acuity does not ensure that person is a high criterion inspector, merely that the chances are relatively high'.

It is not altogether surprising that a perfect relationship between acuity and performance was not obtained. Being a laboratory-based measure the acuity task does not test the operator's performance within a work system: most acuity tasks use stationary stimuli whereas the objects in many inspection tasks are moving; most acuity tests are carried out under 'ideal' environmental conditions whereas this is not necessarily so at work; and most acuity tasks carry no reward or punishment for the testee. Again, this is not necessarily the case at work.

Given these drawbacks it is unlikely that a simple relationship can, or will, be found. Nevertheless some attempts at more realism have been made. For example, Nelson and Barany (1969) developed a dynamic visual acuity test in which the test material and conditions incorporated many of the features of the inspection task for which inspectors are being selected. As Megaw points out, however, such tests are difficult and expensive to develop if they are to be in any way predictive.

Another approach has been taken by some workers who feel that the size of the inspector's visual field (essentially a test of peripheral acuity) should be related to inspection performance. For example, Johnston (1965) investigated the relationship between the size of observers' visual fields and the time required to locate targets on static displays. Her data suggested that people with large visual fields can find targets more rapidly than those with small fields.

Other studies have indicated that an important difference between best and poorest performance is the length of time taken by the observer between eye fixations during the search task. For example, Boynton, Elworth and Palmer (1958) found that their best subject averaged nearly twice the saccadic length of their 'worst' subject, and so they concluded that longer sweeps are an aid to efficient search. This is presumably because longer sweeps between fixations will result in fewer eyeball fixations. It takes a shorter time to scan the material so that more scans can be made in the time available.

It still remains the case, however, that such results were obtained from subjects in the laboratory and have not been validated for industrial tasks.

Age and Experience

When considering features such as safety and accidents, difficulties involved in isolating age as a single variable were noted. Increasing age is often associated both with failing health (which can detrimentally affect performance) and increased experience (which can improve performance). It is not surprising, therefore, that few studies are available which have investigated the effects of ageing on inspectors.

Jamieson (1966) recorded the ages of his inspectors when carrying out two types of task: either inspecting switches for mechanical faults as they left the assembly line (which involved a minimum of 190 discriminations per switch), or checking telephone exchange racks for faulty soldered joints and connections. (Unfortunately no indication was given of the experience of his subjects.) In both types of task, inspection performance increased with increasing age, although the relationship was significant only in the telephone rack task. These results were confirmed with a further group of workers. Unfortunately, however, since it is likely that the sight of many of the older workers would have begun to fail, the study did not answer the question of whether experience and other variables such as conscientiousness outweighed the negative factors of ageing.

Although useful in illustrating the effects of age on inspector performance, Jamieson's experiments do not enable the positive effects of increased experience and the negative effects of reduced abilities to be tested. Nevertheless, work by Czaja and Drury (1981) suggests that any negative effects may be able to be overcome with appropriate training before the inspection task. In their study, pre-training took the form firstly of subjects organising a list of words and then learning them, and secondly sorting objects into different sized groups. Following this pre-training regime, subjects were required to inspect displayed characters and reject those which did not conform to particular sizes. Pre-trained older subjects performed better on this task than those who had no previous training.

Personality

Personality is a variable which has received considerable attention in the past, particularly in studies of its relationship with vigilance. In this case the evidence appears to suggest that along an introversion–extraversion dimension at least some differences may be apparent, with introverts performing slightly better than extraverts. Along another dimension—locus of control—Sanders et al. (1976) demonstrated that people with low scores (that is, who tend to internalise their view of the world) tend to make fewer errors on a vigilance task than do externals.

Unfortunately, there are fewer studies that have attempted to relate personality measures to quality control/inspection tasks, although two that were reported by Wolke and DuCette (1974) could be placed under this heading. They used a proof-reading task and also measured their subjects' locus of control. As with the vigilance studies, internals were shown to produce better performance in both the paced and unpaced versions of the task. Eskew and Riche (1982) later demonstrated that this superiority is because internals use more appropriate decision criteria and make fewer 'false alarms' (i.e. rejecting an otherwise perfect item).

PHYSICAL AND ENVIRONMENTAL VARIABLES

Lighting

Because inspection is largely a visual task, it should be obvious that the inspector's main environmental needs are for adequate illumination. This implies providing enough light to be able to view the objects without undue fatigue, but not so much light as to cause glare. All of the factors discussed in the previous chapter which can affect visual performance should be considered, therefore. However, two additional aspects ought to be emphasised: first the type of lighting and secondly its position.

Regarding the type of lighting Lion (Lion, 1964; Lion, Richardson and Browne, 1968) compared inspection and manipulation performance using two kinds of illumination: fluorescent and tungsten lights. In the first experiment she asked her subjects to perform a variety of tasks (grading ballbearings, threading needles, reading numbers, and measuring the lengths of rods) using either an 80-watt 'warm' fluorescent tube or a 100-watt clear tungsten bulb. Both lights produced illumination of 14 lumens/sq ft at the work surface. Her subjects were significantly quicker completing the tasks using a fluorescent than a tungsten bulb, although the number of errors made in each case were not significantly affected. Since all tasks used stimuli which had a high degree of reflectivity, Lion argued that the performance difference was due to the filament (tungsten) light producing a concentrated light source and thus more glare. This was insufficient to increase errors but it was enough to slow down the rate of work.

In a second series of experiments Lion and her colleagues used tasks more similar to those encountered in an inspection task, that is, searching for defects in small objects moving on a conveyor belt. The defective objects were either buttons with off-centred holes or black plastic discs with a broken white design etched onto their surface. Again, tungsten and fluorescent room lighting were compared, this time producing equivalent illumination levels of 30 lumens/sq ft at the working level.

In this experiment the results were slightly less conclusive. Lion's subjects overlooked significantly fewer faulty broken designs on the disc-sorting task under fluorescent compared to tungsten lighting, but there were no significant differences on the button-sorting task. The authors explain the discrepancy by pointing to the type of task involved in each case. The 'faulty design' task required the operator to perceive a break in a line, which is essentially an acuity task, while the button-sorting task required a more 'global' perception of the object. In this case, the rejection criterion was whether or not the four buttonholes were central. The authors suggest that it is only the visual acuity task which is at a disadvantage under point-source illumination, possibly because of the glaring effects.

With respect to the position of the light source, Fox (1977) describes a series of experiments designed to investigate problems experienced in the quality control of coins produced at the Royal Mint. In one study he compared the error detection rate when a bank of five 40-watt fluorescent lights was placed immediately above the workplace in a horizontal arrangement, and when the bank was angled on its supports. This second condition purposefully produced specular glare from the coin surfaces.

The interesting feature of this arrangement was that the quality of the glare changed with the absence, presence and even type of coin defect. Thus, because the effect was to vary the contrast between the faulty part of the item and its background, to detect a damaged or misshapen coin the inspectors' task becomes one of detecting the glare type (intensity) rather than comparing the coin with an internalised model. Although the fault detection rate did not differ using the two arrangements, Fox argues that the angled position allowed a more 'standard' performance from the inspectors. Unfortunately, he provides no details of the angle used, and did not attempt to carry out any controlled study of this question. Nevertheless the use of glare to benefit the inspector is an interesting concept, although it should be pointed out that prolonged use may well cause visual fatigue.

Perceptual Aids

Although the level and type of illumination are extremely important aspects of the visual environment, as was pointed out in Chapter 1 the inspector's task can often be assisted by using visual aids such as magnifiers or visual overlays.

Magnification is an obvious aid for the inspector—particularly if the task includes significant acuity components. Increasing the apparent size of the object will also increase the size of the defect to be detected. However, the term 'magnification' should not be limited solely to discussing 'size'. Thus the term can be used in its broadest sense to denote a form of increase which enhances the perceived magnitude of the object or event being examined. So an inspection task that involves detecting small colour differences may be aided (i.e. the differences 'magnified') by using different coloured lights; a specific signal in an auditory discrimination task can be 'magnified' (i.e. the tone made more apparent) by modulation; and so on.

If the apparent size of an object is magnified by a magnifying glass, it is sensible to use a jig or holder for the object being inspected. This has two advantages. First, because most optical magnifiers have a restricted depth of field, the jig will immediately place the object at the appropriate distance from the magnifying glass, ensuring a standard appearance of all the inspected objects. Secondly, although the natural hand tremor does not interfere with the normal perception of objects, behind a magnifying glass any movement caused by tremor is increased. This might affect visual acuity performance in the way discussed in Chapter 10 when considering the effects of vibration.

A note of caution must be sounded, however, against the 'unrestricted' use of linear, optical magnification. From the scanty data available it would appear that, as with most encounters with the physical world, there is an optimum level of magnification. Both higher and lower magnification levels tend to result in reduced performance. Early investigators to demonstrate this effect were Nayyar and Simon who, in 1963, asked subjects to perform a task which consisted of picking up, transporting and assembling metal dots of 0.01 in diameter. Their subjects performed the task under three magnifications: $20\times$, $30\times$ and $40\times$, and the results indicated that the subjects picked up the dots more quickly when using the $30\times$ magnification than either of the other two. In a subsequent study Simon (1964) demonstrated that this optimum magnification was strongly related to the size of the object to be manipulated. Again comparing $20\times$ and $30\times$ magnification, he demonstrated the advantage of the $30\times$ magnification for a 0.01 in dot but, when a larger dot was used (0.015 in), the relative advantages of the two magnification sizes were reversed.

These results suggest, therefore, that it is the image size on the retina that is important rather than the magnification size. This contention is supported by Smith and Adams' (1971) results when they demonstrated that no matter what size object was used, the optimum magnification always produced an image which subtended an angle of about 8–9 min of arc at the eye. This factor remained constant even under different illumination levels.

Visual aids in the form of overlays have also been shown to benefit inspection performance. Using such aids it is often possible to help the inspector spot defects by making them stand out from the background. Like Fox's coin inspection, the inspection task thus becomes one of looking for things that are highlighted rather than looking at each and every individual item.

Noise

The effects of noise on performance have already been discussed in Chapter 10, and will not be discussed further here. However, it should be remembered that under some conditions noise may actually increase performance. Thus Poulton (1977) has suggested that noise may act as an arouser when dealing with boring, repetitive tasks, while Chapter 10 discussed the effects of background music on performance.

ORGANISATIONAL VARIABLES

As well as the factors which the physical environment brings to the inspection task (in particular the illumination quality and the noise), the social and organisational environments should not be forgotten. These include how the inspector interacts with colleagues and the organisation, and the job arrangements as a whole.

Social Factors

The inspection model described earlier relies heavily on the inspector's subjective judgement of whether or not the object perceived matches the ideal model in the 'mind'. However, it is well known that judgements of this type can be greatly influenced by social pressures on the observer to conform to the group norm. As a famous example, Asch (1952) asked subjects to judge the length of a line. When exposed to various types of group pressure, individual's estimates conformed strongly to the group's estimates even when, by manipulating 'stooges' in the group, the group decision was widely in error.

As an example of the ways in which such pressures to conform may influence an inspector's judgement, Belbin (1957) describes how in a knitwear factory inspectors reported very few 'seconds'; instead they classified nearly all defective work as 'mendable'. In this factory, although the knitters lost pay for defective work they lost more for 'seconds' than for 'menders'. It would appear, therefore, that lacking clear standards the inspectors were unable to resist the knitters' pressure to class most defects as 'menders' rather than as 'seconds'.

In addition to pressures from the workforce, an inspector often has to face similar types of coercion from the production management. As part of the production team the inspector's task includes maintaining a certain production flow. As Thomas and Seaborne (1961) point out, when the production department is in difficulties there will be considerable pressure to maintain a certain output by accepting some components which, in more favourable circumstances, might have been rejected. On the other hand, when output is high the criterion for acceptance could be made more stringent without an appreciable reduction in the productive flow.

McKenzie (1957) summarises some of these aspects by pointing out that, particularly when objects are individually made, 'in the factory inspection is always, if implicitly, of people; inspection decisions about a man's work directly reflect on him'. Again, therefore, the implication is made that there are a number of social pressures placed on the inspector not to reject an item. These pressures may arise from the workplace (increased rejection might result in reduced bonuses; increased rejection implies reduced work quality) or even from the production management (increased rejection means reduced output schedules and higher cost).

Feedback

The benefit to performance of adequate feedback has been stressed throughout this book and its effects on inspection performance are no different. Since inspection involves comparing an external object with an 'internal' model, it is essential that the inspector is given every opportunity to 'update' the model in the light of experience. Two separate roles can be identified for feedback: first to maintain motivation and second to provide information about efficiency.

The value of feedback as a motivator is difficult to assess in any controlled way. However, Megaw (1978) considers that there is a 'general consensus of opinion' that feedback helps inspectors to appreciate the importance of their work and thus become more involved in their task.

As with most tasks, giving inspectors details of their performance is likely to improve accuracy: operators who realise that too many good items are being rejected, too many faulty items missed, or even that their performance is accurate can adjust their 'internal model'—the rejection criterion—accordingly. That feedback is effective in this role was demonstrated by Drury and Addison (1973) for inspecting complex glass items. During a specified period the inspectors' output was checked by a second group of inspectors who informed the first group immediately they had made an error. Introducing this undelayed feedback resulted in increased performance for the first group such that the probability of missing a fault was halved. However, the authors rightly caution that the improvement may not have occurred solely as a result of improved feedback, since the new feedback arrangement was part of other procedural changes, including in supervision methods.

Rest Pauses

Inspection is normally a light, repetitive task, the speed of which is governed by the speed of the industrial process producing the objects to be inspected. It is also a task with a high vigilance component. Since even highly motivated people require a short break after prolonged activity, it would be quite reasonable to suggest that the same principle holds for industrial inspectors.

Murrell (1962b) has proposed the concept of an 'actile period', which he defines as 'a period during which there is a state of preparedness to respond optimally to stimulation either discretely or continuously'—in other words, the period during which a worker can maintain concentration on the task in hand. He further suggests that this period has a finite duration depending on the individual involved and the task undertaken. At the end of the actile period, performance will start to deteriorate and, with continued activity, the deterioration will become serious and output will begin to fall. In addition to the projected fall in output, a further important consideration of an actile period concept is that without a break the operator will individually impose such a break of a few seconds at a time. Thus, Branton and Oborne (1979) have inferred the presence of 'mini-sleeps' among anaesthetists who had to monitor long and often boring operations.

A number of studies have demonstrated the need for rest pauses throughout the working day (see for example Murrell, 1971). However, Colquohoun (1958) demonstrated the necessity for such pauses at more frequent intervals during inspection work. In a laboratory study in which his subjects were required to spot faulty discs on a moving drum, his results indicated that when the work was performed uninterrupted for a period of an hour the efficiency, although initially high, declined after about 30 minutes. If a five-minute rest period was inserted at this point, however, the performance was maintained at a high level throughout the hour.

TASK VARIABLES

So far, consideration has been given to aspects of the inspection task which the inspector brings as an individual, and those which are added by the physical, social and organisational environments. Finally, factors supplied by the task itself should be considered. In this respect, important considerations are the pace of the work, its complexity, and the likelihood of a fault being present.

Speed of Working

Drury (1973) has pointed out that the rate at which an inspector can work is likely to be one of the most vital pieces of information required when designing industrial inspection systems. For a fixed production rate, knowing the time required to inspect an item determines the staffing level and hence, to a large extent, the design of the physical facilities. Poor quality control is likely to occur if too slow or too fast a pace is imposed or too many inspectors are installed. In his investigation of the quality control of coin production, Fox (1977) varied the speed at which the coins passed the inspector's field of view, either in pairs or in triplets. Whereas no significant difference in inspection accuracy was obtained between the inspection speeds when only two coins appeared at any one time (inspection time/coin varied between 0.05 and 0.125 s), when three coins were presented at a time a significant increase from 70.8 to 82.7 per cent correct detection occurred (inspection time/coin ranged between 0.033 and 0.83 s).

The increase in detection efficiency with inspection time, however, is not linear. In fact, most of the studies reviewed by Drury (1973) demonstrate an exponential increase in fault detection as the time available for inspection is increased. The curve flattens out below perfect detection, with the critical inspection time unfortunately depending largely on the task complexity and the conspicuity of the fault. So no general guidelines can be given for appropriate times. In addition to this trend, however, there appears to be a very slight, although generally non-significant, increase in the probability of making the other type of inspection error (for instance, rejecting a good item rather than a bad one) with time. Although this trend is very slight, and in some studies completely absent, it does imply again that slight changes may occur in the inspector's criterion of a 'good' item.

Product Complexity

The importance of the product's complexity as a variable which affects the time available to inspect each item has already been considered. However, even when inspectors are allowed long inspection periods, the product's complexity can have a detrimental effect on performance. Thus, Harris (1966) demonstrated an almost linear reduction in detection performance with increasing item complexity (complexity was defined in two ways; either according to a rated complexity index, or in terms of the number of components—circuit boards, transistors, wires, etc.—in the equipment). Since the detection decrease could not be overcome simply by increasing the inspector's time, Harris suggests using visual aids with complex equipment. As has already been demonstrated, these can be useful in such circumstances.

The Probability of a Defect Occurring

Since most aspects of human behaviour are shaped by the probability of an event occurring or not occurring, it is not unreasonable for this also to be the case for inspection tasks. In a vigilance test, for example, Jenkins (1958) demonstrated that as the signals to be detected became more frequent, so the number of correct detections also increased. This view was later altered slightly, however, to suggest that it was not the frequency of 'wanted' signals in themselves which was the important criterion, but the ratio of wanted to the total number of signals (i.e. the probability of a wanted signal occurring) (for example Jerison, 1966).

These assertions were tested in a factory environment by Fox and Haslegrave (1969) who varied the probability of a defect occurring in batches of screws and bolts. Their results indicated that detection efficiency increased almost linearly with an increase in the fault probability. However, a corresponding increase in false detections (i.e. rejecting a good item) also occurred. Again, therefore, it appears that the inspectors were altering their rejection criteria rather than simply becoming more efficient detectors. Increasing the probability of a defective item occurring simply causes more items to be rejected rather than more items to be rejected correctly.

MAINTENANCE

From the discussion so far, it is clear that inspection is essentially a perceptual problem—the operator's task is to perceive faulty aspects of an object and to make judgements on the basis of these perceptions. Any part of the task, operator, environment, or organisation which affects perceptual ability is also likely to affect inspection performance. Similarly, any way in which the ergonomist can increase the operator's perceptual acuity should help to increase inspection performance.

If this very crude analogy is extended, it could be argued that maintenance performance is largely composed of motor and control components. Thus, although the maintenance operator perhaps needs to scan 'faulty' equipment to isolate the fault, subsequent problems are likely to centre around the component's accessibility, the equipment's controllability and/or an individual's ability to manipulate, lift or pull out the relevant machinery. In essence, therefore, this crude distinction could be explained in terms of the aspects of the body's sensory nervous structure discussed in Chapter 2 (inspection) and its motor control structure considered in Chapter 3 (maintenance).

It is a fact of life that no machine or component is likely to survive the life of the total system and unless we accept the concept of a totally 'throw-away' society in which any machine which breaks down is discarded for a new model, faulty parts will continually have to be maintained or replaced. However, although great strides have been made in reducing the failure rate of various components (particularly in the electronics industry), such advances have not kept pace with system complexity or costs. As the system becomes more complex, maintaining parts of it is likely to become more difficult and costly. Maintenance, therefore, costs money, and it is in the interests of all who operate a system to reduce the costs by considering (or having others consider) at an early stage in the product or system design the ease with which it can be maintained.

The rest of this chapter will discuss some of the ways that this ideal state of affairs can be approached but, before doing so, it is as well to consider the conditions under which equipment often has to be maintained.

First, there are extremes of environmental conditions. When having to locate faulty components or otherwise maintain systems under field conditions, the environmental considerations discussed in Chapters 10 and 11 may be far from optimum. In particular, illumination levels in the interiors of machines are often very low, usually requiring the maintenance engineer to have to cope with some kind of torch. At the other end of the illumination scale, bright sunlight or even unguarded lights in the machine mean that maintenance often has to be carried out under conditions of sometimes high disability glare. Other environmental conditions, for example temperature and weather, can also vary with the site of the equipment when it breaks down. A long-distance lorry driver, for example, may have to carry out vehicle repairs on an isolated, cold, windswept road in the highlands of Scotland on one day, and then in the middle of a burning desert a few days later.

Secondly, the workplace of the maintenance engineer is often very cramped, and this point becomes more salient with the impact of miniaturisation. The problem applies not only to the difficulty of climbing into appropriate parts of the equipment as necessary, but to difficulties in being able to reach, grasp and manipulate components within the machine itself.

Finally, it should be remembered that maintenance is often carried out under conditions of stress, which can take many forms. Since a machine which is out of operation is costing money, the maintenance engineer is often under time stress from both the operator and management to rectify the fault. There is also the possibility of danger from the immediate work environment. In armed combat this danger is clear and takes the form of enemy action, but other examples may be adduced from civilian maintenance, for example the presence of high-voltage electricity or perhaps toxic chemicals. Stress can also take the form of some fear of failure to rectify the fault. When the machine breaks down it is the maintenance engineer's profession which is called upon to make an unworkable machine workable. 'Professional pride' and concern about an inability to carry out the task as the job progresses may themselves create a stressful environment.

Clearly, therefore, it is important to consider maintainability when designing equipment. The length of time for which a machine is out of operation is wasted time for that machine. The more difficult the maintenance task, the longer the engineer is likely to take, and this increases call-out costs and reduces the machine's value.

DESIGNING FOR MAINTAINABILITY

Although it is so important to consider ease of maintenance at an early stage in the design process, in many respects the techniques for doing so have evolved through common sense rather than through scientific investigation. Unfortunately it can be argued that even today designing for maintainability is more an art than a science, and that good maintenance design is more a state of mind than an established procedure.

However, various suggestions can be made to help the designer produce equipment which is easily maintainable, and all tend to follow very closely the various suggestions made throughout this book; for example, considerations of display and control design and arrangement; appropriate workplace and workspace design; the effect of various environmental parameters, etc.

Anthropometric Considerations

As was discussed earlier, with the increasing trend towards miniaturisation the problem of the accessibility of the machine or the component in question to the maintenance worker becomes paramount. This applies equally well to large pieces of machinery which the operator might need to climb into or crouch behind, as to small machines (usually electronic machines) in which the operator may have to be able to manipulate fingers or hands. At both extremes, and in all cases between, efficiency is likely to be reduced if insufficient consideration is given to the anthropometric dimensions of the appropriate body or limb, plus its associated (protective) clothing.

Communication: Maintenance Manuals, Labelling and Symbols

Since a maintenance engineer is likely to have to service a number of different machines, it is not unreasonable to expect to be provided with detailed information about the machine to be mended—its performance characteristics, mode of construction, possible faults, details and values of its components, etc. This is likely to be obtained from the maintenance manual. As Sinaiko and Brislin (1973) demonstrated, however, a poorly designed manual is likely to lead to reduced performance in terms of increased errors and maintenance time. Thus much of the information provided in Chapter 4 (man–man communication) is important in this context.

Being provided with a good maintenance manual, however, is only half the battle for the maintenance operator. Having located a possible fault using, perhaps, a diagram, the appropriate image from the diagram has to be 'translated' to the machine so that the relevant component can be found. Labels, numbers, symbols and so on can greatly expedite matters in this respect.

Information Displays

As well as being a means of communication between the operator and the machine, displays can also be used to inform the maintenance engineer whether the system, or parts of it, is performing normally. In this respect the principles important in display design were considered in detail in Chapter 5.

Controls

Again, most of the controls which are likely to be used by maintenance engineers will also be used by the normal operator, and the important principles in control design were considered in both Chapters 3 and 6.

One type of 'control' which is likely to be used more by the maintenance operator, however, is the connector or fastener. In the strict sense of the word, of course, connectors are not controls since they perform no controlling function between the operator and the machine. However, they have to be operated in much the same way as controls (using the limbs) and their design involves many of the same principles (for example, measuring that the connector size is appropriate to fit the limb (fingers) operating it; ensuring that the forces required to connect two connectors together are within the abilities of the operator).

Each of the principles which have been suggested for the appropriate design and location of connectors and fasteners follow two main themes, the first of which is ease of connection and disconnection. For easy maintenance, plug-in electrical connectors are likely to be better than screw terminals, and screw terminals better than solder connections. Similarly, U-shaped lugs at the ends of cables which can be connected without removing the securing screw are likely to be easier to maintain than O-shaped lugs containing a hole through which the screw is inserted. For connectors used to fasten equipment together, wing-nuts are easier to move than bolts, while a bolt which can be unscrewed using either a spanner or a screwdriver (i.e. which has both hexagonal sides and a screwdriver slot) is likely to be more easily operated than a bolt which has only one such feature.

Secondly, it is helpful if the connectors are not easily connected either the 'wrong way round' or to the wrong socket. Various techniques are available to ensure that the appropriate connections are made. These include using connectors and sockets of different sizes and colours; cutting and shaping cables so that a connector cannot reach a wrong socket; and using lugs or other aligning pins inside the connector and socket. If lugs are used, however, it is sensible for them to be arranged symmetrically so that the plug cannot be inserted 180 degrees from the correct position.

Arranging the Workspace and Workplace

Whereas the normal operator has to contend with a number of groups of humans and machines in the environment, the nature of the maintenance operator's problems with respect to the workspace and workplan are much the same, although often scaled down in size since they concern only the particular machine being mended. Thus the problems involve access to the appropriate parts of the machine (primarily anthropometric problems) and the layout of components inside the machine. Each of these have been considered in Chapters 8 and 9.

Finally, with regard to the layout of components within the machine, McKendry, Corso and Grant (1960) have demonstrated that an appropriate arrangement can considerably reduce the time required to locate a fault. In their experiment the components in either a simple radio receiver or a complex radar simulator were arranged according to one of four principles:

(1) *Component packaging*, in which all similar components, for example all tubes and all transistors, were grouped together in one place on the equipment. Using this procedure, once the area of a fault is determined, for cheap components at least, a whole plug-in section could be replaced.

(2) *Circuit packaging*, in which components relating to the various circuits (for example amplification, tuning, trimming) were placed together.

(3) *Logical flow*, which represents a combination of two approaches: first the use of modules and subassemblies so that only a single, simple input and output check is necessary to isolate trouble to that unit, and secondly the modules are arranged in a clear sequence representing the 'flow' through the circuitry, for example tuning–amplification– speaker.

(4) *The 'standard' packaging method*, which did not employ any grouping or modules nor did it attempt to suggest a logical flow in components. The parts of the equipment on top of the chassis were appropriately spaced to distribute weight and heat.

In all conditions the subject's task was to isolate a fault to a given component. The results demonstrated that the subjects found the faulty component significantly faster when using the logical flow method than the standard arrangement. The 'circuit' and 'component' arrangements produced intermediate times. Clearly, therefore, simply varying the arrangement of the components to be maintained can have significant effects on maintenance time.

SUMMARY

Both of the topics discussed in this chapter, inspection and maintenance, provide fitting summaries for many of the topics discussed elsewhere in the book. In their own right, both represent problems in the design of man–machine systems. However, the solution of these problems involves considering all aspects of the man–machine system—communication, displays, controls, workspace and workplace design, and the physical and social environment—and ensuring that they interact to the benefit of the operator.

14

ERGONOMICS INVESTIGATIONS: SOME PROBLEMS AND TECHNIQUES

The aim of this final chapter is not to present the reader with a list of different techniques for studying the multitude of features and questions that may occur when interactions between people and the environment are considered. These are covered well enough by a number of specific books in this area, such as Chapanis (1959) or Wilson and Corlett (1990), or in specialised journals such as Applied Ergonomics. Rather, the aim is to illustrate and emphasise pitfalls and problems about which the unsuspecting investigator may be unaware—particularly when studying the behaviour of people at work.

When faced with a problem there are normally two avenues available to the intelligent inquisitor. First, attempts can be made to discover how other people have solved similar problems, by reading accounts of their investigations or by applying their techniques to the particular situation. The information in this book will be useful as a starting point for these kinds of activities. The other approach, and the two are not necessarily mutually exclusive, is for the enquirer to solve the problem by independent study. This has the great advantage that the investigation will relate to the problems experienced in a specific environment and the results and conclusions obtained will be applicable to that particular problem. If just one message has been extracted from the book so far, it should be that ergonomics is a discipline which aims to fit together the person and the environment within a system, and that the results and conclusions from one system are not always applicable to another.

By deciding to study a particular relationship within the system, however, the potential investigator immediately encounters a multitude of further problems—all of which are generated by the human part of the system. There are many ways in which an individual's complex nature can bias or distort the outcome of experiments designed to study human behaviour within a particular setting. Indeed, by adopting some of these approaches—consciously or unconsciously—subjects can make the investigator's task so difficult that it becomes impossible.

Perhaps the first bias, about which any aspiring psychologist is taught, is that of respondent bias (sometimes called volunteer error). For obvious reasons, any experiment normally has to be carried out on a sample of subjects which has been selected from the population being studied. For example, if the investigation is concerned with the response speed of women workers on a shop-floor, it would be sensible only to use those workers in the experiment and not to draw subjects from any other population. However, it may not be feasible to measure the response speed of all women workers in the factory, and so a sensible solution might be to select randomly a dozen or so individuals as a representative sample. But how does the investigator go about the selection?

Since it is the normal expectation in a democratic society to be asked to participate in a study, rather than to be commanded, the random sample is likely to be drawn from those individuals who were actually asked and who agreed to participate. Unfortunately, however, although observing such democratic principles meets the ethical requirements of research, it leaves open the question of whether the 'representative' sample was truly representative or whether it could have been biased: the sample contains only those subjects who agreed to be studied (the volunteers). But why were *they* chosen and why did *they* volunteer? Do they have characteristics which make them different from individuals who refused, or were not asked (perhaps because of personality, fears, age, intellectual level, etc.)? Why were some not asked? Answers to any of these questions could raise serious doubts regarding the impartiality of the sample selected.

Although some degree of volunteer bias normally has to be accepted, other biases can also easily be introduced into the investigation. These can occur simply *because* the investigation is being carried out: because of the interest which is being shown towards the human being who is in the system. Perhaps the most appropriate example of this bias is illustrated by a series of studies conducted at the Hawthorne plant of the Western Electric Company in the 1920s, under the direction of Elton Mayo. The studies began by examining ways in which change in the worker's physical environment would affect production, and the first feature to be investigated was the factory's illumination level. The results obtained, however, proved to be rather surprising: they indicated that changes to the illumination levels resulted in productivity increases *whatever the direction of the changes*. Indeed, in one experiment the illumination level was reduced considerably, almost to moonlight levels, and productivity still increased.

These paradoxical results have since been explained by suggesting that the individuals increased their output because they were in an experimental situation. Perhaps they acted in this way because they felt that the experimenters were taking an interest in them. Whatever the reason, this 'Hawthorne effect'—that performance may vary solely as a result of the experimental situation—has now become a recognised pitfall in psychological investigations.

If these biases were constant and always acted in one direction (for example, always caused the subject to perform better or worse), the problems they cause would not be too great. Unfortunately the biases are neither constant nor consistent. For a number of reasons the same pressures which produced the 'Hawthorne effect' can act in the reverse direction—to cause subjects to perform at a slower, less accurate rate than normal.

One reason for this effect may be the attitudes which the workforce, the unions and/or the management may have towards the investigation. In some respects, for example, ergonomics has many features in common with work study and time and motion study. Unfortunately, however, both these disciplines enjoy considerable popular notoriety which could interfere with the investigation. If the interference is extreme enough to be symptomatised by a complete withdrawal of cooperation and work, then this is bad enough. From the point of view of the investigator, however, a worse situation would be if the apparently cooperative subjects are actually antagonistic to the aims of the study. In such cases the investigator has no idea of the effect of these antagonistic attitudes on the subject's behaviour.

Another negative 'Hawthorne effect' can arise when studies are carried out in industrial premises and measures of workers' productivity are recorded, particularly if the operators feel that the investigation's results might affect future productivity and payment norms (again the memory of time and motion study is difficult to assess). In this case productivity may be depressed purposefully during the investigation period so that, once the norms have been set and after the investigation has ended, 'normal' production will appear to be increased productivity.

The message that arises from these biases suggests that as far as possible the subjects' confidence (whether they be subjects in the laboratory or operators at work) should be sought. For many reasons it may not be possible to explain all the reasons for the experiment (for example, telling subjects that an experiment will investigate the effects of noise on behaviour may cause them to react differently to the noise than they otherwise might have done). However, in many cases it should be possible to allay fears, to discuss the aims of the investigation, and to ensure the subjects that their results are likely to be of benefit (if, indeed, they are).

At this stage it is as well to consider where the study can be carried out—in the laboratory or *in situ*, in the field. Both environments have their advantages and disadvantages.

If the research is to be carried out in the laboratory, precise questions can be asked and controlled stimuli can be presented to the subjects, ensuring that all receive the same stimulus. In the field, however, the investigator is not so well acquainted with the nature of the stimulus which the operator is receiving. Different operators might be receiving (either subjectively or physically) different stimuli owing to factors outside the investigator's control, such as variations in seating positions or even the operators' states of health at the time.

In contrast, however, field investigations have one main advantage over laboratory studies. This concerns the validity of the results that are eventually obtained and have to be related back to the working situation. In this respect it is appropriate to notice that in the preceding paragraph 'subjects' were discussed as receiving stimuli in the laboratory, while 'operators' were said to receive the stimulus in the field. This simple semantic distinction highlights the advantage of the field over the laboratory investigation—namely that if the investigation is to benefit any particular section of the community, then members of that group should be used in the investigation.

The advantage of field studies, therefore, relate to the fact that a laboratory experiment cannot take account of all of the extraneous variables which may influence the operator at work. For example, laboratory subjects do not have to earn a living at that particular time; they may not fully understand the various consequences of their actions; they are not likely to be at ease—in fact, they may enter the laboratory fearing the worst; and they are not being subjected to all the extraneous stimuli that occur in normal work, for example noise, temperature and even pressures from management and colleagues.

It is possible, of course, to combine the two research environments of 'laboratory' and 'field' to produced a third arrangement. In this case subjects' responses are measured under field conditions—that is, personnel are 'employed' specifically to carry out an experiment (they then become 'subjects')—but the investigation is carried under field conditions. This field (subject) approach has been used quite extensively in the past and has much to recommend it. At least the experiment is carried out in the appropriate environment with all the relevant extraneous stimuli. However, it still suffers from the drawback that 'subjects' rather than operators are used.

Before discussing some of the techniques suitable for an ergonomics investigation, one further problem should be posed—whether it is possible to investigate behaviour at all, without affecting the behaviour being investigated.

The question is perhaps better understood by nuclear physicists following the proposition of the 'uncertainty principle' by Heisenberg in the 1930s. Heisenberg was concerned with measuring the behaviour of atoms but concluded that it is not possible to measure their behaviour without affecting them: 'Every subsequent observation ... will alter the momentum [of the atom] by an unknown and indeterminable amount such that after carrying out the experiment our knowledge of the electronic motion is restricted by the uncertainty relation.' The same is also true, unfortunately, for human behaviour. As soon as the investigator enters the system and inserts measuring equipment (whether the equipment is in the form of 'hardware' such as meters or probes, or 'software' such as questions or observation), the subsequent behaviour of the system (including the human operator) will be affected in an uncertain manner. Unfortunately, this cannot be totally overcome, although it can be reduced by using unobtrusive techniques such as observation.

OBSERVATION AND OTHER UNOBTRUSIVE MEASURES

Whatever technique is chosen to investigate the human operator's performance within the system, Heisenberg's uncertainty principle still operates. However, some techniques create less interference than others and, providing it is carried out properly, perhaps the least intrusive in this respect is simply to observe behaviour or its concomitants.

Direct Observation

Directly observing what the operator does when interactions take place within the environment is possibly one of the most commonly used techniques. At a basic level it is simple, requires little equipment and often produces data that can be easily interpreted. However, direct observation can be misused and produce misleading results—particularly if the observer intrudes into the system. Then any of the biases and hindrances discussed earlier can occur.

The most important principle of direct observation, therefore, is that the observer (and any equipment used) should be unobtrusive. This is not to say that the observer should be invisible—merely that the system being observed should not be interfered with in any way. Of course, an invisible observer (for example, one who is behind a screen) is also likely to be unobtrusive. However, situations can arise in which the absence of an observer who would otherwise have been expected could lead to mistrust or worry. A subject could be upset more by knowing (or feeling) that he or she is being observed, for example, through a one-way screen, than if the observer was visible.

The second important principle of direct observation is that a permanent record of the behaviour should be made for future, detailed analysis. This is normally done in one of two ways: either by recording all the activities using videotape, or by sampling the operator's activities and recording aspects of the behaviour on either precoded paper sheets or directly into a computer.

The advantages of using filming techniques should be obvious: all the operator's activities are recorded and the film can subsequently be played back many times during the analysis. As long as the camera has been positioned appropriately, therefore, the investigator is ensured of obtaining a complete, permanent record of the operator's behaviour. Furthermore, when analysing the record the film can be played back at a slower speed than normal (again ensuring that no activity, however slight, is missed), or at a speed which is faster than normal.

The ability to play back the record faster than it was recorded has two advantages. First, it speeds up the analysing time. By the time the tape has been stopped, started and re-run a few times, a two-hour record, for example, is likely to take at least three or four times as long to analyse at normal speed. Playing it back at a faster rate should reduce this time. Secondly, fast playback allows the observer to 'see' motions which might otherwise be too slow to observe at normal speeds. For example, Branton and Grayson (1967) used cinefilm to record the sitting behaviour of passengers in two types of train seat throughout a five-hour journey. When the films were played back at a faster speed than normal it became apparent that one kind of seat caused the sitter to slip forward gradually and out of the seat, requiring the seating position to be adjusted constantly. This 'slipping' action, however, was too slow to be observed in 'real' time. As a further example Branton and Oborne (1979) recorded the behaviour of anaesthetists during various operations. When the video film was speeded up (20× normal speed) a 'head nodding' behaviour was observed which the authors suggest could be related to the onset and continuation of fatigue and monotony.

A disadvantage of using film recording techniques has already been discussed, namely the mass of data which is obtained and which has to be analysed. For example, Lovesey (1975) used a cinefilm to record pilot activity during different types of helicopter flying. Just over two hours of flying was recorded, which then had to be analysed on a frame-by-frame basis. Since the film speed was eight frames per second, Lovesey needed to analyse the head and hand positions of his pilots in each of 63 370 frames.

Another, perhaps less obvious, disadvantage of visual recording lies in the (often) fixed positions required to set up the cameras. To be unobtrusive they should not be too visible and the presence of a camera operator is likely to make them apparent. Unfortunately, however, environmental conditions do not remain constant as those which prevailed when the equipment was set up. For example, during Branton and Oborne's anaesthetist study mentioned above, some operations were filmed which required the theatre lights so be extinguished while the surgeon used a particular light source. During these periods, of course, the video camera was unable to record the anaesthetist's activities. Rennie and Wilson (1980) discuss similar problems using videofilms to record pedestrian behaviour. Movements of the sun (or at least of the earth in relation to the sun) and clouds can cause illumination levels that are too high or too low for the camera.

Analysing the behaviour as it is carried out obviates these problems. This is the one advantage of sampling behaviour and recording the operator's activities, say, every minute on a precoded sheet or directly into a computer. Unless the observer is fully conversant with the activities which are likely to have to be recorded, however, and unless the sampling periods are sufficiently long, this method can place the observer under considerable stress.

Indirect Observation

No matter how well the observer is integrated into the system, the potential still exists to bias the results in many of the ways discussed above. For this reason, other techniques may sometimes have to be used in which the subject(s) are observed indirectly.

Physical traces

If an activity is carried out frequently then over time the equipment, or the part of it which is operated, is likely to become well used. To an observant individual this is useful data. For example, it is possible to judge the popularity of library books by their condition: less popular books remain in a newer condition than books which are borrowed frequently, and the page corners and edges of the popular parts of the book are likely to be dirtier and more dog-eared than the less popular parts. As a further example, the wear and tear on various parts of a floor can indicate the extent to which particular machines are used.

The same type of approach can be used to determine the nature of the activity that is carried out. For example, dial settings left on the machine by the operator, say at night, may indicate how the machine has been used; as may the positions in which movable machines and components are left after use.

Statistical records

In many respects by using statistical records the investigator is merely observing what has happened in the past rather than what is happening at present. As was discussed in Chapter 12, records are most frequently used to study accident trends, their types, places and personnel involvement. They can be very useful in locating areas of potential danger—either in the person or in the environment. As long as a large enough pool of accidents is sampled, useful statistical analyses can be computed and, of course, an investigator who is never at the scene of the accident cannot be intrusive.

Statistical records, however, have limited value. Accidents or near accidents are infrequent events and it may take years to collect enough instances to form any kind of reasonable classification of the troubles that can occur. Secondly, it is virtually impossible to compare or contrast different accident situations because of the difficulty of assessing exposure risks. This point was emphasised, for example, when considering the concept of accident proneness—'accident-prone' individuals may simply be in riskier situations. Thirdly, the statistics tell us simply that an event (accident) had occurred. It is difficult, if not impossible, to construct what happened or why. For these reasons, statistical evidence is only useful as 'back-up' information or for helping to generate hypotheses which can later be tested by more controlled observation or experimentation.

SUMMARY

This chapter has not attempted to equip the reader with the practical or statistical skills required to carry out an ergonomic investigation. The techniques available are so numerous and diverse that to do so would require a separate book. Instead this chapter has provided the reader with a background to the problems involved in human experimentation, the interpersonal problems which can occur but about which the investigator may be unaware. It has also suggested simple, unobtrusive measures which can be used. Armed with an understanding of these problems, the potential ergonomist will be equipped to investigate further the multitude of ways in which people and their environments interact.

REFERENCES

Abrahams, C. F. Jr. and Suggs, C. W. (1969). *Chain Saw Vibration: Isolation and Transmission Through the Human Arm*, Paper presented to Annual Meeting of the American Society of Agricultural Engineers, Indiana, June.

Adams, L. and Zuckerman, D. (1991). The effect of lighting conditions on personal space requirements, *Journal of General Psychology*, **118**, 335–40.

Adler, A. (1941). The psychology of repeated accidents in industry, *American Journal of Psychiatry*, **98**, 99–101.

Agate, J. N. (1949). An outbreak of cases of Raynaud's phenomenon of occupational origin, *British Journal of Industrial Medicine*, **6**, 144–63.

Alden, D. G., Daniels, R. W. and Kanarick, A. F. (1972). Keyboard design and operation: a review of the major issues, *Human Factors*, **14**, 275–93.

Alexander, C. (1972). *Performance Changes Due to the Single and Dual Frequency Vibration of Reading Material*, Ph.D. Thesis, University of Southampton.

Allgeier, A. R. and Byrne, D. (1973). Attraction towards the opposite sex as a determinant of physical proximity, *Journal of Social Psychology*, **90**, 213–19.

American Society of Heating and Refrigeration Engineers. (1965). *ASHRAE Guide and Data Book: Fundamentals and Equipment*. Atlanta, Georgia: ASHRAE.

American Standards Association. (1960). *American Standards Acoustical Terminology S1*. New York: ASA.

Anderson, J. R. (1980). *Cognitive Psychology*. San Francisco: W. H. Freeman.

Andersson, G. B. J. (1980). The load on the lumbar spine in sitting postures. In D. J. Oborne and J. A. Levis (eds). *Human Factors in Transport Research Vol. II*. London: Academic Press.

Andersson, G. B. J. and Örtengren, R. (1974). Lumbar disc pressure and myoelectric back muscle activity during sitting. Studies on an office chair, *Scandinavian Journal of Rehabilitation Medicine*, **3**, 104–14; 122–7; 128–35.

Andersson, G. B. J., Örtengren, R. and Nachemson, A. (1982). Disc pressure measurements when rising and sitting down on a chair, *Engineering in Medicine*, **11**, 189–90.

Andersson, G. B. J., Örtengren, R., Nachemson, A. L., Elfstrom, G. and Broman, H. (1975). The sitting posture: an electromyographic and discometric study, *Orthopaedic Clinics of North America*, **6**, 105–20.

Andrew, I. and Manoy, R. (1972). Anthropometric survey of British Rail footplate staff, *Applied Ergonomics*, **3**, 132–5.

Anglin, J. M. and Miller, G. A. (1968). The role of phrase structure in the recall of meaningful verbal material, *Psychonomic Science*, **10**, 340.

Arborelius, U. P., Wretenberg, P. and Lindberg, F. (1992). The effects of armrests and high seat heights on lower-limb joint load and muscular activity during sitting and rising, *Ergonomics*, **35**, 1377–91.

Argyle, M. and Cook, M. (1976). *Gaze and Mutual Gaze.* Cambridge: Cambridge University Press.

Arroyo, F. V. (1982). Negatives in context, *Journal of Verbal Learning and Verbal Behavior*, **21**, 118–26.

Asch, S. E. (1952). *Social Psychology.* N.J.: Prentice-Hall.

Åstrand, P. O. and Rodahl, K. (1986). *Textbook of Work Physiology*, 3rd edn. New York: McGraw-Hill.

Ayoub, M. A. and Wittels, N. E. (1989). Cumulative trauma disorders, *International Reviews of Ergonomics*, **3**, 217–72.

Baddeley, A. D. (1966). Time estimation at reduced body temperature, *American Journal of Psychology*, **79**, 475–9.

Bahrick, H. P. (1957). An analysis of stimulus variables influencing the proprioceptive control of movements, *Psychological Review*, **64**, 324–8.

Barkala, D. (1961). The estimation of body measurements of British population in relation to seat design, *Ergonomics*, **4**, 123–32.

Barnard, P. and Marcel, A. (1976). The effects of spaced character formats on the production and legibility of handwritten names, *Ergonomics*, **19**, 81–92.

Barnard, P. and Marcel, A. (1983). Representation and understanding in the use of symbols and pictograms. In R. Easterby and H. Zwaga (eds). *Information Design.* Chichester: John Wiley.

Barnard, P. and Wright, P. (1977). A preliminary investigation of factors influencing the interpretation of pictorial instructions for the use of apparatus, *Proceedings of the 8th International Symposium on Human Factors in Telecommunications*, Cambridge, September, 379–92.

Barnes, G. R., Benson, A. J. and Prior, A. R. J. (1978). Visual–vestibular interaction in the control of eye movement, *Aviation, Space and Environmental Medicine*, **49**, 557–64.

Bartlett, F. C. (1950). Programme for experiments of thinking, *Quarterly Journal of Experimental Psychology*, **2**, 145–52.

Bauer, D. and Cavonius, C. R. (1980). Improving the legibility of visual display units through contrast reversal. In E. Grandjean and E. Vigliani (eds). *Ergonomic Aspects of Visual Display Terminals.* London: Taylor and Francis.

Baughn, W. L. (1966). Noise control—percent of population protected, *International Audiology*, **5**, 331–8.

Bearham, J. (1976). *The Cost of Accidents Within the Port Industry.* London: Manpower Services Commission.

Bednall, E. S. (1992). The effect of screen format on visual search list, *Ergonomics*, **35**, 369–83.

Beevis, D. and Slade, I. M. (1970). Ergonomics—costs and benefits, *Applied Ergonomics*, **1**, 79–85.

Begault, D. R. and Wenzel, E. M. (1993). Headphone localization of speech, *Human Factors*, **35**, 361–76.

Begg, I. and Paivio, A. (1969). Concreteness and imagery in sentence meaning, *Journal of Verbal Learning and Verbal Behavior*, **8**, 821–7.

Belbin, R. M. (1957). New fields for quality control, *British Management Review*, **15**, 79–89.

Beldie, L. P., Pastoor, S. and Schwarz, E. (1983). Fixed versus variable letter width for televised text, *Human Factors*, **25**, 273–7.

Bell, C. R., Crowder, M. J. and Walters, J. D. (1971). Durations of safe exposure for men at work in high temperature environments, *Ergonomics*, **14**, 121–8.

Bellingar, T. and Slocum, A. (1993). Effect of protective gloves on hand movement: an exploratory study, *Applied Ergonomics*, **24**, 244–50.

Bendix, T. and Eid, S. F. (1983). The distance between the load and the body with three bi-manual lifting techniques, *Applied Ergonomics*, **14**, 185–92.

Benn, R. T. and Wood, P. H. N. (1975). Pain in the back: an attempt to estimate the size of the problem, *Rheumatology and Rehabilitation*, **14**, 733–57.

Benson, A. J., Huddleston, J. H. F. and Rolfe, J. M. (1965). A psychophysiological study of compensatory tracking on a digital display, *Human Factors*, **7**, 457–72.

Bergenthal, J. (1971). Preferred push button switch operating forces, *IEEE Transactions Man and Cybernetics*, **1**, 385–7.

Berlyne, D. E., Borsa, D. M., Craw, M. A., Gelman, R. S. and Mandell, E. E. (1965). Effects of stimulus complexity and induced arousal on paired-associate learning, *Journal of Verbal Behavior and Verbal Learning*, **4**, 291–9.

Berry, P. C. (1961). The effect of colored illumination upon perceived temperature, *Journal of Applied Psychology*, **45**, 248–50.

Beshir, M. Y. and Ramsey, J. D. (1981). Comparison between male and female subjective estimates of thermal effects and sensations, *Applied Ergonomics*, **12**, 29–33.

Bever, T. G., Garrett, M. F. and Hartig, R. (1973). The interaction of perceptual processes and ambiguous sentences, *Memory and Cognition*, **1**, 277–86.

Biegel, R. A. (1934). An improved typewriter keyboard, *The Human Factor*, **8**, 2805.

Bilger, R. C. and Hirsh, I. J. (1956). Masking of tones by bands of noise, *Journal of the Acoustical Society of America*, **28**, 623–30.

Bird, P. F. (1977). 'Digilux' touch sensitive panel. In *Displays for Man–machine Systems*. IEE Conference Publication No. 150. London: IEE.

Bjerver, K. and Goldberg, L. (1950). Effects of alcohol ingestion on driving ability, *Quarterly Journal on the Study of Alcohol*, **11**, 1–30.

Blake, M. J. F. (1971). Temperament and time of day. In W. P. Colquhoun (ed.). *Biological Rhythms and Human Performance*. London: Academic Press.

Bodmann, H. W. (1962). Illumination levels and visual performance, *International Lighting Review*, **13**, 41–7.

Boggs, D. H. and Simon, J. R. (1968). Differential effect of noise on tasks of varying complexity, *Journal of Applied Psychology*, **52**, 148–53.

Booher, H. R. 1975). Relative comprehensibility of pictorial information and printed words in proceduralized instructions, *Human Factors*, **17**, 266–77.

Boudrifa, H. and Davies, B. T. (1987). The effect of bending and rotation of the trunk on the intra-abdominal pressure and the erector spinae muscle when lifting while sitting, *Ergonomics*, **30**, 103–9.

Bouma, H. (1973). Visual interference in the parafoveal recognition of initial and final letters of words, *Vision Research*, **13**, 767–82.

Bouma, H. (1980). Visual reading processes and the quality of text displays. In E. Grandjean and E. Vigliani (eds). *Ergonomic Aspects of Visual Display Terminals*. London: Taylor & Francis.

Bowen, H. M. and Guiness, G. V. (1965). Preliminary experiments on keyboard design for semi-automatic mail sorting, *Journal of Applied Psychology*, **49**, 194–8.

Boyce, P. R. (1981). *Human Factors in Lighting*. London: Applied Science Publishers.

Boynton, R. M., Elworth, C. and Palmer, R. M. (1958). *Laboratory Studies Pertaining to Visual Air Reconnaissance*. Ohio: USAF, WADC TR 55-304.

Bradley, J. W. (1967). Tactual coding of cylindrical knobs, *Human Factors*, **9**, 483–96.

Bradley, J. W. (1969a). Glove characteristics influencing control manipulability, *Human Factors*, **11**, 21–36.

Bradley, J. W. (1969b). Optimum knob diameter, *Human Factors*, **11**, 353–60.

Bradley, J. W. (1969c). Desirable dimensions for concentric controls, *Human Factors*, **11**, 213–26.

Bradley, J. W. (1969d). Optimum knob crowding, *Human Factors*, **11**, 227–38.

Branton, P. (1966). The comfort of easy chairs. *Furniture Industry Research Report No. 22.*.

Branton, P. (1969). Behaviour, body mechanics and discomfort, *Ergonomics*, **12**, 316–27.

Branton, P. (1972). *Ergonomic Research Contributions to the Design of the Passenger Environment*. Paper presented to the Institute of Mechanical Engineers Symposium on Passenger Comfort, London.

Branton, P. (1983). Process control operators as responsible persons. Invited paper to Symposium on Human Reliability in the Process Control Centre. Institution of Chemical Engineers, Manchester. In D. J. Oborne, R. Branton, F. Leal, P. Shipley and T. Steward (eds). *Person-centred Ergonomics: A Brantonian View of Human Factors*. London: Taylor & Francis.

Branton, P. (1984). Backshapes of seated persons—how close can the interface be designed?, *Applied Ergonomics*, **15**, 105–107.

Branton, P. and Grayson, G. (1967). An evaluation of train seats by an observation of sitting behaviour, *Ergonomics*, **10**, 35–41.

Branton, P. and Oborne, D. J. (1979). A behavioural study of anaesthetists at work. In D. J. Oborne, M. M. Gruneberg and J. R. Eiser (eds). *Research in Psychology and Medicine Vol. I*. London: Academic Press.

Branton, P. and Shipley, P. (1986). VDU stress: is 'Houston Man' addicted, bored or mystic? Paper presented to International Conference on Work with Display Units, Stockholm. In D. J. Oborne, R. Branton, F. Leal, P. Shipley and T. Steward (eds). *Person-centred Ergonomics: A Brantonian View of Human Factors*. London: Taylor & Francis.

Brebner, J. and Sandow, B. (1976). The effect of scale side on population stereotype, *Ergonomics*, **19**, 571–80.

Brenner, B. (1967). Alcoholism and fatal accidents, *Quarterly Journal on Studies of Alcohol*, **28**, 517–28.

Bridger, R. S. (1988). Postural adaptations to a sloping chair and work surface, *Human Factors*, **30**, 237–47.

Brinkmann, P. (1985). Pathology of the vertebral column, *Ergonomics*, **28**, 77–80.

British Standards Institute. (1964). *Recommendations for the Design of Scales and Indexes. Part I Instruments of Bold Presentation and for Rapid Reading*. BS 3693. London: BSI.

British Standards Institute. (1969). *Recommendations for the Design of Scales and Indexes. Part II Indicating Instruments to be Read to 0.33–1.25% Resolution*. BS 3693. London: BSI.

Broadbent, D. E. (1977). Language and ergonomics, *Applied Ergonomics*, **8**, 15–18.

Broadbent, D. E. and Gregory, M. (1965). Effects of noise and of signal rate upon vigilance analysed by means of decision theory, *Human Factors*, **7**, 155–62.

Brookes, M. J. (1972). Office landscape: does it work?, *Applied Ergonomics*, **3**, 224–36.

Brookes, M. J. and Kaplan, A. (1972). The office environment: space planning and effective behaviour, *Human Factors*, **14**, 373–91.

Brown, C. R. (1974). Human factors problems in the design and evaluation of key-entry devices for the Japanese language. In A. Chapanis (ed.). *Ethnic Variables in Human Factors Engineering*. Baltimore: The John Hopkins University Press.

Buchholz, B. and Armstrong, R. J. (1991). An ellipsoidal representation of human hand anthropometry, *Human Factors*, **33**, 429–41.

Buck, P. C. and Coleman, V. P. (1985). Slipping, tripping and falling accidents at work: a national picture, *Ergonomics*, **28**, 949–58.

Buckhout, R. (1964) Effect of whole body vibration on human performance, *Human Factors*, **6**, 157–63.

Buckler, A. T. (1977). *A Review on the Legibility of Alphanumerics on Electronic Displays.* May. AD A040-624.

Burrows, A. A. (1965). Control feel and the dependent variable, *Human Factors*, **7**, 413–21.

Burt, C. (1959). *A Psychological Study of Typography.* Cambridge: Cambridge University Press.

Burton, A. K. (1984). Electromyography and office-chair design: a pilot study, *Behaviour and Information Technology*, **3**, 353–7.

Buswell, G. T. (1935). *]How People Look at Pictures.* Chicago: University of Chicago Press.

Butterworth, G. and Henty, C. (1991). Origins of the proprioceptive function of vision: visual control of posture in one day old domestic chicks, *Perception*, **20**, 381–6.

Byrne, D., Baskett, G. D. and Hodges, L. (1971). Behavioural indicators of interpersonal attraction, *Journal of Applied Social Psychology*, **1**, 137–49.

Cakir, A., Hart, D. J. and Stewart, T. F. M. (1980). *Visual Display Terminals.* Chichester: John Wiley.

Caldwell, L. S. (1963). Relative muscle loading and endurance, *Journal of Engineering Psychology*, **2**, 155–61.

Caldwell, L. S. (1964). Measurement of static muscle endurance, *Journal of Engineering Psychology*, **3**, 16–22.

Card, S. K., English, W. K. and Burr, B. J. (1978). Evaluation of mouse, rate-controlled isometric joystick, step keys and text keys for text selection on a CRT, *Ergonomics*, **21**, 601–13.

Carlson, B. R. (1969). Level of maximum isometric strength and relative load isometric endurance, *Ergonomics*, **12**, 429–35.

Carlsoo, S. (1972). *How Man Moves.* London: Heinemann.

Carroll, J. M. (1982). Learning, using and designing command paradigms, *Human Learning*, **1**, 31–62.

Cashen, V. M. and Leicht, K. L. (1970). Role of the isolation effect in a formal education setting, *Journal of Educational Psychology*, **61**, 484–6.

Castle, P. F. C. (1956). Accidents, absence and withdrawal from the work situation, *Human Relations*, **9**, 223–33.

Catovic, A., Kosovel, Z., Catovic, E. and Muftic, O. (1989). A comparative investigation of the influence of certain arm positions on hand pinch grips in the standing and sitting positions of dentists, *Applied Ergonomics*, **20**, 109–14.

Catterson, A. D., Hoover, G. N. and Asche, W. F. (1962). Human psychomotor performance during prolonged vertical vibration, *Aerospace Medicine*, **33**, 598–602.

Cavanaugh, W. J., Farrell, W. R., Hirtle, P. W. and Walters, B. G. (1962). Speech privacy in buildings, *Journal of the Acoustical Society of America*, **34**, 475–92.

Chambers, J. B. and Stockbridge, H. C. W. (1970). Comparison of indicator components and push-button recommendations, *Ergonomics*, **13**, 401–20.

Chapanis, A. (1951). Studies of manual rotary positioning movements. II: The accuracy of estimating the position of an indicator knob, *Journal of Psychology*, **31**, 65.

Chapanis, A. (1959). *Research Techniques in Human Engineering.* Baltimore: The Johns Hopkins University Press.

Chapanis, A. (1960). Human engineering. In C. D. Flagle, W. H. Higgins and R. N. Roy (eds) *Operations Research and Systems Engineering.* Baltimore: The Johns Hopkins University Press.

Chapanis, A. (1965a). On the allocation of functions between men and machines, *Occupational Psychology*, **39**, 1–11.

Chapanis, A. (1965b). Words, words, words, *Human Factors*, **7**, 1–17.

Chapanis, A. (1974). National and cultural variables in ergonomics, *Ergonomics*, **17**, 153–75.

Chapanis, A. (1976). Engineering psychology. In M. D. Dunnette (ed.). *Handbook of Industrial Psychology*. Chicago: Rand McNally Corp.

Chapanis, A. and Lindenbaum, L. E. (1959). A reaction time study of four control–display linkages, *Human Factors*, **1**, 1–7.

Chapanis, A. and Lockhead, G. R. (1965). A test of the effectiveness of sensor lines showing linkages between displays and controls, *Human Factors*, **7**, 219–29.

Chapanis, A. and Mankin, D. A. (1967). Tests of ten control–display linkages, *Human Factors*, **9**, 119–26.

Christ, R. E. (1975). Review and analysis of colour coding research for visual displays, *Human Factors*, **17**, 542–70.

Christie, B. (1981). *Face-to-File Communication: A Psychological Approach to Information Systems*. Chichester: John Wiley.

Cirello, V. M. and Snook, S. H. (1983). A study of size, distance, height and frequency effects on manual handling tasks, *Human Factors*, **25**, 473–83.

Clark, R. E. (1961). The limiting hand skin temperature for unaffected manual performance in the cold, *Journal of Applied Psychology*, **45**, 193–4.

Clark, R. E. and Cohen, A. (1960). Manual performance as a function of rate of change in hand skin temperature, *Journal of Applied Psychology*, **44**, 496–8.

Clark, R. P. and Edholm, O. G. (1985). *Man and His Thermal Environment*. London: Edward Arnold.

Cochran, D. J., Albin, I. J., Riley, M. W. and Bishu, R. R. (1986). Analysis of grasp force degradation with commercially available gloves. *Proceedings of the Human Factors Society 1986*. Human Factors Society.

Coe, J. B., Cuttle, K., McClellon, W. C., Warden, N. J. and Turner, P. J. (1980). *Visual Display Units*. Report W/1/80. Wellington: New Zealand Department of Health.

Cohen, E. and Follert, R. L. (1970). Accuracy of interpolation between scale gradations, *Human Factors*, **12**, 481–3.

Cohen, S., Glass, D. C. and Singer, J. E. (1973). Apartment noise, auditory discrimination and reading ability in children, *Journal of Experimental Social Psychology*, **9**, 40.

Coles, A. R. A., Garinther, G. R., Hodge, D. C. and Rice, C. G. (1968). Hazardous exposure to impulse noise, *Journal of the Acoustical Society of America*, **43**, 336–43.

Coleshaw, S. R. K., Van Someren, R. N. M., Wolff, A. H., Davis, H. M. and Keatinge, W. R. (1983). Impaired memory registration and speed of reasoning caused by low body temperature, *Journal of Applied Psychology: Respiration, Environmental and Exercise Physiology*, **55**, 27–31.

Colquhoun, W. P. (1958). The effect of short rest pauses on inspection accuracy, *Ergonomics*, **2**, 367–72.

Colquhoun, W. P. (1975a). Evaluation of auditory, visual and dual mode displays for prolonged sonar monitoring in repeated sessions, *Human Factors*, **17**, 425–37.

Colquhoun, W. P. (1975b). *Accidents, injuries and shiftwork*. Paper presented to NIOSH Symposium on Shiftwork and Health, Cincinnati.

Conrad, R. and Hull, A. J. (1968). The preferred layout for data-entry keysets, *Ergonomics*, **11**, 165–73.

Conrad, R. and Longman, D. J. A. (1965). Standard typewriter versus chord keyboard. An experimental comparison, *Ergonomics*, **8**, 77–88.

Cooper, M. B. (1976). The effect of keypad angle of a table telephone on keying performance, *Applied Ergonomics*, **7**, 205–11.

Corlett, E. N. (1989). Aspects of the evaluation of industrial seating, *Ergonomics*, **32**, 257–69.

Corlett, E. N. and Bishop, R. P. (1975). Foot pedal forces for seated operators, *Ergonomics*, **18**, 687–92.

Corlett, E. N., Hutcheson, C., DeLugan, M. A. and Rogozenski, J. (1972). Ramps or stairs: the choice using physiological and biomechanical criteria, *Applied Ergonomics*, **3**, 195–201.

Corlett, E. N., Morcombe, V. J. and Chanda, B. (1970). Shielding factory noise by work-in-progress storage, *Applied Ergonomics*, **1**, 73–8.

Corlett, E. N. and Parsons, A. T. (1978). Measurement of changes: what criteria do we adopt?, *International Journal of Management Sciences*, **6**, 399–406.

Cowley, D. M. (1976). International standards in the vibration field. In W. Tempest (ed.). *Infrasound and Low Frequency Vibration*. London: Academic Press.

Craske, S. (1968). A study of the relation between personality and accident history, *British Journal of Medical Psychology*, **41**, 399–404.

Crawford, B. H. and Stiles, W. S. (1937). The effect of a glaring light source on extrafoveal vision, *Proceedings of the Royal Society (Series B)*, **122**, 255–80.

Creamer, L. R. and Trumbo, D. A. (1960). Multifinger tapping performance as a function of the direction of tapping movements, *Journal of Applied Psychology*, **44**, 376–80.

Cromer, W. (1960). The difference model: a new explanation for some reading difficulties, *Journal of Educational Psychology*, **61**, 471–83.

Crook, M. A. and Langdon, F. J. (1974). The effects of aircraft noise in schools around London airport, *Journal of Sound and Vibration*, **12**, 221–32.

Crossman, E. R. F. W. (1956). The information capacity of the human operator in symbolic and nonsymbolic control processes. In *Information Theory and the Human Operator*. Ministry of Supply Publication WR/D2/56.

Crouse, J. H. and Idstein, P. (1972). Effects of encoding cues on prose learning, *Journal of Educational Psychology*, **61**, 484–6.

Cunningham, D. J., Berglund, L. G. and Fobelets, A. (1985). Skin wettedness under clothing and its relation to thermal comfort in men and women. In P. O. Fanger (ed.). *Clima 2000*. Copenhagen: V.V.S. Congress.

Cushman, W. H. (1980). Selection of filters for dark adaptation goggles in the photographic industry, *Applied Ergonomics*, **11**, 93–9.

Cushman, W. H. and Rosenberg, D. J. (1991). *Human Factors in Product Design*. Amsterdam: Elsevier.

Czaja, S. J. and Drury, C. G. (1981). Training programs for inspection, *Human Factors*, **23**, 473–84.

Dainoff, M. J. (1982). Occupational stress factors in visual display terminal (VDT) operation: a review of empirical research, *Behaviour and Information Technology*, **1**, 141–76.

Damon, A. and Stoudt, H. W. (1963). The functional anthropometry of old men, *Human Factors*, **5**, 485–91.

Damon, A., Stoudt, H. W. and McFarland, R. A. (1971). *The Human Body in Equipment Design*. Mass: Harvard University Press.

Daniels, G. S. (1952). *The Average Man?* Ohio: Wright Patterson Airforce Base Technical Note WCRD 53-7.

Dashevsky, S. G. (1964). Check reading accuracy as a function of pointer alignment, patterning and viewing angle, *Journal of Applied Psychology*, **48**, 344–7.

David, G. C. (1985a). U.K. national statistics on handling accidents and lumbar injuries at work, *Ergonomics*, **28**, 9–16.

David, G. C. (1985b). Intra-abdominal pressure measurements and load capacities for females, *Ergonomics*, **28**, 345–58.

Davies, H. T. (1972). Moving loads manually, *Applied Ergonomics*, **3**, 190–4.

Davis, P. R. (1983a). Slipping, tripping and falling accidents: an introduction, *Ergonomics*, **26**, 1–2.

Davis, P. R. (1983b). Human factors contributing to slips, trips and falls, *Ergonomics*, **26**, 51–60.

Davis, P. R., Ridd, J. E. and Stubbs, D. A. (1980). *Acceptable Loading Levels for British Workers*. Paper presented at the Annual Conference of the Ergonomics Society, Nottingham.

Davis, P. R. and Stubbs, D. A. (1977a). Safe levels of manual forces for young males (1), *Applied Ergonomics*, **8**, 141–50.

Davis, P. R. and Stubbs, D. A. (1977b). Safe levels of manual forces for young males (2), *Applied Ergonomics*, **8**, 219–28.

Davis, P. R. and Stubbs, D. A. (1978). Safe levels of manual forces for young males (3), *Applied Ergonomics*, **9**, 33–7.

Davis, P. R. and Troup, J. D. G. (1964). Pressures in the trunk cavities when pulling, pushing and lifting, *Ergonomics*, **7**, 465–74.

Deatherage, B. H. and Evans, T. R. (1969). Binaural masking: backward, forward and simultaneous effects, *Journal of the Acoustical Society of America*, **46**, 362–71.

De Boer, J. B. (1977). Performance and comfort in the presence of veiling reflections, *Lighting Research and Technology*, **9**, 169.

Deeb, J. M., Drury, C. G. and Pendergast, D. R. (1992). An exponential model of isometric muscular fatigue as a function of age and muscle groups, *Ergonomics*, **35**, 899–918.

Deininger, R. L. (1960). Human factors engineering studies of the design and use of pushbutton telephone sets, *The Bell System Technical Journal*, **39**, 995–1012.

Dempsey, C. A. (1963). The design of body support and restraint systems. In E. Bennett, J. Degan and J. Spiegel (eds). *Human Factors in Technology*. New York: McGraw-Hill.

Dempster, W. T. (1955). *Space Requirements of the Seated Operator: Geometrical, Kinematic, and Mechanical Aspects of the Body with Special Reference to the Limbs*, WADC Technical Report 55-159. Ohio: WPAFB.

De Wall, M., van Riel, M. P. J. M., Snijders, C. J. and van Wingerden, J. P. (1991). The effect on sitting posture of a desk with a 10 degree inclination for reading and writing, *Ergonomics*, **34**, 575–84.

Dewar, M. E. (1977). Body movements when climbing a ladder, *Ergonomics*, **1**, 347–55.

Dickinson, J. (1974). *Proprioceptive Control of Human Movement*. London: Lepus Books.

Diebschlag, W. and Müller-Limroth, W. (1980). Physiological requirements on car seats: some results of experimental studies. In D. J. Oborne and J. A. Levis (eds). *Human Factors in Transport Research, Vol. II*. London: Academic Press.

Diffrient, N., Tilley, A. R. and Bargady, J. C. (1974). *Humanscale 1/2/3*. Mass: MIT Press.

Dixon-Ward, W. (1984). Noise-induced hearing loss. In D. Jones and A. Chapman (eds). *Noise in Society*. Chichester: John Wiley.

Drazin, D. H. (1962). Factors affecting vision during vibration, *Research*, **15**, 275–80.

Droege, R. C. and Hill, B. M. (1961). Comparison of performance on manual and electric typewriters, *Journal of Applied Psychology*, **45**, 268–70.

Drury, C. G. (1973). The effect of speed of working on industrial inspection accuracy, *Applied Ergonomics*, **4**, 2–7.

Drury, C. G. (1985). The role of the hand in manual materials handling, *Ergonomics*, **28**, 213–27.

Drury, C. G. and Addison, J. L. (1973). An industrial study of the effects of feedback and fault density on inspection performance, *Ergonomics*, **16**, 159–69.

Drury, C. G., Begbie, K., Ulate, C. and Dreeb, J. M. (1985). Experiments on wrist deviation in manual materials handling, *Ergonomics*, **28**, 577–89.

Drury, C. G. and Pitzella, T. (1983). Hand placement in manual materials handling, *Human Factors*, **25**, 551–62.

Drury, C. G., Roberts, D. P., Hansgen, R. and Bayman, J. R. (1983). Evaluation of a palletising aid, *Applied Ergonomics*, **14**, 242–6.

Drury, C. G. and Sinclair, M. A. (1983). Human and machine performance in an inspection task, *Human Factors*, **25**, 391–9.

Dudek, R. A., Ayoub, M. M. and El-Nawawi, M. A. (1973). Optimal work–rest schedules under prolonged vibration, *Ergonomics*, **16**, 469–79.

Dunbar, H. F., Wolfe, T. P. and Rioch, J. (1936). The psychic component in fracture. Part I, *American Journal of Psychiatry*, **93**, 649–79.

Dunbar, H. F., Wolfe, T. P., Tauber, E. S. and Brush, A. C. (1939). The psychic component in fracture. Part II., *American Journal of Psychiatry*, **95**, 1319–42.

Duncan, K. D. and Gray, M. J. (1975). An evaluation of a fault finding training course for refinery process operators, *Journal of Occupational Psychology*, **48**, 199–218.

Dunn, A. G. (1971). Engineering the keyboard from the human factors viewpoint, *Computers and Automation*, February, 32–3.

Dwyer, F. M. (1967). Adapting visual illusions for effective learning, *Harvard Educational Review*, **37**, 250–63.

Earl, W. K. and Goff, J. D. (1965). Comparison of two data entry methods, *Perceptual and Motor Skills*, **20**, 369–84.

Eason, K. D. (1991). Ergonomic perspectives on advances in human–computer interaction, *Ergonomics*, **34**, 721–42.

Easterbrook, J. A. (1959). The effect of emotion on cue utilization and the organization of behavior, *Psychological Review*. **66**, 183–201.

Easterby, R. S. (1970). The perception of symbols for machine displays, *Ergonomics*, **13**, 149–58.

Easterby, R. S., Kroemer, K. H. E. and Chaffin, D. B. (1982). *Anthropometry and Biomechanics: Theory and Application*. New York: Plenum Press.

Easterby, R. S. and Hakiel, S. R. (1981). Field testing of consumer safety signs: the comprehension of pictorially presented messages, *Applied Ergonomics*, **12**, 143–52.

Eckstrand, G. A. and Morgan, R. L. (1956). *The Influence of Training on the Tactual Discriminability of Knob Shapes*. Ohio: WADC Technical Report 56-8.

Eddy, J. K. and Glass, A. L. (1981). Reading and listening to high and low imagery sentences, *Journal of Verbal Learning and Verbal Behaviour*, **20**, 333–45.

Edholm, O. G. and Murrell, K. F. H. (1973). *The Ergonomics Society: A History 1949–1970*. London: Ergonomics Research Society.

Edworthy, J., Loxley, S. and Dennis, I. (1991). Improving auditory warning design: relationship between warning sound parameters and perceived urgency, *Human Factors*, **33**, 205–31.

Eilam, Z. (1989). Human engineering the one-handed keyboard, *Applied Ergonomics*, **20**, 225–9.

Ekholm, J., Arborelius, U. P. and Németh, G. (1982). The load on the lumbo-sacral joint and trunk muscle activity during lifting, *Ergonomics*, **25**, 145–62.

Elias, M. F., Snadowski, A. M. and Rizy, E. F. (1965). Identification of televised symbols as a function of symbol resolution, *Perceptual and Motor Skills*, **21**, 91–9.

Ellis, H. D. (1982). The effects of cold on the performance of serial choice reaction time and various discrete tasks, *Human Factors*, **24**, 559–98.

Ellis, J. G. and Dewar, R. E. (1979). Rapid comprehension of verbal and symbolic traffic sign messages, *Human Factors*, **21**, 161–8.

Ellis, M. I., Seedhom, B. B., Amis, A. A., Dowson, D. and Wright, V. (1979). Forces in the knee joint whilst rising from normal and motorized chairs, *Engineering in Medicine*, **8**, 33–40.

Ellis, N. C. and Hill, S. E. (1978). A comparative study of seven segment numerics, *Human Factors*, **20**, 655–60.

Engel, F. L. (1980). Information selection from visual display units. In E. Grandjean and E. Vigliani (eds). *Ergonomic Aspects of Visual Display Terminals*. London: Taylor & Francis.

Ernest, C. H. (1979). Visual imagery ability and the recognition of verbal and non verbal stimuli, *Acta Psychologist*, **43**, 253–69.

Eskew, R. T. and Riche, C. V. (1982). Pacing and locus of control in quality control inspection, *Human Factors*, **24**, 411–15.

Estes, W. K. and Wolford, G. L. (1971). Effects of spaces on responses from tachistoscopically presented letter strings, *Psychonomic Science*, **75**, 77–80.

Evans, G. W. and Howard, R. B. (1973). Personal space, *Psychological Bulletin*, **80**, 334–44.

Fanger, P. O. (1970). *Thermal Comfort*. New York: McGraw-Hill.

Fanger, P. O., Breum, N. O. and Jerking, E. (1977). Can colour and noise influence man's thermal comfort?, *Ergonomics*, **20**, 11–18.

Farmer, E. and Chambers, E. G. (1939). *A Study of Accident Proneness Amongst Motor Drivers*, Industrial Health Research Board Report No. 84. London: IHRB.

Fellmann, Th., Bräuninger, U., Giere, R., and Grandjean, E. (1982). An ergonomic evaluation of VDT's, *Behaviour and Information Technology*, **1**, 69–80.

Fellows, G. L. and Freivalds, A. (1991). Ergonomics evaluation of a foam rubber grip for tool handles, *Applied Ergonomics*, **22**, 225–30.

Ferguson, D. and Duncan, J. (1974). Keyboard design and operating posture, *Ergonomics*, **17**, 731–44.

Fernandez, J. E. and Uppugonduri, K. G. (1992). Anthropometry of South Indian industrial workmen, *Ergonomics*, **35**, 1393–8.

Fidell, S. (1978). Effectiveness of audible warning signals for emergency vehicles, *Human Factors*, **20**, 19–26.

Fine, B. J. (1963). Introversion, extraversion and motor vehicle driver behavior, *Perceptual and Motor Skills*, **12**, 95–100.

Fitch, J. M., Templer, J. and Corcoran, P. (1974). The dimensions of stairs, *Scientific American*, **231**, 82–90.

Fitts, P. M. (1962). Functions of man in complex systems, *Aerospace Engineering*, **21**, 34–9.

Fitts, P. M. and Jones, R. E. (1947a). Psychological aspects of instrument display. I: Analysis of 270 'pilot error' experiences in reading and interpreting aircraft instruments. Aeromedical Laboratory report AMRL-TSEAA-694-12A, July. In W. Sinaiko (ed.). *Selected Papers in the Design and Use of Control Systems*. (1961). New York: Dover.

Fitts, P. M. and Jones R. E. (1947b). Analysis of factors contributing to 460 'pilot error' experiences in operating aircraft controls. Aeromedical Laboratory Report AMRL-TSEAA-694-12, July. In W. Sinaiko (ed.). *Selected Papers in the Design and*

Use of Control Systems. (1961). New York: Dover.

Fitts, P. M. and Seeger, C. M. (1953). S-R compatibility: spatial characteristics of stimulus and response codes, *Journal of Applied Psychology,* **46,** 199–200.

Fleishmann, E. A. (1966). Human abilities and the acquisition of skill. In E. A. Bilodeau (ed.). *Acquisition of Skill.* New York: Academic Press.

Flesch, R. (1948). A new readability yardstick, *Journal of Applied Psychology,* **32,** 221–33.

Fletcher, H. (1940). Auditory patterns, *Reviews of Modern Physics,* **12,** 47–65.

Floyd, W. F. and Ward, J. S. (1969). Anthropometric and physiological considerations in school, office and factory seating, *Ergonomics,* **12,** 132–9.

Folkard, S. and Monk, T. H. (1979). Shiftwork and performance, *Human Factors,* **21,** 483–92.

Folkard, S. and Monk, T. H. (1985). *Hours of Work: Temporal Factors in Work-scheduling.* Chichester: John Wiley.

Folkard, S., Monk, T. H. and Chobban, M. C. (1978). Short and long term adjustment of circadian rhythms in 'permanent' night nurses, *Ergonomics,* **21,** 785–99.

Foster, J. and Bruce, M. (1982). Reading upper and lower case on viewdata, *Applied Ergonomics,* **13,** 145–9.

Foster, J. and Coles, P. (1977). An experimental study of typographic cueing in printed text, *Ergonomics,* **20,** 57–66.

Fowler, R. L. and Barker, A. S. (1974). Effectiveness of highlighting for retention of text material, *Journal of Applied Psychology,* **63,** 309–13.

Fowler, R. L., Williams, W. E., Fowler, M. G. and Young, D. D. (1968). *An Investigation of the Relationship between Operator Performance and Operator Panel Layout for Continuous Tasks.* Ohio: USAF AMRL-TR-68-170.

Fox, J. G. (1963). A comparison of gothic elite and standard elite typefaces, *Ergonomics,* **6,** 193–8.

Fox, J. G. (1971). Background music and industrial productivity—a review, *Applied Ergonomics,* **2,** 70–3.

Fox, J. G. (1977). Quality control of coins. In J. S. Weiner and H. G. Maule (eds). *Human Factors in Work, Design and Production.* London: Taylor & Francis.

Fox, J. G. (1983). Industrial music. In D. J. Oborne and M. M. Gruneberg (eds). *The Physical Environment at Work.* Chichester: John Wiley.

Fox, J. G. and Embrey, E. D. (1972). Music—an aid to productivity, *Applied Ergonomics,* **3,** 202–5.

Fox, J. G. and Haslegrave, C. M. (1969). Industrial inspection efficiency and the probability of a defect occurring, *Ergonomics,* **12,** 713–21.

Fox, W. F. (1967). Human performance in the cold, *Human Factors,* **9,** 203–20.

Fraser, T. M., Hoover, G. N. and Asche, W. F. (1961). Tracking performance during low frequency vibration, *Aerospace Medicine,* **31,** 829–35.

Frazier, L. and Rayner, K. (1982). Making and correcting errors during sentence comprehension. Eye movements in the analysis of structurally ambiguous sentences, *Cognitive Psychology,* **14,** 178–210.

Freivalds, A. (1987). The ergonomics of tools, *International Reviews of Ergonomics,* **1,** 43–75.

Freudenthal, A., van Riel, M. P. J., Molenbroek, F. J. M. and Snijders, C. J. (1991). The effect on sitting posture of a desk with a ten-degree inclination using an adjustable chair and table, *Applied Ergonomics,* **22,** 329–336.

Fried, M. L. and DeFazio, V. J. (1974). Territoriality and boundary conflicts in the subway, *Psychiatry,* **37,** 47–59.

Frymoyer, J. W., Pope, M. H., Costanzu, M. C., Rosen, J. C., Goggin, J. E. and Wilder,

D. G. (1980). Epidemiologic studies of low back pain, *Spine*, **5**, 419–22.

Fukuzumi, S. and Hayashi, Y. (1989). Luminance and stimulus purity of VDT display color in terms of readability, *International Journal of Human–Computer Interaction*, **1**, 115–35.

Fukuzumi, S., Yamamoto, I. and Hayashi, Y. (1987). Study on VDT display color and readability. In G. Salvendy (ed.). *Social Ergonomics and Stress Aspects of Work with Computers*. Amsterdam: Elsevier.

Furness, T. H. and Lewis, C. H. (1978). *Helmet Mounted Display Reading Performance under Whole-body Vibration*. Paper presented to Human Response to Vibration Meeting, Silsoe, Beds.

Gagge, A. P., Stolwijk, J. A. J. and Nishi, Y. (1971). An effective temperature scale based on a simple model of human physiological regulatory response, *ASHRAE Transactions*, **77**, 247–62.

Galitz, W. O. (1965). CRT keyboard human factors evaluation. UNIVAC Systems Application Engineering, Roseville DPD, March.

Gane, C. P., Horabin, I. S. and Lewis, B. N. (1966). The simplification and avoidance of instruction, *Industrial Training*, **1**, 160–6.

Garg, A., Sharma, D., Chaffin, D. B. and Schmidler, J. M. (1983). Biomechanical stresses as related to motion trajectory of lifting, *Human Factors*. **25**, 527–39.

Garrett, J. W. (1971). The adult human hand: some anthropometric and biomechanical considerations, *Human Factors*, **13**, 117–31.

Gerbert, K. and Kemmler, R. (1986). The causes of causes: determinants and background variables of human factor incidents and accidents, *Ergonomics*, **29**, 1439–53.

Ghiringhelli, L. (1980). Collection of subjective opinions on use of VDUs. In E. Grandjean and E. Vigliani (eds). *Ergonomic Aspects of Visual Display Terminals*. London: Taylor & Francis.

Gibbs, C. B. (1970). Servo-control systems in organisms and the transfer of skill. In D. Legge (ed.). *Skills*. Harmondsworth, Penguin.

Gibson, J. J. (1950). The perception of visual surfaces, *American Journal of Psychology*, **63**, 367–84.

Giddings, B. J. (1972). Alpha-numerics for raster displays, *Ergonomics*, **15**, 65–72.

Giesbrecht, G. G., Arnett, J. L., Vela, E. and Bristow, G. K. (1993). Effect of task complexity on mental performance during immersion hypothermia, *Aviation, Space and Environmental Medicine*, **64**, 206–11.

Gilbert, B. G., Hahn, H. A., Gilmore, W. E. and Schurman, D. L. (1988). Thumbs up: anthropometry of the first digit, *Human Factors*, **30**, 747–50.

Gilbert, M. and Hopkinson, R. G. (1949). The illumination of the Snellen Chart, *British Journal of Ophthalmology*, **33**, 305–10.

Gilchrest, B. and Shenkin, A. (1981). The impact of scanners on employment in supermarkets–an update, *Computers and Society*, **11**. 31–3.

Gittelson, B. (1978). *Biorhythm: A Personal Science*, 2nd edn. New York: Arco.

Glass, D. C. and Singer, J.E. (1972). *Urban Stress*. London: Academic Press.

Goldman, R. F. (1988). Standards for human exposure to heat. In B. Makjavic, E. W. Bannister and J. B. Morrison (eds). *Environmental Ergonomics: Sustaining Human Performance in Harsh Environments*. Philadelphia: Taylor & Francis.

Goodwin, N. C. (1975). Cursor positioning on an electronic display using lightpen, lightgun, or keyboard for three basic tasks, *Human Factors*, **17**, 289–95.

Gough, P. B. (1965). Grammatical transformations and speed of understanding, *Journal of Verbal Learning and Verbal Behaviour*, **4**, 107–11.

Gould, J. D. (1976). Looking at pictures. In R. A. Monty and J. W. Senders (eds). *Eye*

Movements and Psychological Processes. Hillsdale, N.J.: Lawrence Erlbaum Associates.

Gould, J. D., Alfaro, L., Barnes, V., Finn, R., Grischkowsky, N. and Minuto, A. (1987). Reading is slower from CRT displays than from paper: attempts to isolate a single-variable explanation, *Human Factors*, **29**, 269–99.

Gould, J. G. (1968). Visual factors in the design of computer-controlled CRT displays, *Human Factors*, **10**, 359–76.

Graf, R. and Torrey, J. W. (1966). Perception of phase structure in written language, *American Psychological Association Convention Proceedings*, 83–8.

Grandjean, E. (1973). *Ergonomics in the Home*. London: Taylor & Francis.

Grandjean, E., Hünting, W. and Hedernann, M. (1983). VDT workstations design: preferred settings and their effects, *Human Factors*, **25**, 161–75.

Grandjean, E., Nishiyama, K., Hünting, W. and Hedernann, M. (1982). A laboratory study on preferred and imposed settings of a VDT workstation, *Behaviour and Information Technology*, **1**, 289–304.

Grant, R. and Davey, B. (1991). How do headings affect text-processing?, *Reading Research and Instruction*, **31**, 12–21.

Green, A. E. (1988). Human factors in industrial risk assessment—some early work. In L. P. Goodstein, H. B. Andersen and S. E. Olsen (eds). *Tasks, Errors and Mental Models*. London: Taylor & Francis.

Green, H. F. and Anderson, L. K. (1956). Color coding in a visual search task, *Journal of Experimental Psychology*, **51**, 19–24.

Greene, J. M. (1970). The semantic function of negatives and passives, *British Journal of Psychology*, **61**, 17–22.

Greenwood, M., Woods, H. M. and Yule, G. U. (1919). A report on the incidence of industrial accidents upon individuals with special reference to multiple accidents. Report No. 4. Industrial Health Research Board. In W. Haddon, E. A. Suchmann and D. Flein (eds). (1964). *Accident Research*. New York: Harper.

Gregoire, H. and Trimble, R. (1986). Anthropometric design variables and performance, *Perceptual and Motor Skills*, **63**, 867–72.

Gregory, M. and Poulton, E. C. (1970). Even versus uneven right-hand margins and the rate of comprehension in reading, *Ergonomics*, **13**, 427–34.

Grether, W. F. (1949). Instrument reading I. The design of long-scale indicators for speed and accuracy of quantitative readings, *Journal of Applied Psychology*, **33**, 363–72.

Grether, W. F. (1973). Human performance at elevated environmental temperatures, *Aerospace Medicine*, **44**, 747–55.

Grieve, D. W. and Pheasant, S. T. (1981). Biomechanics. In W. T. Singleton (ed.). *The Body at Work—Biological Ergonomics*. London: Cambridge University Press.

Griffin, M. J. (1975). Levels of whole-body vibration affecting human vision, *Aviation, Space and Environmental Medicine*, **46**, 1033–40.

Griffin, M. J. (1976a). Vibration and visual acuity. In W. Tempest (ed.). Infrasound and Low Frequency Vibration. London: Academic Press.

Griffin, M. J. (1976b). Eye motion during whole-body vibration, *Human Factors*, **18**, 601–6.

Griffin, M. J. (1990). *Handbook of Human Vibration*. London: Academic Press.

Griffin, M. J. and Lewis, C. H. (1978). A review of the effects of vibration on visual acuity and continuous manual control: Part I Visual acuity, *Journal of Sound and Vibration*, **56**, 383-413.

Griffiths, I. D. and Langdon, F. J. (1968). Subjective response to road traffic noise, *Journal of Sound and Vibration*, **8**, 16–32.

Guignard, J. C. and Irving, A. (1960). Effects of low frequency vibration on man, *Engineering*, 9 September, 364–7.

Guignard, J. C., Landrum, C. J. and Reardon, R. E. (1976). *Experimental Evaluation of International Standard (ISO 2631) for Whole-body Vibration Exposures*. University of Dayton Research Institute. UDRI-TR-76-79.

Guillien, J. and Rebiffé, R. (1980). Anthropometric models of a population of bus drivers. In D. J. Oborne and J. A. Levis (eds). *Human Factors in Transport Research, Vol. I*. London: Academic Press.

Haaland, J., Wingert, J. and Olsen, B. A. (1963). Force required to actuate switches, maximum finger pushing force, and coefficient of friction on Mercury globes, *Honeywell Memo*, February.

Haber, R. N. and Haber, L. R. (1981). Visual components of the reading process. *Visible Language*, **15**, 147–82.

Haberman, P. W. (1987). Alcohol and alcoholism in traffic and other accidental deaths, *American Journal of Drug and Alcohol Abuse*, **13**, 475–84.

Hackmeister, R. (1979). Focus on keyboards, *Electronic Design*, **11**, 169–75.

Haines, R. F. and Gilliland, K. (1973). Response time in the full visual field, *Journal of Applied Psychology*, **58**, 289–95.

Hakkinen, M. T. and Williges, B. H. (1984). Synthesized warning messages: effects of an alerting cue in single- and multiple-function voice synthesis systems, *Human Factors*, **26**, 185–95.

Hale, A. R. and Hale, M. (1972). *A Review of the Industrial Accident Research Literature*. Committee on Safety and Health at Work Paper. London: HMSO.

Hall, E. T. (1959). *The Silent Language*. New York: Doubleday.

Hall, E. T. (1976). The anthropology of space: an organizing model. In H. M. Proshansky, W. H. Ittleson and L. G. Rivlin (eds). *Environmental Psychology*, 2nd edn. New York: Holt, Rinehart and Winston.

Hansen, C. P. (1988). Personality characteristics of the accident involved employee, *Journal of Business and Psychology*, **2**, 346–65.

Hardyck, C. and Petrinovich, L. F. (1977). Left-handedness, *Psychological Bulletin*, **84**, 385–404.

Harnett, R. M., Pruitt, J. R. and Sias, F. R. (1983a). A review of the literature concerning resuscitation from hypothermia: Part I - The problem and general approaches, *Aviation Space and Environmental Medicine*, **54**, 425–34.

Harnett, R. M., Pruitt, J. R. and Sias, F. R. (1983b). A review of the literature concerning resuscitation from hypothermia: Part II - Selected rewarming protocols, *Aviation, Space and Environmental Medicine*, **54**, 487–95.

Harris, C. S., Sommer, H. C. and Johnson, D. L. (1976). Review of the effects of infrasound on man, *Aviation, Space and Environmental Medicine*, **47**, 430–4.

Harris, D. (1966). Effect of equipment complexity on inspection performance, *Journal of Applied Psychology*, **50**, 236–7.

Hartley, J. and Burnhill, P. (1976). *Textbook Design: A Practical Guide*. Paris: UNESCO.

Hartley, J., Young, M. and Burnhill, P. (1975). On the typing of tables, *Applied Ergonomics*, **6**, 39–42.

Harwood, K. and Foley, P. (1987). Temporal Resolution: an insight into the video display terminal (VDT) 'problem', *Human Factors*, **29**, 447–52.

Haslegrave, C. M. (1979). An anthropometric survey of British drivers, *Ergonomics*, **22**, 145–53.

Haubner, P. J. (1986). A workshop on spatial and temporal visual aspects of VDUs, *Behaviour and Information Technology*, **5**, 301–7.

Hayward, M. G. and Keatinge, W. R. (1981). Roles of subcutaneous fat and thermoregulatory reflexes in determining ability to stabilise body temperature in water, *Journal of Physiology*, **320**, 229–51.

Hemingway, J. C. and Erickson, R. A. (1969). Relative effects of raster scan lines and image subtense on symbol legibility on television, *Human Factors*, **11**, 331–8.

Hepburn, H. A. (1958). Portable ladders. I: The quarter-length rule, *British Journal of Industrial Safety*, **4**, 155–8.

Hertzberg, H. T. E. (1958). *Annotated Bibliography of Applied Physical Anthropometry in Human Engineering*, Report No. WADC-TTt-56-30. Ohio: Wright Patterson Airforce Base.

Hertzberg, H. T. E. and Burke, F. E. (1971). Foot forces exerted at various aircraft brake-pedal angles, *Human Factors*, **13**, 445–56.

Hettinger, T. (1961). *Physiology of Strength*, Springfeld, Ill: Charles C. Thomas.

Hetu, R., Truchon-Gagnon, C. and Bilodeau, S. A. (1990). Problems of noise in school settings: a review of literature and the results of an exploratory survey, *Journal of Speech Language Pathology and Audiology*, **14**, 31–9.

Hildebrandt, G. Rohmert, W. and Rutenfranz, J. (1974). Twelve and twenty four hour rhythms in error frequency of locomotive drivers and the influence of tiredness, *International Journal of Chronobiology*, **2**, 175–80.

Hill, J. M. M. and Trist, E. L. (1953). A consideration of industrial accidents as a means of withdrawal from work situation, *Human Relations*, **6**, 357–80.

Hirsch, R. S. (1970). Effects of standards versus alphabetical keyboard formats on typing performance, *Journal of Applied Psychology*, **54**, 484–90.

Hitt, W. D. (1961). An evaluation of five different abstract coding methods, *Human Factors*, **3**, 120–30.

Hochberg, J, and McAlister, E. (1953). *A Quantitative Approach to Figural 'Goodness' Characteristics*. Paper presented to IEE Man–Machine Systems Conference. London: IEE.

Hochberg, J. and Silverstein, A. (1956). A quantitative index of stimulus-similarity: proximity vs. differences in brightness, *American Journal of Psychology*, **69**, 456–8.

Hockey, G. R. J. (1970). Signal probability and signal location as possible bases for increased selectivity in noise, *Quarterly Journal of Experimental Psychology*, **22**, 37–42.

Hoffman, M. and Cramer, M. L. (1981), Workstation design optimization through a stimulation model, *Proceedings of 25th Annual Meeting of the Human Factors Society*, Baltimore: HFS.

Hoffman, M. and Heimstra, N. W. (1972). Tracking performance with visual, auditory or electrocutaneous displays, *Human Factors*, **14**, 131–8.

Holladay, L. L. (1926). The fundamentals of glare and visibility, *Journal of the Optical Society of America*, **12**, 271–319.

Holland, C. A. and Rabbitt, P. M. (1992). People's awareness of their age-related sensory and cognitive deficits and the implications for road safety, *Applied Cognitive Psychology*, **6**, 217–31.

Holland, C. L. (1965). Performance effects of long term random vertical vibration, *Human Factors*, **9**, 93–104.

Holmes, V. M. and Langford, J. (1976). Comprehension and recall of abstract and concrete sentences, *Journal of Verbal Learning and Verbal Behavior*, **15**, 559–66.

Hopkin, V. D. (1971). The evaluation of touch displays for air traffic control tasks, *IEE Conference on Displays: Publication No. 80*.

Hopkinson, R. G. (1940). Discomfort glare in lighted streets, *Transactions of the Illuminating Engineering Society*, **15**, 1–30.

Hopkinson, R. G. (1956). Glare discomfort and pupil diameter, *Journal of the Optical*

Society of America, **46**, 594–656.

Hopkinson, R. G. (1972). Glare from daylight in buildings, *Applied Ergonomics*, **3**, 206–15.

Hopkinson, R. G. and Collins, J. B. (1970). *The Ergonomics of Lighting*. London: McDonald Technical and Scientific.

Hopkinson, R. G., Waldram, J. M. and Stevens, W. R. (1941). Brightness and contrast in illuminating engineering, *Transactions of the Illuminating Engineering Society*, **6**, 37–47.

Hornick, R. J. (1962). The effects of whole body vibration in three directions upon human performance, *Journal of Engineering Psychology*, **1**, 93–101.

Hornick, R. J. and Lefritz, N. M. (1966). A study and review of human reaction to prolonged random vibration, *Human Factors*, **8**, 481–91.

Houghton, F.C. and Yaglou, C.P. (1923). Determining lines of equal comfort. *ASHRAE Transactions*, **29**, 163–76.

Huddleston, J. H. F. (1964). *Human Performance and Behavior in Vertical Sinusoidal Vibration*. Farnborough, Hants: Institute of Aviation Medicine Report 303.

Huddleston, J. H. F. (1965). *Effects of 4.8 and 6.7 c.p.s. Vertical Vibration on Handwriting and a Complex Mental Task, With and Without Abdominal Restraint*. Farnborough, Hants: Institute of Aviation Medicine Memo 60.

Huddleston, J. H. F. (1970). Tracking performance on a visual display apparently vibrating at 1–10 Hz, *Journal of Applied Psychology*, **54**, 401–8.

Huddleston, J. H. F. (1974). A comparison of two 7x9 matrix alphanumeric designs for TV displays, *Applied Ergonomics*, **5**, 81–3.

Hunt, D. P. (1953). *The Coding of Aircraft Controls*. USAF, WADC Technical Report 53-331.

Illuminating Engineering Society. (1977). *IES Code for Interior Lighting*. London: IES.

Imrhan, S. N. (1989). Trends in finger pinch strength in children, adults and the elderly, *Human Factors*, **31**, 689–701.

International Organization for Standardization. (1978). *Guide to the evaluation of human exposure to whole-body mechanical vibration and shock*. Geneva: International Organization for Standardization.

International Organization for Standardization (1985). *Evaluation of Human Exposure to Whole-body Vibration–Part 1: General Requirements*. ISO 2631/1-1985. Geneva: International Organization for Standardization.

International Organization for Standardization (1986). *Mechanical Vibration– Guidelines for the Measurement and the Assessment of Human Exposure to Hand-transmitted Vibration*. ISO 5349. Geneva: International Organization for Standardization.

Irvine, C. H., Snook, S. H. and Sparshatt, J. H. (1990). Stairway risers and treads: acceptable and preferred dimensions, *Applied Ergonomics*, **21**, 215–25.

Isensee, S. H. and Bennett, C. A. (1983). The perception of flicker and flare on computer CRT displays, *Human Factors*, **25**, 177–84.

Jackson, A. (1982). *Some Problems in the Specification of Rolling Ball Operating Characteristics*. Paper presented to IEE Man–Machine Systems Conference. London: IEE.

James, D. I. (1983). Rubbers and plastics in shoes and flooring: the importance of kinetic friction, *Ergonomics*, **26**, 83–89.

Jamieson, G. H. (1966). Inspection in the telecommunications industry: a field study of age and other performance variables, *Ergonomics*, **9**, 297–303.

Jansen, G. (1961). Aversive effects of noise in iron and steel workers, *StahlundEisen*, **81**, 217–20.

Jeavons, P. M. and Harding, G. F. A. (1975). *Photosensitive Epilepsy.* London: Heinemann.

Jenkins, H. M. (1958). The effect of signal rate on performance in visual monitoring, *American Journal of Psychology*, **71**, 647–61.

Jenkins, N. T. (1956). The accident prone personality, *Personnel*, **33**, 29–32.

Jenkins, W. L. and Connor, M. B. (1949). Some design factors in making settings on a linear scale, *Journal of Applied Psychology*, **33**, 395–409.

Jenkins, W. O. (1947). The tactual discrimination of shapes for coding aircraft-type controls. In P. M. Fitts (ed.). *Psychological Research on Equipment Design.* Ohio: USAF Research Report No. 19.

Jerison, H. J. (1959). Effects of noise on human performance, *Journal of Applied Psychology*, **43**, 96–101.

Jerison, H. J. (1966). Remarks on Colquhoun's 'Effect of unwanted signals on performance in a vigilance task', *Ergonomics*, **9**, 413–16.

Johnsgard, K. W. (1953). Check reading as a function of pointer symmetry and uniform alignment, *Journal of Applied Psychology*, **37**, 407–11.

Johnson, D. L., Nixon, C. W., Stephenson, M. R. R. (1976). Long-duration exposure to intermittent noises, *Aviation, Space and Environmental Medicine*, **47**, 987–90.

Johnson, S. L. and Roscoe, S. N. (1972). What moves, the airplane or the world?, *Human Factors*, **14**, 107–29.

Johnston, D. M. (1965). Search performance as a function of peripheral activity, *Human Factors*, **7**, 527–35.

Jones, I. (1976). The technology of visual display units. In D. Grover (ed.). *Visual Display Units.* Guildford: IPC Science and Technology Press Ltd.

Jones, A. J. and Saunders, D. J. (1972). Equal comfort contours for whole-body, vertical, pulsed sinusoidal vibration, *Journal of Sound and Vibration*, **23**, 1–4.

Jones, D. M. (1979). Stress and memory. In M. M. Gruneberg and P. E. Morris (eds). *Applied Problems in Memory.* London: Academic Press.

Jones, D. M. (1983). Noise. In R. Hockey (ed.). *Stress and Fatigue in Human Performance.* Chichester: John Wiley.

Jones, J. C. (1969). Methods and results of seating research, *Ergonomics*, **12**, 171–81.

Jones, M. R. (1962). Colour coding, *Human Factors*, **4**, 355–65.

Jones, S. (1968). *Design of Instruction.* Training Information Paper 1. London: HMSO.

Kadefors, R., Areskoug, A., Dahlman, S., Kilbom, A., Sperling, L., Wikstrom, L. and Oster, J. (1993). An approach to ergonomics evaluation of hand tools, *Applied Ergonomics*, **24**, 203–11.

Kak, A. V. and Knight, J. K. (1980). Text formatting effects in speed reading. *Proceedings of the 24th Human Factors Society Meeting.* Baltimore: HFS.

Kamman, R. (1975). The comprehensibility of printed instructions and the flowchart alternative, *Human Factors*, **17**, 183–91.

Keegan, J. J. and Radke, O. (1964). Designing vehicle seats for greater comfort. *SEA Journal*, September, **72**, 50–5.

Keisler, S. and Finholt, T. (1988). The mystery of RSI, *American Psychologist*, **43**, 1004–15.

Kelly, D. H. (1961). Visual responses to time-dependent stimuli. I Amplitude sensitivity measurements, *Journal of the Optical Society of America*, **51**, 422–9.

Kember, P. and Varley, D. (1987). The legibility and readability of a visual display unit at threshold, *Ergonomics*, **30**, 925–31.

Kemsley, W. F. F. (1950). Weight and height of a population in 1943, *Annals of Eugenics*, **15**, 161–83.

Kennedy, K. W. (1975). International anthropometric variability and its effects on aircraft cockpit design. In A. Chapanis (ed.). *Ethnic Variables in Human Factors Engineering*. Baltimore: Johns Hopkins University Press.

Khalil, T. A. and Ayoub, M. M. (1970). *On prolonged vibration and work-rest schedule*. Paper to Human Factors Society Annual Conference, San Francisco.

Khalil, T. M. and Kurucz, C. N. (1977). The influence of 'biorhythm' on accident occurrence and performance, *Ergonomics*, **20**, 389–98.

Kimura, D. and Vanderwolf, C. H. (1970). The relation between hand preference and the performance of individual finger movements by left and right hands, *Brain*, **93**, 767–94.

King, L. E. (1971). A laboratory comparison of symbol and ward roadway signs, *Traffic Engineering and Control*, **12**, 519–20.

Kinkead, R. (1975). Typing speed, keying rates and optimal keyboard layouts. In *Proceedings of 1975 Human Factors Society Annual Meeting*. Baltimore: HFS.

Klare, G. R. (1963). *The Measurement of Readability*. Des Moines, Iowa: Iowa State University Press.

Klemmer, E. T. (1971). Keyboard entry, *Applied Ergonomics*, **2**, 2–6.

Knave, B. G. (1983). The visual display unit. In *Ergonomic Principles in Office Automation*, Stockholm: Ericsson International.

Kobrick, J. L. and Fine, B. J. (1983). Climate and human performance. In D. J. Oborne and M. M. Gruneberg (eds). *The Physical Environment at Work*. Chichester: John Wiley.

Koelega, H. S. and Brinkman, J.-A. (1986). Noise and vigilance: an evaluative review, *Human Factors*, **28**, 465–81.

Kolers, P. A. (1976). Buswell's discoveries. In R. A. Monty and J. W. Senders (eds). *Eye Movements and Psychological Processes*. Hillsdale, New Jersey: Lawrence Erlbaum Associates.

Konz, S. A. and Mital, A. (1990). Carpal tunnel syndrome, *International Journal of Industrial Ergonomics*, **5**, 175–80.

Koonce, J. M., Gold, M. and Moroze, M. (1986). Comparison of novice and experienced pilots using analog and digital flight displays, *Aviation, Space and Environmental Medicine*, **57**, 1181–4.

Kosslyn, S. M. (1989). Understanding charts and graphs. *Applied Cognitive Psychology*, **3**, 185–226.

Kroemer, K. H. E. (1965). Comparison of a keyboard of a normal typewriter with a 'K' keyboard, *Internat. Zeitschrift angewandt Physiologie*, **20**, 453–64.

Kroemer, K. H. E. (1970). Human strength: terminology, measurement, and interpretation of data, *Human Factors*, **12**, 297–313.

Kroemer, K. H. E. (1972). Human engineering the keyboard, *Human Factors*, **14**, 51–63.

Kroemer, K. H. E. (1974). Horizontal push and pull forces, *Applied Ergonomics*, **5**, 94–102.

Kroemer, K. H. E. (1983). Work space and equipment to fit the user. In D. J. Oborne and M. M. Gruneberg (eds). *The Physical Environment at Work*. Chichester: John Wiley.

Kroemer, K. H. E. (1989a). Engineering anthropometry, *Ergonomics*, **32**, 767–84.

Kroemer, K. H. E. (1989b). Cumulative trauma disorders: their recognition and ergonomics measures to avoid them, *Applied Ergonomics*, **20**, 274–80.

Kroemer, K. H. E. and Robinette, J. C. (1968). *Ergonomics in the Design of Office Furniture: A Review of European Literature*. Ohio: AMRL-TR-68-80.

Krohn, G. S. (1983). Flowcharts used for procedural instructions, *Human Factors*, **25**, 573–81.

Krug, D., George, B., Hannon, S. and Glover, J. A. (1991). The effect of outlines and headings on reader's recall of text, *Contemporary Educational Psychology*, **14**, 111–23.

Kryter, K. D. (1970). *The Effects of Noise on Man*. New York: Academic Press.

Kryter, K. D. and Pearsons, K. S. (1966). Some effects of spectrum content and duration on perceived noise level, *Journal of the Acoustical Society of America*, **39**, 451–64.

Kryter, K. D., Ward, W. D., Miller, J. D. and Eldredge, D. H. E. (1966). Hazardous exposure to intermittent and steady-state noise, *Journal of the Acoustical Society of America*, **39**, 451–64.

Kunce, J. T. (1967). Vocational interests and accident proneness, *Journal of Applied Psychology*, **3**, 223–5.

Kuorinka, I. and Viikari-Juntura, E. (1982). Prevalence of neck and upper limb disorders (NLD) and work load in different occupational groups. Problems in classification and diagnosis, *Journal of Human Ergology*, **11**, 65–72.

Kurke, M. I. (1956). Evaluation of a display incorporating quantitative and check reading characteristics, *Journal of Applied Psychology*, **40**, 233–6.

Lauback, L. L. (1976). Comparative muscular strength of men and women: a review of the literature, *Aviation, Space and Environmental Medicine*, **47**, 534–42.

Läubli, Th., Hünting, W. and Grandjean, E. (1981). Postural and visual loads of VDT workplaces. II Lighting conditions and visual impairment, *Ergonomics*, **24**, 933–44.

Lee, J. and Moray, N. (1992). Trust, control strategies and allocation of function in human–machine systems, *Ergonomics*, **35**, 1243–70.

Lee, R. A. and King, A. I. (1971). Visual vibration response, *Journal of Applied Physiology*, **30**, 281–6.

Lerman, S. (1984). Biophysical aspects of corneal and lenticular transparency, *Current Eye Research*, **3**, 3–14.

Leskinen, T. P. J., Stalhanimar, H. R., Kuorinka, I. A. A. and Troup, J. D. G. (1983). A dynamic analysis of spinal compression with different lifting techniques, *Ergonomics*, **26**, 595–604.

Levenson, H., Hirschfield, M. L. and Hirschfield, A. S. (1980). Industrial accidents and recent life events, *Journal of Occupational Medicine*, **22**, 53–7.

Leventhall, H. G. and Kyriakides, K. (1976). Environmental infrasound: its occurrence and measurement. In W. Tempest (ed.). *Infrasound and Low Frequency Vibration*. London: Academic Press.

Levison, W. H. (1976). *Biomechanical Response and Manual Tracking Performance in Sinusoidal Sum of Sines and Random Vibration Environments*. Ohio: Army Medical Research Laboratories Report, AMRL-TTt-75-94.

Levy-Leboyer, C. and Naturel, V. (1991). Neighbourhood noise annoyance, *Journal of Environmental Psychology*, **11**, 75–86.

Lewin, T. (1969). Anthropometric studies on Swedish industrial workers when standing and sitting, *Ergonomics*, **12**, 883–902.

Lewis, C. H. (1980). *The Interaction of Control Dynamics and Display Type with the Effect of Vibration Frequency on Manual Tracking Performance*. Paper presented to Human Response to Vibration Meeting, Swansea.

Lewis, C. H. and Griffin, M. J. (1978). A review of the effects of vibration on visual acuity and manual control. Part II. Continuous manual control, *Journal of Sound and Vibration*, **56**, 415–57.

Lewis, C. H. and Griffin, M. J. (1979a). The effect of character size on the legibility of numeric displays during vertical whole-body vibration, *Journal of Sound and Vibration*, **67**, 562–5.

Lewis, C. H. and Griffin, M. J. (1979b). Mechanisms of the effects of vibration frequency, level and duration on continuous manual control performance, *Ergonomics*, **22**, 855–89.

Lewis, C. H. and Griffin, M. J. (1980a). Predicting the effects of vertical vibration frequency, combinations of frequencies used and visual distance on the reading of numeric displays, *Journal of Sound and Vibration*, **70**, 355–77.

Lewis, C. H. and Griffin, M. J. (1980b). Predicting the effects of vibration frequency and axis and seating conditions on the reading of numeric displays, *Ergonomics*, **23**, 485–501.

Licklider, J. C. (1948). The influence of interaural phase relations upon the masking of speech by white noise, *Journal of the Acoustical Society of America*, **20**, 150–9.

Licklider, J. C. R. (1961). *Audio warning signals for air force weapon systems*, Technical Report WADD TR 60-814. Ohio: Wright-Patterson AFB.

Liebman, M. (1970). The effects of sex and race norms on personal space, *Environmental Behaviour*, **2**, 208–46.

Lim, D. J. and Dunn, D. E. (1979). Anatomic correlates of noise-induced hearing loss. In Symposium on Noise—Its Effects and Control, *Otolaryngologic Clinics of North America*, **12**, No. 3. Philadelphia.

Lion, J. S. (1964). The performance of manipulative and inspection tasks under tungsten and fluorescent lighting, *Ergonomics*, **7**, 51–61.

Lion, J. S., Richardson, E. and Browne, R. C. (1968). A study of the performance of industrial inspectors under two kinds of lighting, *Ergonomics*, **11**, 23–34.

Litterick, I. (1981). QWERTYUIOP—dinosaur in a computer age, *New Scientist*, **89**, 66–89.

Little, K. B. (1965). Personal space, *Journal of Experimental Social Psychology*, **1**, 237–47.

Lockhart, J. M. (1968). Extreme body cooling and psychomotor performance, *Ergonomics*, **11**, 249–60.

Lockhart, J. M. and Keiss, H. O. (1971). Auxiliary heating of the hands during cold exposure and manual performance, *Human Factors*, **13**, 457–65.

Lodge, G. T. (1973). *Pilot stature in relation to cockpit size: a hidden factor in Navy jet aircraft accidents*. Norfolk, VA: Naval Safety Center.

Loveless, N. E. (1962). Direction-of-motion stereotypes: a review, *Ergonomics*, **5**, 357–83.

Lovesey, E. J. (1971). *An Investigation into the Effects of Dual Axis Vibration, Restraining Harness, Visual Feedback and Control Force on a Manual Positioning Task*. Farnborough, Hants: Royal Aircraft Establishment Technical Report 71213.

Lovesey, E. J. (1974). The occurrence and effects upon performance of low frequency vibration. In W. Tempest (ed.). *Infrasound and Low Frequency Vibration*. London: Academic Press.

Lovesey, E. J. (1975). The helicopter—some ergonomic factors, *Applied Ergonomics*, **6**, 139–46.

Luczak, H. (1991). Work under extreme conditions, *Ergonomics*, **34**, 687–720.

Lukiesh, M. and Holladay, L. L. (1925). Glare and visibility, *Transactions of the Illuminating Engineering Society*, **20**, 221–52.

Lundberg, U. (1976). Urban commuting: crowdedness and catecholamine excretion, *Journal of Human Stress*, **2**, 36–42.

Mackay, G. M., Defoneka, C. P., Blair, I. and Clayton, A. B. (1969). *Causes and Effects of Road Accidents*. Department of Transportation, University of Birmingham.

Mackworth, N. H. and Morandi, A. J. (1967). The gaze selects informative details within pictures, *Perception and Psychophysics*, **2**, 547–52.

Maddox, M. E., Burnette, J. T. and Gutman, J. C. (1977). Font comparisons for 5×7 dot matrix characters, *Human Factors*, **19**, 89–93.

Magora, A. (1972). Investigation of the relation between low back pain and occupation. Three physical requirements: sitting, standing and weight lifting, *Industrial Medicine*, **41**, 5–9.

Mahoney, E. R. (1974). Compensatory reactions to spatial immediacy, *Sociometry*, **37**, 423–31.

Maki, B. E., Bartlett, S. A. and Fernie, G. R. (1984). Influence of stairway handrail height on the ability to generate stabilizing forces and moments, *Human Factors*, **26**, 705–14.

Mandal, A. C. (1976). Work chair with tilting seat, *Ergonomics*, **19**, 157–64.

Mandal, A. C. (1981). The seated man (Homo Sedens), *Applied Ergonomics*, **12**, 19–26.

Manning, D. P. (1983). Deaths and injuries caused by slipping, tripping and falling, *Ergonomics*, **26**, 3–10.

Marshark, M. and Paivio, A. (1977). Integrative processing of concrete and abstract sentences, *Journal of Verbal Learning and Verbal Behavior*, **16**, 217–31.

Martin, A. (1972). A new keyboard layout, *Applied Ergonomics*, **3**, 48–51.

Maslen, K. R. (1972). *Efficiency Under Prolonged Vibration and the ISO 'Guide'*. Farnborough, Hants: Royal Aircraft Establishment Technical Memo EP 512.

Mathews, K. and Cannon, L. (1975). Environmental noise level as a determinant of helping behavior, *Journal of Personality and Social Psychology*, **32**, 571–7.

Matin, E. (1974). Saccadic suppression: a review and analysis, *Psychological Bulletin*, **81**, 899–917.

McAteer, E. (1992). Typeface emphasis and information focus in written language, *Applied Cognitive Psychology*, **6**, 345–59.

McBride, G., King, M. G. and James, J. W. (1965). Social proximity effects on GSR in adult humans, *Journal of Psychology*, **61**, 153–7.

McClelland, I. and Ward, J. S. (1976). Ergonomics in relation to sanitary ware design, *Ergonomics*, **4**, 465–78.

McConkie, G. W., Kerr, P. W., Reddix, M. D. and Zola, D. (1988). Eye movement control during reading: 1. The location of initial fixations of words, *Vision Research*, **28**, 1107–18.

McCormick, E. J. (1950). An analysis of visual requirements in industry, *Journal of Applied Psychology*, **34**, 54–61.

McCormick, E. J. (1976). *Human Factors in Engineering and Design*. New York: McGraw-Hill.

McDermott, F. T. (1986). Repetition strain injury: a review of current understanding, *The Medical Journal of Australia*, **144**, 196–200.

McEwing, R. W. (1977). Touch displays in industrial computer systems. In *Displays for Man–machine systems*. London: IEEE.

McIntyre, D. R. and Bates, B. T. (1982). Effects of rung spacing on the mechanics of ladder ascent, *Journal of Human Movement Studies*, **8**, 55–72.

McKendry, J. M., Corso, J. F. and Grant, G. (1960). The design and evolution of maintainable packaging methods for electronic equipment, *Ergonomics*, **3**, 255–72.

McKenzie, R. M. (1957). On the accuracy of inspectors, *Ergonomics*, **1**, 258–72.

McLaughlin, G. H. (1966). Comparing styles of presenting technical information, *Ergonomics*, **9**, 257–9.

McLean, N. V. (1965). Brightness contrast, colour contrast and legibility, *Human Factors*, **7**, 521–6.

McLeod, R. W. and Griffin, M. J. (1989). A review of the effects of translational whole-body vibration on continuous manual control performance, *Journal of*

Sound and Vibration, **133**, 55–115.

McLeod, R. W. and Griffin, M. J. (1993). Effects of duration and vibration on performance of a continuous manual control task, *Ergonomics*, **36**, 645–59.

McNall, P. E., Ryan, P. W., Rohles, F. H., Nevins, R. G. and Springer, W. E. (1968). Metabolic rates at four activity levels and their relationship to thermal comfort, *ASHRAE Transactions*, **74**, Part 1, VI.3.1. to IV.3.20.

Mead, P. G. and Sampson, P. B. (1972). Hand steadiness during unrestricted linear arm movements, *Human Factors*, **14**, 45–50.

Meddick, R. D. L. and Griffin, M. J. (1976). The effect of two-axis vibration on the legibility of reading material, *Ergonomics*, **19**, 21–33.

Megaw, E. D. (1978). *Some Factors Affecting Inspection Accuracy*. Paper presented to Symposium on Ergonomics and Visual Inspection, Birmingham.

Megaw, E. D. and Bellamy, L. J. (1983). Illumination at work. In D. J. Oborne and M. M. Gruneberg (eds). *The Physical Environment at Work*. Chichester: John Wiley.

Mehrabian, A. and Diamond, S. G. (1971). Effects of furniture arrangements, props and personality on social interaction, *Journal of Personality and Social Psychology*, **20**, 18–30.

Meisels, M. and Canter, F. M. (1970). Personal space and personality characteristics: a non-confirmation, *Psychological Reports*, **27**, 287–90.

Mekjavic, I. and Bligh, J. (1987). The pathophysiology of hypothermia, *International Reviews of Ergonomics*, **1**, 201–18.

Michael, P. R. and Bienvenue, G. R. (1983). Industrial noise and man. In D. J. Oborne and M. M. Gruneberg (eds). *The Physical Environment at Work*. Chichester: John Wiley.

Michaels, S. E. (1971). QWERTY versus alphabetic keyboards as a function of typing skill, *Human Factors*, **13**, 419–26.

Middlemist, R. D., Knowles, E. S. and Matter, C. F. (1976). Personal space invasions in the lavatory: suggestive evidence for arousal, *Journal of Personality and Social Psychology*, **33**, 541–6.

Miller, G. A. (1956). The magical number seven plus or minus two: some limits on our capacity to process information, *Psychological Review*, **63**, 81–97.

Miller, G. A. and Licklider, J. C. R. (1950). The intelligibility of interrupted speech, *Journal of the Acoustical Society of America*, **22**, 167–73.

Miller, G. R. (1972). *An Introduction to Speech Communication*, 2nd edn. Indianapolis: Bobbs-Merrill.

Miller, R. B. (1983). Transaction structures and format in form design. In R. Easterby and H. Zwaga (eds). *Information Design*. Chichester: John Wiley.

Milroy, R. and Poulton, E. C. (1978). Labeling graphs for improved reading speed, *Ergonomics*, **25**, 55–61.

Mital, A. (1991). Handtools: injuries, illnesses, design and usage. In A. Mital and W. Karwowski (eds). *Workspace, equipment and tool design*. Amsterdam: Elsevier.

Mital, A. and Fard, H. F. (1986). Psychophysical and physiological responses to lifting symmetrical and asymmetrical loads symmetrically and asymmetrically, *Ergonomics*, **29**, 1263–72.

Mital, A., Fard, H. F. and Khaledi, H. (1987). A biomechanical evaluation of staircase riser heights and tread depths during stair-climbing, *Clinical Biomechanics*, **2**, 162–4.

Mital, A. and Manivasagan, I. (1983). Maximum acceptable weight of lift as a function of material density, center of gravity location, hand preference and frequency, *Human Factors*, **25**, 33–42.

Monod, H. (1985). Contractility of muscle during prolonged static repetitive dynamic activity, *Ergonomics*, **28**, 81–9.

Moore, T. G. (1974). Tactile and kinaesthetic aspects of push-buttons, *Applied Ergonomics*, **5**, 66–71.

Moore, T. G. (1975). Industrial push-buttons, *Applied Ergonomics*, **6**, 33–8.

Moore, T. G. (1976). Controls and tactile displays. In K. F. Kraiss and J. Moral (eds). *Introduction to Human Engineering*. Köln: T.W. Rhineland.

Morgan, C. T. (1965). *Physiological Psychology*, 3rd edn. New York: McGraw-Hill.

Morgan, C. T., Cook, J. S., Chapanis, A. and Lund, M. (1963). *Human Engineering Guide to Equipment Design*. New York: McGraw-Hill.

Morgensen, M. F. and English, H. B. (1926). The apparent warmth of colors, *American Journal of Psychology*, **37**, 427–8.

Morris, D. (1977) *Manwatching: A Field Guide to Human Behaviour*. London: Jonathan Cape.

Mortimer, R. G. (1974). Foot brake pedal force capability of drivers, *Ergonomics*, **17**, 509–13.

Morton, R. and Provins, K. A. (1960). Finger numbness after acute local exposure to cold, *Journal of Applied Psychology*, **15**, 149–54.

Murrell, K. F. H. (1958). The relationship between dial size, reading distance and reading accuracy, *Ergonomics*, **1**, 182–90.

Murrell, K. F. H. (1962a). Industrial aspects of ageing, *Ergonomics*, **5**, 147–53.

Murrell, K. F. H. (1962b). Operator variability and its industrial consequence, *International Journal of Production Research*, **1**, 39.

Murrell, K. F. H. (1969). Beyond the panel, *Ergonomics*, **12**, 691–700.

Murrell, K. F. H. (1971). *Ergonomics: Man in his Working Environment*. London: Chapman & Hall.

Murrell, K. F. H. (1980). Occupational psychology through autobiography: Hywell Murrell, *Journal of Occupational Psychology*, **53**, 281–90.

Murrell, K. F. H. and Kingston, P. M. (1966). Experimental comparison of scalar and digital micrometers, *Ergonomics*, **9**, 39–47.

Nakaseko, M., Grandjean, E., Hünting, W. and Grierer, R. (1985). Studies on ergonomically designed alphanumeric keyboards, *Human Factors*, **27**, 175–88.

Nayyar, R. M. and Simon, J. R. (1963). Effects of magnification on a subminiature assembly operation, *Journal of Applied Psychology*, **47**, 190–5.

Nelson, J. D. and Barany, J. W. (1969). A dynamic visual recognition test for paced industrial inspection, *AIIE Transactions*, **1**, 327–32.

Nemecek, J. and Grandjean, E. (1973). Noise in landscaped offices, *Applied Ergonomics*, **4**, 19–22.

Nevins, R. G. and Gagge, A. P. (1972). The new ASHRAE comfort chart, *ASHRAE Journal*, **14**, 19–22.

Newbold, E. M. (1926). *A Contribution to the Study of the Human Factor in the Causation of Accidents*. Report 34 Industrial Health Research Board. London: IHRB.

Nicholson, A. S. (1983). *CEC Workshop: Prevention of Low Back Pain*. Luxembourg: CEC.

Nicolson, R. I. and Gardner, P. H. (1985). The QWERTY keyboard hampers schoolchildren, *British Journal of Psychology*, **76**, 525–31.

Nixon, J. C. and Glorig, A. (1961). Noise-induced permanent threshold shift at 2000 cps and 4000 cps, *Journal of the Acoustical Society of America*, **33**, 904–8.

Norman, D. A. and Fisher, D. (1982). Why alphabetic keyboards are not easy to use: keyboard layout doesn't much matter, *Human Factors*, **24**, 509–19.

Noyes, J. (1983a). The QWERTY keyboard: a review, *International Journal of Man–Machine Studies*, **18**, 265–81.

Noyes, J. (1983b). Chord keyboards, *Applied Ergonomics*, **14**, 55–9.

O'Brien, M. (1985). Women in sport, *Applied Ergonomics*, **16**, 25–39.

O'Hanlon, J. G. and Griffin, M. J. (1971). *Some Effects of the Vibration of Reading Material Upon Visual Performance.* ISVR Technical Report 49. University of Southampton.

O'Regan, J. K. and Levy-Schoen, A. (1987). Eye movement strategy and tactics in word recognition and reading. In M. Coltheart (ed.) *Attention and Performance XII: The Psychology of Reading.* New Jersey: Lawrence Erlbaum Assoc.

Oborne, D. J. (1975). *An Investigation of Passenger Comfort with Particular Reference to the Effects of Vibration.* Ph.D. Thesis. University of Wales.

Oborne, D. J. (1976). A critical assessment of studies relating whole-body vibration to passenger comfort, *Ergonomics*, **19**, 751–74.

Oborne, D. J. (1977). Vibration and passenger comfort, *Applied Ergonomics*, **8**, 97–101.

Oborne, D. J. (1983). Whole-body vibration and ISO 2631: a critique, *Human Factors*, **25**, 55–70.

Oborne, D. J., Branton, R., Leal, F., Shipley, P. and Stewart, T. (1993). *Person-centred Ergonomics: A Brantonian View of Human Factors.* London: Taylor & Francis.

Oborne, D. J. and Humphreys, D. A. (1976). Individual variability in human response to whole-body vibration, *Ergonomics*, **19**, 719–26.

'Observer' and Maxwell, M. A. (1959). A study of absenteeism, accidents and sickness payments in problem drinkers in one industry. *Quarterly Journal of Studies on Alcohol*, **20**, 302–12.

Ohlsson, K., Nilsson, L.-G. and Ronnberg, J. (1981). Speed and accuracy in scanning as a function of combinations of text and background colours, *International Journal of Man–Machine Studies*, **14**, 215–22.

Öhrström, E. (1989). Sleep disturbance, psycho-social and medical symptoms—a pilot survey among persons exposed to high levels of road traffic noise, *Journal of Sound and Vibration*, **133**, 117–28.

Öhrström, E. and Rylander, R. (1990). Sleep disturbance by road traffic noise—a laboratory study on number of noise events, *Journal of Sound and Vibration*, **143**, 93–101.

Olsen, D. R. and Filby, N. (1972). On the comprehension of active and passive sentences, *Cognitive Psychology*, **3**, 361–81.

Orth, B., Weckerle, H. and Wendt, D. (1976). Legibility of numerals displayed in a 4x7 dot matrix and seven-segment digits, *Visible Language*, **10**, 145–55.

Paddan, G. S. (1987). *Transmission of vertical vibration from the floor to the head in standing subjects.* UK Informal Group Meeting on Human Response to Vibration, Royal Military College of Science, Shrivenham.

Paddan, G. S. and Griffin, M. J. (1988). The transmission of translational seat vibration to the head. I. Vertical seat vibration, *Journal of Biomechanics*, **21**, 199–206.

Paivio, A. (1971). *Imagery and Verbal Processes.* New York: Holt, Rinehart & Winston.

Paivio, A. and Begg, I. (1981). *Psychology of Language.* New Jersey: Prentice-Hall.

Paivio, A., Yuille, J. C. and Madigan, S. A. (1968). Concreteness, imagery and meaningfulness values for 925 nouns, *Journal of Experimental Psychology Monograph Supplement 76*, No. 1 Part 2.

Papert, S. (1980). *Mindstorms, Children, Computers and Powerful Ideas.* Brighton: Harvester Press.

Parsons, H. M. (1976). Work environments. In I. Altman and J. F. Wohlwill (eds). *Human Behavior and Environment Vol. I.* New York: Plenum.

Pastoor, S., Schwarz, E. and Beldie, I. P. (1983). The relative suitability of four dot-matrix sizes for text presentation on color television screens, *Human Factors*, **25**, 265–72.

Paterson, D. G. and Tinker, M. A. (1946). Readability of newspaper headlines printed in capitals and lower case, *Journal of Applied Psychology*, **30**, 161–8.

Patterson, M. L., Mullens, S. and Romano, J. (1971). Compensatory reactions to spatial intrusion, *Sociometry*, **34**, 121–4.

Patterson, M. L. and Sechrest, L. B. (1970). Interpersonal distance and impression formation, *Journal of Personality*, **38**, 161–6.

Patterson, R. D. (1985). Auditory warning systems for high-workload environments, *Ergonomics International*, **85**, 163–5.

Pawlak, U. (1986). Ergonomic aspects of image polarity. *Behaviour and Information Technology*, **5**, 335–48.

Peacock, L. J. (1956). *A Field Study of Rifle Aiming Steadiness and Serial Reaction Performance as Affected by Thermal Stress and Activity*. Ohio: US AMRL Report 231.

Pearsons, K. S., Bennett, R. L. and Fidell, S. (1977). *Speech Levels in Various Noise Environments*. US Environmental Protection Agency Report EPA-600/1-77-025. Washington, DC.

Peizer, E. and Wright, D. W. (1974). Human locomotion. In Institute of Mechanical Engineers (ed.). *Human Locomotion Engineering*. London: I.Mech.E.

Perry, D. K. (1952). Speed and accuracy of reading Arabic and Roman numerals, *Journal of Applied Psychology*, **36**, 346–7.

Petherbridge, P. and Hopkinson, R. G. (1950). Discomfort glare and the lighting of buildings, *Transactions of the Illuminating Engineering Society*, **15**, 39–79.

Petropoulos, H. and Brebner, J. (1981). Stereotypes for direction-of-movement of rotary controls associated with linear displays: the effects of scale presence and position, of pointer direction and distances between the control and the display, *Ergonomics*, **24**, 143–51.

Pfauth, M. and Priest, J. (1981). Person–computer interface using touch screen devices. *Proceedings of the 25th Annual Meeting of the Human Factors Society*. Baltimore: HFS.

Pheasant, S. T. (1982a). A technique for estimating anthropometric data from the parameters of the distributions of stature, *Ergonomics*, **25**, 981–92.

Pheasant, S. T. (1982b). Anthropometric estimates for British civilian adults, *Ergonomics*, **25**, 993–1001.

Pheasant, S. T. (1983). Sex differences in strength—some observations on their variability, *Applied Ergonomics*, **14**, 205–11.

Pheasant, S. T. (1991). *Ergonomics, Work and Health*. London: Taylor & Francis.

Pheasant, S. T. and O'Neill, D. (1975). Performance in gripping and turning—a study in hand/handle effectiveness, *Applied Ergonomics*, **6**, 205–8.

Pheasant, S. T. and Stubbs, D. A. (1991). *Lifting and Handling—An Ergonomic Approach*. Teddington, Middlesex: National Back Pain Association.

Phillips, R. J. (1979). Why is lower case better?, *Applied Ergonomics*, **10**, 211–14.

Plath, D. W. (1970). The readability of segmented and conventional numerals, *Human Factors*, **12**, 493–7.

Plummer, L. S. and Das, S. S. (1973). A study of dichotomous thought processes in accident prone drivers, *British Journal of Psychiatry*, **122**, 289–94.

Pollack, I. and Ficks, L. (1954). Information of elementary multi-dimensional auditory displays, *Journal of the Acoustical Society of America*, **26**, 155–8.

Pook, G. K. (1969). Color coding effects in compatible and noncompatible display control arrangements, *Journal of Applied Psychology*, **53**, 301–3.

Porter, C. S. (1988). Accident proneness: a review of the concept, *International Reviews of Ergonomics*, **2**, 177–206.

Porter, C. S. and Corlett, E. N. (1989). Performance differences of individuals classified by questionnaire as accident prone or non-accident prone, *Ergonomics*, **32**, 317—33.

Postman, L. (1975). Verbal learning and memory, *Annual Review of Psychology*, **26**, 291–350.

Pottier, M., Dubreuil, A. and Mond, H. (1969). The effects of sitting posture on the volume of the foot, *Ergonomics*, **12**, 753–8.

Poulsen, T. (1991). Influence of session length on judged annoyance, *Journal of Sound and Vibration*, **145**, 217–24.

Poulton, E. C. (1967). Searching for newspaper headlines printed in capitals or lower-case letters, *Journal of Applied Psychology*, **51**, 417–25.

Poulton, E. C. (1969a). Searching lists of food ingredients printed in different sizes, *Journal of Applied Psychology*, **53**, 55–8.

Poulton, E. C. (1969b). How efficient is print?, *New Society*, 5 June, 869–71.

Poulton, E. C. (1975). Colours for sizes: a recommended ergonomic colour code, *Applied Ergonomics*, **6**, 231–5.

Poulton, E. C. (1976). Continuous noise interferes with work by masking auditory feedback and inner speech, *Applied Ergonomics*, **7**, 79–84.

Poulton, E. C. (1977). Continuous intense noise masks auditory feedback and inner speech, *Psychological Bulletin*, **84**, 977–1001.

Poulton, E. C. (1978). Increased vigilance with vertical vibration at 5 Hz: an alerting mechanism, *Applied Ergonomics*, **9**, 73–6.

Poulton, E. C. and Brown, C. H. (1968). Rate of comprehension of an existing tele-printer output and of possible alternatives, *Journal of Applied Psychology*, **52**, 16–21.

Powell, P. I., Hale, M., Martin, J. and Simon, M. (1971). *2000 Accidents*. London: National Institute of Industrial Psychology.

Prather, K., Crisera, R. A. and Fidell, S. (1975). *Behavioral Analysis of Workers and Job Hazards in the Roofing Industry*. US Department of Health, Education and Welfare. Contract No. HSM-99-72-121, NIOSH 75–176.

Price, H. E. (1985). The allocation of functions in systems, *Human Factors*, **27**, 33–45.

Prince, J. H. (1967). Printing for the visually handicapped, *Journal of Typographic Research*, **1**, 31–47.

Pritchard, D. (1964). Industrial lighting in windowless factories, *Lighting and Lighting Research*, **57**, 265.

Putz-Anderson, V. (ed.). (1988). *Cumulative Trauma Disorders: A Manual for Musculoskeletal Diseases of the Upper Limbs*. London: Taylor & Francis.

Radl, G. W. (1980). Experimental investigations for optimal presentation-mode and colours of symbols on the CRT screen. In E. Grandjean and E. Vigliani (eds). *Ergonomic Aspects of Visual Display Terminals*. London: Taylor & Francis.

Ranney, D. (1993). Work-related chronic injuries of the forearm and hand: their specific diagnosis and management, *Ergonomics*, **36**, 871–80.

Rasmussen, J. (1981). Models of mental strategies in process plant diagnosis. In J. Rasmussen and W. B. Rouse (eds). *Human Detection and Diagnosis of System Failures*. New York: Plenum.

Rasmussen, J. (1984). Strategies for state identification and diagnosis in supervisory control tasks and design of computer-based support systems. In W. V. Rouse (ed.). *Advances in Man–machine Systems Research*. Greenwich: JAI Press.

Raw, G. J. and Griffiths, I. D. (1990). Subjective response to changes in road traffic noise: a model, *Journal of Sound and Vibration*, **141**, 43–54.

Ray, R. D. and Ray, W. D. (1979). An analysis of domestic cooker control design, *Ergonomics*, **22**, 1243–8.

Rayner, K. (1977). Visual attention in reading: eye movements reflect cognitive processes, *Memory and Cognition*, **5**, 443–8.

Rayner, K. (1978). Eye movements in reading and information processing, *Psychological Bulletin*, **85**, 618–60.

Rayner, K. and Morris, R. K. (1992). Eye movement control in reading: evidence against semantic preprocessing, *Journal of Experimental Psychology: Human Perception and Performance*, **18**, 163–72.

Rayner, K., Sereno, S. C., Morris, R. K., Schmauder, A. R. and Clifton, C. (1989). Eye movements and on-line language comprehension processes, *Language and Cognitive Processes*, **4**, 21–49.

Reason, J. T. (1978). Motion sickness—some theoretical and practical considerations, *Applied Ergonomics*, **9**, 163–7.

Reason, J. T. (1979). Actions not as planned: the price of atomization. In G. Underwood (ed.). *Aspects of Consciousness. I Psychological Issues*. London: Academic Press.

Reason, J. T. and Brand, J. J. (1975). *Motion Sickness*. London: Academic Press.

Redgrove, J. (1979). Fitting the job to the woman: a critical review, *Applied Ergonomics*, **10**, 215–23.

Rennie, A. M. and Wilson, J. R. (1980). The observation of behaviour at road crossing facilities. In D. J. Oborne and J. A. Levis (eds). *Human Factors in Transport Research, Vol 2*. London: Academic Press.

Rey, R. P. and Meyer, J. J. (1980). Visual impairments and their objective correlates. In E. Grandjean and E. Vigliani (eds). *Ergonomic Aspects of Visual Display Terminals*. London: Taylor and Francis.

Reynolds, D. D. and Angevine, E. N. (1977). Hand–arm vibration Part II: Vibration transmission characteristics of the hand and arm, *Journal of Sound and Vibration*, **51**, 255–65.

Reynolds, D. D. and Soedel, W. S. (1972). Dynamic response of the hand–arm system to a sinusoidal input, *Journal of Sound and Vibration*, **21**, 339–53.

Reynolds, L. (1983). The legibility of printed scientific information and technical information. In R. Easterby and H. Zwaga (eds). *Information Design*. Chichester: John Wiley.

Riccio, G. E. and Stoffregen, T. A. (1991). An ecological theory of motion sickness and postural instability, *Ecological Psychology*, **3**, 195–240.

Ridd, J. E. (1985). Spatial restraints and intra-abdominal pressure, *Ergonomics*, **28**, 149–66.

Riggs, L. A. (1972). Vision. In J. W. Kling and L. A. Riggs (eds). *Experimental Psychology*. New York: Methuen.

Roberts, D. F. (1960). Functional anthropometry of elderly women, *Ergonomics*, **3**, 321–7.

Roberts, D. F. (1975). Population dimensions, their genetic basis and their relevance to practical problems of design. In A. Chapanis (ed.). *Ethnic Variables in Human Factors Engineering*. Baltimore: The Johns Hopkins University Press.

Robinette, K. M. and McConville, J. T. (1981). An Alternative to Percentile Models. *SAE Technical Paper 810217*. Warrendale, PA: Society of Automotive Engineers.

Rodahl, K. and Guthe, T. (1988). Physiological limitations of human performance in hot environments, with particular reference to work in heat-exposed industry. In B. Mekjavic, E. W. Bannister and J. B. Morrison (eds). *Environmental Ergonomics:*

Sustaining Human Performance in Harsh Environments. Philadelphia: Taylor & Francis.

Rodger, A. and Cavanagh, P. (1962). Training occupational psychologists, *Occupational Psychology*, **36**, 82–8.

Roebuck, J. A., Kroemer, K. H. E. and Thompson, W. G. (1975). *Engineering Anthropometry Methods.* New York: John Wiley.

Rogers, J. G. (1963). The effects of target distance and direction on maximum velocity of the rolling ball control, *Human Factors*, **5**, 379–83.

Rogers, Y. (1989). Icon design for the user interface, *International Reviews of Ergonomics*, **3**, 129–54.

Rohles, F. H. (1967). Environmental psychology, *Psychology Today*, June, 54–63.

Rohles, F. H. (1969). Preference for the thermal environment by the elderly, *Human Factors*, **11**, 37–41.

Rolfe, J. M. (1969a). Human factors and the display of height information, *Applied Ergonomics*, **1**, 16–24.

Rolfe, J. M. (1969b). *Some Investigations into the Effectiveness of Numerical Displays for the Presentation of Dynamic Information.* Farnborough, Hants: IAM Technical Report R470.

Rolfe, J. M. and Allnutt, M. F. (1967). Putting the man in the picture, *New Scientist*, **16**, February, 401–6.

Rose, M. J. (1991). Keyboard operating posture and actuation force: implications for muscle over-use, *Applied Ergonomics*, **22**, 198–203.

Ross, S., Katchmar, L. T. and Bell, H. (1955). Multiple-dial check reading: pointer symmetry compared with uniform alignment, *Journal of Applied Psychology*, **39**, 215–18.

Rowlands, G. F. (1977). *The Transmission of Vertical Vibration to the Heads and Shoulders of Seated Men.* Farnborough, Hants: Royal Aircraft Establishment Technical Report TR 77068.

Royal Society for the Prevention of Accidents. (1977). *Factory Accidents.* London: ROSPA.

Rutenfranz, J. and Colquhoun, W. P. (1979). Circadian rhythms in human performance, *Scandinavian Journal of Work, Environment and Health*, **5**, 167–77.

Ruys, T. (1970). *Windowless Offices.* MA Thesis, University of Washington.

Sah, A. P. (1989) Personality characteristics of accident free and accident involved Indian railway drivers, *Journal of Personality and Clinical Studies*, **5**, 203–6.

Sanders, H. G. and Hoffman, M. A. (1975). Personality aspects of involvement in pilot error accidents, *Aviation, Space and Environmental Medicine*, February, 186–90.

Sanders, M. G., Halcomb, C. G., Fray, J. M. and Owens, J. M. (1976). Internal–external locus of control and performance on a vigilance task, *Perceptual and Motor Skills*, **42**, 939–43.

Saunders, J. E. (1969). The role of the level and diversity of horizontal illumination in an appraisal of a simple office task, *Lighting Research and Technology*, **1**, 37.

Savinar, J. (1975). The effect of ceiling height on personal space, *Man–environment Systems*, **5**, 321–4.

Scales, E. M. and Chapanis, A. (1954). The effect on performance of tilting the toll operator's keyset, *Journal of Applied Psychology*, **38**, 452–6.

Schiepers, C. W. J. (1980). Response latency and accuracy in visual word recognition, *Perception and Psychophysics*, **27**, 71–81.

Schmidtke, H. (1980). Ergonomic design principles of alphanumeric displays. In E. Grandjean and E. Vigliani (eds). *Ergonomic Aspects of Visual Display Terminals.* London: Taylor & Francis.

Schohan, B., Rawson, H. E. and Soliday, S. M. (1965). Pilot and observer performance in simulated low altitude high speed flight, *Human Factors*, **7**, 257–65.

Seibel, R. (1962). Performance on a five-finger chord keyboard, *Journal of Applied Psychology*, **46**, 165–9.

Seibel, R. (1964). Data entry through chord, parallel entry devices, *Human Factors*, **6**, 189–92.

Seidel, H. and Heide, R. (1986). Long-term effects of whole-body vibration: a critical survey of the literature, *International Archives of Occupational and Environmental Health*, **58**, 1–26.

Sell, R. G. (1977). Ergonomics as applied to crane cabs. In J. S. Weiner and H. G. Maule (eds). *Human Factors in Work, Design and Production*. London: Taylor & Francis.

Seminara, J. L. (1979). A survey of ergonomics in Poland, *Ergonomics*, **22**, 479–505.

Shackel, B. (1962). Ergonomics in the design of a large digital computer console, *Ergonomics*, **5**, 229–41.

Sharp, E. D. and Hornseth, J. P. (1965). *The Effect of Control Location upon Performance Time for Knob, Toggle Switch and Push Button*. Ohio: AMRL Technical Report TR-65-41.

Shaw, L. and Sichel, H. S. (1971). *Accident Proneness: Research in the Occurrence, Causation and Prevention of Road Accidents*. Oxford: Pergamon.

Sheehy, M. P. and Marsden, C. D. (1982). Writer's cramp: a focal dystonia, *Brain*, **107**, 461–80.

Shibolet, S., Lancaster, M. C. and Danon, Y. (1976). Heat stroke: a review, *Aviation, Space and Environmental Medicine*, **47**, 280–301.

Shinar, D. and Acton, M. B. (1978). Control–display relationships on the four-burner range: population stereotypes versus standards, *Human Factors*, **20**, 13–17.

Shoenberger, R. W. (1970). *Human Performance as a Function of Direction and Frequency of Whole-body Vibration*. Ohio: Army Medical Research Laboratories Report, AMRL-TR-70-7.

Shoenberger, R. W. (1974). An investigation of human information processing during whole-body vibration, *Aerospace Medicine*, **45**, 143–53.

Siegel, A. I. and Brown, F. R. (1958). An experimental study of control console design, *Ergonomics*, **1**, 251–7.

Simon, C. W. and Roscoe, S. N. (1956). *Altimeter Studies Part II. A Comparison of Integrated versus Separated Displays*. Hughes Aircraft Co., Culver City, California. Technical Memo. No. 435.

Simon, J. R. (1964). Magnification as a variable in subminiature work, *Journal of Applied Psychology*, **48**, 20–4.

Simon, J. R. and Rudell, A. P. (1967). Auditory S-R compatibility: the effects of an irrelevant cue on information processing, *Journal of Applied Psychology*, **51**, 300–4.

Simons, A. K. and Schmitz, M. A. (1958). *The Effect of Low Frequency, High Amplitude Whole Body Vibration on Human Performance*. Washington DC: Office of the Surgeon General, Research and Development Div.

Simpson, C. A. and Marchionda-Frost, K. (1984). Synthesized speech rate and pitch effects on intelligibility of warning messages for pilots, *Human Factors*, **26**, 509–17.

Sinaiko, H. W. and Brislin, R. W. (1973). Evaluating language translations: experiments on 3 assessment methods, *Journal of Applied Psychology*, **57**, 328–34.

Sinha, S. P. and Sinha, S. P. (1991). Personal space and density as factors in task performance and feeling of crowding, *Journal of Social Psychology*, **131**, 831–7.

Slobin, D. I. (1966). Grammatical transformations and sentence comprehension in childhood and adulthood, *Journal of Verbal Learning and Verbal Behaviour*, **5**, 219–27.

Smiley, J. A. (1955). A clinical study of group accident-prone workers, *British Journal of Industrial Medicine*, **12**, 263–78.

Smith, G. L. and Adams, S. K. (1971). Magnification and microminiature inspection, *Human Factors*, **13**, 247–54.

Smith, G. L. and Thomas, D. W. (1964). Color versus shape coding in information displays, *Journal of Applied Psychology*, **48**, 137–46.

Smith, M. J. (1987). Mental and physical strain at VDT workstations, *Ergonomics*, **6**, 243–55.

Smith, M. M. and Marriott, A. M. (1982). Vision and proprioception in simple catching, *Journal of Motor Behavior*, **14**, 143–52.

Smith, S. L. (1978). The limited readability of Lansell numerals, *Human Factors*, **20**, 57–64.

Smith, S. L. (1979). Letter size and legibility, *Human Factors*, **21**, 661–70.

Smith, S. W. and Rea, M. S. (1979). *Relationships between office task performance and ratings of feelings and task evaluation under different light sources and levels.* Proceedings of the CIE 19th Session, Kyoto.

Sommer, H. C. and Harris, C. S. (1970). *Combined Effects of Noise and Vibration on Mental Performance as a Function of Time of Day.* Ohio: Army Medical Research Laboratories Report, AMRL-TR-70-36.

Sommer, R. (1968). Intimacy ratings in five countries, *International Journal of Man–Machine Studies*, **3**, 109–14.

Sommer, R. (1969). *Personal Space: The Behavioral Basis of Design.* New York: Prentice-Hall.

Sommer, R. (1974). *Tight Spaces: Hard Architecture and How to Humanize It.* New Jersey: Prentice-Hall.

Sommerich, C. M., McGlothlin, J. D. and Marras, W. S. (1993). Occupational risk factors associated with soft tissue disorders of the shoulder: a review of recent investigations of the literature, *Ergonomics*, **36**, 697–717.

Spencer, J. (1963). Pointers for general purpose indicators, *Ergonomics*, **6**, 35–49.

Spiker, A., Rogers, S. P. and Cicinelli, J. (1986). Selecting colour codes for a computer-generated topographic map based on perception experiments and functional requirements, *Ergonomics*, **29**, 1313–28.

Spoor, A. (1967). Presbyacusis values in relation to noise-induced hearing loss, *International Audiology*, **6**, 48–57.

Sprent, N., Crawshaw, M. and Bartram, D. (1983). Structuring timetable information, *Ergonomics*, **26**, 505–16.

Stammerjohn, L., Smith, M. J. and Cohen, B. (1981). Evaluation of workstation design factors in VDT operations, *Human Factors*, **23**, 401–12.

Starr, S. J., Thompson, C. R. and Shute, S. J. (1982). Effects of video display terminals on telephone operators, *Human Factors*, **24**, 699–712.

Stephens, S. D. G. (1970). Studies on the uncomfortable loudness level, *Sound*, **4**, 203.

Sternberg, S. (1966). High-speed scanning in human memory, *Science*, **153**, 652–4.

Stevens, S. S. (1972). Stability of human performance under intense noise, *Journal of Sound and Vibration*, **21**, 35–56.

Stiles, W. S. (1929). The scattering theory of glare, *Proceedings of the Royal Society (Series B)*, **105**, 131–46.

Stockbridge, H. C. W. and Lee, M. (1973). The psycho-social consequences of aircraft noise, *Applied Ergonomics*, **4**, 44–5.

Stott, J. R. R. (1980). *Mechanical Resonance of the Eyeball.* Paper presented to Human Response to Vibration Meeting, Swansea.

Stoudt, H. W. (1981). The anthropology of the elderly, *Human Factors,* **21**, 29–37.

Strandberg, L. (1983). On accident analysis and slip-resistance measurement, *Ergonomics,* **26**, 11–32.

Stubbs, D. A. (1985). Human constraints on manual working capacity: effects of age on intratruncal pressure, *Ergonomics,* **28**, 107–14.

Stubbs, D. A., Buckle, P. W., Hudson, M. P., Rivers, R. M. and Worrington, R. N. (1983). Back pain in the nursing profession: Part 1, Epidemiology and pilot methodology, *Ergonomics,* **26**, 755–65.

Swensen, E. E., Purswell, J. L., Schlegel, R. E. and Stanevich, R. L. (1992). Coefficient of friction and subjective assessment of slippery work surfaces, *Human Factors,* **34**, 67–77.

Szlichcinski, K. P. (1977a). Diagrams and illustrations as aids to problem solving, *Instructional Science,* **8**, 253–74.

Szlichcinski, K. P. (1977b). Telling people how things work, *Applied Ergonomics,* **10**, 2–8.

Szlichcinski, K. P. (1977c). Symbols and pictograms: a review of their usefulness and the methodology of their design, *Proceedings of the 8th International Symposium on Human Factors in Telecommunications.* Harlow: STL Ltd.

Tanner, J. (1962). *Growth at Adolescence.* Oxford: Blackwell Scientific.

Tanner, J. (1978). *Foetus into Man—Physical Growth from Conception to Maturity.* London: Opus Books.

Tapagaporn, S. and Saito, S. (1990). How polarity and lighting conditions affect the pupil size of VDT operators, *Ergonomics,* **33**, 201–8.

Taylor, W. (1974). The vibration syndrome: introduction. In W. Taylor (ed.). *The Vibration Syndrome.* London: Academic Press.

Teel, K. S. (1971). Is human factors engineering worth the investment?, *Human Factors,* **13**, 17–21.

Teichener, W. H. and Kobrick, J. L. (1955). Effects of prolonged exposure to low temperature on visual-motor performance, *Journal of Experimental Psychology,* **49**, 122–6.

Teichener, W. H. and Krebs, M. J. (1974). Visual search for simple targets, *Psychological Bulletin,* **81**, 15–28.

Terrana, T., Merluzzi, F. and Guidici, E. (1980). Electromagnetic radiation emitted by visual display units. In E. Grandjean and E. Vigliani (eds). *Ergonomic Aspects of Visual Display Terminals.* London: Taylor & Francis.

Thomas, L. F. (1968). Setting subjective and objective standards and making judgments. In *Human Factors in the Management of Industrial Inspection.* Paper presented to the Industrial Section of the Ergonomics Research Society and the Institute of Mechanical Engineering.

Thomas, L. F. and Seaborne, A. E. M. (1961). The socio-technical context of industrial inspection, *Journal of Occupational Psychology,* **35**, 36–43.

Tichauer, E. R. (1978). *The Biomechanical Basis of Ergonomics.* New York: John Wiley.

Tillman, W. A. and Hobbs, G. E. (1949). The accident prone automobile driver, *American Journal of Psychiatry,* **106**, 321–31.

Timbal, J., Loncle, M. and Boutelier, C. (1976). Mathematical model of man's tolerance to cold using morphological factors, *Aviation, Space and Environmental Medicine,* **47**, 958–64.

Timmers, H., van Nes, F. L. and Blommaert, F. J. J. (1980). Visual word recognition as a function of contrast. In E. Grandjean and E. Vigliani (eds). *Ergonomic Aspects of Visual Display Terminals.* London: Taylor & Francis.

Tinker, M. A. (1960). Legibility of mathematical tables, *Journal of Applied Psychology.* **44**, 83–7.

Tinker, M. A. (1965a). *Legibility of Print.* Iowa: Iowa State University Press.

Tinker, M. A. (1965b). *Bases for Effective Reading.* Iowa: Iowa State University Press.

Toms, M. and Patrick, J. (1987). Some components of fault-finding, *Human Factors,* **29**, 587–97.

Toms, M. and Patrick, J. (1989). Components of fault-finding: symptom interpretation, *Human Factors,* **31**, 465–83.

Torle, G. (1965). Tracking performance under random acceleration: effects of control dynamics, *Ergonomics,* **8**, 481–6.

Totman, R. G. and Kiff, J. (1979). Life stress and the susceptibility to colds. In D. J. Oborne, M. M. Gruneberg and J. R. Eiser (eds). *Research in Psychology and Medicine, Vol I.* London: Academic Press.

Trice, H. M. and Roman, P. M. (1972). *Spirits and Demons at Work: Alcohol and Other Drugs on the Job.* New York: New York School of Industrial and Labor Relations, Cornell University.

Ulin, S. S., Armstrong, T. J., Snook, S. H. and Keyserling, W. M. (1993). Perceived exertion and discomfort associated with driving screws at various work locations and at different work frequencies, *Ergonomics,* **36**, 833–46.

Umbers, I. G. and Collier, G. D. (1990). Coding techniques for process plant VDU formats, *Applied Ergonomics,* **21**, 187–98.

Usher, D. M. (1982). *A touch sensitive VDU compared with a computer-aided keypad for controlling power generating plant.* Paper presented to IEE Conference on Man/machine Systems.

Van Heusden, E., Plomp, R. and Pols, L. C. W. (1979). Effect of ambient noise on the vocal output and the preferred listening level of conversational speech, *Applied Acoustics,* **12**, 31–43.

Vartabedian, A. G. (1971). Legibility of symbols on CRT displays, *Applied Ergonomics,* **2**, 130–2.

Vartabedian, A. G. (1973). Developing a graphic set for cathode ray tube display using a 7x9 dot pattern, *Applied Ergonomics,* **4**, 11–16.

Vaughan, W. S. (1975). Diver temperature and performance changed during long-duration, cold water exposure, *Undersea Biomedical Research,* **2**, 75–88.

Verhaegen, P., Vanhalst, B., Derycke, H. and VanHoeke, M. (1976). The value of some psychological theories of industrial accidents, *Journal of Occupational Psychology,* **1**, 39–45.

Verhoef, L. W. M. (1993). A new conceptual structure for travel information, *Applied Ergonomics,* **24**, 263–9.

Vernon, H. M. and Warner, C. G. (1932). The influence of the humidity of the air on capacity for work at high temperatures, *Journal of Hygiene (Cambridge),* **32**, 431.

Vickers, D. (1979). *Decision Processes in Visual Perception.* New York: Academic Press.

Wagenaar, W. A., Schreuder, R. and Wijlhuizen, G. J. (1987). Readability of instructional text, written for the general public, *Applied Cognitive Psychology,* **1**, 155–67.

Wallace, M. and Buckle, P. (1987). Ergonomic aspects of neck and upper limb disorders, *International Reviews of Ergonomics,* **1**, 173–200.

Waller, R. A. (1969). Office acoustics–effect of background noise, *Applied Acoustics,* **2**, 121–30.

Waltzman, S. B. and Levitt, H. (1978). Speech interference level as a predictor of face-to-face communication in noise, *Journal of the Acoustical Society of America,* **63**, 581–90.

Ward, J. S. (1984). Women at work—ergonomic considerations, *Ergonomics*, **27**, 475–80.

Ward, J. S. and Bealding, W. (1970). Optimum dimensions for domestic staircases, *Architects Journal*, **152**, 513–20.

Ward, J. S. and Fleming, P. (1964). Changes in body wright and body composition in African mine recruits, *Ergonomics*, **7**, 83–90.

Ward, J. S. and Kirk, N. S. (1967). Anthropometry of elderly women, *Ergonomics*, **10**, 17–24.

Warner, H. D. and Mace, K. C. (1974). Effects of platform fashion shoes on brake response time, *Applied Ergonomics*, **5**, 143–6.

Warrick, M. J. (1947). Direction of movement in the use of control knobs to position visual indicators. In P. M. Fitts (ed.). *Psychological Research on Equipment Design.* Ohio: US Army Air Force Aviation Program Research Department Report No. 19.

Wason, P. C. (1965). The contexts of plausible denials, *Journal of Verbal Learning and Verbal Behavior*, **4**, 7–11.

Watten, R. G. and Lie, I. (1992). Time factors in VDT-induced myopia and visual fatigue: an experimental study, *Journal of Human Ergology*, **21**, 13–20.

Weale, R. A. (1963). *The Ageing Eye.* London: H. K. Lewis.

Webster, J. C. (1973). S. I. L.–past, present and future, *Journal of Sound and Vibration*, **3**, 22–6.

Weidman, B. (1970). *Effect of safety gloves on simulated work tasks.* AD 738981. Springfield, VA: National Technical Information Service.

Weisz, A. Z., Goddard, C. and Allen, R. W. (1965). *Human Performance under Random and Sinusoidal Vibration*, Ohio: Aerospace Medical Research Laboratories, Report AMRL-TR-65-209.

Welford, A. T. (1976). *Skilled Performance: Perceptual and Motor Skills.* Illinois: Scott, Foresman.

Welford, A. T. (1984). Theory and application in visual displays. In R. Easterby and H. Zwaga (eds). *Information Design.* Chichester: John Wiley.

Wells, J. and Storey, N. (1980). *Investigations of Vibration-induced Eye Movements under Whole-Body Vibration.* Paper presented to Human Response to Vibration Meeting, Swansea.

Wertheimer, M. (1958). Principles of perceptual organization. In D. C. Beardslee and M. Wertheimer (eds). *Readings in Perception.* Princeton: Van Nostrand.

Wesner, C. E. (1972). Induced arousal and word-recognition learning by mongoloids and normals, *Perceptual and Motor Skills*, **35**, 586.

Wetherall, A. (1981). The efficacy of some auditory–vocal subsidiary tasks as measures of the mental load on male and female drivers, *Ergonomics*, **24**, 197–214.

White, M. J. (1989). Effect of calendar layout on calendar search, *Ergonomics*, **32**, 15–25.

White, R. M. (1975). Anthropometric measures of selected populations of the world. In A. Chapanis (ed.). *Ethnic Variables in Human Factors Engineering.* Baltimore: The Johns Hopkins University Press.

White, W. J., Warrick, M. J. and Grether, W. F. (1953). Instrument reading II: check reading of instrument groups, *Journal of Applied Psychology*, **37**, 302–7.

Whitfield, D., Ball, R. G. and Bird, J. M. (1983). Some comparisons of on-display and off-display touch input devices for interaction with computer-generated displays, *Ergonomics*, **26**, 1033–53.

Whitlock, F. O., Stoll, J. R. and Rekhdahl, R. J. (1977). Crisis, life events and accidents, *Australian and New Zealand Journal of Psychiatry*, **11**, 127–32.

Wickens, C. D., Vidulich, M. and Sandry-Garza, D. (1984). Principles of S-R compatibility with spatial and verbal tasks: the role of display–control location and voice interactive display–control interfacing, *Human Factors*, **26**, 533–43.

Wilkins, A. J. (1978). *Epileptogenic Attributes of TV and VDUs*. Paper presented to Ergonomics Society Conference on Eyestrain and VDUs, Loughborough.

Wilkins, A. J., Darby, C. E. and Binnie, C. D. (1979). On the triggering of photosensitive epilepsy. In D. J. Oborne, M. M. Gruneberg and J. R. Eiser (eds). *Research in Psychology and Medicine, Vol. I*. London: Academic Press.

Wilkinson, R. T. and Gray, R. (1974). *Effects of duration of vertical vibration beyond the proposed ISO fatigue-decreased proficiency time on the performance of various tasks*, AGARD CP-145 Paper B19.

Willis, F. N. (1966). Initial speaking distance as a function of the speaker's relationship, *Psychonomic Science*, **5**, 221–2.

Wilmore, J. H. (1975). Inferiority of female athletes: myth or reality?, *Journal of Sports Medicine*, **3**, 1–6.

Wilson, A. (1963). *Noise–Final Report*. London: HMSO.

Wilson, J. R. (1983). Pressures and procedures for the design of safer consumer products, *Applied Ergonomics*, **14**, 109–16.

Wilson, J. R. and Corlett, N. (eds). (1990). *Evaluation of Human Work: A Practical Ergonomics Methodology*. London: Taylor & Francis.

Wilson, J. R. and Grey, S. M. (1984). Reach requirements and job attitudes at laser-scanner checkout systems, *Ergonomics*, **27**, 1247–66.

Wing, A. (1979). The slowing of handwritten responses made in spaced character formats, *Ergonomics*, **22**, 465–8.

Winkel, J. and Oxenburgh, M. (1989). Towards optimising physical activity in VDT/office work. In S. Sauter, M. Dainoff and M. Smith (eds). *Promoting Health and Productivity in the Computerized Office*. London: Taylor & Francis.

Winsemius, W. (1965). Some ergonomic aspects of safety, *Ergonomics*, **8**, 151–62.

Wisner, A. (1989). Fatigue and human reliability revisited in the light of ergonomics and work psychopathology, *Ergonomics*, **32**, 891–8.

Wohlwill, J. F., Nasar, J. L., De Joy, D. M. and Foruzami, H. H. (1976). Behavioral effects of a noisy environment: task involvement versus passive exposure, *Journal of Applied Psychology*, **61**, 67–74.

Wolcott, J. H., McMeekin, R. R., Burgin, R. E. and Yanowitch, R. E. (1977a). Correlation of occurrence of aircraft accidents with biorhythmic criticality and cycle phase in US Air Force, US Army and civilian aviation pilots, *Aviation, Space and Environmental Medicine*, **48**, 976–83.

Wolcott, J. H., McMeekin, R. R., Burgin, R. E. and Yanowitch, R. E. (1977b). Correlation of general aviation accidents with biorhythm theory, *Human Factors*, **19**, 382–93.

Wolf, C. G. (1992). A comparative study of gestural, keyboard and mouse interfaces, *Behaviour and Information Technology*, **11**, 13–23.

Wolford, G. and Hollingsworth, S. (1974a). Retinal location and string position as important variables in visual information processing, *Perception and Psychophysics*, **16**, 437–42.

Wolford, G. and Hollingsworth, S. (1974b). Lateral masking in visual information processing, *Perception and Psychophysics*, **16**, 315–20.

Wolke, S. and DuCette, J. (1974). Intentional performance and incidental learning as a function of personality and task dimensions, *Journal of Personality and Social Psychology*, **29**, 90–101.

Wong, W. A. and Hobbs, G. W. (1949). Personal factors in industrial accidents: a survey of accident proneness in an industrial group, *Industrial Medicine and Surgery*, **18**, 291–4.

Wood, P. H. N. and McLeish, C. L. (1974). Statistical appendix 5: morbidity in industry and rheumatism in general practice, *Annals of Rheumatic Diseases*, **33**, 93–105.

Wright, P. (1977a). Presenting technical information: a survey of research findings, *Instructional Science*, **6**, 93–134.

Wright, P. (1977b). Decision making as a factor in the ease of using numerical tables, *Ergonomics*, **20**, 91–6.

Wright, P. (1980). The comprehension of tabulated information: some similarities between reading prose and reading tables, *National Society for Performance and Instruction Journal*, **19**, 25–9.

Wright, P. (1983). Informed design for forms. In R. Easterby and H. Zwaga (eds). *Information Design*. Chichester: John Wiley.

Wright, P. and Barnard, P. (1978). Asking multiple questions about several items: the design of matrix structures on application forms, *Applied Ergonomics*, **9**, 7–14.

Wright, P. and Fox, K. (1970). Presenting information in tables, *Applied Ergonomics*, **1**, 234–42.

Wright, P. and Reid, F. (1973). Written information: some alternatives to prose for expressing the outcomes of complex contingencies, *Journal of Applied Psychology*, **57**, 160–6.

Wyndham, C. H. (1966). A survey of the causal factors in heat stroke and of their prevention in the gold mining industry, *Journal of the South African Industry of Mining and Metallurgy*, **1**, 245–58.

Wyndham, C. H., Strydom, N. B., Benade, A. J. S. and Van Rensburg, A. J. (1970). Tolerance times of high wet bulb temperatures by acclimatized and unacclimatized men, *Environmental Research*, **3**, 339–52.

Wyon, D. P., Andersen, I. and Lundqvist, G. R. (1979). The effects of moderate heat stress on mental performance, *Scandinavian Journal of Work and Environmental Health*, **5**, 352.

Yaglou, C. P. (1947). A method for improving the effective temperature index, *ASHVE Transactions*, **53**, 307–26.

Yarbus, A. L. (1967). *Eye Movements and Vision*. New York: Plenum.

Young, L. R. and Sheena, D. (1975). Survey of eye movement recording techniques, *Behavior Research Methods and Instrumentation*, **7**, 397–429.

Zeff, C. (1965). Comparison of conventional and digital time displays, *Ergonomics*, **8**, 339–45.

Zipp, P., Haider, E., Halpern, N. and Rohmert, W. (1983). Keyboard design through physiological strain measurements, *Applied Ergonomics*, **14**, 117–22.

Zuboff, S. (1988). *In the Age of the Smart Machine: The Future of Work and Power*. New York: Basic Books.

Zwaga, H. and Easterby, R. (1983). Developing effective symbols for public information. In R. Easterby and H. Zwaga (eds). *Information Design*. Chichester: John Wiley.

INDEX

Wiley Titles of Related Interest

COGNITIVE ABILITY OF COMPUTER SUPPORTED TASKS

Yvonne Waern

Reviews current knowledge and theories about how computer systems are used for the cognitive tasks of learning, problem solving, storing and organizing information. The emphasis is on the processes, and on the difficulties associated with the interaction of human systems with computer systems.

0-471-93066-0 paper 352pp 1991

EXPLORING STATISTICS WITH MINITAB: A WORKBOOK FOR THE BEHAVIOURAL SCIENCES

Andrew Monk

Provides students with the background and practical skills needed to take advantage of statistical packages now available for mainframes and microcomputers. Specifically designed for students of psychology and ergonomics, the book shows how such packages can be used to learn introductory statistics.

0-471-93002-4 266pp 1991

WORK, STRESS, DISEASE AND LIFE EXPECTANCY

Ben Fletcher

Evaluates the effects of work stress on the major physical disease clusters, focusing on the role of occupational stress in life expectancy.

0-471-91970-5 268pp 1991

TRAINING FOR PERFORMANCE: PRINCIPLES OF APPLIED LEARNING

John Morrison

Presents recent theory and research relating to the process of human learning and training, including topics such as skill acquisition, transfer, retention, individual differences and social and organizational factors.

0-471-92248-X 324pp 1991

HANDBOOK OF LIFE STRESS, COGNITION AND HEALTH

Edited by Shirley Fisher and James Reason

A comprehensive and authoritative review of experience, theory and management/therapy of the stresses associated with life events, with the focus on the role of cognitive and psychological factors.

0-471-91269-7 784pp 1988